Lecture Notes in Artificial Intelligence   5118

Edited by R. Goebel, J. Siekmann, and W. Wahlster

Subseries of Lecture Notes in Computer Science

Mehdi Dastani   Amal El Fallah Seghrouchni
João Leite   Paolo Torroni (Eds.)

Languages, Methodologies and Development Tools for Multi-Agent Systems

First International Workshop, LADS 2007
Durham, UK, September 4-6, 2007
Revised Selected and Invited Papers

 Springer

Series Editors

Randy Goebel, University of Alberta, Edmonton, Canada
Jörg Siekmann, University of Saarland, Saarbrücken, Germany
Wolfgang Wahlster, DFKI and University of Saarland, Saarbrücken, Germany

Volume Editors

Mehdi Dastani
Utrecht University, Intelligent Systems Group
3508 TB Utrecht, The Netherlands
E-mail: mehdi@cs.uu.nl

Amal El Fallah Seghrouchni
LIP6, University Pierre and Marie Curie
104, Avenue du Président Kennedy
75016 Paris, France
E-mail: amal.elfallah@lip6.fr

João Leite
Universidade Nova de Lisboa
Departamento de Informática
2829-516 Caparica, Portugal
E-mail: jleite@di.fct.unl.pt

Paolo Torroni
DEIS, University of Bologna
V.le Risorgimento 2, 40136 Bologna, Italy
E-mail: paolo.torroni@unibo.it

Library of Congress Control Number: 2008931313

CR Subject Classification (1998): I.2.11, I.6, H.3.5

LNCS Sublibrary: SL 7 – Artificial Intelligence

ISSN   0302-9743
ISBN 978-3-540-85057-1 Springer Berlin Heidelberg New York

Springer is a part of Springer Science+Business Media

springer.com

© Springer-Verlag Berlin Heidelberg 2008

Typesetting: Camera-ready by author, data conversion by Scientific Publishing Services, Chennai, India
Printed on acid-free paper   SPIN: 12442829   06/3180   5 4 3 2 1 0

Preface

This book contains the proceedings of the first international workshop on languages, methodologies and development tools for multi-agent systems (LADS 2007), which took place on 4–6 September 2007 in Durham, UK. This workshop was part of MALLOW 2007, a federation of workshops on Multi-Agent Logics, Languages, and Organisations.

The LADS 2007 workshop addressed both theoretical and practical issues related to developing and deploying multi-agent systems. It constituted a rich forum where leading researchers from both academia and industry could share their experiences on formal approaches, programming languages, methodologies, tools and techniques supporting the development and deployment of multi-agent systems. From a theoretical point of view, LADS 2007 aimed at addressing issues related to theories, methodologies, models and approaches that are needed to facilitate the development of multi-agent systems ensuring their predictability and verification. Formal declarative models and approaches have the potential of offering solutions for the specification and design of multi-agent systems. From a practical point of view, LADS 2007 aimed at stimulating research and discussion on how multi-agent system specifications and designs can be effectively implemented and tested.

This book is the result of a strict selection and review process. From 32 papers originally submitted to LADS 2007, and after 2 rounds of reviews, we selected 15 high-quality papers covering important topics related to multi-agent programming technology, such as: theories, methodologies, techniques and principles of multi-agent systems. The book also contains an invited paper, in which Dave Robertson reports on the aims and achievements of the OpenKnowledge project.

We would like to thank all authors, invited speakers, programme committee members, and additional reviewers for their outstanding contribution to the success of LADS 2007. We would also like to thank all the sponsors. We are particularly grateful to Rafael Bordini and the MALLOW organisers for their technical support and for hosting LADS 2007.

May 2008

Mehdi Dastani
Amal El Fallah Seghrouchni
João Leite
Paolo Torroni

Conference Organisation

Programme Chairs

Mehdi Dastani (Utrecht University, The Netherlands)
Amal El Fallah Seghrouchni (University of Paris 6, France)
João Leite (Universidade Nova de Lisboa, Portugal)
Paolo Torroni (University of Bologna, Italy)

Programme Committee

Marco Alberti (University of Ferrara, Italy)
Natasha Alechina (University of Nottingham, UK)
José Júlio Alferes (New University of Lisbon, Portugal)
Matteo Baldoni (University of Turin, Italy)
Federico Bergenti (University of Parma, Italy)
Juan A. Botía (Murcia University, Spain)
Lars Braubach (University of Hamburg, Germany)
Jean-Pierre Briot (University of Paris 6, France)
Keith Clark (Imperial College London, UK)
Yves Demazeau (Institut IMAG, Grenoble, France)
Jürgen Dix (Clausthal University, Germany)
Ulle Endriss (University of Amsterdam, The Netherlands)
Michael Fisher (The University of Liverpool, UK)
Paolo Giorgini (University of Trento, Italy)
Jorge J. Gómez-Sanz (Universidad Complutense Madrid, Spain)
Shinichi Honiden (NII, Tokyo, Japan)
Jomi F. Hübner (Universidade Regional de Blumenau, Brazil)
Peep Küngas (SOA Trader, Ltd., Tallin, Estonia)
Jiming Liu (Hong Kong Baptist University, Hong Kong)
John W. Lloyd (Australian National University, Canberra, Australia)
Alessio Lomuscio (Imperial College London, UK)
Viviana Mascardi (University of Genova, Italy)
John-Jules Ch. Meyer (Utrecht University, The Netherlands)
Juan Pavón (Universidad Complutense de Madrid, Spain)
Alexander Pokahr (University of Hamburg, Germany)
Birna van Riemsdijk (Ludwig Maximilians Universität München, Germany)
Sebastian Sardiña (RMIT University, Melbourne, Australia)
Ichiro Satoh (NII, Kyoto, Japan)
Leon Sterling (University of Melbourne, Australia)
Patrick Taillibert (Thales Airborne Systems, Elancourt, France)
Leon van der Torre (University of Luxembourg, Luxembourg)

Gerhard Weiß (Software Competence Center Hagenberg, Austria)
Michael Winikoff (RMIT University, Melbourne, Australia)
Pinar Yolum (Bogazici University, Istanbul, Turkey)
Yingqian Zhang (Delft University, The Netherlands)

Local Organisation

Rafael H. Bordini (Local Chair, Durham University, UK)
Berndt Farwer (Durham University, UK)
Patricia Shaw (Durham University, UK)

External Reviewers

Samir Aknine
Dirk Bade
Cristina Baroglio
Nils Bulling
Federico Chesani
Enrico Denti
Akin Gunay
James Harland
Peter Novak
Katia Potiron
Yasuyuki Tahara
John Thangarajah
Sicco Verwer
Gregory Wheeler

Sponsoring Institutions

Department of Electronics, Computer Sciences and Systems, University of
    Bologna
Centro de Inteligência Artificial (CENTRIA), Universidade Nova de Lisboa

Table of Contents

Development Frameworks

Open Knowledge

Coordinating Knowledge Sharing through Peer–to–Peer Interaction

Dave Robertson[1], Fausto Giunchiglia[2], Frank van Harmelen[3],
Maurizio Marchese[2], Marta Sabou[4], Marco Schorlemmer[5], Nigel Shadbolt[6],
Ronnie Siebes[3], Carles Sierra[5], Chris Walton[1], Srinandan Dasmahapatra[6],
Dave Dupplaw[6], Paul Lewis[6], Mikalai Yatskevich[2], Spyros Kotoulas[3],
Adrian Perreau de Pinninck[5], and Antonis Loizou[6]

[1] Informatics, University of Edinburgh, UK
[2] Information and Communication Technology, University of Trento, Italy
[3] AI Department, Vrije Universiteit Amsterdam, Netherlands
[4] Knowledge Media Institute, Open University, UK
[5] Institut d'Investigació en Intel·ligència Artificial, Barcelona, Spain
[6] Electronics and Computer Science, University of Southampton, UK

Abstract. The drive to extend the Web by taking advantage of automated symbolic reasoning (the so-called Semantic Web) has been dominated by a traditional model of knowledge sharing, in which the focus is on task-independent standardisation of knowledge. It appears to be difficult, in practice, to standardise in this way because the way in which we represent knowledge is strongly influenced by the ways in which we expect to use it. We present a form of knowledge sharing that is based not on direct sharing of "true" statements about the world but, instead, is based on sharing descriptions of interactions. By making interaction specifications the currency of knowledge sharing we gain a context to interpreting knowledge that can be transmitted between peers, in a manner analogous to the use of electronic institutions in multi-agent systems. The narrower notion of semantic commitment we thus obtain requires peers only to commit to meanings of terms for the purposes and duration of the interactions in which they appear. This lightweight semantics allows networks of interaction to be formed between peers using comparatively simple means of tackling the perennial issues of query routing, service composition and ontology matching. A basic version of the system described in this paper has been built (via the OpenKnowledge project); all its components use established methods; many of these have been deployed in substantial applications; and we summarise a simple means of integration using the interaction specification language itself.

1 Introduction

To coordinate the sharing of knowledge in an automated way on a large scale is an aim shared by many areas of computing. In some areas the challenge of scale is especially difficult because the environment for knowledge sharing is open,

M. Dastani et al. (Eds.): LADS 2007, LNAI 5118, pp. 1–18, 2008.

in the sense that we cannot prescribe which programs will choose to interact in sharing knowledge. One solution to this problem would be to develop sophisticated agent architectures to make individual programs more adaptive and resilient. In practice, however, the architectures of most internet-based systems are not specifically agent-oriented. A second approach, and the one taken in this paper, is to take the approach adopted in electronic institutions and use a formal model of the intended interaction in different social contexts in order to provide the necessary constraints on interaction and synchronisation of message passing. We motivate our approach by comparison to the aspirations of semantic web systems but, in Section 6, we discuss the relevance of our approach across a broader range of large scale coordination systems.

Semantic Web efforts encourage designers to specify pages and programs in a knowledge representation language. What fundamentally distinguishes the Semantic Web from traditional knowledge representation is not the formal representations of pages and programs but the way these representations are used in automated processing. The use we have in mind is to improve the accuracy of Web searches and to allow components (especially those that are programs operating as Web services) to be connected automatically rather than simply be discovered individually. It simplifies our explanation, without loss of generality, if we think of all components (pages and programs) as peers[1] capable of supplying information in some formal language: a page supplies information about that page; a program generates information, perhaps requiring input information in order to do so (we return to the data-centric versus process-centric view in Section 6.1). This way of attempting to share knowledge between peers encounters elementary problems, familiar from traditional software and knowledge engineering:

- When two different components supply exactly the same formal expression this does not imply that they mean the same thing. Conversely, when they supply different formal expressions they may mean the same thing. In traditional knowledge (and software) engineering we avoid this problem by reaching a consensus amongst component designers on an ontology. To obtain an ontology one needs an oracle to decide which formal terms to use. There are only two sources of oracle: human or mechanical. Neither source scales well. Human oracles can only agree in small groups for narrow tasks or domains. Mechanical oracles need to acquire domain knowledge via automated learning methods, none of which has scaled beyond narrow tasks or domains.
- Only some combinations of components work well together, even when the meanings of their appropriate inputs and outputs correspond, because of assumptions made deep within the design of components. In traditional knowledge (and software) engineering this problem is detected through integration

---

[1] We use the word "peer" in this paper simply to underline that no component is given special authority over others, other than via the manner in which components interact with humans and with each other. We use "peer" rather than "agent" in order to emphasise that the programs we coordinate need not be built to an agent architecture.

testing: by running assemblies of components comprising the system and checking for defects such as range errors (where the type of an input is correct but its value is outside the range anticipated by the component's designers). It is infeasible to test all ranges for all variables for all components so integration testing only covers some small subset of the possible interactions.

- Components may fail without warning, either because they are removed or as a consequence of their environment. Traditionally this problem is solved by ensuring that the components are in a shared, controlled environment. No such controls are available in an open environment, in which we may not always know who, what or where are our peers.
- Even without the problems above, theoretical results (*e.g.* [8]) show that in general it is impossible to guarantee consistently shared common knowledge in asynchronous distributed systems. The engineering solution to this problem is to provide mechanisms for establishing synchronisation between appropriate components, but for this we must have a frame of reference to bound the synchronisation - otherwise synchronisation itself falls foul of the general consistency problem.

As an example, suppose we want to find the addresses of expert researchers on wave energy in Scotland. A conventional Web search using Google doesn't find this information easily because the information about who is an expert is hard to infer from conventional Web pages and the large number of pages discussing wave energy tend to swamp out the few home pages of expert researchers and their groups. A semantic web approach might do better if appropriate information services could be combined. Suppose that an expert finding service does exist and it offers to supply as output a set, S, of names of specialists if given as input a request for experts in some country, X, and discipline, D. A simple specification of this service (made much simpler then, say, an OWL-S, specification since we need only a simple example here) might be this:

$$
\begin{array}{l}
\text{service} : expert\_finder \\
\quad \text{input} : request\_experts(country(X), discipline(D)) \\
\quad \text{output} : specialists(X, D, S) \\
\text{operation} : get\_experts(X, D, S)
\end{array}
$$

Suppose also that two address finding services exist in Scotland, allowing one to send a request for the address of a person with a given name, P, and receive an address, A, for him or her. One of these services is run by a UK address company (*uk_address*); the other by the University of Edinburgh (*univ_ed*). Both, by coincidence, have identical specifications:

$$
\begin{array}{l}
\text{service} : address\_finder \\
\quad \text{input} : request\_address(person(P)) \\
\quad \text{output} : address(P, A) \\
\text{operation} : get\_address(P, A)
\end{array}
$$

A semantic web search engine could not obtain the set of addresses we require using only these service specifications (assuming that the specifications connect to actual services via some grounding mechanism not discussed here) because it is missing some vital functionality:

Functionality 1. Interaction specification: *Wherever there is distributed computation there is an issue of control over message passing between services. The expert_finder service supplies a set, S, of names of experts but the address_finder service deals with individual names. Something must infer that we should take each element of S and pass it to the address_finder, collecting the results. We cannot always infer this by examining only the types and values of variables - just like normal programming, someone or something must supply the necessary control structure.*

Functionality 2. Interaction coordination: *We need to know that some form of interaction involving expert_finder and address_finder would be useful for the task. Notice that our task is not, and could not be, specified with the services because the engineers of those services could not be assumed to predict all the possible tasks of which they might be a part. To provide any automation we must separately obtain a formal description of the interaction we might need. And this description will most likely be provided using language terms that are different from those used by the services which want to interact with a given service. Some mechanism must make sure that the services are fed appropriate information. The variable, D, in the expert_finder service will need to be bound to the name of some scientific discipline that the service recognises and it is unlikely to recognise all conceivable discipline descriptions. Will it accept "wave energy"? We don't know simply by looking at the type of the variable.*

We have described major problems associated with the aspiration of semantic web efforts. These are traditional engineering problems but their traditional solutions do not apply in open environments. The key to solving these, we shall argue, is in making specifications of interactions an integral part of knowledge exchange between peers. In Section 2 we summarise a compact but expressive formal language for specifying and computing interactions. We then describe the basic mechanisms needed to support this computation in an open environment: ontology alignment (Section 3.1), discovery (Section 3.2) and visualisation (Section 3.3). Section 4 then combines these elements within a minimal model of interaction, shareable between peers. Finally, since we view this as an evolutionary manifesto, in Section 6 we compare our approach to the major existing paradigms.

2   Interaction Specification

The functional requirement we must satisfy here is: given that a peer has been given a model of interaction, use this computationally to control its own behaviour and communicate to other relevant peers the behaviours expected of them for this interaction.

$$
\begin{aligned}
Model &:= \{Clause, \ldots\} \\
Clause &:= Role :: Def \\
Role &:= a(Type, Id) \\
Def &:= Role \mid Message \mid Def \ then \ Def \mid Def \ or \ Def \\
Message &:= M \Rightarrow Role \mid M \Rightarrow Role \leftarrow C \mid M \Leftarrow Role \mid C \leftarrow M \Leftarrow Role \\
C &:= Constant \mid P(Term, \ldots) \mid \neg C \mid C \wedge C \mid C \vee C \\
Type &:= Term \\
Id &:= Constant \mid Variable \\
M &:= Term \\
Term &:= Constant \mid Variable \mid P(Term, \ldots) \\
Constant &:= \text{lower case character sequence or number} \\
Variable &:= \text{upper case character sequence or number}
\end{aligned}
$$

Fig. 1. LCC syntax

From previous implementations by the authors using the system described below, there are several different ways in which a peer might exploit an interaction model with a precise computational behaviour:

- It might simply run this model locally, sending messages to other peers but not allowing them to be privy to the broader picture of interaction contained in the model. This is a traditional server-based style of coordination.
- It might distribute appropriate components of the model to those peers with which it interacts, on the assumption that each of them will separately run that component - producing a distributed computation.
- It might use the model as a form of script which it passes entire to the next peer with which it needs to interact - producing complex interactions amongst many peers via pairwise interactions between peers.

None of these computational models is optimal. Server or script based computation keeps the interaction model in one piece, giving advantages in imposing constraints on interaction that apply across groups of peers. On the other hand, a server based computation means that peers other than the one acting as server have little control over the course of the interaction; while a script based computation only works for interactions that can be deconstructed into a series of pairwise interchanges. Since no winning execution strategy is known, it makes sense to use an interaction modelling language that has a semantics independent of any one of these strategies but that is capable of being executed by any of them.

The need to supply this sort of information has been recognised by many in the semantic web community. The most direct solution is to specify the process of service combination, and the roles undertaken by the services in that process, in an executable language. We give in Figure 2 a specification for our running example in one such language: the Lightweight Coordination Calculus (LCC) which is the core language used in the OpenKnowledge project. Figure 1 defines the syntax of LCC. An interaction model in LCC is a set of clauses, each of which

$a(expert\_locator(X, D, L), C) ::$
  $request\_experts(X, D) \Rightarrow a(expert\_finder, E)$ *then*
  $specialists(X, D, S) \Leftarrow a(expert\_finder, E)$ *then*
  $a(address\_collector(S, L), C)$

$a(address\_collector(S, L), C) ::$
$$\left(\begin{array}{l} request\_address(P) \Rightarrow a(address\_finder, F) \leftarrow S = [P|Sr] \wedge L = [A|Lr] \; then \\ address(P, A) \Leftarrow a(address\_finder, F) \; then \\ a(address\_collector(Sr, Lr), C) \end{array} \right) \quad or$$
  $null \leftarrow S = [] \wedge L = []$

$a(expert\_finder, E) ::$
  $request\_experts(X, D) \Leftarrow a(expert\_locator(X, D, L), C)$ *then*
  $specialists(X, D, S) \Rightarrow a(expert\_locator(X, D, L), C) \leftarrow get\_experts(X, D, S)$

$a(address\_finder, F) ::$
  $request\_address(P) \Leftarrow a(address\_collector(S), C)$ *then*
  $address(P, A) \Rightarrow a(address\_collector(S), C) \leftarrow get\_address(P, A)$ *then*
  $a(address\_finder, F)$

Fig. 2. Example interaction model

defines how a role in the interaction must be performed. Roles are described by the type of role and an identifier for the individual peer undertaking that role. The definition of performance of a role is constructed using combinations of the sequence operator ('*then*') or choice operator ('*or*') to connect messages and changes of role. Messages are either outgoing to another peer in a given role ('$\Rightarrow$') or incoming from another peer in a given role ('$\Leftarrow$'). Message input/output or change of role can be governed by a constraint defined using the normal logical operators for conjunction, disjunction and negation. Notice that there is no commitment to the system of logic through which constraints are solved - so different peers might operate different constraint solvers (including human intervention).

Returning to the example of Figure 2, each of the four clauses defines the message passing behaviour of a role in the interaction. The first clause defines the role we wish some peer (identified by name C) to perform: that of a locator for experts which, given a country, X and a discipline, D, identifies a list of addresses, L. To undertake this role, C must send a message to an expert finder, E, requesting names of experts and then receive a set of names, S from E before taking the role of an address collector. The second clause defines the address collector role which involves recursing through the set of names, requesting, and then receiving, an address for each from an address finder, F. The third and fourth clauses define our earlier *expert_finder* and *address_finder* services in terms of the message passing required by each of them. Note that these make specific commitments to the temporal behaviours of the services in our interaction (for instance we prescribe that an *expert_finder* is contacted only once in this interaction while an *address_finder* may be contacted many times).

It is not the task of this paper to explain LCC in detail or to justify its use rather than some other process specification language (for that argument see [16]). For our current purposes, the salient features of LCC are:

- It is an executable specification language, providing the features common to such languages (such as variables, data structures and recursion). All of these were needed to deal with even our simple running example.
- Despite its specificity in terms of data and control structure, so we know precisely how we want our services to interact, there remain obstacles to achieving that interaction:
  - Which specific terms will work when communicating between services? This is discussed in Section 3.1.
  - How do we know which actual services to use? In our LCC specification the variables E and F are unbound but messages must be sent to specific services. This is discussed in Section 3.2.
  - What happens if our peers are human operated? For example, the operation $get\_experts(X, D, S)$ in the third clause of Figure 2 might involve asking a human who the experts are. At that point the human needs to know enough of the interaction's context to give an informative reply (see Section 3.3).

Principle 1. *Interaction models are declarative, executable specifications that may be understood independently of any particular peer or execution model. The conditions under which they are run, however, requires more run-time support than a traditional executable specification language.*

3   Interaction Coordination

The functional requirement we must satisfy here is: given a peer with no knowledge of how to interact with others to perform some task, obtain for it a description of an appropriate interaction.

One way to do this might be through synthesis, either fully automated (*e.g.* [4]) or interactive (*e.g.* [12]), so that peers could compose appropriate service clusters for whatever task arises. Although an important means of initiating some kinds of interaction specification, synthesis is unlikely to be the main source of this functionality for three reasons. First, as in Section 1, the specifications we need are non-trivial to synthesise automatically and would require specialist expertise to synthesise interactively. Second, synthesis can be time consuming and peers in a semantic web are likely to need fast responses. Third, and perhaps most importantly, sharing information about useful interactions is a way to propagate experience about effective knowledge sharing - so obtaining a model of interaction that has been widely used and is popular with one's peers may in many cases be better (and much easier) than building one from scratch. We now consider two key enablers for this from of sharing: dynamic ontology matching and peer-to-peer interaction model sharing.

3.1   Dynamic Ontology Matching

In our introduction we argued that traditional methods of ontology matching do not scale to open knowledge sharing systems. Our focus on interaction has not, however, eradicated the issue. Instead, we have a different form of ontology matching problem to consider: matching terms that appear dynamically in the course of an interaction. Being autonomously and independently defined inside each peer, most of these terms will be semantically heterogeneous. Thus, while one peer could have *expert_finder* as its service role, the others could have *person_finder*, *expertICT_finder*, *expert_broker*, and so on. Notice that while the first and the fourth role denote services which are essentially equivalent, the second is more general than *expert_finder*, while the third is less general. It is a fact that these terms are always used in the context of some local, a priori defined, often left implicit, ontological description of the world. And this influences not only the specific equivalent terms used to describe a concept but also the level of generality of the concept itself.

The solution we propose is to construct semantic mappings (*e.g.* more or less general, equivalent to, disjoint from) existing between the terms used during interaction. One such example is the mapping $\langle expert\_finder, person\_finder, LG \rangle$, stating that *expert_finder* is less general (*LG*) than *person_finder*. These mappings are those defined and used in C-OWL [14]. Their main advantage over "syntactic mappings", namely mappings which return an affinity measure in the interval [0,1] (see, e.g., the mappings constructed by the state of the art system COMA [9]), is that the information carried by the semantic relation can then be exploited in many ways, for instance when fixing mismatches (see "Term matching" below).

We discover semantic mappings, using the method implemented in the S-Match system [7]. This is applied in at least three different phases:

- *Role matching*: Aligns the different ways in which roles are described when initiating or joining an interaction. An example is the mapping $\langle expert\_finder, person\_finder, LG \rangle$.
- *Term matching*: Aligns (structured) terms within the clause defining a role in order to undertake an interaction. An example is matching *get_address*, which in one peer could take two arguments (*e.g.* name of a person and his/her address) and in another three arguments, where the third argument (*e.g. Type_of_Comm*) could discriminate whether we need an address for personal or work communication.
- *Query / Answer matching*: Takes place when running an interaction model and deals with the semantic heterogeneity arising from the statement of a query and in the values returned in its answers. For example, an interaction model specifying that the *address_finder* needs to look up the address for Stephen Salter by invoking the *get_address*('*Stephen Salter*', A) operation is not guaranteed (as we are with the ontology of messages) to match perfectly to the operation the peer actually can perform. Perhaps the operation used by the peer is *find_address* and the surname is expected first (as in '*Salter, Stephen*').

The kind of (semantic) matching that we need here differs from the previous approaches in that it is not done once and for all, at design time on statically defined ontologies, but, rather, it is performed at run-time. This moves the problem of *ontology* (and data) *integration*, widely studied in the literature, to the problem of *ontology coordination*. As discussed in [6], the problem of data and ontology coordination is characterised by various new difficulties (beyond the obvious requirement of very fast response times). Coordination is dynamic so exactly what needs to be coordinated depends on what is interacting. Peers have partial knowledge of their network so cannot always predict which other peers will interact with them. Ontology matches made in this way without prior consensus are therefore intended to support query answer sets that are *good enough* for the interaction in hand but not necessarily complete or always correct.

This form of dynamic semantic matching might at first sight seem a harder problem than conventional static matching. We can, however, utilise our coordination framework to turn it into a more limited, easier problem. From Principle 1, interaction models are shareable resources. So too are mappings used with them. This cuts down the number of new mappings that are needed as models are reused. Furthermore, the context in which mappings are constructed is much more limited than with traditional ontology mapping. Since the purpose of mappings is to ensure that a specific interaction model functions correctly then the only issue is whether the meaning associated with the particular use of an operation required of a peer corresponds to an operation it can do. This is a much less demanding task than the general task of mapping entire ontologies between peers, for two reasons. First, we need consider only the fragment of the ontology that applies to a specific interaction. Second, the commitments we make in a mapping can be weaker and more easily judged: for instance, mapping "visit to Italy" to "holiday trip" may make perfect sense for an interaction with a holiday service even though the mapping does not hold in general.

Principle 2. *Models of interactions are developed locally to peers. However, they must be shared in order to achieve interaction coordination. This is achieved by dynamically matching, at run time, terms in the interaction models. This happen both when synthesising them and when running them to answer specific queries. Dynamic semantic matching does this by considering the terms in the context (defined as a local ontology) of the involved peers.*

3.2 Interaction Model Sharing and Discovery

The obstacle to a peer wishing to acquire an interaction model in an open system is knowing who to ask and how to ask. We cannot expect a peer to know all other peers or to know the details of an interaction. We can expect, however, that each peer knows about some distributed discovery service(s) and that each peer knows some features of the interaction in which it is willing to participate. These features need not be complex - keyword matching may suffice. In our running example, a peer with no knowledge of how to find addresses of experts might ask the discovery service for interaction models described by the keywords {*expert, address*}. The task of the semantic discovery system is then to locate interaction models with these features and peers that want to participate in these interactions across the peer network.

Principle 2 separates interaction models from services, with the advantage that interactions can be shared. To make them work, however, they must connect to specific services. This requires choice. In our running example we must choose, when binding F (the *address_finder*) whether we use *uk_address* or *univ_ed*? That may depend on the names suggested as wave energy experts by the *expert_finder* service. If 'Stephen Salter' were a name suggested then *univ_ed* might be the best choice (since Salter is a professor at Edinburgh). If not, then *uk_address* might be a better bet because it is more general. Hence the context set by earlier interactions conditions subsequent choices of services.

There are three (non–exclusive) ways to tackle this issue:

Sharing of experience between peers: The most direct way to overcome problems like those above is (like traditional Web search engines) to refer to records of past experience. If we know, for example, that someone else had used the LCC specification in our example successfully with the variable bindings $E = e\_find$, $F = univ\_ed$, $X = 'Scotland'$ and $D = 'wave\ energy'$ then if we were to ask a similar query we might follow a similar binding pattern. A detailed description of the method currently used for this appears in [2].

Using the semantic discovery service: To facilitate ranking of peers or interaction models, the semantic discovery service can calculate and maintain statistical information about keywords and contexts from all interaction models and all peers in the system. A description of the semantic discovery service appears in [19].

Collaborative recommendation of interaction models and services: By identifying emergent groups amongst peers, based on sharing of interaction models between peers, groups of users that are likely to use services under similar contexts can be inferred. In addition we can require that the local ontologies of peers in the same cluster (or at least those segments relevant to the candidate interaction protocols) can be automatically mapped to each other. In this setting the problem of choosing the best candidate component is reduced to collaborative filtering. The appropriateness of interaction models retrieved by the system and specific services can be assessed based on the frequency of their use within the community, while the added mapping requirement can ensure that the input parameters will be provided in the format expected by the service.

Principle 3. *The choice of interaction models and peers to occupy roles in them is determined by a distributed discovery service. Evidence of role performance in interactions may be routed to this service. Interaction models in need of role performers and role performers in need of related interaction models consult this service.*

In recent years, a wide variety of resource discovery systems have been proposed and developed. Most of them, like UDDI and Napster, support attribute-based retrieval. Their major disadvantage is that they are centralised approaches. To alleviate these problems, many peer-to-peer indexing systems have been proposed, and basic methods such as distributed hash tables, latent semantic indexing and semantic overlays have been developed.

We assume that data or services are described through sets of terms which we call *descriptions* and that the system contains a large number of such descriptions. Our routing methods extend the work described in [18] to provide statistical information about terms. Initially, peers use a distributed hash table to muster data and group descriptions by term. Since we make no assumptions of shared ontologies, different terms may be used for similar concepts. In [17] a method for automatic word sense discrimination is proposed. Words (or in our case terms) and their senses are represented in a real-valued high-dimensional space where closeness in the space corresponds to semantic similarity. As input for this method we use the descriptions for each term. From the representations of terms in the high-dimensional space, we can then extract information about term generality, term popularity, related terms and homonyms.

3.3 Visualisation for User Interaction and Interaction Monitoring

There are two constraints in the interaction model for our running example of Figure 2: $get\_experts(X, D, S)$ in the third clause and $get\_address(P, A)$ in the fourth clause. We have assumed that each of these would be satisfied automatically via a service call. Sometimes, however, constraints may need to be satisfied by human interaction if all automated means of constraint satisfaction fail. A variant of our example might involve the satisfaction of $get\_experts(X, D, S)$ by a human expert who expresses an opinion on the set, S, of experts in a given country, X, in domain of expertise, D. When these interactive constraints must be satisfied then it is necessary to link interaction model specifications to visualisation specifications (which then can be interpreted via a Web browser or similar mechanism). There are several (non-exclusive) ways to do this:

- By carrying the visualisation specification with the interaction model. This allows interaction model designers to customise visualisations to interactions.
- By providing alternative visualisation methods on peers. This allows limited local customisation to account for style choices.
- By building customised visualisers for very heavily used interaction models. This is appropriate for tasks where the visualisation is the inspiration for the interaction model - for example if we wished to have a complex geospatial visualisation on peers but maintain consistency across peers of information viewed within that visualisation framework.
- By generating visualisation directly from the structure of an interaction model. This is appropriate for tasks such as monitoring the state of an interaction or investigating a failure - a facility not essential to all users but essential for some.

Principle 4. *Interaction models must permit versatility in visualisation: providing default visualisations for common structures but also allowing customisation of visualisation by both peers and interaction model designers. This can be* *achieved by adopting a standard, declarative markup language for visualisation that each peer may interpret without needing to understand the deeper semantics of the constraints themselves.*

4   A Minimal, Most General Interaction Model

We have used the interaction model of Figure 2 as an illustrative example of the various reasoning components needed for peer-to-peer discovery, sharing and collaboration. This example is domain specific (as are most interactions) but we can also specify more general forms of interaction. The most general of these describes how a peer manages other interaction models.

Figure 3 gives a minimal specification of peer interaction (reduced to its essentials to save space). It describes the key roles of a peer: discovery and sharing of interaction models; and collaboration driven from interaction models communicated between peers. In the definition: $\mathcal{P}$ is an interaction model; $\mathcal{S}$ is the state of the interaction in which the peer currently is engaged; $\mathcal{O}$ is the set of onology mapping applying to $\mathcal{S}$; M is a message; X, is the unique identifier of a peer; $locate(K, \mathcal{P})$ means the peer can find a $\mathcal{P}$, described by keyword list, K; $add\_to\_interaction\_cache(\mathcal{P})$ adds $\mathcal{P}$, to the cache known to the peer; $in\_interaction\_cache(\mathcal{P})$ select $\mathcal{P}$, from the cache known to the peer; $match(M, \mathcal{P}, \mathcal{S}, \mathcal{O}, M', \mathcal{P}', \mathcal{S}', \mathcal{O}')$ extends $\mathcal{O}$, adapting $(\mathcal{P}, \mathcal{S})$, to peer giving $(\mathcal{P}', \mathcal{S}', \mathcal{O}')$; $expand(M, \mathcal{P}, \mathcal{S}, \mathcal{S}', M', Z)$ expands $\mathcal{S}$ given M, yielding M' sent to per Z; and $completed(M, \mathcal{P}', \mathcal{S}')$ means that M completes this interaction for this peer.

$a(peer, X)$ ::
    $(a(discoverer, X)$ or $a(collaborator, X)$ or $a(sharer, X))$ then
    $a(peer, X)$

$a(discoverer, X)$ ::
$$\begin{pmatrix} descriptors(K) \ \Leftarrow\ a(discoverer, Y) \text{ then} \\ discovered(\mathcal{P}) \ \Rightarrow\ a(discoverer, Y) \leftarrow locate(K, \mathcal{P}) \end{pmatrix} \text{ or}$$
$$\begin{pmatrix} descriptors(K) \ \Rightarrow\ a(discoverer, Y) \text{ then} \\ add\_to\_interaction\_cache(\mathcal{P}) \leftarrow discovered(\mathcal{P}) \ \Leftarrow\ a(discoverer, Y) \end{pmatrix}$$

$a(collaborator, X)$ ::
    $m(M, \mathcal{P}, \mathcal{S}, \mathcal{O}) \ \Leftarrow\ a(collaborator, Y)$ then
$$\begin{pmatrix} m(M', \mathcal{P}'', \mathcal{S}'', \mathcal{O}') \ \Rightarrow\ a(collaborator, Z) \leftarrow \begin{pmatrix} match(M, \mathcal{P}, \mathcal{S}, \mathcal{O}, M', \mathcal{P}', \mathcal{S}', \mathcal{O}') \ \wedge \\ expand(M', \mathcal{P}', \mathcal{S}', \mathcal{P}'', \mathcal{S}'', Z) \end{pmatrix} \text{ or} \\ m(M, \mathcal{P}, \mathcal{S}, \mathcal{O}) \ \Rightarrow\ a(collaborator, Z) \leftarrow routing(M, \mathcal{P}, \mathcal{S}, \mathcal{O}, Z) \text{ or} \\ null \leftarrow completed(M', \mathcal{P}', \mathcal{S}') \end{pmatrix}$$

$a(sharer, X)$ ::
    $share(\mathcal{P}) \ \Rightarrow\ a(sharer, Y) \leftarrow in\_interaction\_cache(\mathcal{P})$ or
    $add\_to\_interaction\_cache(\mathcal{P}) \leftarrow share(\mathcal{P}) \ \Leftarrow\ a(sharer, Y)$

Fig. 3. Interaction model for a basic peer

Figure 3, of course, is not complete because it does not define important aspects of routing, ontology matching, *etc.* that we discussed in earlier sections. For these the reader is referred to the papers cited in appropriate earlier sections. Our point here is that even the basic knowledge sharing operations of a peer can be understood in terms of shareable interaction models.

5   The OpenKnowledge Kernel

The previous sections are language oriented - they discuss the issues tackled in the OpenKnowledge project with respect to interaction models expressed in LCC. Many different systems could address these issues but the first (to our knowledge) actually to do is the OpenKnowledge kernel system, currently available to download as open source Java code from www.openk.org. In this section we briefly sketchthe main functional elements of the kernel system from the point of view of the subscribe-bootstrap-run cycle through which interactions are deployed. Readers with an interest in more detailed description of the kernel are referred to the tutorial and manual sections of www.openk.org.

Interactions in OpenKnowldge take place via a cycle of subscription (when peers say they want to take part in interactions); bootstrapping (to initiate a fully subscribed interaction) and running (to perform the bootstrapped interaction):

Subscription to an interaction model: When a peer needs to perform a task it asks the discovery service for a list of interaction models matching the description of the task. Then, for each received interaction model, the peer compares the (Java) methods in its local component library with the constraints in the entry role in which it is interested. If the peer finds an interaction model whose constraints (in the role the peer needs to perform) are covered by these methods, then the peer can subscribe (via subscription negotiator) to that interaction model in the discovery service. The subscription, through a subscription adaptor, binds the Interaction Model to a set of methods in the peer. A subscription can endure for only a single interaction run or for many, possibly unlimited, interaction runs (for example, a buyer will likely subscribe to run a purchase interaction once, while a vendor may want to keep selling its products or services).

Bootstrapping an interaction: When all the roles in the interaction model have subscriptions, the discovery service selects a random peer as a coordinator. The coordinator then bootstraps and runs the interaction. The bootstrap involves first asking the peers who they want to interact with, among all the peers that have subscribed to the various roles, then creating a team of mutually compatible peers and finally - if possible - asking the selected group of peers to commit to the interaction.

Running an Interaction: This part of the cycle is handled by the randomly chosen coordinator peer. The coordinator peer runs the interaction locally with messages exchanged between local proxies of the peers. However, when the coordinator encounters a constraint in a role clause, it sends a message, containing the constraint to be solved, to the peer performing the role, The subscription adaptor on the peer calls the corresponding method - found during the comparison at subscription time (see above). The peer then sends back a message to the coordinator with the updated values of variables and the boolean result obtained from satisfying the constraint. The kernel's matcher allows the components on the peer and the interaction models to be decoupled. The peer compares the constraints in the roles in which it is interested with the methods in its local components and creates a set of adaptors that maps the constraint in the roles to similar methods.

The OpenKnowledge kernel is intended as the main vehicle for deploying LCC and as the point of reference for programmers (particularly Java programmers) who wish to extend on our framework. Although the current paper focuses on issues connected to deployment of coordination in a peer to peer setting, an equally important aspect of our use of interaction models is at the level of specification and analysis. Here we have found that by viewing interactions as shareable specifications we can re-apply traditional formal methods in novel ways, for example in model checking [13], matchmaking [10], dynamic ontology mapping [3] and workflow [11]. In this activity it is crucial to have a compact, declarative language in which we can specify interactions independent of the infrastructure used to deploy them.

6   Comparison to Current Paradigms

In the main part of this paper we have motivated, through example, the use of shared, explicit models of interaction to provide context for knowledge sharing. We used the aspirations of the semantic web community as a focus for our arguments but our approach has relevance more broadly across communities involved in the coordination of knowledge sharing. We consider some of these below.

6.1   The Data-Centric and Process-Centric Semantic Web

One view of the Semantic Web is data-centric, where nodes are data sources with which we associate formal specifications of content. The onus is on curators of data (or engineers of services supplying data) to author their specifications appropriately so that generic systems can discover and use data, guided by this additional information. The intention in doing this is to describe key aspects of the semantics of content - so called, semantic annotations. The difficulty in practise with using only semantic annotations is that to gain consensus on what the annotations should be it is necessary for them to be used for practical purposes by the peer group to which they are relevant. From this it follows that the data-centric paradigm needs to be supported by a way of sharing patterns of usage and knitting them into semantic annotations. The interaction models described in this paper are a means of expressing such patterns. Peer-to-peer routing makes it possible to share these on a large scale. Various forms of ontological alignment (including manual alignment) can then be applied to allow peers to select (and collectively reinforce) specific patterns of usage that work when combining data.

The need to represent potential interactions has long been recognised, hence the process specification elements of OWL-S. In OWL-S, however, an interaction process is associated with a service (and with its data) rather than being separately defined. By separating interaction specifications from data annotations we obtain three crucial advantages:

- We no longer have to define generic processes for services. Instead we expect to have many, perhaps very domain specific, interaction models that we then align more narrowly with services.
- We no longer have to aim for broad ontological consensus across services because data is used via narrow alignments.
- By losing the above two restrictions we are able to knit together services with less sophisticated formal languages.

6.2   Web Service Architecture

Our approach is intended to complement and extend a traditional Web service architecture by addressing a number of restrictions. The key extensions that we are proposing, and the restrictions that they address, are summarised below:

- The Web Service Architecture, while distributed, is not inherently peer-to-peer. In particular, there is no support for efficient routing of messages between services, service discovery is performed in a centralised manner using registries, and there is the assumption that services will always be available at a fixed location. In our Peer-based architecture we relax these restrictions. We provide efficient query routing between components to prevent bottlenecks, we support component discovery using distributed search techniques, and we can cope with components that are not always available through dynamic substitution.
- The lightweight interaction models that we define avoid problems associated with dynamic service composition. Our models define precisely how interaction should be performed with individual components, and also how composition of components should be performed. We do not rely upon complex planning operations or require the construction of detailed workflows by users, although our methods do not exclude these methods where appropriate.
- The basic Web services architecture does not contain any support for assessing trust across services when conducting interactions. Because our methods maintain explicit models of interaction to coordinate services we can apply a repertoire of trust assessment methods to these: from evidence based or provenance-based methods through to methods based on statistical analysis (on groups of interactions) or social analysis (on groups of peers with shared interactions). Importantly, we can associate different measures of trust with appropriate interactions, since one measure will not fit all situations.

6.3   Grids

In [1] three generations of grids are identified: first generation, where proprietary solutions are aimed mainly at sharing computational resources of large super-computing centres for high-performance applications; second generation, where (through middleware and standardisation) grids have become more ubiquitous; and third generation, which shifts to a service-oriented architecture, and the use of meta-data to describe these services. In this third generation, services are given well-defined, machine-processable meaning so as to enable autonomic configuration of the grid and assembly of services - the so-called "semantic grid" elaborated in [5].

Our approach is consistent with the semantic grid vision but without our methods being predicated on sophisticated underlying Grid infrastructure. Traditional grid systems connect together specific services (or types of service) in stable networks - the aim being to do as much as possible to make these networks robust, secure and resistant to failure. We concentrate on specifying interactions, which may take place with different combinations of services in an open, peer-to-peer environment where the only essential infrastructure requirement is the ability to pass messages between peers. In this sense, our aim is an "everyman's grid" in the sense that we aim to maintain integrity of interaction (a key grid objective) without requiring specialist (centralised) infrastructure or computing resources to do so and at a very low entry cost.

7   Conclusions

The need for coordinated interactions between software components is growing quickly with the increase in numbers and diversity of programs capable of supplying data on the Internet. Although multi-agent, semantic web and grid communities have traditionally taken different approaches to tackling this problem, we have argued in this paper that a substantial area within these communities is (from a coordination point of view) a shared problem that may be tackled by developing shareable, formal models of interaction. In Section 2 we described a simple language (LCC) for this purpose. In Section 3 we described the demands placed on this language for automated inference during knowledge sharing. To conclude the language description, we use LCC to describe the bare essentials of the peer interaction process; then in Section 5 we briefly describe the implemented OpenKnowledge kernel system currently available from www.openk.org. Finally, in Section 6, we compared this approach across semantic web, web service and grid approaches to coordination. Our aim throughout has been to demonstrate that a basic, common core of interaction specification is appropriate across these areas.

The methods described in this paper have already been applied to a variety of domains. For example, [20] describes how to use interaction models for experiment specification in astrophysics and [15] describes a novel result in protein structure prediction using our methods. Despite these early successes we still have a long way to go before achieving these sorts of peer to peer coordination routinely on a large scale. What we now know is that the basic infrastructure can be built. What remains to be seen is whether this infrastructure has resonance with the social settings in which people wish to share knowledge.

Acknowledgements

This research is funded by the OpenKnowledge project (`www.openk.org`).

References

1. Berman, F., Fox, G., Hey, A. (eds.): Grid Computing: Making the Global Infrastructure a Reality. John Wiley & Sons, New York (2003)
2. Besana, P., Robertson, D.: How service choreography statistics reduce the ontology mapping problem. In: Aberer, K., Choi, K.-S., Noy, N., Allemang, D., Lee, K.-I., Nixon, L., Golbeck, J., Mika, P., Maynard, D., Mizoguchi, R., Schreiber, G., Cudré-Mauroux, P. (eds.) ISWC 2007. LNCS, vol. 4825, pp. 44–57. Springer, Heidelberg (2007)
3. Besana, P., Robertson, D.: How service choreography statistics reduce the ontology mapping problem. In: Aberer, K., Choi, K.-S., Noy, N., Allemang, D., Lee, K.-I., Nixon, L., Golbeck, J., Mika, P., Maynard, D., Mizoguchi, R., Schreiber, G., Cudré-Mauroux, P. (eds.) ISWC 2007. LNCS, vol. 4825, pp. 44–57. Springer, Heidelberg (2007)
4. Blyth, J., Deelman, E., Gil, Y.: Automatically composed workflows for grid environments. IEEE Intelligent Systems (July/August 2004)
5. De Roure, D., Jennings, N.R., Shadbolt, N.R.: The semantic grid: A future e-science infrastructure. In: Berman, F., Fox, G., Hey, A.J.G. (eds.) Grid Computing - Making the Global Infrastructure a Reality, pp. 437–470. John Wiley and Sons Ltd., Chichester (2003)
6. Giunchiglia, F., Zaihrayeu, I.: Making peer databases interact: A vision for an architecture supporting data coordination. In: Klusch, M., Ossowski, S., Shehory, O. (eds.) CIA 2002. LNCS (LNAI), vol. 2446. Springer, Heidelberg (2002)
7. Giunchiglia, F., Shvaiko, P., Yatskevich, M.: S-match: an algorithm and an implementation of semantic matching. In: Bussler, C., Davies, J., Fensel, D., Studer, R. (eds.) ESWS 2004. LNCS, vol. 3053, pp. 61–75. Springer, Heidelberg (2004)
8. Halpen, J.Y., Moses, Y.: Knowledge and common knowledge in a distributed environment. Journal of the ACM 37(3), 549–587 (1990)
9. Do, H.H., Rahm, E.: COMA - a system for flexible combination of schema matching approaches. In: Proceedings of Very Large Data Bases Conference (VLDB), pp. 610–621 (2001)
10. Lambert, D., Robertson, D.: Matchmaking and brokering multi-party interactions using historical performance data. In: Fourth International Joint Conference on Autonomous Agents and Multi-agent Systems (2005)
11. Li, G., Chen-Burger, J., Robertson, D.: Mapping a business process model to a semantic web services model. In: IEEE International Conference on Web Services (2007)
12. Oinn, T., Addis, M., Ferris, J., Marvin, D., Senger, M., Greenwood, M., Carver, T., Glover, K., Pocock, M., Wipat, A., Li, P.: Taverna: a tool for the composition and enactment of bioinformatics workflows. Bioinformatics 20(17), 3045–3054 (2004)

13. Osman, N., Robertson, D.: Dynamic verification of trust in distributed open systems. In: Twentieth International Joint Conference on Artificial Intelligence (2007)
14. Bouquet, P., Giunchiglia, F., Van Harmelen, F., Serafini, L., Stuckenschmidt, H.: C-OWL: contextualizing ontologies. In: Fensel, D., Sycara, K.P., Mylopoulos, J. (eds.) ISWC 2003. LNCS, vol. 2870, pp. 164–179. Springer, Heidelberg (2003)
15. Quang, X., Walton, C., Gerloff, D., Sharman, J., Robertson, D.: Peer-to-peer experimentation in protein structure prediction: an architecture, experiment and initial results. In: International Workshop on Distributed, High-Performance and Grid Computing in Computational Biology (2007)
16. Robertson, D.: Multi-agent coordination as distributed logic programming. In: Demoen, B., Lifschitz, V. (eds.) ICLP 2004. LNCS, vol. 3132, pp. 416–430. Springer, Heidelberg (2004)
17. Schutze, H.: Automatic word sense discrimination. Computational Linguistics 24(1), 97–123 (1998)
18. Siebes, R.: pnear - combining content clustering and distributed hash tables. In: Proceedings of the IEEE 2005 Workshop on Peer-to-Peer Knowledge Management, San Diego, CA, USA (July 2005)
19. Siebes, R., Dupplaw, D., Kotoulas, S., Perreau de Pinninck, A., van Harmelen, F., Robertson, D.: The openknowledge system: an interaction-centered approach to knowledge sharing. In: Proceedings of the 5th International Conference on Cooperative information Systems, Portugal (November 2007)
20. Walton, C., Barker, A.: An Agent-based e-Science Experiment Builder. In: Proceedings of the 1st International Workshop on Semantic Intelligent Middleware for the Web and the Grid, Valencia, Spain (August 2004)

Probabilistic and Logical Beliefs

J.W. Lloyd[1] and K.S. Ng[2]

[1] Computer Sciences Laboratory
College of Engineering and Computer Science
The Australian National University
jwl@cecs.anu.edu.au
[2] National ICT Australia
keesiong.ng@nicta.com.au

Abstract. This paper proposes a method of integrating two different concepts of belief in artificial intelligence: belief as a probability distribution and belief as a logical formula. The setting for the integration is a highly expressive logic. The integration is explained in detail, as its comparison to other approaches to integrating logic and probability. An illustrative example is given to motivate the usefulness of the ideas in agent applications.

1 Introduction

The term 'belief' has two meanings in artificial intelligence: in robotics and vision [1], a 'belief' is generally a probability distribution; in logical artificial intelligence, a 'belief' is a logical formula. In this paper, we give a definition of belief that encompasses both meanings and investigate the use of this concept for agent applications.

This work is set in the context of the more general problem of integrating logic and probability, a problem that is currently attracting substantial interest from researchers in artificial intelligence [2,3,4,5,6,7]. Consequently, to set the scene and also to provide a contrast with the approach to integration adopted in this paper, we now briefly discuss the most common approach in literature.

Unfortunately, there does not seem to be any widely agreed statement of exactly what the problem of integrating logic and probability actually is, much less a widely agreed solution to the problem [8,9,10,11]. However, the following quote from [10], which contains an excellent overview of the problem especially from the philosophical point of view, captures the generally agreed essence of the problem: "Classical logic has no explicit mechanism for representing the degree of certainty of premises in an argument, nor the degree of certainty in a conclusion, given those premises". Thus, intuitively, the problem is to find some way of effectively doing probabilistic reasoning in a logical formalism that may involve the invention of 'probabilistic logics'. The discussion below is restricted to recent approaches that have come from the artificial intelligence community; these approaches usually also include a significant component of learning [11].

The standard logical setting for these approaches is first-order logic. Imagine that an agent is operating in some environment for which there is some

M. Dastani et al. (Eds.): LADS 2007, LNAI 5118, pp. 19–36, 2008.
© Springer-Verlag Berlin Heidelberg 2008

uncertainty (for example, the environment might be partially observable). The environment is modelled as a probability distribution over the collection of first-order interpretations (over some suitable alphabet for the application at hand). The intuition is that any of these interpretations could be the actual environment but that some interpretations are more likely than others to correctly model the actual world and this information is given by the distribution on the interpretations. If the agent actually knew this distribution, then it could answer probabilistic questions of the form: if (closed) formula ψ holds, what is the probability that the (closed) formula φ holds? In symbols, the question is: what is $Pr(\varphi \mid \psi)$?

We formalise this situation. Let $\mathfrak{I}$ be the set of interpretations and p a probability measure on the σ-algebra of all subsets of this set. Define the random variable $X_\varphi : \mathfrak{I} \to \mathbb{R}$ by

$$X_\varphi(I) = \begin{cases} 1 & \text{if } \varphi \text{ is true in } I \\ 0 & \text{otherwise,} \end{cases}$$

with a similar definition for X_ψ. Then $Pr(\varphi \mid \psi)$ can be written in the form

$$p(X_\varphi = 1 \mid X_\psi = 1)$$

which is equal to

$$\frac{p(X_\varphi = 1 \wedge X_\psi = 1)}{p(X_\psi = 1)}$$

and, knowing p, can be evaluated.

Of course, the real problem is to know the distribution on the interpretations. To make some progress on this, most systems intending to integrate logical and probabilistic reasoning in artificial intelligence make simplifying assumptions. For a start, most are based on Prolog. Thus theories are first-order Horn clause theories, maybe with negation as failure. Interpretations are limited to Herbrand interpretations and often function symbols are excluded so the Herbrand base (and therefore the number of Herbrand interpretations) is finite. Let $\mathfrak{I}$ denote the (finite) set of Herbrand interpretations and $\mathcal{B}$ the Herbrand base. We can identify $\mathfrak{I}$ with the product space $\{0, 1\}^{\mathcal{B}}$ in the natural way. Thus the problem amounts to knowing the distribution on this product space. At this point, there is a wide divergence in the approaches. For example, either Bayesian networks or Markov random fields can be used to represent the product distribution. In [4], the occurrences of atoms in the same clause are used to give the arcs and the weights attached to clauses are used to give the potential functions in a Markov random field. In [6], conditional probability distributions are attached to clauses to give a Bayesian network. In [3], a program is written that specifies a generative distribution for a Bayesian network. In all cases, the logic is exploited to give some kind of compact representation of what is usually a very large graphical model. Generally, the theory is only used to construct the graphical model and reasoning proceeds probabilistically, as described above.

Here we follow a different approach. To begin with, we use a much more expressive logic, modal higher-order logic. The higher-orderness will be essential to achieve the desired integration of logic and probability. Also, the modalities will be important for agent applications. Furthermore, in our approach, the theory plays a central role and probabilistic reasoning all takes place in the context of the theory.

The next section gives a brief account of the logic we employ. In Section 3, the definition of a density and some of its properties are presented. Section 4 presents our approach to integrating logic and probability. Section 5 considers the idea that beliefs should be function definitions. Section 6 gives an extended example to illustrate the ideas. Section 7 gives some conclusions and future research directions.

2   Logic

We outline the most relevant aspects of the logic, focussing to begin with on the monomorphic version. We define types and terms, and give an introduction to the modalities that will be most useful in this paper. Full details of the logic, including its reasoning capabilities, can be found in [12].

Definition 1. *An* alphabet *consists of three sets:*

1. *A set $\mathfrak{T}$ of type constructors.*
2. *A set $\mathfrak{C}$ of constants.*
3. *A set $\mathfrak{V}$ of variables.*

Each type constructor in $\mathfrak{T}$ has an arity. The set $\mathfrak{T}$ always includes the type constructor Ω of arity 0. Ω is the type of the booleans. Each constant in $\mathfrak{C}$ has a signature. The set $\mathfrak{V}$ is denumerable. Variables are typically denoted by $x, y, z, \ldots$. Types are built up from the set of type constructors, using the symbols $\rightarrow$ and $\times$.

Definition 2. *A* type *is defined inductively as follows.*

1. *If T is a type constructor of arity k and $\alpha_1, \ldots, \alpha_k$ are types, then $T\,\alpha_1 \ldots \alpha_k$ is a type. (Thus a type constructor of arity 0 is a type.)*
2. *If α and β are types, then $\alpha \rightarrow \beta$ is a type.*
3. *If $\alpha_1, \ldots, \alpha_n$ are types, then $\alpha_1 \times \cdots \times \alpha_n$ is a type.*

Int is the type of the integers and *Real* is the type of the reals. (*List* σ) is the type of lists whose items have type σ. Also $\sigma \rightarrow \Omega$ is the type of sets whose elements have type σ, since sets are identified with predicates; $\{\sigma\}$ is a synonym for $\sigma \rightarrow \Omega$ used when we are intuitively thinking of a term as a set of elements rather than as a predicate.

The set $\mathfrak{C}$ always includes the following constants.

1. $\top$ and $\bot$, having signature Ω.
2. $=_\alpha$, having signature $\alpha \rightarrow \alpha \rightarrow \Omega$, for each type α.
3. $\neg$, having signature $\Omega \rightarrow \Omega$.

4. $\wedge$, $\vee$, $\longrightarrow$, $\longleftarrow$, and $\longleftrightarrow$, having signature $\Omega \to \Omega \to \Omega$.
5. Σ_α and Π_α, having signature $(\alpha \to \Omega) \to \Omega$, for each type α.

The intended meaning of $=_\alpha$ is identity (that is, $=_\alpha x\ y$ is $\top$ iff x and y are identical), the intended meaning of $\top$ is true, the intended meaning of $\bot$ is false, and the intended meanings of the connectives $\neg$, $\wedge$, $\vee$, $\longrightarrow$, $\longleftarrow$, and $\longleftrightarrow$ are as usual. The intended meanings of Σ_α and Π_α are that Σ_α maps a predicate to $\top$ iff the predicate maps at least one element to $\top$ and Π_α maps a predicate to $\top$ iff the predicate maps all elements to $\top$.

We assume there are necessity modality operators $\square_i$, for $i = 1, \dots, m$.

Definition 3. *A* term, *together with its type, is defined inductively as follows.*

1. *A variable in $\mathfrak{V}$ of type α is a term of type α.*
2. *A constant in $\mathfrak{C}$ having signature α is a term of type α.*
3. *If t is a term of type β and x a variable of type α, then $\lambda x.t$ is a term of type $\alpha \to \beta$.*
4. *If s is a term of type $\alpha \to \beta$ and t a term of type α, then $(s\ t)$ is a term of type β.*
5. *If $t_1, \dots, t_n$ are terms of type $\alpha_1, \dots, \alpha_n$, respectively, then $(t_1, \dots, t_n)$ is a term of type $\alpha_1 \times \cdots \times \alpha_n$.*
6. *If t is a term of type α and $i \in \{1, \dots, m\}$, then $\square_i t$ is a term of type α.*

Terms of the form $(\Sigma_\alpha\ \lambda x.t)$ are written as $\exists_\alpha x.t$ and terms of the form $(\Pi_\alpha\ \lambda x.t)$ are written as $\forall_\alpha x.t$ (in accord with the intended meaning of Σ_α and Π_α). Thus, in higher-order logic, each quantifier is obtained as a combination of an abstraction acted on by a suitable function (Σ_α or Π_α).

The polymorphic version of the logic extends what is given above by also having available parameters which are type variables (denoted by $a, b, c, \dots$). The definition of a type as above is then extended to polymorphic types that may contain parameters and the definition of a term as above is extended to terms that may have polymorphic types. We work in the polymorphic version of the logic in the remainder of the paper. In this case, we drop the α in $\exists_\alpha$, $\forall_\alpha$, and $=_\alpha$, since the types associated with $\exists$, $\forall$, and $=$ are now inferred from the context.

An important feature of higher-order logic is that it admits functions that can take functions as arguments and return functions as results. (First-order logic does not admit these so-called higher-order functions.) This fact can be exploited in applications, through the use of predicates to represent sets and densities to model uncertainty, for example.

As is well known, modalities can have a variety of meanings, depending on the application. Some of these are indicated here; much more detail can be found in [13], [14] and [12], for example.

In multi-agent applications, one meaning for $\square_i \varphi$ is that 'agent i knows φ'. In this case, the modality $\square_i$ is written as $\boldsymbol{K}_i$. A weaker notion is that of belief. In this case, $\square_i \varphi$ means that 'agent i believes φ' and the modality $\square_i$ is written as $\boldsymbol{B}_i$.

The modalities also have a variety of temporal readings. We will make use of the (past) temporal modalities ● ('last') and ■ ('always in the past').

Modalities can be applied to terms that are not formulas. Thus terms such as $B_i 42$ and ●A, where A is a constant, are admitted. We will find to be particularly useful terms that have the form $\Box_{j_1} \cdots \Box_{j_r} f$, where f is a function and $\Box_{j_1} \cdots \Box_{j_r}$ is a sequence of modalities. The symbol $\Box$ denotes a sequence of modalities.

Composition is handled by the (reverse) composition function ∘ defined by $((f \circ g) \, x) = (g \, (f \, x))$.

The logic has a conventional possible-worlds semantics with higher-order interpretations at each world.

3 Densities

This section presents some standard notions of measure theory, particularly that of a density, which will be needed later [15].

Definition 4. *Let $(X, \mathcal{A}, \mu)$ be a measure space and $f : X \to \mathbb{R}$ a measurable function. Then f is a* density *(on $(X, \mathcal{A}, \mu)$) if (i) $f(x) \geq 0$, for all $x \in X$, and (ii) $\int_X f \, d\mu = 1$.*

There are two main cases of interest. The first is when μ is the counting measure on X, in which case $\int_X f \, d\mu = \sum_{x \in X} f(x)$; this is the discrete case. The second case is when X is $\mathbb{R}^n$, for some $n \geq 1$, and μ is Lebesgue measure; this is the continuous case.

A density f gives a probability ν on $\mathcal{A}$ by the definition

$$\nu(A) = \int_A f \, d\mu,$$

for $A \in \mathcal{A}$. In the common discrete case, this definition specialises to

$$\nu(A) = \sum_{x \in A} f(x).$$

If $(X, \mathcal{A}, \mu)$ is a measure space, then *Density X* denotes the set of densities on $(X, \mathcal{A}, \mu)$.

Some (higher-order) functions that operate on densities will be needed. The following two definitions give natural ways of 'composing' functions whose codomains are densities.

Definition 5. *Let $(X, \mathcal{A}, \mu)$, $(Y, \mathcal{B}, \nu)$, and $(Z, \mathcal{C}, \xi)$ be measure spaces. The function ♮ : $(X \to$ Density $Y) \to (Y \to$ Density $Z) \to (X \to$ Density $Z)$ is defined by*

$$(f \, ♮ \, g)(x)(z) = \int_Y f(x)(y) \times g(y)(z) \, d\nu(y),$$

for $f : X \to$ Density Y, $g : Y \to$ Density Z, $x \in X$, and $z \in Z$.

Specialised to the discrete case, the definition is

$$(f \natural g)(x)(z) = \sum_{y \in Y} f(x)(y) \times g(y)(z).$$

Definition 6. *The function*

$$\S : Density\ Y \to (Y \to Density\ Z) \to Density\ Z$$

is defined by

$$(f \S g)(z) = \int_Y f(y) \times g(y)(z)\ d\nu(y),$$

where $f : Density\ Y$, $g : Y \to Density\ Z$, *and* $z \in Z$.

Specialised to the discrete case, the definition is

$$(f \S g)(z) = \sum_{y \in Y} f(y) \times g(y)(z).$$

We can define conditional densities. Consider a function $f : Density\ X \times Y$ that defines a product density. Then we can express the conditional density obtained by conditioning on values in X by the function $f_1 : X \to Density\ Y$ defined by

$$f_1(x)(y) = \frac{f(x,y)}{\int_Y f(x,y)\ d\nu(y)},$$

for $x \in X$ and $y \in Y$. Clearly, $f_1(x)$ *is* a density. Conditioning on the other argument is analogous to this.

Marginal densities can also be defined. Consider a function

$$f : Density\ X \times Y \times Z$$

that defines a product density. Then we can form the marginal density over the first argument by the function $f_1 : Density\ X$ defined by

$$f_1(x) = \int_Z \int_Y f(x,y,z)\ d\nu(y)\ d\xi(z),$$

for $x \in X$. By Fubini's theorem, f_1 *is* a density. This is easily extended to marginalising in arbitrary products.

4   Integrating Logic and Probability

This section provides an overview of our approach to integrating logic and probability. The key idea is to allow densities to appear in theories. For this reason, we first set up some logical machinery for this. In the logic, we let *Density σ* denote the type of densities whose arguments have type σ. Any term of type *Density* σ, for some σ, is called a *density*. We also make available the functions from Section 3 that compose functions whose codomains are densities. Conditionalisation and marginalisation are also easily expressed.

The idea is to model uncertainty by using densities in the definitions of (some) functions in theories. Consider a function $f : \sigma \to \tau$ for which there is some uncertainty about its values that we want to model. We do this with a function

$$f' : \sigma \to Density\ \tau,$$

where, for each argument t, $(f'\ t)$ is a suitable density for modelling the uncertainty in the value of the function $(f\ t)$. The intuition is that the actual value of $(f\ t)$ is likely to be where the 'mass' of the density $(f'\ t)$ is most concentrated. Of course, (unconditional) densities can also be expressed by functions having a signature of the form *Density* τ.

This simple idea turns out to be a powerful and convenient way of modelling uncertainty with logical theories in diverse applications, especially agent applications. Note carefully the use that has been made of the expressive logic here. Functions whose values are densities are higher-order functions that cannot be modelled directly in first-order logic.

As well as representing knowledge, it is necessary to reason with it. We employ a declarative programming language called Bach for this purpose. Bach is a probabilistic modal functional logic programming language. Programs in the language are equational theories in modal higher-order logic. The reasoning system for the logic underlying Bach combines a theorem prover and an equational reasoning system [12,16]. The theorem prover is a fairly conventional tableau theorem prover for modal higher-order logic. The equational reasoning system is, in effect, a computational system that significantly extends existing declarative programming languages by adding facilities for computing with modalities and densities. The proof component and the computational component are tightly integrated, in the sense that either can call the other. Furthermore, this synergy between the two makes possible all kinds of interesting reasoning tasks. For agent applications, the most common reasoning task is a computational one, that of evaluating a function call. In this case, the theorem-prover plays a subsidiary role, usually that of performing some rather straightforward modal theorem-proving tasks. However, in other applications it can just as easily be the other way around with the computational system performing subsidiary equational reasoning tasks for the theorem prover.

Here is an example to illustrate the ideas introduced so far.

Example 1. We model the following scenario, which is one of the main examples used in [3]. An urn contains an unknown number of balls that have the colour blue or green with equal probability. Identically coloured balls are indistinguishable. An agent has the prior belief that the distribution of the number of balls is a Poisson distribution with mean 6. The agent now draws some balls from the urn, observes their colour, and then replaces them. The observed colour is different from the actual colour of the ball drawn with probability 0.2. On the basis of these observations, the agent should infer certain properties about the urn, such as the number of balls it contains.

It was claimed in [3] that this problem cannot be modelled in most existing first-order probabilistic languages because the number of balls in the urn is unknown. Interestingly, the problem can be modelled rather straightforwardly if we define densities over structured objects like sets and lists. The following is a suitable graphical model.

$$\boxed{numOfBalls} \longrightarrow \boxed{setOfBalls} \longrightarrow \boxed{ballsDrawn_d} \longrightarrow \boxed{observations}$$

In the simulation given by the following Bach program, a number n is selected from the Poisson distribution and a set s of balls of size n is constructed. A ball is represented by an integer identifier and its colour: $Ball = Int \times Colour$. The balls in s are labelled 1 to n, and the colours are chosen randomly. Given s, a list is constructed consisting of d balls by drawing successively at random with replacement from s. The observed colours of the drawn balls are then recorded.

$colour : Colour \rightarrow \Omega$

$(colour \ x) = (x = Blue) \vee (x = Green)$

$numOfBalls : Density \ Int$

$(numOfBalls \ x) = (poisson \ 6 \ x)$

$poisson : Int \rightarrow Density \ Int$

$(poisson \ x \ y) = e^{-x}x^y/y!$

$setOfBalls : Int \rightarrow Density \ \{Ball\}$

$(setOfBalls \ n \ s) = if \ \exists x_1 \cdots \exists x_n.((colour \ x_1) \wedge \cdots \wedge (colour \ x_n) \wedge$
$$(s = \{(1, x_1), \ldots, (n, x_n)\}) \ then \ 0.5^n \ else \ 0$$

$ballsDrawn : Int \rightarrow \{Ball\} \rightarrow Density \ (List \ Ball)$

$(ballsDrawn \ d \ s \ x) =$

$\quad if \ \exists x_1 \cdots \exists x_d.((s \ x_1) \wedge \cdots \wedge (s \ x_d) \wedge (x = [x_1, \ldots, x_d])) \ then \ (card \ s)^{-d} \ else \ 0$

$observations : (List \ Ball) \rightarrow Density \ (List \ Colour)$

$(observations \ x \ y) = if \ (length \ x) = (length \ y) \ then \ (obsProb \ x \ y) \ else \ 0$

$obsProb : (List \ Ball) \rightarrow (List \ Colour) \rightarrow Real$

$(obsProb \ [] \ []) = 1$

$(obsProb \ (\# \ (x_1, y_1) \ z_1) \ (\# \ y_2 \ z_2)) =$
$$(if \ (y_1 = y_2) \ then \ 0.8 \ else \ 0.2) \cdot (obsProb \ z_1 \ z_2)$$

$joint : Int \rightarrow Density \ (Int \times \{Ball\} \times (List \ Ball) \times (List \ Colour))$

$(joint \ d \ (n, s, x, y)) =$

$\quad (numOfBalls \ n) \cdot (setOfBalls \ n \ s) \cdot (ballsDrawn \ d \ s \ x) \cdot (observations \ x \ y)$

The function *card* returns the cardinality of a set and *length* returns the size of a list. The functions *setOfBalls* and *ballsDrawn* are defined informally above; formal recursive definitions can be given.

Marginalisations and conditionalisations of the given density can be computed to obtain answers to different questions. For example, the following gives the probability that the number of balls in the urn is m after the colours $[o_1, o_2, \ldots, o_d]$ from d draws have been observed:

$$\frac{1}{K} \sum_s \sum_l \left(joint\ d\ (m, s, l, [o_1, o_2, \ldots, o_d]) \right),$$

where K is a normalisation constant, s ranges over $\{\, s \mid (setOfBalls\ m\ s) > 0\,\}$, and l ranges over $\{\, l \mid (ballsDrawn\ d\ s\ l) > 0\,\}$. The elements of these two sets are automatically enumerated by Bach during execution of the query.

At this stage, it is interesting make a comparison with other approaches to integrating logic and probability. Perhaps the main point is the value of working in a higher-order logic. All other logical approaches to this integration that we know of use first-order logic and thereby miss the opportunity of being able to reason about densities in theories. This is an important point. (Classical) logic is often criticised for its inability to cope with uncertainty: witness the quote in the introduction. In contrast, our view is that higher-order logic is quite capable of modelling probabilistic statements about knowledge directly in theories themselves, thus providing a powerful method of capturing uncertainty. In first-order logic, there is a preoccupation with the truth or falsity of formulas, which does seem to preclude the possibility of capturing uncertainty. However, looked at from a more general perspective, first-order logic is impoverished. It is not natural to exclude higher-order functions – these are used constantly in everyday (informal) mathematics. Also the rigid dichotomy between terms and formulas in first-order logic gets in the way. In higher-order logic, a formula is a term whose type just happens to be boolean; also it is just as important to compute the value of arbitrary terms, not only formulas. Higher-order logic is essentially the language of everyday mathematics and no-one would ever claim situations involving uncertainty and structural relationships between entities cannot be modelled directly and in an integrated way using mathematics – therefore they can also be so modelled using higher-order logic.

Another significant difference concerns the semantic view that is adopted. In the most common approach to integration explained above there is assumed to be a distribution on interpretations and answering queries involves performing computations over this distribution. In principle, this is fine; given the distribution, one can answer queries by computing with this distribution. But this approach is intrinsically more difficult than computing the value of terms in the traditional case of having *one* intended interpretation, the difficulty of which has already led to nearly all artificial intelligence systems using the proof-theoretic approach of building a theory (that has the intended interpretation as a model) and proving theorems with this theory instead. Here we adopt the well-established method of using a theory to model a situation and relying on the soundness of theorem proving to produce results that are correct in the intended interpretation [12]. We simply have to note that this theory, if it is higher-order, can include densities that can be reasoned with. *Thus no new conceptual machinery at all needs to be invented.* In our approach, whatever the situation, there is a single intended interpretation, which would include densities in the case where uncertainty is being modelled, that is a model of the theory. Our approach also gives fine control over exactly what uncertainty is modelled – we only introduce densities in those parts of the theory that really need them. Furthermore, the probabilistic and non-probabilistic parts of a theory work harmoniously together.

5   Beliefs

In this section, we discuss suitable syntactic forms for beliefs. There are no generally agreed forms for beliefs in the literature, other than the basic requirement that they be formulas. For the purpose of constructing multi-agent systems, we propose the following definition.

Definition 7. *A belief is the definition of a function $f : \sigma \to \tau$ having the form*

$$\Box\forall x.((f\ x) = t),$$

where $\Box$ is a (possibly empty) sequence of modalities and t is a term of type τ.

The function f thus defined is called a belief function. In case τ has the form Density ν, for some ν, we say the belief is probabilistic.

A belief base is a set of beliefs.

Typically, for agent j, beliefs have the form $\boldsymbol{B}_j\varphi$, with the intuitive meaning 'agent j believes φ', where φ is $\forall x.((f\ x) = t)$. Other typical beliefs have the form $\boldsymbol{B}_j\boldsymbol{B}_i\varphi$, meaning 'agent j believes that agent i believes φ'. If there is a temporal component to beliefs, this is often manifested by temporal modalities at the front of beliefs. Then, for example, there could be a belief of the form $\bullet^2\boldsymbol{B}_j\boldsymbol{B}_i\varphi$, whose intuitive meaning is 'at the second last time, agent j believed that agent i believed φ'. (Here, $\bullet^2$ is a shorthand for $\bullet\bullet$.)

To motivate Definition 7, we now consider a probabilistic extension of the rational agent architecture described in [17].

For this purpose, let S be the set of states of the agent and A the set of actions that the agent can apply. The set S is the underlying set of a measure space that has a σ-algebra $\mathcal{A}$ and a measure μ on $\mathcal{A}$. Often $(S, \mathcal{A}, \mu)$ is discrete so that $\mathcal{A}$ is the powerset of S and μ is the counting measure. The dynamics of the agent is captured by a function

$$transition : A \to S \to Density\ S.$$

In the discrete case, $transition(a)(s)(s')$ is the conditional probability that, given the state is s and action a is applied, there will be a transition to state s'.

Various specific rationality principles could be used; a widely used one is the principle of maximum expected utility [18, p.585] (namely, a rational agent should choose an action that maximises the agent's expected utility, where the utility is a real-valued function on the set of states). If this principle is used, it is assumed that the utility function is known to the agent and that the maximum expected value of the utility corresponds closely to the external performance measure. Under the principle of maximum expected utility, the policy function

$$policy : Density\ S \to A$$

is defined by

$$policy(\boldsymbol{s}) = \underset{a\in A}{\operatorname{argmax}}\ \mathbb{E}_{\boldsymbol{s}\ \S\ transition(a)}(utility),$$

for each $\boldsymbol{s} \in Density\ S$. Here $\mathbb{E}_{\boldsymbol{s}\ \S\ transition(a)}(utility)$ denotes the expectation of the random variable $utility : S \to \mathbb{R}$ with respect to the density $\boldsymbol{s}\ \S\ transition(a)$ (where $\S$ was defined in Section 3). If the current state density is $\boldsymbol{s}$, then the action selected is thus the one given by $policy(\boldsymbol{s})$.

In many complex applications, the agent is not given the definition of the function $transition$ (or cannot be given this definition because it is impractical to specify it precisely enough); in such cases, the agent essentially has to learn the transition function from its experience in the environment. A common complication then is that the number of states may be very large, so large in fact that it is quite impractical to attempt to learn *directly* the definition of the function $transition$. Instead, an obvious idea is to partition the set of states into a much smaller number of subsets of states such that the states in each subset can be treated uniformly and learn a transition function over equivalence classes of states. We now explore this idea, showing how the expressivity of the logic can be exploited to turn this idea into a practical method that assists in the construction of agents.

It will be important to employ two different ways of partitioning the states. For this reason, two collections of functions on states are introduced. These are

$$e_i : S \to V_i,$$

where $i = 1, \ldots, n$, and

$$r_j : S \to W_j,$$

where $j = 1, \ldots, m$. Each function e_i, for $i = 1, \ldots, n$, is called an *evidence feature* and each function r_j, for $j = 1, \ldots, m$, is called a *result feature*. Each e_i and r_j is a feature that picks out a specific property of a state that is relevant to selecting actions. Evidence features are so-called because they pick out properties of the state that suggest the action that ought to be selected. Result features are so-called because they pick out properties of the state which result from applying an action that can be usefully employed in the calculation of its utility. An interesting fact that emerges from applying these ideas to practical applications is how different the evidence features are compared with the result features [17].

Typically, the cardinality of the product spaces $V_1 \times \cdots \times V_n$ and $W_1 \times \cdots \times W_m$ are much smaller than the cardinality of S. Often, some V_i and W_j are simply the set of booleans. In an application that is at least partly continuous, they could be $\mathbb{R}$. There are two key functions associated with this construction. The function

$$(e_1, \ldots, e_n) : S \to V_1 \times \cdots \times V_n$$

is defined by

$$(e_1, \ldots, e_n)(s) = (e_1(s), \ldots, e_n(s)),$$

for each $s \in S$. The space $V_1 \times \cdots \times V_n$ is assumed to have a suitable σ-algebra of measurable sets on it, so that $(e_1, \ldots, e_n)$ is a measurable function. If μ is the measure on S, then $(e_1, \ldots, e_n)^{-1} \circ \mu$ is the measure imposed on $V_1 \times \cdots \times V_n$. (Note that $(f \circ g)(x)$ means $g(f(x))$.) Similarly, the function

$$(r_1, \ldots, r_m) : S \to W_1 \times \cdots \times W_m$$

is defined by

$$(r_1, \ldots, r_m)(s) = (r_1(s), \ldots, r_m(s)),$$

for each $s \in S$. The space $W_1 \times \cdots \times W_m$ is also assumed to have a suitable σ-algebra of measurable sets on it, so that $(r_1, \ldots, r_m)$ is a measurable function. Similarly, $(r_1, \ldots, r_m)^{-1} \circ \mu$ is the measure imposed on $W_1 \times \cdots \times W_m$.

Now, instead of the transition function

$$transition : A \to S \to Density\ S,$$

one works with a function

$$transition' : A \to V_1 \times \cdots \times V_n \to Density\ W_1 \times \cdots \times W_m.$$

The motivation for doing this is that *transition'* should be more amenable to being learned because of the much smaller cardinalities of its domain and codomain. Some precision is lost in working with $V_1 \times \cdots \times V_n$ and $W_1 \times \cdots \times W_m$ instead of S in this way, as discussed below; to make up for this, informative choices of the evidence and result features need to be made. The policy is now defined by

$$policy(s) = \operatorname*{argmax}_{a \in A} \mathbb{E}_{s\ \S\ ((e_1, \ldots, e_n)\ \circ\ transition'(a))}(utility'),$$

for each $s \in Density\ S$. Here

$$utility' : W_1 \times \cdots \times W_m \to \mathbb{R}.$$

The result features are intended to be chosen so that $(r_1, \ldots, r_m) \circ utility'$ gives the utility of each state. Note that

$$(e_1, \ldots, e_n) \circ transition'(a) : S \to Density\ W_1 \times \cdots \times W_m,$$

so that $s \S ((e_1, \ldots, e_n) \circ transition'(a))$ is a density on $W_1 \times \cdots \times W_m$.

If the action selected by the policy is a_{max}, then the state density that results by applying this action is

$$s \S ((e_1, \ldots, e_n) \circ transition'(a_{max}) \circ \overline{(r_1, \ldots, r_m)}).$$

Here, since $(r_1, \ldots, r_m) : S \to W_1 \times \cdots \times W_m$, it follows from [15, Theorem 4.1.11] that one can define the function

$$\overline{(r_1, \ldots, r_m)} : Density \ W_1 \times \cdots \times W_m \to Density \ S$$

by

$$\overline{(r_1, \ldots, r_m)}(h) = (r_1, \ldots, r_m) \circ h,$$

for each $h \in Density \ W_1 \times \cdots \times W_m$. Thus

$$(e_1, \ldots, e_n) \circ transition'(a_{max}) \circ \overline{(r_1, \ldots, r_m)} : S \to Density \ S$$

and so

$$s \S ((e_1, \ldots, e_n) \circ transition'(a_{max}) \circ \overline{(r_1, \ldots, r_m)}) : Density \ S,$$

as required.

Now consider this question: what makes up the belief base of such an agent? Clearly, the definitions of the evidence and (some of the) result features should be in the belief base. Further, the definitions of the functions *transition*, *utility* and *policy* should also be in the belief base. And these are all the beliefs the agent needs to maintain about the environment in order to act rationally. This concludes our motivation for Definition 7.

At this point, the advantages and disadvantages of introducing features are clearer. The main advantage is that they can make learning the transition function feasible when otherwise it wouldn't be because of the vast size of the state space. The main disadvantage is that some precision in the update of the state density during the agent cycle is lost since this is now mediated by passing through $V_1 \times \cdots \times V_n$ and $W_1 \times \cdots \times W_m$. This shows the crucial importance of finding suitable features; if these can be found, and experience has shown that this can be hard for some applications, then the loss of precision is likely to be small and there is everything to gain. Choosing the 'right' (general form of) features is generally a problem that has to be solved before deployment by the designer of the agent, although some techniques are known that allow agents to discover such information autonomously. For example, it is likely that the features will need to capture beliefs about the beliefs of other agents, beliefs about temporal aspects of the environment, and will have to cope with uncertainty. The logic of this paper is ideal for the representation of such properties. Agents can learn the precise definition of a feature (whose general form is given by an hypothesis language) during deployment by machine learning techniques. This eases the task of the designer since only the general forms of the features need specifying before deployment. In a dynamic environment, this adaptive capability of an agent is essential, of course.

The above description generalises the agent architecture presented in [17] by admitting probabilistic beliefs in addition to non-probabilistic ones. Using a density to model the uncertain value of a function on some argument is better than using a single value (such as the mean of the density). For example, if the density is a normal distribution, then it may be important that the variance is large or small: if it is large, intuitively, there is less confidence about its actual value; if it is small, then there could be confidence that the actual value is the mean. Such subtleties can assist in the selection of one action over another. Similarly, learning tasks can exploit the existence of the density by including features based on the mean, variance, higher moments, or other parameters of the density in hypothesis languages.

We now examine the form that beliefs can take in more detail. Some beliefs can be specified directly by the designer and the body of the definition can be any term of the appropriate type. In particular, some of these beliefs may be compositions of other probabilistic beliefs in which case the composition operators introduced in Section 3 will be useful. Some beliefs, however, need to be acquired from training examples, usually during deployment. We propose a particular form for beliefs of this latter type. We consider beliefs that, for a function $f : \sigma \to \tau$, are definitions of the following form.

$$\Box \forall x.((f\ x) = \tag{1}$$
$$\quad if\ (p_1\ x)\ then\ v_1$$
$$\quad else\ if\ (p_2\ x)\ then\ v_2$$
$$\quad \vdots$$
$$\quad else\ if\ (p_n\ x)\ then\ v_n$$
$$\quad else\ v_0),$$

where $\Box$ is a (possibly empty) sequence of modalities, $p_1, \ldots, p_n$ are predicates that can be modal and/or higher order, and $v_0, v_1, \ldots, v_n$ are suitable values. Such a belief is a definition for the function f in the context of the modal sequence $\Box$. Note that in the case when τ has the form $Density\ \nu$, for some ν, the values $v_0, v_1, \ldots, v_n$ are densities.

While the above form for acquired beliefs may appear to be rather specialised, it turns out to be convenient and general, and easily encompasses beliefs in many other forms [19,20]. Also this decision-list form of beliefs is highly convenient for acquisition using some kind of learning algorithm [21,22,23,24]. Towards that end, the Alkemy machine learning system [22,23] is being extended with the ability to acquire modal and probabilistic beliefs.

6   Illustration

Here is an extended example to illustrate the ideas that have been introduced.

Example 2. Consider a majordomo agent that manages a household. There are many tasks for such an agent to carry out including keeping track of occupants, turning appliances on and off, ordering food for the refrigerator, and so on.

Here we concentrate on one small aspect of the majordomo's tasks which is to recommend television programs for viewing by the occupants of the house. Suppose the current occupants are Alice, Bob, and Cathy, and that the agent knows the television preferences of each of them in the form of beliefs about the function *likes* : *Program* → *Density* Ω. Let $\boldsymbol{B_m}$ be the belief modality for the majordomo agent, $\boldsymbol{B_a}$ the belief modality for Alice, $\boldsymbol{B_b}$ the belief modality for Bob, and $\boldsymbol{B_c}$ the belief modality for Cathy. Thus part of the majordomo's belief base has the following form:

$$\boldsymbol{B_m B_a} \forall x.((likes\ x) = \varphi) \tag{2}$$
$$\boldsymbol{B_m B_b} \forall x.((likes\ x) = \psi) \tag{3}$$
$$\boldsymbol{B_m B_c} \forall x.((likes\ x) = \xi) \tag{4}$$

for suitable φ, ψ, and ξ. We will now look at the form of a belief about *likes*. Methods for acquiring these beliefs were studied in [25].

Figure 1 is a typical definition acquired incrementally using real data. In the beginning, the belief base contains the formula

$$\boldsymbol{B_m}\blacksquare\boldsymbol{B_a}\forall x.((likes\ x) = \lambda y.if\ (y = \top)\ then\ 0.5\ else\ if\ (y = \bot)\ then\ 0.5\ else\ 0).$$

The meaning of this formula is "the agent believes that, at all times in the past, Alice has no preference one way or another over any program". After 3 time steps, this formula has been transformed into the last formula in Figure 1. In

---

$\boldsymbol{B_m}\,\boldsymbol{B_a}\,\forall x.((likes\ x) =$

  if $(projTitle \circ (= $ *"NFL Football") x) then $\lambda y.if$ $(y = \top)$ then 1 else if $(y = \bot)$ then 0 else 0*

  else if $(projTitle \circ (existsWord\ (= $ *"sport")) x) then $\lambda y.if$ $(y = \top)$ then 0.7*

                                                     else if $(y = \bot)$ *then 0.3 else 0*

  else $(\bullet likes\ x))$

$\bullet\boldsymbol{B_m}\,\boldsymbol{B_a}\,\forall x.((likes\ x) =$

  if $(projGenre \circ (= $ *Documentary) x) then $\lambda y.if$ $(y = \top)$ then 0.9 else if $(y = \bot)$ then 0.1 else 0*

  else if $(projGenre \circ (= $ *Movie) x) then $\lambda y.if$ $(y = \top)$ then 0.75 else if $(y = \bot)$ then 0.25 else 0*

  else $(\bullet likes\ x))$

$\bullet^2\boldsymbol{B_m}\,\boldsymbol{B_a}\,\forall x.((likes\ x) =$

  if $(projGenre \circ (= $ *Documentary) x) then $\lambda y.if$ $(y = \top)$ then 1 else if $(y = \bot)$ then 0 else 0*

  else if $(projGenre \circ (= $ *Drama) x) then $\lambda y.if$ $(y = \bot)$ then 0.8 else if $(y = \top)$ then 0.2 else 0*

  else $(\bullet likes\ x))$

$\bullet^3\boldsymbol{B_m}\blacksquare\boldsymbol{B_a}\forall x.((likes\ x) = \lambda y.if\ (y = \top)\ then\ 0.5\ else\ if\ (y = \bot)\ then\ 0.5\ else\ 0).$

Fig. 1. Part of the belief base of the agent

general, at each time step, the beliefs about *likes* at the previous time steps each have another ● placed at their front to push them one step further back into the past, and a new current belief about *likes* is acquired. Note how useful parts of previously acquired beliefs are recycled in forming new beliefs.

We have seen the general form of beliefs (2)-(4). Given these beliefs about the occupant preferences for TV programs, the task for the majordomo agent is to recommend programs that all three occupants would be interested in watching together. To estimate how much the group as a whole likes a program, the agent simply counts the number of positive preferences, leading to the definition of *aggregate* below. To deal with the fact that user preferences are not definite but can only be estimated, we compose *aggregate* with the function *combinePrefs* to form *groupLikes*, where *combinePrefs* brings the individual preferences together.

$$combinePrefs : Program \rightarrow Density\ \Omega \times \Omega \times \Omega$$

$$\boldsymbol{B}_m \forall p.\forall x.\forall y.\forall z.((combinePrefs\ p\ (x,y,z)) =$$
$$(\boldsymbol{B}_a likes\ p\ x) \times (\boldsymbol{B}_b likes\ p\ y) \times (\boldsymbol{B}_c likes\ p\ z))$$

$$aggregate : \Omega \times \Omega \times \Omega \rightarrow Density\ \Omega$$

$$\boldsymbol{B}_m \forall x.\forall y.\forall z.((aggregate\ (x,y,z)) =$$
$$\lambda v.\frac{1}{3}((\mathbb{I}\ (x=v)) + (\mathbb{I}\ (y=v)) + (\mathbb{I}\ (z=v))))$$

$$groupLikes : Program \rightarrow Density\ \Omega$$

$$\boldsymbol{B}_m \forall x.((groupLikes\ x) =$$
$$((combinePrefs\ \natural\ aggregate)\ x)).$$

Here, $\mathbb{I} : \Omega \rightarrow Int$ is the indicator function defined by $(\mathbb{I}\ \top) = 1$ and $(\mathbb{I}\ \bot) = 0$.

The version of *combinePrefs* given above makes an independence assumption amongst the densities $\boldsymbol{B}_a likes\ p$, and so on. It may be that there are some dependencies between these densities that could be learned. In this case, a more complicated definition of *combinePrefs* would be substituted for the one above. Analogous comments apply to *aggregate*.

Now let us look more closely at what the architecture of the agent would look like if the rational agent architecture were used for this task. The function *groupLikes* is the latter component of one of the evidence features, say e_1. (The initial component of e_1 maps from states to programs.) There are likely to be other evidence features as well. For example, there may be an evidence feature that determines whether all the occupants are free to watch the program at the time it is on. Once all the evidence and result features have been determined, the function

$$transition' : A \rightarrow V_1 \times \cdots \times V_n \rightarrow Density\ W_1 \times \cdots \times W_m$$

that is learned by Alkemy would be used along with the utility to give a rational policy to select an appropriate action (to recommend or not recommend any particular program.)

Note that, for this example, elements in V_1 have type *Density* Ω. This means that the hypothesis language used to learn *transition'* should take account of properties of the density. In such a simple case as a density on the booleans, there are not many possibilities; different thresholds on the probability of $\top$ could be tried, for example.

7 Conclusion

This paper has shown how to integrate logical and probabilistic beliefs in modal higher-order logic. The key point is that the expressive power of the logic allows densities and other probabilistic concepts to appear in beliefs. Our approach is based on the well-established method that uses theories to model situations, and reasoning procedures, such as theorem-proving and equational reasoning, to determine the values of terms (in the intended interpretation). The integration of logic and probability does not force any restriction on the logic employed; indeed, it is the expressive power of the logic that makes the integration actually possible. In fact, the logic we employ is considerably more expressive than those used in all other approaches to integration that we are aware of. Reasoning about probabilistic beliefs is realised through the Bach programming language that has special implementational support for this. In particular, there is support for operations, such as marginalisation, on large product densities. Also the standard compositional operations on densities can be neatly encoded in Bach. Beliefs can be acquired with the Alkemy learning system.

Future work includes completing the implementations of Bach and Alkemy, and applying the technology in challenging application areas, such as cognitive robotics and vision.

Acknowledgments

NICTA is funded through the Australian Government's Backing Australia's Ability initiative, in part through the Australian Research Council.

References

1. Thrun, S., Burgard, W., Fox, D.: Probabilistic Robotics. MIT Press, Cambridge (2005)
2. Muggleton, S.: Stochastic logic programs. In: De Raedt, L. (ed.) Advances in Inductive Logic Programming, pp. 254–264. IOS Press, Amsterdam (1996)
3. Milch, B., Marthi, B., Russell, S., Sontag, D., Ong, D., Kolobov, A.: BLOG: Probabilistic models with unknown objects. In: Kaelbling, L., Saffiotti, A. (eds.) Proceedings of the 19th International Joint Conference on Artificial Intelligence, pp. 1352–1359 (2005)
4. Richardson, M., Domingos, P.: Markov logic networks. Machine Learning 62, 107–136 (2006)
5. Milch, B., Russell, S.: First-order probabilistic languages: Into the unknown. In: Muggleton, S., Otero, R., Tamaddoni-Nezhad, A. (eds.) ILP 2006. LNCS (LNAI), vol. 4455, pp. 10–24. Springer, Heidelberg (2007)

6. Kersting, K., De Raedt, L.: Bayesian logic programming: Theory and tool. In: Getoor, L., Taskar, B. (eds.) Introduction to Statistical Relational Learning. MIT Press, Cambridge (2007)

7. Shirazi, A., Amir, E.: Probabilistic modal logic. In: Holte, R., Howe, A. (eds.) Proceedings of the 22nd AAAI Conference on Artificial Intelligence, pp. 489–495 (2007)

8. Nilsson, N.: Probabilistic logic. Artificial Intelligence 28(1), 71–88 (1986)

9. Halpern, J.: An analysis of first-order logics of probability. Artificial Intelligence 46, 311–350 (1989)

10. Williamson, J.: Probability logic. In: Gabbay, D., Johnson, R., Ohlbach, H., Woods, J. (eds.) Handbook of the Logic of Inference and Argument: The Turn Toward the Practical. Studies in Logic and Practical Reasoning, vol. 1, pp. 397–424. Elsevier, Amsterdam (2002)

11. De Raedt, L., Kersting, K.: Probabilistic logic learning. SIGKDD Explorations 5(1), 31–48 (2003)

12. Lloyd, J.: Knowledge representation and reasoning in modal higher-order logic (2007), http://users.rsise.anu.edu.au/~jwl

13. Fagin, R., Halpern, J., Moses, Y., Vardi, M.: Reasoning about Knowledge. MIT Press, Cambridge (1995)

14. Gabbay, D., Kurucz, A., Wolter, F., Zakharyaschev, M.: Many-Dimensional Modal Logics: Theory and Applications. Studies in Logic and The Foundations of Mathematics, vol. 148. Elsevier, Amsterdam (2003)

15. Dudley, R.: Real Analysis and Probability. Cambridge University Press, Cambridge (2002)

16. Lloyd, J., Ng, K.S.: Reflections on agent beliefs. In: Baldoni, M., Son, T., van Riemsdijk, M.B., Winikoff, M. (eds.) DALT 2007. LNCS(LNAI), vol. 4897, pp. 122–139. Springer, Heidelberg (2007)

17. Lloyd, J., Sears, T.: An architecture for rational agents. In: Baldoni, M., et al. (eds.) DALT 2005. LNCS (LNAI), vol. 3904, pp. 51–71. Springer, Heidelberg (2006)

18. Russell, S., Norvig, P.: Artificial Intelligence: A Modern Approach. 2nd edn. Prentice-Hall, Englewood Cliffs (2002)

19. Rivest, R.: Learning decision lists. Machine Learning 2(3), 229–246 (1987)

20. Eiter, T., Ibaraki, T., Makino, K.: Decision lists and related boolean functions. Theoretical Computer Science 270(1-2), 493–524 (2002)

21. Lloyd, J., Ng, K.S.: Learning modal theories. In: Muggleton, S., Otero, R., Tamaddoni-Nezhad, A. (eds.) ILP 2006. LNCS (LNAI), vol. 4455, pp. 320–334. Springer, Heidelberg (2007)

22. Lloyd, J.: Logic for Learning. Cognitive Technologies. Springer, Heidelberg (2003)

23. Ng, K.S.: Learning Comprehensible Theories from Structured Data. PhD thesis, Computer Sciences Laboratory, The Australian National University (2005)

24. Buntine, W.L.: A Theory of Learning Classification Rules. PhD thesis, School of Computing Science, University of Technology, Sydney (1992)

25. Cole, J., Gray, M., Lloyd, J., Ng, K.S.: Personalisation for user agents. In: Dignum, F., et al. (eds.) Fourth International Conference on Autonomous Agents and Multiagent Systems (AAMAS 2005), pp. 603–610 (2005)

An Argumentation Based Semantics for Agent Reasoning

Sanjay Modgil

Department of Computer Science, Kings College London

Abstract. A key challenge for agent architectures and programming paradigms is to account for defeasible reasoning over mental attitudes and to provide associated conflict resolution mechanisms. A growing body of work is looking to address these challenges by proposing argumentation based approaches to agent defeasible and practical reasoning. This work conforms to Dung's seminal argumentation semantics. In this paper we review our previous work in which we extend Dung's semantics to allow for inclusion of arguments that express preferences between other arguments. In this way we account for the fact that preference information required to resolve conflicts is itself defeasible and may be conflicting. We then propose the extended semantics as a semantics for agent defeasible and practical reasoning, and substantiate this claim by showing how our semantics can characterise, and indeed provide a framework for extending, existing approaches to agent reasoning over beliefs, goals, and actions.

1 Introduction

A key challenge for agent architectures and programming paradigms is the need to formalise defeasible (non-monotonic) and practical reasoning, and associated conflict resolution mechanisms for mental attitudes such as beliefs, desires, intentions and obligations. Conflicts can arise within mental attitudes. For example, two beliefs may logically contradict, or two goals may logically preclude realisation of each other. Plans can be represented in terms of atomic actions related to the adopted goals (intentions) they are intended to realise [9],[20]. Alternative plans for realising a given intention can be viewed as conflicting (in the sense that one must be chosen at the expense of the other), or two plans for realising different intentions can be said to conflict if resource bounds preclude their joint execution. Conflicts can also arise *between* mental attitudes; e.g. a desire derived goal conflicting with an obligation derived goal [8]. Hence, non-monotonic formalisms such as Default Logic [21], have been adopted as a semantics for agent reasoning [23]. For example, the BOID architecture characterises generated candidate goal sets as extensions of a prioritised default logic theory in which rules for inferring goals are modelled as defaults, and a prioritisation of these defaults resolves conflicts between mental attitudes [8]. Consider two default rules respectively inferring the conflicting desire derived goal of 'being on the beach' and obligation derived goal of 'being at work'. Prioritising the former rule over the later will result in the generation of a single extension containing the goal to be on the beach. Indeed, goals are generated through the interaction of beliefs, intentions, desires and obligations, and prioritisations on these attitudes to resolve conflicts, correspond to different agent *types*

M. Dastani et al. (Eds.): LADS 2007, LNAI 5118, pp. 37–53, 2008.

(12 primitive types are identified in [8]). For example, a selfish agent will prioritise desire over obligation derived goals, whereas a social agent will adopt the reverse prioritisation. Default Logic semantics have also been proposed for primitives in agent programming languages [22]. For example, the GenGoals and GenPlan primitives in [9] are defined in terms of generation of prioritised default logic extensions of goals, respectively plans.

In recent years, a growing body of work (e.g. [2],[4],[12],[14],[20]) has proposed argumentation based approaches to agent defeasible and practical reasoning. These works propose logical formalisms that conform to Dung's seminal argumentation semantics [11] (and its variants). A Dung argumentation framework consists of a set of arguments $Args$ and a binary conflict based relation $\mathcal{R}$ on $Args$ ($\mathcal{R} \subseteq Args \times Args$). A 'calculus of opposition' is then applied to the framework to evaluate the winning (justified) arguments under different extensional semantics. The underlying logic, and definition of the logic's constructed arguments $Args$ and relation $\mathcal{R}$, is left unspecified, thus enabling instantiation of a framework by various logical formalisms. Dung's semantics have thus become established as a general framework for non-monotonic reasoning, and, more generally, reasoning in the presence of conflict. A theory's inferences can be defined in terms of the claims of the justified arguments constructed from the theory (an argument essentially being a proof of a candidate inference - the argument's claim - in the underlying logic). Indeed, many of the major species of logic programming and non-monotonic logics (e.g. default, autoepistemic, non-monotonic modal logics) turn out to be special forms of Dung's theory [6,11]. Hence, Dung's semantics can be seen to generalise and subsume the above Default Logic semantics proposed for agent architectures and programming languages.

To determine a unique set of justified arguments invariably requires preference information to resolve conflicts between pairs of attacking arguments. The role of preferences has been formalised in both the underlying logical formalisms that instantiate a Dung framework, and at the abstract level of the framework itself. Examples of the former (e.g., [19]) define the relation $\mathcal{R}$ in terms of the conflict based interaction between two arguments, and a preference based on their relative strength. Examples of the latter (e.g., [1] [5]) augment Dung's framework to include a preference ordering on arguments. Hence, given a conflict based *attack* relation $\mathcal{R}$ on the arguments, a *defeat* relation $\mathcal{R}'$ is defined, where defeat represents a successful attack by additionally accounting for the relative strengths of (preferences between) attacking arguments. The justified arguments are then evaluated on the basis of the defeat relation $\mathcal{R}'$.

However, the preference information required to determine the success of an attack is often assumed pre-specified as a given ordering, and external to the logical formalism. This does not account for the fact that preferences may vary according to context, and because information sources (be they agents or otherwise) may disagree as to the criteria by which the strengths of arguments should be valuated, or the valuations assigned for a given criterion. Hence, to facilitate agent flexibility and adaptability, requires argumentation based reasoning *about*, as well as *with*, defeasible and possibly conflicting preference information. For example, a 'social' agent uniformly prioritises arguments for obligation derived goals above arguments for desire derived goals. However, certain contexts may warrant selfish behavior. Such behavioural heterogeneity requires argumentation based reasoning as to which prioritisation (agent type) is appropriate in a given context. In a practical reasoning context, consider two 'instrumental' arguments (that can be understood as denoting unscheduled plans as in [12],[20],[?]) each of which relate alternative drugs for realising a medical treatment goal. Different clinical trials reporting on the relative efficacy of the drugs may lead to contradictory preferences, requiring that the agent justify selecting one clinical trial valuation over another.

Requirements for reasoning about preferences have been addressed in works extending the object level logical languages for argument construction with rules for deriving priorities amongst rules, e.g., in default logic [7] and logic programming [14,19]. One can then construct 'priority arguments' whose claims determine preferences between other mutually attacking arguments to determine the successful attacks (defeats). Arguments claiming conflicting priorities may be constructed and preferences between these can be established on the basis of other priority arguments. However, these works are restricted to basing argument strength on a single criterion; one based on the priorities of the argument's constituent rules. In previous work [16] we extended Dung's abstract argumentation theory so as to allow for argumentation about preferences between arguments. An extended framework can include 'preference arguments' that *claim preferences between other arguments*. This is achieved by defining a new attack relation that originates from a preference argument, and *attacks an attack* between the arguments that are the subject of the preference claim. In section 2 of this paper we present an improved (in the sense that it simplifies) version of the extended semantics described in [16] (more fully described, with associated proofs, in [17]). In the spirit of Dung's abstract approach, no commitment is made to how preferences are defined in the underlying logical formalism instantiating the extended framework. Thus, if C is a preference argument expressing that an argument A is preferred to an argument B, then this preference may be based on any criterion for valuating argument strength, including criteria that relate to the argument as a whole, such as the value promoted by the argument [5]. We therefore claim that the extended semantics can serve as a general semantics for flexible and adaptive agent defeasible and practical reasoning. We substantiate this claim in sections 3 and 4. In section 3 we show how logic programming approaches such as [14,19] can be formalised as instances of our extended framework. We illustrate with examples demonstrating reasoning about preferences between conflicting arguments for beliefs and goals. In section 4 we show how our framework provides for extending an existing argumentation based formalism for agent practical reasoning ([4]) so as to accommodate defeasible reasoning about preference information that is assumed pre-defined in [4]. Finally, we conclude and discuss future work in section 5.

2 Argumentation Semantics That Accommodate Defeasible Reasoning about Preferences

A Dung argumentation framework is of the form $(Args, \mathcal{R})$ where $\mathcal{R} \subseteq (Args \times Args)$ can denote either attack or defeat. A **single** argument $A \in Args$ is defined as acceptable w.r.t. some $S \subseteq Args$, if for every B such that $(B, A) \in \mathcal{R}$, there exists a $C \in S$ such that $(C, B) \in \mathcal{R}$. Intuitively, C 'reinstates' A. Dung then defines the acceptability of a **set** of arguments under different extensional semantics. The definition is given here, in which $S \subseteq Args$ is conflict free if no two arguments in S are related by $\mathcal{R}$, and F is a characteristic function of a framework, such that:

- $F : 2^{Args} \mapsto 2^{Args}$
- $F(S) = \{A \in Args | A$ is acceptable w.r.t. $S\}$.

Definition 1. *Let $S \subseteq Args$ be a conflict free set. Then:*

- *S is admissible iff each argument in S is acceptable w.r.t. S (i.e. $S \subseteq F(S)$)*
- *S is a preferred extension iff S is a set inclusion maximal admissible extension*
- *S is a complete extension iff each argument which is acceptable w.r.t. S is in S (i.e. $S = F(S)$)*
- *S is a stable extension iff $\forall B \notin S$, $\exists A \in S$ such that $(A, B) \in \mathcal{R}$*
- *S is the grounded extension iff S is the least fixed point of F.*

Consider the following example in which two individuals **P** and **Q** exchange arguments $A, B \ldots$ about the weather forecast:

P : "Today will be dry in London since the BBC forecast sunshine" $= A$
Q : "Today will be wet in London since CNN forecast rain" $= B$
P : "But the BBC are more trustworthy than CNN" $= C$
Q : "However, statistics show that CNN are more accurate than the BBC" $= C'$
Q : "And basing a comparison on statistics is more rigorous and rational than basing a comparison on your instincts about their relative trustworthiness" $= E$

Arguments A and B symmetrically attack, i.e., $(A, B),(B, A) \in \mathcal{R}$. $\{A\}$ and $\{B\}$ are admissible. We then have an argument C that claims that A is preferred to B. Hence B does not successfully attack (defeat) A, but A does defeat B. Evaluating admissibility on the basis of this binary defeat relation, $\{A\}$ and not $\{B\}$ is admissible. The impact of argument C could conceivably be modelled by letting C attack B (see $\Delta1$ in figure 1 in which an attack is visualised as an arrow from the attacker to the attacked). This would yield the required result, but if an argument D then attacked A (e.g. $D = $ "the BBC forecast is for Glasgow and not London") then $\{B\}$ would still not be admissible ($\Delta2$ in figure 1). This is clearly inappropriate. C expresses a preference for A over B, but if A is attacked (and defeated) by another argument, then we should recover B. Intuitively, C is an argument about the relationship between A and B. Specifically, in expressing a preference for A over B, C is an argument for A's repulsion of, or defence against, B's attack on A, i.e., C *defence* attacks B's ***attack on*** A ($\Delta3$ in figure 1) so that B's attack on A does not succeed as a defeat. B's attack on A is, as it were, cancelled out, and we are left with A defeating B. Now, if D attacks A we will recover $\{B\}$ as an admissible extension ($\Delta4$ in figure 1). Of course, given C' claiming a preference for B over A and so *defence* (d) attacking A's attack on B, then we will have that $\{A\}$ and $\{B\}$ are now both admissible, since neither defeats the other. Intuitively, C and C' claim contradictory preferences and so attack each other ($\Delta5$ in figure 1). These attacks can themselves be subject to d attacks in order to determine the defeat relation between C and C' and so A and B. In the example, E d attacks the attack from C to C' ($\Delta6$ in figure 1), and so determines that C' defeats C. Hence, C's d-attack on B's attack on A is cancelled out, and we are left with B defeating A; the discussion concludes in favour of **Q**'s argument that it will be a wet day in London.

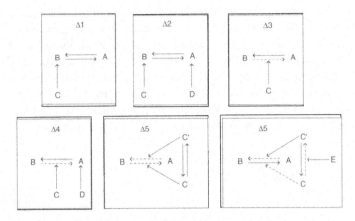

Fig. 1.

We now formally define the elements of an *Extended Argumentation Framework*:

Definition 2. *An* Extended Argumentation Framework *(EAF) is a tuple (Args, $\mathcal{R}$, $\mathcal{D}$) such that Args is a set of arguments, and:*

- $\mathcal{R} \subseteq Args \times Args$
- $\mathcal{D} \subseteq (Args \times \mathcal{R})$
- *If $(C, (A, B))$, $(C', (B, A)) \in \mathcal{D}$ then (C, C'), $(C', C) \in \mathcal{R}$*

Notation 1. We may write $A \rightharpoonup B$ to denote $(A, B) \in \mathcal{R}$. If in addition $(B, A) \in \mathcal{R}$, we may write $A \rightleftharpoons B$. We may also write $C \twoheadrightarrow (A \rightharpoonup B)$ to denote $(C, (A, B)) \in \mathcal{D}$, and say that C *defence* (d) attacks A's attack on B.

From hereon, definitions are assumed relative to an *EAF* (Args, $\mathcal{R}$, $\mathcal{D}$), where arguments $A, B, \ldots$ are assumed to be in *Args*, and S is a subset of *Args*. We now formally define the defeat relation that is parameterised w.r.t. some set S of arguments. This accounts for an attack's success as a defeat being relative to preference arguments already accepted in some set S, rather than relative to some externally given preference ordering.

Definition 3. *A S-defeats B, denoted by $A \rightarrow^s B$, iff $(A, B) \in \mathcal{R}$ and $\neg \exists C \in S$ s.t. $(C,(A, B)) \in S$. A strictly S-defeats B iff A S-defeats B and B does not S-defeat A.*

Example 1. Let Δ be the *EAF*: $A \rightleftharpoons B, C \twoheadrightarrow (A \rightharpoonup B)$

A and B S-defeat each other for $S = \emptyset$, $\{A\}$ and $\{B\}$.
B $\{C\}$-defeats A but A does not $\{C\}$-defeat B (B strictly $\{C\}$-defeats A).

We now define the notion of a conflict free set S of arguments. One might define such a set as one in which no two arguments attack each other. However, when applying argumentation to practical reasoning, it may be that if B asymmetrically attacks A, but A is preferred to B, then neither B or A defeat each other, and so both may end up being justified arguments. This is appropriate only when the arguments are not inherently contradictory. For example, in [4], arguments relating to deciding a course of action appeal to values [5]. If A is an argument for a medical action a, appealing to the value of *health*, and B is an argument claiming that a is prohibitively expensive, then B asymmetrically attacks A, and B appeals to the value of *cost*. If a given value ordering ranks the value of *health* above *cost*, then B does not defeat A, and both arguments may then be justified; one commits to the action while accepting that it is expensive. Since in what follows, an admissible extension of an *EAF* is defined on the basis of a conflict free set, we need to allow for the above when defining a conflict free set:

Definition 4. *S is conflict free iff* $\forall A, B \in S$: *if* $(B, A) \in \mathcal{R}$ *then* $(A, B) \notin \mathcal{R}$, *and* $\exists C \in S$ *s.t.* $(C,(B, A)) \in \mathcal{D}$.

In [16] we suggest that special attention be given to symmetric *EAF*s in which preference arguments can only *d*-attack attacks between arguments that symmetrically attack:

Definition 5. *Let* $\Delta = (Args, \mathcal{R}, \mathcal{D})$ *be an* EAF. *We say that* Δ *is a symmetric EAF iff: if* $(C, (B, A)) \in \mathcal{D}$, *then* $(A, B) \in \mathcal{R}$.

The restriction on $\mathcal{D}$ is appropriate when the arguments are inherently contradictory, as when arguing about beliefs. This is because no conflict free subset S of $Args$ in a symmetric *EAF* (and so admissible extension) can contain arguments that attack, since it could not satisfy the condition in definition 4. [1]

We now define the acceptability of an argument A w.r.t. a set S for an *EAF*. Consider figure 2-a) in which the acceptability of $A1$ w.r.t. S is under consideration. $B1 \rightarrow^s A1$, and $A1$ reinstates itself via the defeat $A1 \rightarrow^s B1$. However, the latter defeat is based on an attack $A1 \rightharpoonup B1$ that is itself under attack: $B2 \twoheadrightarrow (A1 \rightharpoonup B1)$. We therefore need to check that $A1 \rightarrow^s B1$ is 'defeat reinstated' by an argument in S that S-defeats $B2$. In general, $X \rightarrow^S Y$ is *defeat reinstated* iff for any Z s.t. $(Z,(X, Y)) \in \mathcal{D}$, there is a $Z' \in S$ s.t. $Z' \rightarrow^S Z$.

In figure 2-a) $A1 \rightarrow^s B1$ is 'defeat reinstated' by $A2 \in S$. In general, an argument X can then be said to be 'locally' acceptable w.r.t. a set S if for any Y that S-defeats X, there is a $Z \in S$ such that Z S-defeats Y and this defeat is defeat reinstated. However,

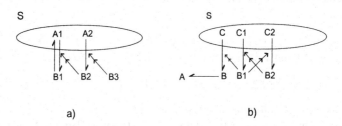

a)   b)

Fig. 2. $A1$ is not acceptable w.r.t. S in a). A is acceptable w.r.t. S in b).

---

[1] Note that other restrictions on $\mathcal{D}$ may be appropriate. E.g in logic programming systems such as [19], if B claims what was assumed non-provable (through negation as failure) by a rule in A, then B asymmetrically attacks A, and defeats A irrespective of their relative preference. One would then preclude such attacks from being *d*-attacked by preference arguments.

local acceptability does not suffice in the sense that the obtained notion of admissibility (as defined in definition 1) does not satisfy the property that if X is acceptable w.r.t. an admissible S, then $S \cup \{X\}$ is admissible. This result is shown by Dung's *fundamental lemma* in [11]. Intuitively, S represents a coherent 'position' defending each of its contained arguments. Having established such a position in the course of an argument, one would want that a proposed argument A that is defended by the position, does not, when included in the position, undermine the position that defends it. Referring to figure 2-a), S is admissible under local acceptability. $B3$ is locally acceptable w.r.t S, but $S' = S \cup \{B3\}$ is not admissible since $A1$ is not locally acceptable w.r.t S' (because the presence of $B3$ now invalidates the defeat from $A2$ to $B2$). What is required when checking the acceptability of $A1$ w.r.t. S is not only that $A1 \rightarrow^S B1$ is defeat reinstated, but that the defeat's reinstater $A2 \rightarrow^S B2$ is itself defeat reinstated. It is not, since no argument in S S-defeats $B3$. In general:

Definition 6. *Let $S \subseteq Args$ in $(Args, \mathcal{R}, \mathcal{D})$. Let $R_S = \{X_1 \rightarrow^S Y_1, \ldots, X_n \rightarrow^S Y_n\}$ where for $i = 1 \ldots n$, $X_i \in S$. Then R_S is a reinstatement set for $C \rightarrow^S B$, iff:*

- $C \rightarrow^S B \in R_S$, *and*
- $\forall X \rightarrow^S Y \in R_S, \forall Y'$ *s.t.* $(Y', (X, Y)) \in \mathcal{D}$, *there* $\exists X' \rightarrow^S Y' \in R_S$

Definition 7. *A is acceptable w.r.t. $S \subseteq Args$ in $(Args, \mathcal{R}, \mathcal{D})$, iff $\forall B$ s.t. $B \rightarrow^S A$, $\exists C \in S$ s.t. $C \rightarrow^S B$ and there is a reinstatement set for $C \rightarrow^S B$.*

Under this definition of acceptability, Dung's fundamental lemma is satisfied (see [16]). In figure 2-b), A is acceptable w.r.t. S given the reinstatement set $\{C \rightarrow^S B, C1 \rightarrow^S B1, C2 \rightarrow^S B2\}$ for $C \rightarrow^S B$. With the above definition of acceptability, extensional semantics for *EAF*s are now given by definition 1, where conflict free defined as in definition 4, for the stable semantics, 'A S-defeats B' replaces '$(A, B) \in \mathcal{R}$', and (for technical reasons) the domain of an *EAF*'s characteristic function F is restricted to the set of all *conflict free* subsets of $Args$.

For the complete, preferred and stable semantics, an argument is sceptically justified if it belongs to all extensions, and credulously justified if it belongs to at least one extension. The grounded semantics return a single extension, and so are inherently sceptical. In [16] we show that for symmetric *EAF*s, S is an admissible extension obtained on the basis of local acceptability iff S is an admissible extension obtained on the basis of acceptability in definition 7. Hence, the extensions of a symmetric *EAF* can equivalently be defined under local acceptability, and Dung's fundamental lemma holds for such *EAF*s under local acceptability. In [16] we also show the following results that have been shown to hold for Dung argumentation frameworks (the importance of these results are discussed in more detail in [16] and [11]). Let Δ be any *EAF*. Then:

1. The set of all admissible extensions of Δ form a complete partial order w.r.t. set inclusion
2. For each admissible S there exists a preferred extension S' of Δ such that $S \subseteq S'$
3. Δ possesses at least one preferred extension.
4. Every stable extension of Δ is a preferred extension but not vice versa.
5. Defining a sequence $F^1 = F(\emptyset)$, $F^{i+1} = F(F^i)$, then $F^{i+1} \supseteq F^i$ (where each F^j in the sequence is conflict free)

Suppose an *EAF* Δ is defined as finitary iff for any argument A or attack (B, C), the set of arguments attacking A, respectively (B, C), is finite. Referring to the sequence in 5 above, one can also show that the least fixed point (grounded extension) of a symmetric Δ is given by $\bigcup_{i=1}^{\infty}(F^i)$. For arbitrary *EAF*s we can not guarantee that the fixed point obtained in 5 is the least fixed point (the existence of a least fixed point is guaranteed by the monotonicity of F, which only holds for symmetric EAFs). This means that the grounded extension of an EAF that is not symmetric is defined by the sequence in 5.

To conclude, we have defined an extended semantics that allows for representation of arguments that express preferences between other arguments. No commitments are made to the underlying logics for argument construction, or to the criteria used to valuate the strength of, and so preferences between, arguments. This work is to be contrasted with approaches that extend the underlying **object level** logical languages with rules for deriving priorities amongst rules. In the following section we provide support for our claim that the above extended semantics can serve as a semantics for agent defeasible and practical reasoning, in the sense that given an agent theory T defined in a logic based formalism L, then α is an inferred belief or goal, or chosen action iff α is the claim of a justified argument of the extended argumentation framework instantiated by the arguments and attacks defined by the theory T in L.

3   Argumentation Based Reasoning about Goals

In this section we illustrate how inferences obtained in logic programming formalisms that facilitate defeasible reasoning about rule priorities (e.g.[14],[19]), can be characterised in terms of the claims of the justified arguments of an instantiated *EAF*. We will adopt an approach to reasoning about goals in [14], in which subsets of a set of agent rules for deriving goals are associated with one of five agent's *needs* or *motivations* (based on Maslow's work in cognitive psychology [15]): **Physiological**, **Safety**, **Affiliation (Social)**, **Achievement (Ego)** and **Self-Actualisation**. Simplifying the representation in [14], one can express an agent's default personality by rules of the form $R_{def} : true \Rightarrow hp(r_X^m, r_Y^{m'})$ expressing that a rule with name r_X associated with motivation m has higher priority than a rule with name r_Y associated with motivation m' (where X and Y range over the rule name indicies used). Exceptional circumstances may warrant prioritisation of a specific m' over m goal: $R_{excep} : S \Rightarrow hp(r_Y^{m'}, r_X^m)$ (where S denotes a conjunction of first order literals with explicit negation). Hence, if S holds, then one can construct an argument $A1$ based on R_{def} and $A2$ based on R_{excep}. Given an argument based on $R_{overide} : true \Rightarrow hp(R_{excep}, R_{def})$, then $A2$ defeats $A1$, so that an argument for a goal based on $r_Y^{m'}$ will now defeat an argument for a goal based on r_X^m. Note that in agent architectures [8]and programming paradigms [9] that address conflict resolution amongst goals, rules for deriving goals are expressed as conditionals of the form $a \rightarrow^M b$ [8] or modal rules of the form $a \rightarrow Mb$ [9] where a and b are propositional, respectively propositional modal, wff, and $M \in \{B(Belief), O(Obligation), I(Intention), D(Desire)\}$. As mentioned in the introduction, a prioritised default logic semantics resolves conflicts amongst the goals generated by different mental attitudes.The relationship with [14] is clear. Agent personalities represented by orderings on motivations, correspond with agent types represented by orderings on mental attitudes in [9] and [8]. However, behavioural heterogeneity and adaptability is limited in the latter works, in the sense that an altruistic agent's goals will always be characterised by default extensions that contain obligation (social) derived goals at the expense of conflicting desire (ego) derived goals.

In what follows we formalise reasoning of the above type in [19]'s *argument based logic programming with defeasible priorities* (ALP-DP). To simplify the presentation, we present a restricted version of ALP-DP - ALP-DP* - that does not include negation as failure (as this is not needed for any of the examples). We describe ALP-DP* arguments, their attacks, and how priority arguments define preferences. We refer the reader to [19] for details of the proof theory.

Definition 8. *Let (S, D) be a ALP-DP* theory where S is a set of strict rules of the form $s : L_0 \wedge \ldots \wedge L_m \rightarrow L_n$, D a set of defeasible rules $r : L_0 \wedge \ldots \wedge L_j \Rightarrow L_n$, and:*

- *Each rule name r (s) is a first order term. From hereon we may write* head(r) *to denote the consequent L_n of the rule named r.*
- *Each L_i is an atomic first order formula, or such a formula preceded by strong negation $\neg$.*

We also assume that the language contains a two-place predicate symbol $\prec$ for expressing priorities on rule names. Strict rules are intended to represent information that is beyond debate. We assume that any S includes the following strict rules expressing properties on the relation $\prec$.

- $o1 : (x \prec y) \wedge (y \prec z) \rightarrow (x \prec z)$ • $o2 : (x \prec y) \wedge \neg(x \prec z) \rightarrow \neg(y \prec z)$
- $o3 : (y \prec z) \wedge \neg(x \prec z) \rightarrow \neg(x \prec y)$ • $o4 : (x \prec y) \rightarrow \neg(y \prec x)$

Definition 9. *An argument A based on the theory (S, D) is:*

1. *a finite sequence $[r_0, \ldots, r_n]$ of ground instances of rules such that:*
   - *for every i ($0 \leq i \leq n$), for every literal L_j in the antecedent of r_i there is a $k < i$ such that* head(r_k) $= L_j$. *If* head(r_n) $= x \prec y$ *then A is called a 'singleton priority argument'.*
   - *no distinct rules in the sequence have the same head;*

   or:
2. *a finite sequence $[r_{0_1}, \ldots r_{n_1}, \ldots, r_{0_m}, \ldots r_{n_m}]$, such that for $i = 1 \ldots m$, $[r_{0_i}, \ldots r_{n_i}]$ is a singleton priority argument. We say that A is a 'composite priority argument' that concludes the ordering $\bigcup_{i=1}^{m}$ head(r_{n_i})*

In [19], arguments are exclusively defined by 1). Here, we have additionally defined composite priority arguments so that an ordering, and hence a preference, can be claimed (concluded) by a single argument rather than a set of arguments. Note that from hereon we will, for ease of presentation, show only propositional examples. Also, abusing the notation, arguments will be represented as sequences of *rule names* rather that the rules these names identify. The following example adopts the categorisation of goals in the BOID architecture [8] and programming paradigm [9]. Rules named int_i represent goals committed to in previous deliberations. Rules named bel_i allow for derivation of beliefs, and act as a filter on desire and obligation derived goals derived by rules named des_i and

ob_i respectively. The filtering rules ensure that agents do not engage in wishful thinking. This could be expressed as an agent type, by prioritising these filtering rules above desire and obligation rules. Here, we make the filtering rules strict.

Example 2. Let $S = \{o1 \ldots o4\} \cup \{bel_1 : cheap\_room \rightarrow \neg close\_to\_conf,$
$bel_2 : close\_to\_conf \rightarrow \neg cheap\_room\}$, and D be the set of rules:

- $bel_3 :\Rightarrow remaining\_budget\_high$ $soc_1 :\Rightarrow des_1 \prec ob_1$
- $int_1 :\Rightarrow go\_to\_conference$ $self_1 :\Rightarrow ob_1 \prec des_1$
- $des_1 : go\_to\_conference \Rightarrow close\_to\_conf$ $def\_agent\_type :\Rightarrow self_1 \prec soc_1$
- $ob_1 : go\_to\_conference \Rightarrow cheap\_room$
- $exception\_soc : remaining\_budget\_high \Rightarrow soc_1 \prec self_1$
- $overide\_social :\Rightarrow def\_agent\_type \prec exception\_soc$

The following are a subset of the arguments that can be constructed:

$A1 = [int_1, des_1]$ is an argument for the desire derived goal to be close to the conference, given the intention to go to the conference.
$A2 = [int_1, ob_1]$ is an argument for the obligation derived goal to book a cheap room.
$B1 = [soc_1]$ and $B2 = [self_1]$ respectively express social and selfish agent types.
$C1 = [def\_agent\_type]$ expresses that the reasoning agent is by default a social agent, and $C2 = [bel_3, exception\_soc]$ expresses exceptional conditions (when the remaining project funds are high) under which the agent behaves selfishly. Finally, $D1 = [overide\_social]$ expresses that the selfish agent type warranted by exceptional conditions overrides the default social behaviour.

The following definitions assume arguments are relative to a theory (S, D). [19] defines:

Definition 10. *For any arguments A, A' and literal L:*

- *A is strict iff it does not contain any defeasible rule; it is defeasible otherwise.*
- *L is a conclusion of A iff L is the head of some rule in A*
- *If T is a sequence of rules, then A + T is the concatenation of A and T*

[19] motivates definition of attacks between arguments that account for the ways in which arguments can be extended with strict rules:

Definition 11. *A1 attacks A2 iff there are sequences S1 and S2 of strict rules such that A1 + S1 is an argument with conclusion L and A2 + S2 is an argument with a conclusion ¬L.*

By definition, if $A1$ attacks $A2$ then $A2$ attacks $A1$. Note that A1 may attack A2 on a number of conclusions and corresponding concatenations of strict rules. In example 2, $A1$ and $A2$ attack each other since $A1 + [bel_2]$ has the conclusion $\neg cheap\_room$ and $A2$ has the conclusion $cheap\_room$. Also $B1 + [o4]$ has the conclusion $\neg(ob_1 \prec des_1)$ and so $B1$ attacks and is attacked by $B2$. To determine a preference amongst attacking arguments ALP-DP* defines the sets of relevant defeasible rules to be compared:

Definition 12. *If $A + S$ is an argument with conclusion L, the defeasible rules $R_L(A + S)$ **relevant** to L are:*

1. $\{r_d\}$ iff A includes defeasible rule r_d with head L
2. $R_{L_1}(A+S) \cup \ldots \cup R_{L_n}(A+S)$ iff A is defeasible and S includes a strict rule s
* $: L_1 \wedge \ldots \wedge L_n \to L$*

For example, $R_{cheap\_room}(A2) = \{ob_1\}$ and $R_{\neg cheap\_room}(A1 + [bel_2]) = \{des_1\}$. We define ALP-DP*'s ordering on these sets and hence preferences amongst arguments, w.r.t. an ordering concluded (as defined in definition 9-2) by a priority argument:

Definition 13. *Let C be a priority argument concluding the ordering $\prec$. Let R and R' be sets of defeasible rules. Then $R' > R$ iff $\forall r' \in R'$, $\exists r \in R$ such that $r \prec r'$.*

The intuitive idea behind the above definition is that R can be made better by replacing some rule in R with any rule in R', while the reverse is impossible. Now, given two arguments A and B, it may be that they attack on more than one conclusion. Given a priority ordering $\prec$ concluded by an argument C, we say that A is preferred$_\prec$ to B if for every pair (L, L') of conclusions on which they attack, the set of A's defeasible rules relevant to L is stronger $(>)$ than the set of B's defeasible rules relevant to L'.

Definition 14. *Let C be a priority argument concluding $\prec$. Let $(L_1, L_1'), \ldots, (L_n, L_n')$ be the pairs on which A and B attack, where for $i = 1 \ldots n$, L_i and L_i' are conclusions in A and B respectively. Then A is preferred$_\prec$ to B if for $i = 1 \ldots n$, $R_{L_i}(A + S_i) > R_{L_i'}(B + S_i')$*

In example 2, $B1$ concludes $des1 \prec ob1$, and so $R_{cheap\_room}(A2) > R_{\neg cheap\_room}(A1)$, and so $A2$ is preferred$_{des1 \prec ob1}$ to $A1$. We can now instantiate a symmetric *EAF* with the arguments, their attacks, and priority arguments claiming preferences and so d attacking attacks:

Definition 15. *The EAF $(Args, \mathcal{R}, \mathcal{D})$ for a theory (S, D) is defined as follows. Args is the set of arguments given by definition 9, and $\forall A, B, C \in Args$:*

1. $(C,(B, A)) \in \mathcal{D}$ iff C concludes $\prec$ and A is preferred$_\prec$ to B
2. $(A, B),(B, A) \in \mathcal{R}$ iff A and B attack as in definition 11

Note that it can be shown that if $(C,(B, A))$ and $(C',(A, B)) \in \mathcal{R}_d$ then C and C' attack each other as in definition 11. The following result is a special case of proposition 8 in [16] which shows an equivalence for full ALP-DP with negation as failure:

Proposition 1. *Let Δ be the EAF defined by a theory (S, D) as in definition 15. Then L is the conclusion of a justified argument as defined in [19] iff L is the conclusion of an argument in the grounded extension of Δ.[2]*

For example 2 we obtain the *EAF* $\Delta1$ in figure 3. $D1$, $C2$, $B2$ and $A1$ are sceptically justified under all the semantics. Intuitively, the normally social agent can behave selfishly if the remaining budget for the project is high. We conclude with another example that illustrates argumentation to resolve conflicts amongst goals derived from the same class of mental attitudes. The example also illustrates how argumentation over beliefs is incorporated into argumentation over goals.

---

[2] Note that all of Dung's extensional semantics can be defined for an ALP-DP theory's *EAF*. In [19] only the grounded, stable and complete semantics can be defined.

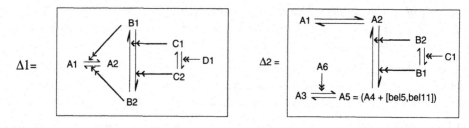

Fig. 3. *EAFs* $\Delta 1$ *and* $\Delta 2$

Example 3. Let (S, D) be a theory where $S = \{o1 \dots o4\} \cup \{bel_7 : forecast\_storm \rightarrow \neg forecast\_calm, bel_8 : forecast\_calm \rightarrow \neg forecast\_storm, bel_9 : close\_to\_conf \rightarrow \neg close\_to\_beach, bel_{10} : close\_to\_beach \rightarrow \neg close\_to\_conf\}$

D is the set of defeasible rules:

- $int_1 :\Rightarrow go\_to\_conference$
- $des_1 : go\_to\_conference \Rightarrow close\_to\_conf$
- $des_2 : go\_to\_conference \Rightarrow close\_to\_beach$
- $bel_3\_bravo :\Rightarrow forecast\_calm$
- $bel_4\_bbc :\Rightarrow forecast\_storm$
- $bel_5 : forecast\_storm \Rightarrow beach\_hotel\_closed$
- $bel_{11} : beach\_hotel\_closed \rightarrow \neg close\_to\_beach$
- $bel_6 :\Rightarrow bel_3\_bravo \prec bel_4\_bbc$
- $realistic :\Rightarrow des_2 \prec bel_{11}$
- $wishful :\Rightarrow bel_{11} \prec des_2$
- $def\_agent\_type :\Rightarrow wishful \prec realistic$

Amongst the arguments that can be constructed, we obtain:

$A1 = [int_1, des_1]$ and $A2 = [int_1, des_2]$ are mutually attacking arguments for the desire derived goals of being close to the conference and being close to the beach respectively.

$A3 = [bel_3\_bravo]$ and $A4 = [bel_4\_bbc]$ are also mutually attacking arguments for contradictory weather forecasts, and $A3$ also mutually attacks $A5 = [bel_4\_bbc, bel_5, bel_{11}]$ which expresses the belief that if the forecast is for storms then the beach side hotel will be closed and so the agent cannot be close to the beach. Hence, $A5$ also mutually attacks $A2$.

$A6 = [bel_3\_bravo \prec bel_4\_bbc]$ claims that the bbc is acknowledged to be the more reliable than the bravo channel, and so expresses that $A4$ and $A5$ are preferred to $A3$.

$B1 = [realistic]$ and $B2 = [wishful]$ characterise agent types that respectively give priority to belief over desire, and desire over belief derived goals. $C1 = [def\_agent\_type]$ expresses that the default agent behaviour is realistic.

The EAF $\Delta 2$ instantiated by the above arguments is shown in figure 2. Since the agent is realistic and the BBC more reliable than Bravo, $C1$, $B1$, $A6$, $A5$ and $A1$ are sceptically justified under all the semantics. The agent adopts the goal of being close to the conference.

4 Argumentation Based Reasoning over Actions

A number of works apply argumentation to decide a preferred course of action, including logic programming formalisms of the type described in the previous section, and agent programming paradigms such as [9], in which mutually conflicting or 'incoherent' candidate sets of plans are also characterised in terms of prioritised default logic extensions. In works such as [2] and [12], tree structured *instrumental* arguments are composed by chaining propositional rules, and relate the root node top level goal to sub-goals, and primitive actions in the leaf nodes (these arguments can be thought of as unscheduled plans). Given conflict free sets of instrumental arguments, the preferred sets are chosen solely on the basis of those that maximise the number of agent goals realised. These works have been extended in [20] to accommodate decision theoretic notions. An instrumental argument additionally includes the resources required for execution of the leaf node actions. The strength of, and so preferences amongst, instrumental arguments is then based on their utility defined in terms of numerical valuations of the 'worth' of the goals and cost of the resources represented in the arguments. A more general conception of how to valuate the strength of arguments for action is partially realised in [4]. In this work, arguments for alternative courses of action for realising a given goal instantiate a value based argumentation framework (VAF) [5]. A given ordering on values (an 'audience') advanced by arguments, is then used to determine relative preferences and so defeats amongst arguments:

If A attacks B, then A defeats B only if the value advanced by B is not ranked higher than the value advanced by A according to some audience a.

Examples of values include cost, safety, efficacy (of the action w.r.t. goal) e.t.c. In [18] we proposed an extension to VAF that associates for a given value V, the degree to which an argument promotes or demotes a value. In this way, one can prefer $A1$ for action $a1$ to $A2$ for action $a2$, if both promote the same value, but the later does so to a lesser degree. Note that the same can be seen to apply to goals, so that, for example, a preference between two conflicting arguments for obligation derived goals may be based on the relative 'strength' or 'importance' of the obligations. In general then, one can consider arguments for goals or actions as being associated with, or advancing, meta-level criteria (be they motivations, values, etc), where:

1. The degree to which a criterion is advanced may vary according to context and or perspective
2. The ordering on criteria may vary according to context and or perspective

Both cases may warrant argumentation based resolution of conflicting preferences. In what follows, we illustrate some of the above ideas with an example taken from [18] that we now formalise in an *EAF*. We thus demonstrate how the extended semantics provide for integration of object level argumentation about action and metalevel reasoning about values and value orderings. The example builds on a schemes and critical questions approach to value based argumentation over action [4], whereby an argument for an action instantiates the following presumptive scheme **AS1**:

In the current circumstances R, we should perform action A, to achieve new circumstances S, which will realise some goal G, which will promote some value V

An extensive set of critical questions associated with **AS1** are then described. If $A1$ is an argument instantiating **AS1**, then the critical questions serve to identify arguments that attack $A1$. For example, an argument $A2$ stating that the action in $A1$ has an unsafe side-effect, asymmetrically attacks $A1$. $A2$ is identified with the critical question: *does the action have a side effect which demotes some value?* $A2$ may then itself be attacked by arguments identified by $A2$'s critical questions, and so on. Every argument advances a value. The arguments, their attacks, and a value ordering, instantiate a VAF, and based on the derived defeat relation, the justified arguments are evaluated under Dung's preferred semantics. In the following example, we will assume arguments instantiating schemes and critical questions. [4] described formal construction of these arguments in an underlying BDI type logic. We also assume arguments for possibly conflicting valuations of arguments and value orderings. Formal construction of these arguments is described in [18].

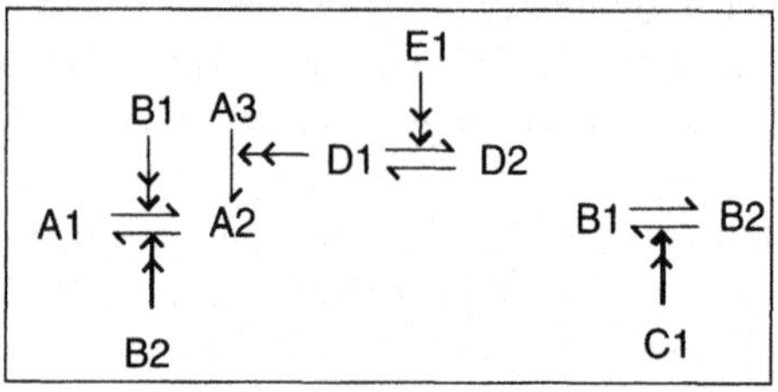

Fig. 4.

Example 4. Consider Δ in fig.3 in which $A1$ and $A2$ are arguments for the medical actions 'give aspirin' and 'give chlopidogrel' respectively. These arguments instantiate **AS1** and refer to beliefs, actions, goals and values, as described in [4]. $A1$ and $A2$ both promote the value of *efficacy*. They symmetrically attack since they claim alternative actions for the goal of preventing blood clotting. Argument $B1$ is based on clinical trial 1's conclusion that $A2$'s chlopidogrel is more efficacious than $A1$'s aspirin at preventing blood clotting. Hence $B1 \twoheadrightarrow (A1 \rightharpoonup A2)$. However, $B2$ is based on clinical trial 2's conclusion that the opposite is the case. Hence $B1 \rightleftharpoons B2$. At this stage neither $A1$ or $A2$ are sceptically justified under any semantics. However, $C1$ is an argument claiming that trial 1 is preferred to trial 2 since the former uses a more statistically robust design. Hence, $C1 \twoheadrightarrow (B2 \rightharpoonup B1)$. Now $A2$ and not $A1$ is sceptically justified. However, $A3$ promoting the value of *cost*, states that chlopidogrel is prohibitively expensive. We now have an example of an asymmetric attack: $A3 \rightharpoonup A2$. However, $D1 \twoheadrightarrow (A3 \rightharpoonup A2)$ where $D1$ is a value ordering ranking *efficacy* over *cost*. Hence, $A3$ does not defeat $A2$ and so $A2$ remains sceptically justified. Here, we see that $A3$ is also sceptically justified. Administering chlopidogrel is the preferred course of action, while acknowledging that it is costly. It's just that efficacy is deemed to be more important than cost. However, $D2$ now ranks *cost* over *efficacy*. Now neither $A2$ or $A1$ are sceptically justified. Finally, $E1$ is a utilitarian argument stating that since financial resources are low, use of chlopidogrel will compromise treatment of other patients, and so one should preferentially rank *cost* over *efficacy* (such a trade of is often made in medical contexts). Hence, $A1$ is now sceptically justified; aspirin is now the preferred course of action.

5 Discussion and Future Work

In this paper we describe an extended Dung semantics that meets requirements for agent flexibility and adaptability, when engaging in defeasible reasoning about beliefs and goals, and practical reasoning about actions. We claim that the extended semantics can serve as a semantics for agent defeasible and practical reasoning. In our view what appropriately accounts for the correctness of an inference for a belief, or goal, or choice of an action, is that the inference or choice can be shown to rationally prevail in the face of opposing inferences or choices. Dung's, and our extended semantics, in abstracting to the level of a 'calculus of opposition', provides logic neutral, rational means for establishing such standards of correctness.

This paper supports the above claim by formalising agent reasoning about goals in an existing logic programming based formalism [19] that facilitates defeasible reasoning about priorities. It remains to show that other non-monotonic formalisms accommodating reasoning about preferences in the object level, can instantiate extended argumentation frameworks. A notable example is the work of [10] in which defeasible logic rules for agent reasoning are extended with graded preferences, so that one can conclude preferences between mental attitudes contingent on mental attitudes in premises of the rules. We also discussed how the BOID architecture [8] and programming paradigm [9], neither of which accommodate defeasible reasoning about preferences, relate to the logic programming formalism described. This suggests that our extended argumentation semantics can serve as a framework in which to further develop existing agent reasoning formalisms of the above kind, in order to facilitate argumentation based reasoning about preferences, and so agent flexibility and adaptability. We also referred to works formalising construction of arguments in a BDI type logic for value based argumentation over action [4], and works formalising construction of arguments for valuations and value orderings [18], and showed how such arguments can instantiate an *EAF*.

The issue of how arguments for goals and actions interact remains to be addressed in future work. For example, a goal g may be selected at the expense of goal g'. However, it may be that no feasible plan exists for realising g (in the sense that resources are not available or that the plan is prohibitively expensive). Of course, arguments about the feasibility of plans can be used to express preferences between arguments for goals. For example, an argument that there is no feasible plan for g expresses a preference for the argument for g' over the argument for g. However, this requires that arguments for plans be constructed for all candidate goals, which may be computationally very expensive. The two stage process whereby goals are selected, and then arguments for plans are constructed and chosen is more efficient.

We also note that the inherently dialectical nature of argumentation has led to development of formal frameworks for argumentation based dialogues (see [3] for a review), where, for example, one agent seeks to persuade another to adopt a belief, or when agents communicate in order to deliberate about what actions to execute, or to negotiate over resources. These dialogues illustrate requirements for communicating and challenging reasons for preferring one argument to another. We aim to address these requirements by developing frameworks for argumentation based dialogues that build on the extended semantics described in this paper.

Acknowledgements. This work was funded by the EU 6th framework project ASPIC (www.argumentation.org). Thanks to Martin Caminada, Trevor Bench-Capon, and P.M. Dung for useful and enjoyable discussions related to the work in this paper.

References

1. Amgoud, L.: Using Preferences to Select Acceptable Arguments. In: Proc. 13th European Conference on Artificial Intelligence, pp. 43–44 (1998)
2. Amgoud, L., Kaci, S.: On the Generation of Bipolar Goals in Argumentation-Based Negotiation. In: Proc. 1st Int. Workshop on Argumentation in Multi-Agent Systems, pp. 192–207 (2004)
3. ASPIC Deliverable D2.1: Theoretical frameworks for argumentation (June 2004), http://www.argumentation.org/PublicDeliverables.htm
4. Atkinson, K.M., Bench-Capon, T.J.M., McBurney, P.: Computational Representation of Practical Argument. Synthese 152(2), 157–206 (2006)
5. Bench-Capon, T.J.M.: Persuasion in Practical Argument Using Value-based Argumentation Frameworks. Journal of Logic and Computation 13(3), 429–448 (2003)
6. Bondarenko, A., Dung, P.M., Kowalski, R.A., Toni, F.: An abstract, argumentation-theoretic approach to default reasoning. Artificial Intelligence 93, 63–101 (1997)
7. Brewka, G.: Reasoning about priorities in default logic. In: Proc. 12th National Conference on Artificial Intelligence (AAAI 1994), pp. 940–945 (1994)
8. Broersen, J., Dastani, M., Hulstijn, J., van der Torre, L.W.N.: Goal Generation in the BOID Architecture. Cognitive Science Quarterly Journal 2(3-4), 428–447 (2002)
9. Dastani, M., van der Torre, L.: Programming BOID-Plan Agents: Deliberating about Conflicts among Defeasible Mental Attitudes and Plans. In: Proc 3rd international Joint Conference on Autonomous Agents and Multiagent Systems, pp. 706–713 (2004)
10. Dastani, M., Governatori, G., Rotolo, A., van der Torre, L.: Preferences of Agents in Defeasible Logic. In: Zhang, S., Jarvis, R. (eds.) AI 2005. LNCS (LNAI), vol. 3809, pp. 695–704. Springer, Heidelberg (2005)
11. Dung, P.M.: On the acceptability of arguments and its fundamental role in nonmonotonic reasoning, logic programming and n-person games. Artificial Intelligence 77, 321–357 (1995)
12. Hulstijn, J., van der Torre, L.: Combining Goal Generation and Planning in an Argumentation Framework. In: 15th Belgium-Netherlands Conference on AI, pp. 155–162 (2003)
13. Hindriks, K., de Boer, F., van der Hoek, W., Ch, J.-J.: Agent Programming in 3APL. In: Autonomous Agents and Multi-Agent Systems, vol. 2(4), pp. 357–401 (1999)
14. Kakas, A., Moraitis, P.: Argumentation based decision making for autonomous agents. In: 2nd Int. Joint Conference on Autonomous Agents and Multiagent Systems, pp. 883–890 (2003)
15. Maslow, A.: Motivation and Personality. Harper and Row, New York (1954)
16. Modgil, S.: An Abstract Theory of Argumentation That Accommodates Defeasible Reasoning About Preferences. In: 9th European Conference on Symbolic and Quantitative Approaches to Reasoning with Uncertainty, pp. 648–659 (2007)
17. Modgil, S.: Reasoning About Preferences in Argumentation Frameworks. Technical Report, http://www.dcs.kcl.ac.uk/staff/modgilsa/ArguingAboutPreferences.pdf
18. Modgil, S.: Value Based Argumentation in Hierarchical Argumentation Frameworks. In: Proc. 1st International Conference on Computational Models of Argument, pp. 297–308 (2006)

19. Prakken, H., Sartor, G.: Argument-based extended logic programming with defeasible priorities. Journal of Applied Non-Classical Logics 7, 25–75 (1997)
20. Rahwan, I., Amgoud, L.: An argumentation based approach for practical reasoning. In: Proc. 5th Int. Joint Conference on Autonomous agents and Multiagent systems, pp. 347–354 (2006)
21. Reiter, R.: A logic for default reasoning. Artificial Intelligence 13, 81–132 (1980)
22. van Riemsdijk, B., Dastani, M., Meyer, J.: Semantics of declarative goals in agent programming. In: 4th Int. Joint Conference on Autonomous agents and Multiagent systems, pp. 133–140 (2005)
23. Thomason, R.: Desires and defaults: a framework for planning with inferred goals. In: 7th International Conference on Knowledge Representation and Reasoning, pp. 702–713 (2002)

Goal Selection Strategies for Rational Agents

Nick A.M. Tinnemeier, Mehdi Dastani, and John-Jules Ch. Meyer

Utrecht University
P.O. Box 80.089
3508 TB Utrecht
The Netherlands

Abstract. In agent theory and agent programming, goals constitute
the motivational attitude of rational agents and form the key concept
in explaining and generating their pro-active behavior. Pursuing multiple goals simultaneously might pose problems for agents as the plans for
achieving them may conflict. We argue that a BDI-based agent programming language should provide constructs to allow an agent programmer
to implement agents that: 1) do not pursue goals with conflicting plans
simultaneously, and 2) can choose from goals with conflicting plans. This
paper presents an explicit and generic mechanism to process incompatible goals, i.e., goals with conflicting plans. The proposed mechanism can
be integrated in existing BDI-based agent programming languages. We
discuss different strategies to process incompatible goals based on a given
conflict relation and show some properties and relations between these
strategies.

1 Introduction

To facilitate the implementation of cognitive agents, BDI-based agent programming languages provide constructs to implement agent concepts such as beliefs,
goals and plans. Examples of these programming languages are Jadex [1], Jack
[2], Jason [3], 3APL [4], IMPACT [5], CLAIM [6], GOAL [7], CANPLAN2 [8]
and 2APL [9]. In these agent programming languages, belief constructs can be
used to implement the (incomplete) information the agent has about its world,
whereas goal constructs can be used to implement the states the agent desires
to achieve. In agent theory and agent programming, goals constitute the motivational attitude of rational agents and form the key concept in explaining and
generating their pro-active behavior [10,11,12]. In pursuing its goals an agent
uses (partial) plans which specify the actions that should be taken to achieve its
goals. In general, most BDI-based agent programming languages allow an agent
to have multiple goals at the same time. When an agent has more than one
goal, different strategies are possible for adopting plans to achieve these goals.
A strategy that is commonly used in many agent programming languages, for
example in both 3APL[4] and 2APL [9], is to adopt a plan for each goal and to
execute all generated plans at the same time (in an interleaving mode).

Pursuing multiple goals simultaneously might be beneficial for an agent, it
also poses problems. Goals might be incompatible with each other in the sense

M. Dastani et al. (Eds.): LADS 2007, LNAI 5118, pp. 54–70, 2008.
© Springer-Verlag Berlin Heidelberg 2008

that the plan for reaching one goal possibly conflicts with the plans for other goals. Consider for example a household agent with the capability of cleaning rooms. Suppose that the agent has two goals: to have cleaned room one and five. Although it is possible for the agent to achieve one goal after the other, trying to achieve them simultaneously by first making a step in the direction of one room and then in the direction of the other would clearly be irrational. So, the goals that an agent has committed to by adopting plans might pose constraints for the adoption of plans to pursue other goals. Furthermore, confronted with different incompatible goals, an agent should still be able to choose among goals. Therefore, we argue that a BDI-based agent programming language should provide constructs to allow an agent programmer to implement agents that: 1) do not pursue incompatible goals simultaneously, and 2) can choose from possibly incompatible goals. Most agent programming languages, however, lack constructions that sufficiently deal with these issues in an explicit way. It should be noted that such constructs are different from a goal (event) selection function as proposed, for example, by Jason [3]. These selection functions are too generic and are not devised to process incompatible goals. In fact, our proposal can be considered as a specific instantiation of such a function.

One might argue that it is the responsibility of the agent programmer to implement its agents in such a way that its goal base will never contain incompatible goals. For example, the programmer should ensure that a goal is added to its goal base after the existing plans for incompatible goals are fully executed and the goals are either achieved or dropped. However, we believe that adding a goal to the goal base should not depend on the existence of incompatible goals, as in agent programming the goals of an agent can in principle be incompatible or even inconsistent (cf. [13,14]). Moreover, we believe that an agent programmer may not know at design time which goals it will adopt during its execution such that it becomes a cumbersome task, if not impossible, to write such an agent program. A generic mechanism to process incompatible goals facilitates the implementation of pro-active agents and eases the task of agent programmers. A different solution to avoid that an agent pursues incompatible goals is to use the notion of atomic plans as introduced in 2APL. Atomicity of a plan ensures that the plan is executed at once without interleaving its actions with the actions of other plans. This mechanism can be used to avoid the interleaved execution of the plans for incompatible goals, i.e., to avoid simultaneous pursuit of incompatible goals. This solution is, however, too restrictive as it does not allow the actions of an atomic plan to be interleaved with the plans of *compatible* goals.

In this paper, we propose an explicit and generic mechanism to process incompatible goals. In order to illustrate that the proposed mechanism can be integrated in arbitrary BDI-based agent programming languages, we present the proposed mechanism in the context of a simple agent programming language that can be extended to existing BDI-based agent programming languages. According to this proposal, an agent programmer should specify a conflict relation between only those *sub*-goals for which a planning rule is specified. It should be noted that in most BDI-based agent programming languages, all (sub-)goals for which planning rules are specified, are known at design time. It should also be noted that these planning rules could be applied to adopt plans for arbitrary goals not known at design time. We discuss different strategies to process incompatible goals based on a given conflict relation and show some properties and relations between these strategies. In particular, we present in section 2 a simple generic BDI-based agent programming language by specifying its syntax and operational semantics. Then, the actual contribution of this paper starts in section 3, in which we extend the programming language with a goal conflict relation, discuss different strategies to process incompatible goals and show their properties and relations. In section 4 we discuss related work and section 5 concludes this paper and discusses some directions for future research.

2   An Agent Programming Language

In this section we provide the syntax and semantics of a logic-based agent programming language that is needed to let us present the notion of goal selection strategies later on. The language provided here is based on 2APL [9], but does not reflect its complete syntax and semantics. Instead, we provide a simplified version that is self-contained and can be used to illustrate the different notions of a goal selection strategy. In contrast to 2APL and many logic-based agent programming languages in which the beliefs and goals of the agent are modelled in a subset of first-order logic, the programming language presented here uses a subset of propositional logic, because the focus of this paper is on goal selection strategies. Extending the language to a computational subset of first-order logic (e.g. Horn clauses) is rather straightforward and does not pose any serious technical difficulties.

Furthermore, 2APL provides external actions by which the agent can change its environment, communicative actions to communicate with other agents, and rules to react to external events. All of these constructs are left out in the language presented here, because they are not needed to illustrate the idea of goal selection strategies. In the next section this simplified language will be extended with some goal selection strategies.

2.1   Syntax

An agent has beliefs about its environment, and goals to denote the desirable situation it wants to realize. As mentioned earlier, these are modelled in a subset of propositional logic.

Definition 1 (belief and goal language). *Let the set $\mathcal{P}$ be the set of atomic propositions. The belief language $\mathcal{L}_B$ with typical element β, and goal language $\mathcal{L}_G$ with typical element κ are then defined as:*

- *if $\varphi \in \mathcal{P}$ then $\varphi, \neg\varphi \in \mathcal{L}_B$*
- *if $\varphi \in (\mathcal{P} \setminus \{\top, \bot\})$ then $\varphi, \neg\varphi \in \mathcal{L}_G$*
- *if $\kappa, \kappa' \in \mathcal{L}_G$ then $\kappa \wedge \kappa' \in \mathcal{L}_G$*

The symbol $\models$ will be used to denote the standard entailment relation for propositional logic.

The beliefs of the agent can thus be represented by literals, i.e. positive and negative atomic propositions. A belief that the agent is in room three, for instance, can be represented as `in_room_3`. The goals of the agent can be represented by a conjunction of literals, for instance, `cleaned1` and `cleaned2` to denote the goals of having cleaned room one and two.

To reach its goals, an agent needs to act. A plan describes a sequence of actions an agent should perform in order to reach its goals. For the sake of simplicity and to focus on goal selection strategies we assume only a set of basic actions by which the agent can modify its beliefs, and an action by which the agent can adopt new goals.

Definition 2 (plan language). *Let $\mathcal{A}ct$ with typical element a be the set of basic actions an agent can perform. The set of plans Plan with typical element π is then defined as:*

- *$\mathcal{A}ct \subseteq$ Plan*
- *if $\kappa \in \mathcal{L}_G$ then $\mathrm{adopt}(\kappa) \in$ Plan*
- *if $\pi_1, \pi_2 \in$ Plan then $\pi_1; \pi_2 \in$ Plan*

In the following we will use ϵ to denote the empty plan and identify $\epsilon; \pi$ and $\pi; \epsilon$ with π. Furthermore, we assume that every plan is ended by ϵ.

An agent can possibly know of more than one plan to pursue a single goal. Which plan is the best depends on the current situation. To choose and generate an appropriate plan, the agent uses so-called planning goal rules. These rules are of the form $\kappa \leftarrow \beta \mid \pi$. The informal meaning of such a rule is that the agent can use a plan π to reach a goal κ in case the agent believes β.

Definition 3 (planning goal rules). *The set of goal planning rules $\mathcal{R}_{PG}$ is defined as:*

$$\mathcal{R}_{PG} = \{(\kappa \leftarrow \beta \mid \pi) : \kappa \in \mathcal{L}_G \text{ and } \beta \in \mathcal{L}_B \text{ and } \pi \in \text{Plan}\}$$

2.2 Semantics

In this section we define the operational semantics of the agent programming language as defined in the previous section in terms of a transition system. A transition system is a set of derivation rules for deriving transitions for this language. A transition is a transformation of one configuration C into another configuration C', denoted by $C \longrightarrow C'$. Each transition corresponds to a single computation step for the presented (agent) programming language. A configuration represents the state of an agent at each point during computation.

Definition 4 (agent configuration). *Let $\Sigma = \{\sigma : \sigma \subseteq \mathcal{L}_B \text{ and } \sigma \not\models \bot\}$ be the set of consistent belief sets, and let $\Gamma = \{\kappa \in \mathcal{L}_G : \kappa \not\models \bot\}$ be the set of goals. An agent configuration is then defined as a tuple $\langle \sigma, \gamma, \Pi, \mathrm{PG} \rangle$ where $\sigma \in \Sigma$ is the belief base, $\gamma \subseteq \Gamma$ is the goal base, $\Pi \subseteq (\mathcal{L}_G \times \text{Plan})$ are the plans, and $\mathrm{PG} \subseteq \mathcal{R}_{PG}$ are the planning goal rules.*

The plan base of the agent is a set of pairs (κ, π), where κ denotes the state of affairs that is supposed to be reached by the sequence of actions denoted by π. We use κ to keep track of the goals the agent is working on.

Note that in contrast to the belief base, the individual goals in the goal base are consistent, but different goals can be inconsistent. An agent can thus have as goal in_room_3 while it also has a goal ¬in_room_3. We say that an agent has a goal κ when κ is derivable from the goal base of that agent. As the goal base can be inconsistent we cannot use the same entailment relation as we use for the belief base. Instead, we define a goal entailment relation to be used for the goal base (cf. [13,14]). As it would be irrational for an agent to have goals that are already believed to be achieved, the belief base of the agent is also used for this goal entailment relation.

Definition 5 (goal entailment). *Let $\gamma \subseteq \Gamma$ be a goal base, and let $\sigma \in \Sigma$ be a belief base. The goal entailment relation $\models_g$ is then defined in the following way:*

$$(\gamma, \sigma) \models_g \kappa \Leftrightarrow (\exists \gamma_i \in \gamma : \gamma_i \models \kappa) \text{ and } \sigma \not\models \kappa$$

An agent with belief base σ and goal base γ is thus said to have a goal κ if and only if κ is derivable from at least one of the goals in goal base γ and is not entailed by the belief base.

The agent can update its belief base by performing basic actions. For this purpose we use a function update : $\mathcal{A}ct \times \Sigma \to \Sigma$ that takes as arguments a basic action and a belief base, and evaluates to a new belief base as a consequence of executing the basic action. The transition rule defined below defines the semantics of executing a basic action, which can be executed in case the goal for which the plan is generated is still a goal of the agent (condition $(\gamma, \sigma) \models_g \kappa$). A goal of the agent is removed from its goal base if the goal is believed to be reached after having executed the belief update operation (3rd *where*-clause of R1). Moreover, it would be irrational for an agent to execute a plan for a goal already believed to be reached. Therefore, the plans that were generated for this goal are removed from the plan base (2nd *where*-clause of R1). In defining the transition rules below an agent configuration $C = \langle \sigma, \gamma, \Pi, \mathtt{PG} \rangle$ is assumed. The set of planning rules $\mathtt{PG}$ will be omitted whenever possible, since this component does not change during the agent's execution.

R1 (belief update). *Let $C = \langle \sigma, \gamma, \Pi, \mathtt{PG} \rangle$ be an agent configuration, and let $a \in \mathcal{A}ct$ and $(\kappa, a; \pi) \in \Pi$.*

$$\frac{\mathtt{update}(a, \sigma) = \sigma' \text{ and } (\gamma, \sigma) \models_g \kappa}{\langle \sigma, \gamma, \Pi \rangle \longrightarrow \langle \sigma', \gamma', \Pi'' \rangle}$$

where
1) $\Pi' = (\Pi \setminus \{(\kappa, a; \pi)\}) \cup \{(\kappa, \pi)\}$
2) $\Pi'' = \Pi' \setminus \{(\kappa', \pi') \in \Pi' : (\gamma, \sigma') \not\models_g \kappa'\}$
3) $\gamma' = \gamma \setminus \{\gamma_i \in \gamma : \sigma' \models \gamma_i\}$

Note that under the interpretation of the goal entailment relation a goal in_room_1 ∧ battery_loaded differs from having two separate goals in_room_1 and battery_loaded in the goal base. The first goal is only achieved once the agent believes in_room_1 ∧ battery_loaded, while the single goal in_room_1 is achieved if it believes in_room_1 even when it does not believe battery_loaded.

Agents can adopt new goals by performing an adopt action. The goal is added to the goal base only if the goal is not already believed to be achieved. The following two transition rules capture a goal adoption. The first rule captures the case in which the goal is not already believed to be achieved, whereas the second rule captures the case in which the goal is already believed to be achieved. In the latter case the plan execution proceeds without any changes in the agent's belief and goal bases.

R2 (goal adoption 1). *Let* $C = \langle \sigma, \gamma, \Pi, \mathtt{PG} \rangle$ *be an agent configuration.*

$$\frac{(\kappa, \mathsf{adopt}(\kappa'); \pi) \in \Pi \text{ and } (\gamma, \sigma) \models_g \kappa \text{ and } \sigma \not\models \kappa'}{\langle \sigma, \gamma, \Pi \rangle \longrightarrow \langle \sigma, \gamma \cup \{\kappa'\}, \Pi' \rangle}$$

where $\Pi' = (\Pi \setminus \{(\kappa, \mathsf{adopt}(\kappa'); \pi)\}) \cup \{(\kappa, \pi)\}$

R3 (goal adoption 2). *Let* $C = \langle \sigma, \gamma, \Pi, \mathtt{PG} \rangle$ *be an agent configuration.*

$$\frac{(\kappa, \mathsf{adopt}(\kappa'); \pi) \in \Pi \text{ and } (\gamma, \sigma) \models_g \kappa \text{ and } \sigma \models \kappa'}{\langle \sigma, \gamma, \Pi \rangle \longrightarrow \langle \sigma, \gamma, \Pi' \rangle}$$

where $\Pi' = (\Pi \setminus \{(\kappa, \mathsf{adopt}(\kappa'); \pi)\}) \cup \{(\kappa, \pi)\}$

When an agent has executed all the actions of a plan, this plan is removed from the plan base. Removing a plan from the plan base does not affect the goal base of the agent. When the plan failed in establishing the desired state, the goal remains in the goal base of the agent, such that the agent can try again to reach its goal with a possibly different plan. The next transition rule is for removing empty plans from the plan base.

R4 (empty plan). *Let* $C = \langle \sigma, \gamma, \Pi, \mathtt{PG} \rangle$ *be an agent configuration.*

$$\frac{(\kappa, \epsilon) \in \Pi}{\langle \sigma, \gamma, \Pi \rangle \longrightarrow \langle \sigma, \gamma, \Pi \setminus \{(\kappa, \epsilon)\} \rangle}$$

As already mentioned, an agent uses planning goal rules for generating plans by which it hopes to reach its goals. An agent can apply a goal planning rule $\kappa \leftarrow \beta \mid \pi$ if κ is a goal of the agent, β is derivable from the agent's belief base, and the agent is not already working on a plan for κ. In defining the transition rule for plan generation we first define the set of applicable planning rules with respect to an agent configuration.

Definition 6 (applicable rules). *Let $C = \langle \sigma, \gamma, \Pi, \mathsf{PG} \rangle$ be an agent configuration, and let $\kappa \in \mathcal{L}_G$. The set of applicable planning goal rules for goal κ w.r.t. configuration C is then defined as:*

$$appl(\kappa, C) =$$

$$\{\kappa \leftarrow \beta \mid \pi \in \mathsf{PG} : (\gamma, \sigma) \models_g \kappa \text{ and } \sigma \models \beta \text{ and } \neg \exists \pi' \in \mathsf{Plan} : (\kappa, \pi') \in \Pi\}$$

When a goal planning rule is applicable the plan will be added to the agent's plan base. The following rule captures this situation.

R5 (plan generation). *Let $C = \langle \sigma, \gamma, \Pi, \mathsf{PG} \rangle$ be an agent configuration.*

$$\frac{(\kappa \leftarrow \beta \mid \pi) \in appl(\kappa, C)}{\langle \sigma, \gamma, \Pi \rangle \longrightarrow \langle \sigma, \gamma, \Pi' \rangle}$$

where $\Pi' = \Pi \cup \{(\kappa, \pi)\}$

In order to show some properties of the behavior of an agent, we define the notion of an agent execution. Given a transition system consisting of a set of transition rules, an execution of an agent is a sequence of configurations that can be generated by applying transition rules to the initial configuration of that agent. An agent execution thus shows a possible behavior of the agent. All possible executions for an initial configuration show the complete behavior of an agent.

Definition 7 (agent execution). *An execution of an agent in transition system $\mathcal{T}$ is a (possibly infinite) sequence of agent configurations $\langle C_0, C_1, \ldots \rangle$ such that for each for $i \in \mathbb{N}$, $C_i \longrightarrow C_{i+1}$ can be derived from $\mathcal{T}$. We use the term initial configuration to refer to C_0.*

Recall that $(\kappa, \pi) \in \Pi$ means that a plan has been generated to achieve a state denoted by κ. We assume that in the initial configuration the associated κ to each plan in the plan base is in fact a goal of the agent. Under this assumption we can show that R1, ..., R5 ensures that the associated κ to each plan in the plan base in all derived configurations is in fact a goal of the agent. In other words, the agent will never adopt a plan for which the corresponding κ is not a goal of the agent.

Proposition 1. *Let $\langle C_0, C_1, \ldots \rangle$ be an agent execution in transition system $\mathcal{T}$, where $C_i = \langle \sigma^i, \gamma^i, \Pi^i, \mathsf{PG} \rangle$, and let $\mathcal{T}$ consist of the rules R1, ..., R5. Given that $\forall (\kappa, \pi) \in \Pi^0 : (\gamma^0, \sigma^0) \models_g \kappa$, then $\forall i \in \mathbb{N}. \forall (\kappa, \pi) \in \Pi^i : (\gamma^i, \sigma^i) \models_g \kappa$*

Proof. By induction on the depth of the execution. We have $\forall (\kappa, \pi) \in \Pi^0 : (\gamma^0, \sigma^0) \models_g \kappa$ by assumption. Now assume that $\forall (\kappa, \pi) \in \Pi^k : (\gamma^k, \sigma^k) \models_g \kappa$ for arbitrary $k \geq 0$. Now we have to prove that after application of one of R1, ..., R5 it holds that $\forall (\kappa, \pi) \in \Pi^{k+1} : (\gamma^{k+1}, \sigma^{k+1}) \models_g \kappa$. For R2, R3 and R4 this is trivial as they do not change the belief and goal bases. Assume that a plan

$(\kappa, \pi) \in \Pi^{k+1}$ *is adopted by application of rule R5. From definition 6 and that* $\gamma^k = \gamma^{k+1}$ *after application of R5 it follows that* $(\gamma^{k+1}, \sigma^{k+1}) \models_g \kappa$. *Now assume that a goal is removed from the goal base by application of rule R1. From the fact that if a goal is removed, also all the plans that are associated to this goal are removed we conclude that* $\forall (\kappa, \pi) \in \Pi^{k+1} : (\gamma^{k+1}, \sigma^{k+1}) \models_g \kappa$ *still holds.* $\square$

3 Goal Selection Strategies

The previous section defined a simplified version of an agent programming language. In this section we consider several possible goal selection strategies for this agent programming language. Central to the notion of a goal selection strategy is that we relate those goals that cannot be pursued simultaneously. For this purpose we extend the previously defined agent configuration with a binary relation $\mathcal{R}$ on the set of goals. We call such an extended agent configuration a goal strategy agent.

Definition 8 (goal strategy agent). *Let* $\langle \sigma, \gamma, \Pi, \mathrm{PG} \rangle$ *be an agent configuration. A goal strategy agent is a tuple* $\langle \sigma, \gamma, \Pi, \mathrm{PG}, \mathcal{R} \rangle$ *where* $\mathcal{R} \subseteq (\mathcal{L}_G \times \mathcal{L}_G)$ *is a goal selection strategy.*

The main idea of $\mathcal{R}$ is thus that it specifies which goals are incompatible with each other. To work on two goals that might hinder the achievement of one another would be irrational. Consequently, we desire that if two goals are incompatible the agent should not be working on plans for these goals at the same time.

Definition 9 (non-conflicting plan base). *Let* $C = \langle \sigma, \gamma, \Pi, \mathrm{PG}, \mathcal{R} \rangle$ *be a goal strategy agent. The plan base in* C *is* $\mathcal{R}$-*non-conflicting iff:*

$$\forall (\kappa, \pi), (\kappa', \pi') \in \Pi : (\kappa, \kappa') \notin \mathcal{R} \text{ and } (\kappa', \kappa) \notin \mathcal{R}$$

In the sequel we consider several notions of a goal selection strategy by introducing the relations $\mathcal{R}^{<>}$ (incompatibility), $\mathcal{R}_d^{\prec}$ (disruptive precedence) and $\mathcal{R}_c^{\prec}$ (cautious precedence) as concrete instances of $\mathcal{R}$. We study some of the possible semantics of these relations by providing alternative definitions of the plan generation rule R5.

3.1 Incompatibility of Goals

Goals the agent has already committed to by having adopted a plan constrain the possibility for the pursuit of other goals [15]. A rational agent is expected to refrain from adopting a plan that hinders the achievement of the goals the agent is currently committed to. In this subsection we define the *incompatibility* relation $\mathcal{R}^{<>}$ to relate goals that cannot be pursued at the same time. We adapt the previously defined plan generation rule R5 to ensure that the agent generates its plans in such a way that the plan base remains non-conflicting.

Definition 10 (goal incompatibility relation). *A goal incompatibility relation* $\mathcal{R}^{<>} \subseteq (\mathcal{L}_G \times \mathcal{L}_G)$ *is a set of pairs of goals such that:*

- $(\kappa, \kappa') \in \mathcal{R}^{<>} \leftrightarrow (\kappa', \kappa) \in \mathcal{R}^{<>}$
- $(\kappa, \kappa') \in \mathcal{R}^{<>} \rightarrow \kappa' \neq \kappa$

Intuitively, when $(\kappa, \kappa') \in \mathcal{R}^{<>}$ this means that the goal κ cannot be pursued in parallel with the goal κ'. Note that the incompatibility relation is symmetric and anti-reflexive, meaning that two distinct goals are always incompatible with each other and no goal can be incompatible with itself. The next transition rule redefines rule R5 for plan generation, now taking the incompatibility of goals into account.

R5.1 (incompatibility). *Let* $C = \langle \sigma, \gamma, \Pi, \texttt{PG}, \mathcal{R}^{<>} \rangle$ *be a goal strategy agent with* $\mathcal{R}^{<>}$ *being an incompatibility relation*

$$\frac{(\kappa \leftarrow \beta \mid \pi) \in appl(\kappa, C) \text{ and } \forall \kappa' \in \mathcal{L}_G : (\kappa', \pi') \in \Pi \rightarrow (\kappa, \kappa') \notin \mathcal{R}^{<>}}{\langle \sigma, \gamma, \Pi \rangle \longrightarrow \langle \sigma, \gamma, \Pi' \rangle}$$

where $\Pi' = \Pi \cup \{(\kappa, \pi)\}$

In words, a plan can be generated for κ if there is an applicable planning rule for κ, and none of the current plans the agent is working on are for a goal that is incompatible with κ. Returning to the example of section 1, in this new transition system we can prevent the household agent from trying to clean the rooms one and five at the same time by defining the goals `clean1` and `clean5` as incompatible with each other, i.e. $(\texttt{clean1}, \texttt{clean5}), (\texttt{clean5}, \texttt{clean1}) \in \mathcal{R}^{<>}$. When the household agent has for example adopted a plan for cleaning room one, it will not adopt a plan for cleaning room five as long as it is still working on cleaning room one. Note that in case the adopted plan finished, but failed to clean room one, the agent can either try again to clean room one or it can start working on cleaning room five instead.

Similar to proposition 1 we show for rules R1, ..., R4, R5.1 that the agent will never adopt a plan for which the corresponding κ is not a goal of the agent when in the initial configuration the associated κ to each plan in the plan base is in fact a goal of the agent. Although not needed for proving that the plan base of the agent remains non-conflicting during its execution, we provide this property for the sake of completeness.

Corollary 1. *Let* $\langle C_0, C_1, \ldots \rangle$ *be an agent execution in transition system* $\mathcal{T}$, *where* $C_i = \langle \sigma^i, \gamma^i, \Pi^i, \texttt{PG}, \mathcal{R}^{<>} \rangle$, *and* $\mathcal{T}$ *consists of the rules* R1, ..., R4 *and* R5.1. *Given that* $\forall (\kappa, \pi) \in \Pi^0 : (\gamma^0, \sigma^0) \models_g \kappa$, *then* $\forall i \in \mathbb{N}. \forall (\kappa, \pi) \in \Pi^i : (\gamma^i, \sigma^i) \models_g \kappa$

Proof. This follows from proposition 1 and the fact that R5.1 is a more restrictive version of R5. □

The bottom line of $\mathcal{R}^{<>}$ is to ensure that if the agent started with a non-conflicting plan base, the plan base of the agent remains non-conflicting. Given that the agent starts with a non-conflicting plan base, we show that the plan base stays non-conflicting for all executions in the transition system consisting of the rules $R1, \ldots, R4, R5.1$.

Proposition 2. *Let $\langle C_0, C_1, \ldots \rangle$ be an agent execution in transition system T consisting of the rules $R1, \ldots, R4$ and R5.1. Given that the plan base in C_0 is $\mathcal{R}^{<>}$-non-conflicting then the plan base in C_i is $\mathcal{R}^{<>}$-non-conflicting $\forall i \in \mathbb{N}$.*

Proof. By induction on the depth of the execution. The plan base of C_0 is non-conflicting by assumption. Now assume that the plan base of C_k is non-conflicting for arbitrary $k \geq 0$. The only way in which the plan base can become conflicting is by adoption of a plan to the plan base. Suppose that in configuration C_{k+1} a plan for goal κ has been adopted by applying R5.1. From the premises of R5.1 it directly follows that $\forall(\kappa', \pi) \in \Pi^{k+1} : (\kappa, \kappa') \notin \mathcal{R}^{<>}$. From the symmetry of $\mathcal{R}^{<>}$ we conclude that $\forall(\kappa', \pi) \in \Pi^{k+1} : (\kappa', \kappa) \notin \mathcal{R}^{<>}$, which means that the plan base of C_{k+1} is also non-conflicting. □

3.2 Precedence of Goals

The above defined incompatibility relation ensures that the agent refrains from adopting plans for goals that hinder the achievement of goals the agent is currently pursuing. It does not, however, guarantee a certain order in which the agent tries to achieve its goals. Under the interpretation of the incompatibility relation $\mathcal{R}^{<>}$ the choice between two incompatible goals for which no plan is adopted yet is non-deterministic. Sometimes, however, when an agent is faced with such a choice, one goal should have precedence over the other. Suppose, for instance, that the household agent cannot clean rooms in case its battery charge is low. Therefore, one would expect the agent to first achieve its goal to have its battery loaded (denoted by **battery_loaded**) before pursuing a goal to clean a room. In this subsection we provide the precedence relation $\mathcal{R}^{\prec}$ enabling the agent not only to avoid pursuing goals that cannot be achieved simultaneously, but also to choose between such incompatible goals. Later we provide two different behaviours for plan generation under $\mathcal{R}^{\prec}$. We will distinct between these two by naming them $\mathcal{R}_d^{\prec}$ and $\mathcal{R}_c^{\prec}$.

Definition 11 (goal precedence relation). *A precedence relation $\mathcal{R}^{\prec} \subseteq (\mathcal{L}_G \times \mathcal{L}_G)$ is a set of pairs of goals such that:*

- $(\kappa, \kappa') \in \mathcal{R}^{\prec}$ *and* $(\kappa', \kappa'') \in \mathcal{R}^{\prec} \rightarrow (\kappa, \kappa'') \in \mathcal{R}^{\prec}$
- $(\kappa, \kappa') \in \mathcal{R}^{\prec} \rightarrow (\kappa', \kappa) \notin \mathcal{R}^{\prec}$ *and* $\kappa' \neq \kappa$

The intuitive meaning of the precedence relation is as follows. When some goals κ and κ' are related by $\mathcal{R}^{\prec}$, i.e. $(\kappa, \kappa') \in \mathcal{R}^{\prec}$, these goals are not to be pursued simultaneously, and when both κ and κ' are goals of the agent the achievement of κ has precedence over the achievement of κ'. Precedence implies an order in which goals are pursued. The relation $\mathcal{R}^{\prec}$ is irreflexive, i.e. no goal can have precedence over itself, and transitive. When, for example, the goal to have the battery loaded precedes the goal to have room one clean (the room of the boss), and cleaning room one on its turn precedes a goal to have cleaned room two, then it seems not unreasonable to assume that the goal of having the battery loaded also precedes the goal to have cleaned room two. Note that irreflexivity and transitivity together imply asymmetry.

Suppose, for example, that in generating its plans an agent is faced with a choice between two goals `battery_loaded` and `clean1`. Furthermore, assume that $(\mathtt{battery\_loaded}, \mathtt{clean1}) \in \mathcal{R}^{\prec}$. If the agent has not adopted a plan for one of them and does not have any goals with higher precedence than `battery_loaded`, then one might expect this agent to adopt a plan to load its battery. If, however, the agent was already working on a plan for cleaning room one before the goal `battery_loaded` was adopted, then applying a planning goal rule for `battery_loaded` results in a conflicting plan base. In the following we propose two different strategies, disruptive and cautious precedence, to keep the plan base non-conflicting by providing two transition rules for plan generation with precedence.

Disruptive Precedence

Disruptive precedence implements a strategy in which the agent stops pursuing goals with less precedence the moment a plan can be adopted for a goal with higher precedence. Plans the agent is already executing might thus be disrupted in case a plan is adopted for a more important goal. The transition rule defined below implements this strategy.

R5.2 (disruptive precedence). *Let* $C = \langle \sigma, \gamma, \Pi, \mathsf{PG}, \mathcal{R}_d^{\prec} \rangle$ *be a goal strategy agent where* $\mathcal{R}_d^{\prec}$ *is a precedence relation.*

$$\frac{(\kappa \leftarrow \beta \mid \pi) \in appl(\kappa, C) \ and \ \forall \kappa' \in \mathcal{L}_G : (\gamma, \sigma) \models_g \kappa' \to (\kappa', \kappa) \notin \mathcal{R}_d^{\prec}}{\langle \sigma, \gamma, \Pi \rangle \longrightarrow \langle \sigma, \gamma, \Pi' \rangle}$$

where $\Pi' = (\Pi \cup \{(\kappa, \pi)\}) \setminus \{(\kappa', \pi') \in \Pi : (\kappa, \kappa') \in \mathcal{R}_d^{\prec}\}$

In words, an applicable planning goal rule for κ is applied if no other goal has precedence over κ. Note that in contrast to transition rule R5.1 in the premises only conflicting goals are taken into account instead of plans in the plan base. It might thus seem that there are plans (κ', π') in the plan base of the agent such that $(\kappa', \kappa) \in \mathcal{R}_d^{\prec}$, which means that the agent has plans for goals that precede κ, and therefore conflict with κ. However, this will never be the case because the premises ensures that the agent has no goal that precedes κ, and as we show by the following corollary, every κ' associated to a plan of the agent is also a goal of the agent.

Corollary 2. *Let* $\langle C_0, C_1, \ldots \rangle$ *be an agent execution in transition system* $\mathcal{T}$, *where* $C_i = \langle \sigma^i, \gamma^i, \Pi^i, \mathsf{PG}, \mathcal{R}_d^{\prec} \rangle$, *and* $\mathcal{T}$ *consists of the rules* $R1, \ldots, R4$ *and* $R5.2$. *Given that* $\forall (\kappa, \pi) \in \Pi^0 : (\gamma^0, \sigma^0) \models_g \kappa$, *then* $\forall i \in \mathbb{N}. \forall (\kappa, \pi) \in \Pi^i : (\gamma^i, \sigma^i) \models_g \kappa$

Proof. This follows from proposition 1 and the fact that R5.2 is a more restrictive version of R5. □

When a planning rule for a goal κ is applied, all plans associated with goals that are to be preceded by κ are dropped. This way it is ensured that the goal κ for which a plan has been adopted does not conflict with plans for goals with less precedence. At this point we are able to show that if the agent starts with an empty plan base, with rules R1, ..., R4 and R5.2 it is guaranteed that the plan base stays non-conflicting in the rest of the execution.

Proposition 3. *Let $\langle C_0, C_1, \ldots \rangle$ be an agent execution in transition system $\mathcal{T}$ consisting of the rules R1, ..., R4 and R5.2 and let the plan base in C_0 be empty. Then the plan base in C_i is $\mathcal{R}_d^{\prec}$-non-conflicting $\forall i \in \mathbb{N}$.*

Proof. By induction on the depth of the execution. In C_0 the plan base is non-conflicting, because $\Pi = \emptyset$. Assume that for arbitrary $k \geq 0$ the plan base of C_k is non-conflicting. Now we have to prove that when a plan for goal κ is adopted by rule R5.2 for all plans in C_{k+1} for a goal κ' it holds that $(\kappa, \kappa'), (\kappa', \kappa) \notin \mathcal{R}_d^{\prec}$. The premises of rule R5.2 ensures that $(\kappa', \kappa) \notin \mathcal{R}_d^{\prec}$ for any goal κ'. From $\Pi^0 = \emptyset$ and corollary 2 it follows that $\forall(\kappa', \pi) \in \Pi^k : (\gamma, \sigma) \models_g \kappa'$, we can thus conclude that $\forall(\kappa', \pi) \in \Pi^{k+1} : (\kappa', \kappa) \notin \mathcal{R}_d^{\prec}$. That there are no plans in the plan base for κ' such that $(\kappa, \kappa') \in \mathcal{R}_d^{\prec}$ follows from the fact that all these plans are dropped once a plan for κ has been adopted. □

When the goal of the household robot to have loaded its battery should precede a goal to have a room clean, and the agent is not cleaning a room already, the agent should postpone the adoption of a plan for cleaning a room until its battery is loaded. In the following we show that for rules R1, ..., R4, R5.2 such behaviour can indeed be expected. More generally, when the agent has adopted a goal κ that has precedence over some other goal κ', then if the agent has not adopted a plan for κ' it will not do so as long as κ is still a goal of the agent. Recall that κ is a goal of the agent as long as the state denoted by κ is not believed to be reached.

Proposition 4. *Let transition system $\mathcal{T}$ consist of the rules R1, ..., R4 and R5.2. Let $C_0 = \langle \sigma^0, \gamma^0, \Pi^0, \text{PG}, \mathcal{R}_d^{\prec} \rangle$ be an initial configuration where $(\gamma^0, \sigma^0) \models_g \kappa$, $(\gamma^0, \sigma^0) \models_g \kappa'$, $\forall \pi \in \text{Plan} : (\kappa', \pi) \notin \Pi^0$ and $(\kappa, \kappa') \in \mathcal{R}_d^{\prec}$. Then for every execution with initial configuration C_0 in $\mathcal{T}$ it holds that $\forall_{i \geq 0} : ((\forall_{0 \leq j \leq i} : (\gamma^j, \sigma^j) \models_g \kappa) \to \forall \pi \in \text{Plan} : (\kappa', \pi) \notin \Pi^i)$*

Proof. By induction on the depth of an execution $\langle C_0, C_1, \ldots \rangle$ with all of the above assumptions about C_0. Then $\forall \pi \in \text{Plan} : (\kappa', \pi) \notin \Pi^0$ by assumption. Assume that up to arbitrary $k \geq 0$ it holds that $\forall_{0 \geq i \geq k} : ((\gamma^i, \sigma^i) \models_g \kappa$ and $\forall \pi \in \text{Plan} : (\kappa', \pi) \notin \Pi^i)$. Now we have to prove that it cannot be that $(\gamma^{k+1}, \sigma^{k+1}) \models_g \kappa$ and $\forall \pi \in \text{Plan} : (\kappa', \pi) \in \Pi^{k+1}$ which can only happen after application of R5.2. As the condition $\forall \kappa \in \mathcal{L}_G : (\gamma^k, \sigma^k) \models_g \kappa \to (\kappa, \kappa') \notin \mathcal{R}_d^{\prec}$ of the premises of rule R5.2 is not satisfied, we can conclude that $\forall \pi \in \text{Plan} : (\kappa', \pi) \notin \Pi^{k+1}$. □

Note that in the above proposition no assumptions are made about whether the agent is already working on a plan for κ or not. Even if no plan is adopted for κ

and there are no applicable planning rules, the agent will not adopt a plan for goals that are to be preceded by κ. As a consequence, the execution of the agent might block when all goals of the agent are to be preceded by a goal for which no plan can be adopted. It is the responsibility of the designer to avoid such behaviour in case this is deemed undesirable. The designer should then ensure that the agent can always find an appropriate plan for such an important goal. A weaker version of R5.2 can be introduced such that a rule for κ' can be applied when there are no *applicable* rules for more important goals.

Cautious Precedence

By dropping plans for goals with less precedence immediately after a PG-rule for some goal with higher precedence is enabled the agent might give up too soon. Particularly in situations in which goals with higher precedence are often adopted the agent might never finish a plan for some of its goals. The agent would then never reach those goals. For example, when the boss' room needs a lot of cleaning, the agent might never finish a plan for cleaning the other rooms. Therefore, we also propose a more cautious form of precedence, in which the agent persists to plans it has already adopted. With such a strategy the agent is more cautious about dropping plans. This strategy is captured by rule R5.3 as defined below.

R5.3 (cautious precedence). *Let* $C = \langle \sigma, \gamma, \Pi, \text{PG}, \mathcal{R}_c^{\prec} \rangle$ *be a goal strategy agent where* $\mathcal{R}_c^{\prec}$ *is a precedence relation.*

$$\frac{(\kappa \leftarrow \beta \mid \pi) \in appl(\kappa, C) \text{ and } \forall \kappa' \in \mathcal{L}_G : (\gamma, \sigma) \models_g \kappa' \rightarrow (\kappa', \kappa) \notin \mathcal{R}_c^{\prec} \text{ and } \\ \forall \kappa' \in \mathcal{L}_G : (\kappa', \pi') \in \Pi \rightarrow (\kappa, \kappa') \notin \mathcal{R}_c^{\prec}}{\langle \sigma, \gamma, \Pi \rangle \longrightarrow \langle \sigma, \gamma, \Pi' \rangle}$$

where $\Pi' = \Pi \cup \{(\kappa, \pi)\}$

The first clause of the premises of R5.3 states that an agent can apply an applicable planning goal rule for a goal κ if no other goal has precedence over κ. The second clause of the premises states that the agent is not already working on a goal κ' with less precedence than κ. The agent will thus persist working on a plan for a goal even though a goal planning rule for a goal with higher precedence is applicable. Note that when the plan for such a conflicting goal κ' failed to achieve this goal, the agent will not retry with another plan as long as κ is still a goal of the agent. Under the assumption that no new goals with higher precedence than κ are adopted, the agent will adopt a plan for κ as soon as all plans for goals with lower precedence than κ are completed.

Note that just like in transition rule R5.2 only conflicting goals are taken into account instead of plans in the plan base. To avoid that a plan for a goal κ is adopted while there already is a plan (κ', π) in the plan base such that $(\kappa', \kappa) \in \mathcal{R}_c^{\prec}$, it is needed that every κ' associated to a plan of the agent is also a goal of the agent. This is shown by the corollary below.

Corollary 3. *Let* $\langle C_0, C_1, \ldots \rangle$ *be an agent execution in transition system* $\mathcal{T}$, *where* $C_i = \langle \sigma^i, \gamma^i, \Pi^i, \text{PG}, \mathcal{R}_c^{\prec} \rangle$, *and* $\mathcal{T}$ *consists of the rules* $R1, \ldots, R4$ *and* $R5.3$. *Given that* $\forall (\kappa, \pi) \in \Pi^0 : (\gamma^0, \sigma^0) \models_g \kappa$, *then* $\forall i \in \mathbb{N}. \forall (\kappa, \pi) \in \Pi^i :$ $(\gamma^i, \sigma^i) \models_g \kappa$.

Proof. This follows from proposition 1 and the fact that R5.3 is a more restrictive version of R5. □

Next, we show that similar to proposition 3, in a transition system consisting of the rules $R1, \ldots, R4$ and $R5.3$ the plan base of the agent stays non-conflicting during the execution of an agent that started with an empty plan base.

Proposition 5. *Let* $\langle C_0, C_1, \ldots \rangle$ *be an agent execution in transition system* $\mathcal{T}$ *consisting of the rules* $R1, \ldots, R4$ *and* $R5.3$ *and let the plan base in* C_0 *be empty. Then the plan base in* C_i *is* $\mathcal{R}_c^{\prec}$*-non-conflicting* $\forall i \in \mathbb{N}$.

Proof. Observe that rule R5.3 is a more restricted version of R5.2 and ensures that no goal κ *is adopted when* $\exists (\kappa', \pi) \in \Pi : (\kappa, \kappa') \in \mathcal{R}_c^{\prec}$. *The proof is therefore similar to the proof of proposition 3.* □

Just like we have shown for rules $R1, \ldots, R4, R5.2$ we show that with rules $R1, \ldots, R4, R5.3$ an agent that has not already adopted a plan for a goal κ' will not do so as long as the agent has a goal κ with higher precedence, i.e. $(\kappa, \kappa') \in \mathcal{R}_c^{\prec}$.

Proposition 6. *Let transition system* $\mathcal{T}$ *consist of the rules* $R1, \ldots, R4$ *and* $R5.3$. *Let* $C_0 = \langle \sigma^0, \gamma^0, \Pi^0, \text{PG}^0, \mathcal{R}_c^{\prec} \rangle$ *be an initial configuration where* $(\gamma^0, \sigma^0) \models_g$ $\kappa, (\gamma^0, \sigma^0) \models_g \kappa', \forall \pi \in \text{Plan} : (\kappa', \pi) \notin \Pi^0$ *and* $(\kappa, \kappa') \in \mathcal{R}_c^{\prec}$. *Then for every execution with initial configuration* C_0 *in* $\mathcal{T}$ *it holds that* $\forall_{i \geq 0} : ((\forall_{0 \leq j \leq i} : (\gamma^j, \sigma^j) \models_g$ $\kappa) \rightarrow \forall \pi \in \text{Plan} : (\kappa', \pi) \notin \Pi^i)$

Proof. Similar to the proof of proposition 4. □

Note that just as with disruptive precedence, the execution of the agent might block when all goals of the agent are to be preceded by a goal for which no plan can be adopted.

3.3 A Brief Comparison of the Proposed Mechanisms

We have already shown that all three transition systems guarantee that if a plan base is non-conflicting initially it remains non-conflicting during the agent's execution. We have not shown, however, to what extent the different transition systems differ from each other. We omit a formal proof that the behaviour of a transition system with disruptive precedence differs from one with cautious precedence, as we believe that the difference should be clear; the first will drop a plan for less important goals immediately after a planning rule is applied for a goal with higher precedence, while the latter will wait for plans associated to goals with less precedence to finish before applying a planning rule for a goal with higher precedence. We will, however, as a final property show that both forms of plan generation with the precedence relation generate different behaviour than plan generation with incompatibility. The crux is that with the rules $R1, \ldots, R4, R5.1$ no order of the pursuit of goals is assured.

Proposition 7. *Let transition system T_1 consist of rules $R1, \ldots, R4$, $R5.1$, transition system T_2 of $R1, \ldots, R4$, $R5.2$, and transition system T_3 of $R1, \ldots, R4$, $R5.3$. Neither transition system T_2 nor T_3 can generate the same behaviour as T_1.*

Proof. Assume that $\forall \pi \in \mathtt{Plan} : (\kappa, \pi) \notin \Pi^0$, $(\kappa' \leftarrow \beta|\pi) \in appl(\kappa', C_0)$, and that $\mathcal{R}^{<>} = \{(\kappa, \kappa'), (\kappa', \kappa)\}$. Recall that if a rule for κ is applicable then κ is a goal of the agent (by definition 6). Then after applying R5.1 for $(\kappa' \leftarrow \beta|\pi)$, in C_1 it holds that $(\kappa', \pi) \in \Pi^1$ and $(\gamma^1, \sigma^1) \models_g \kappa$. According to proposition 4 and proposition 6 such an execution is not possible in T_2 nor in T_3. $\qquad\square$

4   Related Work

Related to our work is the work presented in [16], which describes the structure of a goal model which can be used by an agent to reason about goals during its deliberation process and means-ends reasoning. As part of this model an inconsistency operator is provided to denote that the success of one goal implies the failure of another. Also a preference operator is provided to express that in case of inconsistency between goals one goal is preferred to another.

Also related to our work is the goal deliberation strategy as proposed in [17]. This strategy allows agent developers to specify the relationship between incompatible goals in order to avoid negative interference in pursuing multiple goals. This relation also implies a precedence of one goal over another. In fact, their mechanism of avoiding the pursuit of incompatible goals closely resembles our notion of disruptive precedence, provided that in contrast to our incompatibility relation, their incompatibility relation is not a transitive one.

The main difference between our work and that of [16] and [17] is that our proposal is not limited to a specific platform, but can be integrated in existing BDI-based agent programming language. Furthermore, [16] and [17] do not provide a formal semantics of the proposed constructions. The lack of a formal semantics makes it hard to compare different approaches extensively.

Another solution that involves avoiding negative interference in pursuing multiple goals is the one proposed in [18]. Possible conflicts are detected and avoided by annotating plans and goals with detailed summary information about their effects, pre-conditions, and in-conditions. Just as also observed in [17] we believe that acquiring and assigning such information to goals and plans is a cumbersome task for an agent programmer. Also, in contrast to our approach, it is not possible to enforce that one goal precedes another. Moreover, as we have integrated the goal selection strategies in transition rules we believe that our approach can be directly used to build agent interpreters that can process incompatible goals.

5   Conclusion and Discussion

In this paper, we have introduced three types of goal selection strategies as an explicit and generic mechanism to process incompatible goals. These mechanisms prevent an agent from simultaneously pursuing goals that are incompatible with each other, and enable the agent to choose from possibly incompatible goals in adopting plans to reach its goals. We have presented the proposed mechanism in the context of a simple agent programming language that can be extended to most BDI-based agent programming languages. The three goal selection strategies are implemented as conditions for the application of goal planning rules. These strategies are integrated in the transition rules for PG-rule applications. It should be noted that our account of precedence might look like a preference relation. However, it should be emphasized that the precedence relation is defined as a programming construct to help an agent to choose a goal from a (possibly) incompatible set of goals. It is not a concept agents reason about.

In the current proposal different strategies are studied separately. We emphasise that all proposed mechanisms should be present in an agent programming language. We are currently investigating new relations that can be used to denote the incompatibility of goals. For example, as mentioned before, we also envisage a variant of the precedence rules that does not prevent the generation of new plans for less important goals in case there is no applicable PG-rule for the most important goal.

As for now, $\mathcal{R}$ is defined on only the head of PG-rules, which refer to goals the agent might have. A possible extension would be to define $\mathcal{R}$ on the entire PG-rules, allowing for a more fine grained specification of incompatibility. Our choice for the head of the rules is intentional. There are many cases for which two goals are incompatible irrespective of the plan being used to achieve these goals (in case of our example the agent cannot be in two rooms at the same time). For those cases this would mean that every possible pair of plans should be marked as incompatible. Extending our mechanism to the more fine grained one as mentioned above, is quite straightforward, though.

Further, for now it is the task of the agent programmer to specify which goals are incompatible with each other. We are interested in a mechanism that detects incompatibility automatically. Suppose, for example, that the agent believes that to clean a room it should be in that room. Then when it also believes that it cannot be in two different rooms at the same time, it should deduce that goals to have cleaned different rooms are incompatible.

Finally, we observe that in the current approach the precedence of goals is fixed, while in some cases precedence might depend on a specific context, e.g., the current beliefs of the agent. For example, it may often be the case that the goal κ_1 is preferred to κ_2 in summer and κ_2 to κ_1 in winter, or κ_1 and κ_2 are normally compatible, unless the agent is very short of money. This topic is closely related to preference change, which is not the focus of this paper. Therefore, investigating how the precedence relation can be extended taking the context into account remains for further research.

Acknowledgments

This research was supported by the CoCoMAS project funded through the Dutch Organization for Scientific Research (NWO).

References

1. Pokahr, A., Braubach, L., Lamersdorf, W.: Jadex: A BDI Reasoning Engine. In: [19], pp. 149–174
2. Winikoff, M., Padgham, L., Harland, J., Thangarajah, J.: Jack intelligent agents: An industrial strength platform. In: [19], pp. 175–193
3. Bordini, R., Hübner, J., Vieira, R.: Jason and the Golden Fleece of agent-oriented programming. In: [19], pp. 3–37
4. Dastani, M., van Riemsdijk, M., Meyer, J.: Programming Multi-Agent Systems in 3APL. In: [19], pp. 39–67
5. Dix, J., Zhang, Y.: IMPACT: A Multi-Agent Framework with Declarative Semantics. In: [19], pp. 69–122
6. Fallah-Seghrouchni, A.E., Suna, A.: CLAIM and SyMPA: A Programming Environment for Intelligent and Mobile Agents. In: [19], pp. 95–122
7. de Boer, F., Hindriks, K., van der Hoek, W., Meyer, J.J.: A Verification Framework for Agent Programming with Declarative Goals. Journal of Applied Logic (2007)
8. Sardina, S., Padgham, L.: Goals in the context of BDI plan failure and planning. In: Proc. of AAMAS (2008)
9. Dastani, M., Meyer, J.: A Practical Agent Programming Language. In: Proc. of the fifth Int. Workshop on Programming Multi-agent Systems (2007)
10. Winikoff, M., Padgham, J.H.L., Thangarajah, J.: Declarative and Procedural Goals in Intelligent Agent Systems. In: Proc. of the Eighth Int. Conf. on Principles of Knowledge Representation and Reasoning (KR 2002) (2002)
11. Dastani, M., van Riemsdijk, M.B., Meyer, J.: Goal types in agent programming. In: Proc. of AAMAS, pp. 1285–1287 (2006)
12. van Riemsdijk, M.B., Dastani, M., Meyer, J., de Boer, F.S.: Goal-oriented modularity in agent programming. In: Proc. of AAMAS, pp. 1271–1278 (2006)
13. Hindriks, K.V., de Boer, F.S., van der Hoek, W., Meyer, J.J.C.: Agent programming with declarative goals. In: Castelfranchi, C., Lespérance, Y. (eds.) ATAL 2000. LNCS (LNAI), vol. 1986, pp. 228–243. Springer, Heidelberg (2001)
14. van Riemsdijk, M.B., Dastani, M., Meyer, J.J.C.: Semantics of declarative goals in agent programming. In: Proc. of AAMAS, pp. 133–140 (2005)
15. Bratman, M.: Intentions, Plans, and Practical Reason. Harvard University Press, Cambridge (1987)
16. Morreale, V., Bonura, S., Francaviglia, G., Centineo, F., Cossentino, M., Gaglio, S.: Goal-Oriented Development of BDI Agents: The PRACTIONIST Approach. In: IAT 2006: Proc. of the IEEE/WIC/ACM int. conf. on Intelligent Agent Technology (2006)
17. Pokahr, A., Braubach, L., Lamersdorf, W.: A Goal Deliberation Strategy for BDI Agent Systems. In: Eymann, T., Klügl, F., Lamersdorf, W., Klusch, M., Huhns, M.N. (eds.) MATES 2005. LNCS (LNAI), vol. 3550, pp. 82–93. Springer, Heidelberg (2005)
18. Thangarajah, J., Padgham, L., Winikoff, M.: Detecting & Avoiding Interference Between Goals in Intelligent Agents. In: Proc. of the 18th Int. Joint Conference on Artificial Intelligence (2003)
19. Bordini, R., Dastani, M., Dix, J., Fallah-Seghrouchni, A.E. (eds.): Multi-Agent Programming: Languages, Platforms and Applications. Springer, Heidelberg (2005)

A Common Basis for Agent Organisation in BDI Languages*

Anthony Hepple, Louise Dennis, and Michael Fisher

Department of Computer Science, University of Liverpool, Liverpool, U.K.
{A.J.Hepple,L.A.Dennis,MFisher}@liverpool.ac.uk

Abstract. Programming languages based on the BDI style of agent model are now common. Within these there appears to be some, limited, agreement on the core functionality of agents. However, when we come to multi-agent organisations, not only do many BDI languages have no specific organisational structures, but those that do exist are very diverse. In this paper, we aim to provide a unifying framework for the core aspects of agent organisation, covering groups, teams and roles, as well as organisations. Thus, we describe a simple organisational mechanism, and show how several well known approaches can be embedded within it. Although the mechanism we use is derived from the METATEM programming language, we do not assume any specific BDI language. The organisational mechanism is intended to be independent of the underlying agent language and so we aim to provide a common core for future developments in agent organisation.

1   Introduction

As hardware and software platforms become more sophisticated, and as these are deployed in less predictable environments, so the level of *autonomy* built into such systems has increased. This has allowed systems to work effectively without detailed, and constant, human intervention. However, autonomous systems can be hard to understand and even harder to develop reliably. In order to help in this area, the concept of an *agent* was introduced to capture the abstraction of an autonomously acting entity. Based on this concept, new techniques were developed for analysing, designing and implementing agents. In particular, several new programming languages were developed explicitly for implementing autonomous agents.

We can simply characterise an agent as an autonomous software component having certain goals and being able to communicate with other agents in order to accomplish these goals [29]. The ability of agents to act independently, to react to unexpected situations and to cooperate with other agents has made them a popular choice for developing software in a number of areas. At one extreme there are agents that are used to search the Internet, navigating autonomously in order to retrieve information; these are relatively lightweight agents, with

---

* Work partially supported by EPSRC under grant EP/D052548.

M. Dastani et al. (Eds.): LADS 2007, LNAI 5118, pp. 71–88, 2008.

few goals but significant domain-specific knowledge. At the other end of the spectrum, there are agents developed for independent process control in unpredictable environments. This second form of agent is often constructed using complex software architectures, and has been applied in areas such as real-time process control [20,25]. Perhaps the most impressive use of such agents is in the real-time fault monitoring and diagnosis carried out on NASA Deep Space One [22].

The key reason why an agent-based approach is advantageous for modelling and programming autonomous systems, is that it permits the clear and concise representation, not just of *what* the autonomous components within the system do, but *why* they do it. This allows us to abstract away from low-level control aspects and to concentrate on the key feature of autonomy, namely the goals the component has and the choices it makes towards achieving its goals. Thus, in modelling a system in terms of agents, we often describe each agent's *beliefs* and *goals*, which in turn determine the agent's *intentions*. Such agents then make decisions about what action to perform, given their beliefs and goals/intentions. This kind of approach has been popularised through the influential BDI (Belief-Desire-Intention) model of agent-based systems [25]. This representation of behaviour using *mental* notions has several benefits. The first is that, ideally, it abstracts away from low-level issues: we simply present some goal that we wish to be achieved, and we expect it to act as an agent would given such a goal. Secondly, because we are used to understanding and predicting the behaviour of rational agents, the behaviour of autonomous software should be relatively easy for humans to understand and predict too. Not surprisingly, therefore, the BDI approach to agent modelling has been successful and has led to many novel programming languages based (at least in some part) upon this model; these are often termed *BDI Languages*. Although a wide variety of such languages have been developed [2] few have strong and flexible mechanisms for *organising* multiple agents, and those that do provide no agreement on their organisational mechanisms. Thus, while BDI languages have converged to a common core relating to the activity of individual agents [9], no such convergence is apparent in terms of multi-agent structuring.

Our overall aim is to provide a common logically based framework for BDI style agent programming (which incorporates organisational aspects) to facilitate agent verification [4]. As a result a clear goal is to develop a simple, intuitive and semantically consistent organisation mechanism. In this paper we show how a simple model can, in BDI languages, encompass many proposed models of multi-agent organisation and teamwork. The formal semantics of this approach is considered in detail in [10].

Paper Structure. Section 2 surveys some of the leading approaches to agent organisation that have already been proposed and illustrates their diverse nature. In Section 3 we describe the structuring mechanism we propose for unifying the multi-agent concepts. Section 4 demonstrates how our framework can be used to model concepts such as joint-intentions, roles, etc., which form the basis of the approaches surveyed in Section 2. Finally, in Section 5, we provide concluding remarks and outline future work.

2   Approaches to Agent Organisation

In this section we overview some of the key approaches to the organisation of agents that have been proposed. It is important to note that we are particularly concerned with *rational agents*, predominantly using the BDI model of computation. While we have not listed *all* approaches, the selection we give covers many of the leading attempts at teamwork, organisational structuring and role-based computation. In addition, while we are primarily interested in developing BDI languages with clear logical semantics and logic-based mechanisms, we also consider organisational approaches beyond this class.

2.1   Cohen and Levesque: *Joint Intentions*

With a respected philosophical view on agent co-operation, Cohen and Levesque produced a significant paper 'Teamwork' [8] extending previous work [6,7,21]. They persuasively argue that a team of agents should *not* be modelled as an aggregate agent and propose new (logical) concepts of *joint intentions, joint commitments* and *joint persistent goals* to ensure that teamwork does not break down due to any divergence of individual team members' beliefs or intentions. The authors' proposals oblige agents working in a team to retain team goals until it is mutually agreed amongst team members that a goal has now been achieved, is no longer relevant, or is impossible. This level of commitment is stronger than an agent's commitment to its individual goals which are dropped the moment it (individually) believes they are satisfied. Joint intentions can be reduced to individual intentions if supplemented with mutual beliefs.

2.2   Tidhar, Cavedon and Rao: *Team-Oriented Programming*

Tidhar [27] introduced the concept of *team-oriented programming* with social structure. Essentially this is an agent-centred approach that defines joint goals and intentions for teams but stops short of forcing individual team members to adopt those goals and intentions. An attempt to clarify the definition of a 'team' and what team formation entails is made using concepts such as 'mind-set synchronisation' and 'role assignment'. Team behaviour is defined by a temporal ordering of plans which guide (but do not constrain) agent behaviour. A social structure is proposed by the creation of *command* and *control* teams which assign roles, identify sub-teams and permit inter-team relationships. In [5], the authors formalise their ideas of social structure with concepts of commitment expressed using modal logic. This allows the formal expression of commitment between teams, such as

team A intends to achieve task B for the sake of team C.

2.3   Ferber, Gutknecht and Michel: *Roles and Organisations*

Ferber *et al.* [13] present the case for an organisational-centred approach to the design and engineering of complex multi-agent systems. They cite disadvantages of the predominant agent-centred approaches such as: lack of access rights control; inability to accommodate heterogeneous agents; and inappropriate abstraction for describing organisational scenarios. The authors propose a model for designing language independent multi-agent systems in terms of *agents, roles* and *groups*. Agents and groups are proposed as distinct first class entities although it is suggested that an agent ought to be able to transform itself into a group. (We will see later that this is close to our approach.)

In [14], Ferber continues to argue for an organisational-centred approach, advocating the complete omission of mental states at the organisational level, defining an organisation of agents in terms of its capabilities, constraints, roles, group tasks and interaction protocols. Clearly articulated here is a manifesto of design principles.

2.4   Pynadath and Tambe: *TEAMCORE*

Pynadath *et al.* [24] describe their interpretation of team-oriented programming that aims to organise groups of heterogeneous agents to achieve team goals. A framework for defining teams is given that provides the following concepts:

Team—an agent without domain abilities;
Team-ready—agents with domain abilities that interface with team agents;
Sub-goal—a goal that contributes to the team goal; and
Task—the allocation of a sub-goal to a team-ready agent.

An implementation of their framework, TEAMCORE, provides organisational functionality such as multicast communication between agents, assigning tasks, maintaining group beliefs and maintaining hierarchies of agents (by role). Heterogeneous agents are accommodated by wrapper agents that act as proxies for the domain agent.

2.5   Fisher, Ghidini and Hirsch: *Groups as Agents*

Beginning within the context of executable temporal logics [1], Fisher *et al.* produced a series of papers [15,16,17,18] that developed the METATEM language into a generalised approach for expressing dynamic distributed computations. As we will see more about this model in Section 3, we just provide a brief outline here.

Organisational structuring within the METATEM language [15] consists of a simple nested grouping structure where groups comprise communicating elements (objects, agents, or other software components). The key aspect of this approach is that groups themselves are also agents, providing a homogeneous, simple, yet expressive, model. In [16], it is argued that systems composed of components as diverse as objects, web services and abstract features can be modelled with this general approach.

2.6   Hübner, Sichman and Boissier: *Roles and Permissions*

Hübner *et al.* believed that the agent organisational frameworks proposed prior to their 2002 paper [19] overlooked the significant relationship between structural and functional properties of an organisation. Thus, in [19], they propose a three component approach to the specification of agent organisations that combines independent structural and functional specifications with a deontic specification, the latter defining among other things the roles (structural) having permission to carry out group tasks (functional). The approach provides a proliferation of constructs for specifying multi-agent systems, including the ability to concisely express many additional aspects, such as

- the ability to specify *compatibility* of group membership, akin to the members of a government expressing a conflict of interest.
- enabling the *cardinality* of group membership to be defined and thus defining a well formed group as a group who's membership is between its specified minimum and maximum size.
- control of the organisation's goal(s), with an ability to specify sequential, branching and parallel execution of sub-goals.
- the ability to express a variance in the agents' permissions over time.

It is argued that such an approach improves the efficiency of multi-agent systems by focusing agents on the organisation's goals. Indeed, we note that of all the proposals discussed in this section this approach provides the developer with the widest vocabulary with which to express agent behaviour when defining the organisation.

2.7   Dignum, Esteva, Sierra and Vázquez-Salceda: *Institutions*

These authors made formal [12] and practical [11,28] contributions to a method of agent organisation that enjoys much current popularity [23]. An electronic institution aims to provide an *open* framework in which agents can contribute to the goals of *society* without sacrificing its own self-interest; the implication being that an autonomous agent will be motivated to participate in the institution by its desire to satisfy it own goals, but that its participation will be structured by the framework in such a way that institutional goals are achieved. A key concept is that of institutional norms.

In [12], the institution remains independent of agent-architecture by modelling agents as roles, of which there are two types — internal and external (to the institution) — with different rights. A *dialogue* defines valid locutions, a *scene* is a unit of interaction within an institution and a *performative structure* defines an objective as a network of scenes. In an attempt to allow more agent autonomy these ideas were refined and in [28] more concepts were introduced, including *landmarks* that can be used to guide agents through an interaction when a prescriptive dialogue is considered too constraining.

Perhaps the most noteworthy aspect of these proposals is the change of focus from the agents themselves onto the interactions that take place between agents.

2.8 Summary

It should be noted that none of the above organisational approaches can comprehensively model all forms of co-operative multi-agent systems. Rather they represent attempts to discover practical and beneficial ways of specifying distributed computational systems, and facilitating the focus of computation on a system's main purpose whilst not compromising the autonomy of the system's components. In achieving this aim it may be convenient to categorise groups of agents in terms of cohesion and co-operation. For instance, a *group* of agents may be individually autonomous, existing as a group solely due to their proximity to one another rather than their co-operation. In contrast, the word *team*, implies a high degree of co-operation and adhesion with an *organisation* fitting somewhere in between. As Cohen stated in [8]

"teamwork is more than co-ordinated individual behaviour".

Thus, the more expressive proposals reviewed here enable the specification of more cohesive groups but often at significant cost to the agents involved.

3 Structuring Mechanisms

The approach we propose is based on that of METATEM described previously in [15]. However, we advocate this grouping approach, independent of the underlying language for agents. The aim of our grouping structure is to provide a simple organisational construct that enables the definition of a variety of multi-agent systems, ranging from unstructured collections of uncoordinated agents to complex systems that are often described using the high-level abstractions described in the last section.

The basic restrictions we put on any underlying language is that, as in most BDI-based languages, there are logically coherent mechanisms for explicitly describing *beliefs* and *goals*. As in the METATEM framework, the grouping approach involves very few additional constructs within the language [10]. Specifically, we require just two additional elements within each agent's state. We also, as is common, require that first-class elements such as beliefs, goals and plans, can be communicated between agents. Delivery of messages should be guaranteed, though the delay between send and receipt is not fixed. Finally, we expect asynchronously concurrent execution of agents.

3.1 Extending Agents

Assuming that the underlying agent language can describe the behaviour of an agent, as has been shown for example in [9], we now extend the concept of agent with two sets, **Content** and **Context**. The agent's **Content** describes the set of agents it contains, while the agent's **Context** describes a set of agents it is contained within. Thus, the formal definition of an agent is as follows [17].

```
Agent ::= Behaviour:   Specification
          Content:     P(Agent)
          Context:     P(Agent)
```

Here, $\mathcal{P}$(**Agent**) are sets of agents and **Specification** is the description of the individual agent's behaviour, given as appropriate in the target BDI language.

On the right, we provide a graphical representation of such an agent. The agent (the circle) resides within a **Context** and itself comprises its own behavioural layer and its **Content**. This **Content** can again contain further agents. Note that, for formal development purposes, the **Behaviour** may well be a logical specification.

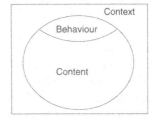

The addition of **Content** and **Context** sets to each agent provides significant flexibility for agent organisation. Agent teams, groups or organisations, which might alternatively be seen as separate entities, are now just agents with non-empty **Content**. This allows these organisations to be hierarchical and dynamic, and so, as we will see later, provides possibilities for a multitude of other co-ordinated behaviours. Similarly, agents can have several agents within their **Context**. Not only does this allow agents to be part of several organisational structures simultaneously, but it allows the agent to benefit from **Context** representing diverse attributes/behaviours. So an agent might be in a context related to its physical locality (i.e. agents in that set are 'close' to each other), yet also might be in a context that provides certain roles or abilities. Intriguingly, agents can be within many, overlapping and diverse, contexts. This gives the ability to produce complex organisations, in a way similar to multiple inheritance in traditional object/concept systems. For example, see Fig. 1 for sample configurations.

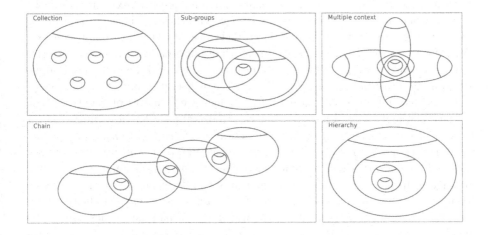

Fig. 1. A selection of possible organisation structures

An important aspect is that this whole structure is very dynamic. Agents can move in and out of `Content` and `Context` sets, while new agents (and, hence, organisations) can be spawned easily and discarded. This allows for a range of structures, from the *transient* to the *permanent*. From the above it is clear that there is no enforced distinction between an agent and an agent organisation. All are agents, all may be treated similarly.

While it may seem counter-intuitive for an organisation to have beliefs and goals, many of the surveyed systems required team constructs such as tasks or goals that can naturally be viewed as belonging to a team/group agent. Some also required *control agents* to manage role assignment and communication which in this framework can be handled by the containing agent itself if so desired. On the other hand it is possible to distinguish between agents (with empty `Content`) and organisations (with non-empty `Content`) and for a programmer to exclude certain constructs from organisations in order to allow an organisation-centred approach, if required.

Finally, it is essential that the agent's internal behaviour, be it a program or a specification, have direct access to both the `Content` and `Context` sets. As we will see below, this allows each agent to become more than just a 'dumb' container. It can restructure, share information and behaviour with, and control access to its `Content`. To describe fragments of the agent's behaviour during the rest of the paper, we will use simple **IF**...**THEN**...**ELSE** statements. Again, this does not prescribe any particular style of BDI language.

3.2   Communication

The core communication mechanism between agents in our model is broadcast message-passing. The use of broadcast is very appealing, allowing agent-based systems to be developed without being concerned about addresses/names of the agents to be communicated with. The potential inefficiency of broadcast communication is avoided by the use of the agents' `Content` and `Context` structures. By default, when an agent broadcasts a message, that message is sent to all members of the agent's `Context` set and forwarded to agents within the same context. This, effectively, produces *multicast*, rather than full broadcast, message-passing.

This is clearly a simple, flexible and intuitive model, and the system developer is encouraged to think in this way. However, it is useful to note that multicast, or 'broadcast within a set', is actually implemented on top of point-to-point message passing! We will assume that the BDI language has a communication construct that can be modelled as the action $send(recipient, m)$ which means that the message m has been sent to the agent $recipient$, and a corresponding $received(sender, m)$ which becomes true when the $recipient$ agent receives the message m from $sender$. Let us consider an example where an agent wishes to broadcast to all other members of one of its `Context` sets. For simplicity, let us term this context set '*group*'. An agent wishing to 'broadcast' a message, m, to members of the *group* sends a message, $send(group, broadcast(m))$, to the group agent alone, as illustrated in Fig. 2.

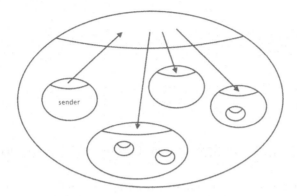

Fig. 2. Broadcast within a Group

The effect of sending a broadcast message to the *group* agent is that the *group* acts as a proxy and forwards the message to its Content, modifying the message such that the message appears to have originated from the proxy. In this way agents maintain their anonymity within the group.

> **IF** $received(from, broadcast(m))$
> **THEN for each** x **in** $\{\text{Content} \setminus from\}$ $send(x, m)$

Being an agent-centred approach to multi-agent organisation there does not exist an (accessible) entity that references *all* agents in the agent space, thus *true* broadcast is not possible. However a number of recursive group broadcasts can be specified, allowing a message to be propagated to all agents with an organisational link to the sender.

For example, reaching all accessible agents requires the sending agent to send a message to all members of its Context and Content sets and for each first-time recipient to recursively forward that message to the union of their Context and Content (excluding the sender). Clearly this is not an efficient method of communication as it is possible for agents to receive multiple copies of the same message, and so it may not be practical in very large societies, but what it lacks in sophistication it makes up for in simplicity and clarity [16].

> **IF** $received(from, broadcastAll(m))$ **AND not** $received(\_, m)$
> **THEN for each** x **in** $\{\text{Content} \cup \text{Context}\}$
> $send(x, m)$ **AND** $send(x, broadcastAll(m))$

Perhaps more useful than indiscriminate broadcasting would be the case of an agent who wants to reach all other members of the 'greatest' organisation to which it belongs. This requires a message to propagate up through the agent structure until it reaches an agent with an empty context, at which point the message is sent downwards until all members and sub-members have been reached.

To illustrate this, consider the situation of agent **E** in Fig. 3(a), who wants to send a message to its entire organisation—the organisation specified by **A**.

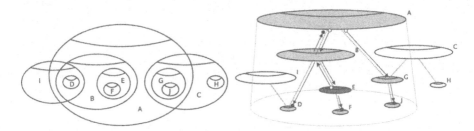

Fig. 3. (a) Nested Organisations. (b) Propagation of Messages

A *propagateUp(m)* message originates from agent E who sends it to agent B. B's context is non-empty so the message continues upwards to A. Since A is the widest organisation to which E belongs (it has an empty `Context` set), it modifies the message, converting it to *propagateDown(message)* and broadcasts it along with the message to all members of its `Content`. Upon receipt of this message, agents B and G send it to their `Content` and so it continues until the message reaches an agent with an empty `Content` as illustrated by Fig. 3(b). This might be specified as follows.

> **IF** *received($\_$, propagateUp(m))* **AND** `Context` $\neq \emptyset$
> **THEN for each** x **in** {`Context`}
>   *send(x, propagateUp(m))*

> **IF** *received($\_$, propagateUp(m))* **AND** `Context` $= \emptyset$
> **THEN for each** x **in** {`Content`}
>   *send(x, m)* **AND** *send(x, propagateDown(m))*

> **IF** *received($\_$, propagateDown(m))* **AND** `Content` $\neq \emptyset$
> **THEN for each** x **in** {`Content`}
>   *send(x, m)* **AND** *send(x, propagateDown(m))*

3.3   Refining and Restricting Communications

Further restriction of communication is possible by, for example, restricting the type of communications agents can make. Employing the concept of speech acts [26] we can use the group agent as a communication filter that restricts intra-group messaging to those messages that conform to permissible protocols or structures.

If, for example, a fact-finding agent contains a number of agents with access to information resources, it may be necessary to restrict their communication to **inform** speech acts. In such circumstances it is possible to modify the default behaviour by imposing a message filter.

> **IF** *received(from, broadcast(m))***AND** *informFilter(m)*
> **THEN for each** x **in** {`Content` $\setminus$ *from*}   *send(x, m)*

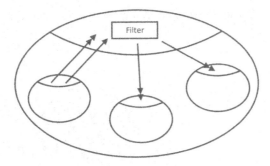

Fig. 4. Filtering communication by group

See Fig. 4 for an example of this. In this way filters can be adapted for many purposes, enabling organisations to maintain:

relevance — ensuring communication is relevant to group goals and intentions;
fairness — allowing each member of a group an equal opportunity to speak; and
legality — assigning permissions to group members to restrict communication.

3.4 Communication Semantics

The above variations on *broadcast* define varying semantics for a message. A key feature of the grouping approach is that the semantics of communication is flexible and, potentially, in the hands of the programmer. Such semantics can also, potentially, be communicated between agents in the form of plans allowing an agent to adopt different semantics for communication as its **Context** changes.

Adherence to particular common communication protocols/semantics also allows groups to establish the extent to which a member is autonomous (e.g., a group can use a semantics for **achieve** speech acts which forces recipients to adopt the communicated goal). This is important because organisational approaches vary from those in which group behaviour is specified by the organisation and imposed on its members with little option for autonomy to those in which group behaviour emerges from an appropriate combination of individual agents without any explicit coordination at all.

4   Common Multi-agent Structures

In this section we will examine some of the key structuring mechanisms that are either explicit or implicit within the approaches surveyed in Section 2, and show how each might be represented appropriately and simply, using the approach outlined above. Table 1 lists the mechanisms identified by our surveyed authors as being useful in the specification of agent co-operation. We believe that our approach is flexible enough to model all of these but for brevity we will only demonstrate a sample of them.

Table 1. Multi-agent organisation concepts

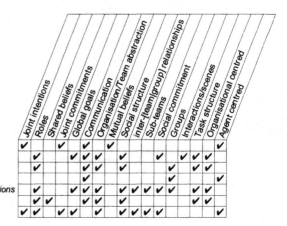

		Joint intentions	Roles	Shared beliefs	Joint commitments	Global goals	Communication	Organisation/Team abstraction	Mutual beliefs	Social structure	inter-[team|group] relationships	Sub-teams	Social commitment	Groups	Interactions/scenes	Task structure	Organisational centred	Agent centred
Cohen & Levesque	*Joint intentions*	✔			✔	✔		✔	✔									✔
Esteva et al	*Institutions*		✔			✔	✔	✔		✔			✔		✔	✔	✔	
Ferber	*Roles and groups*		✔			✔	✔		✔					✔		✔	✔	
Fisher et al.	*Groups*						✔						✔					✔
Hübner	*Roles and permissions*		✔			✔	✔	✔		✔	✔	✔	✔	✔		✔	✔	
Pynadath & Tambe	*Team-oriented*	✔	✔			✔	✔		✔							✔	✔	
Tidhar, Cavedon & Rao	*Team-oriented*	✔	✔		✔	✔		✔		✔	✔	✔	✔					✔

4.1 Sharing Information

Shared beliefs. Being a member of all but the least cohesive groups requires that some shared beliefs exist between its members. Making the contentious assumption that all agents are honest and that joining the group is both individual rational and group rational, let agent i hold a belief set BS_i. When an agent joins a group[1] j it receives beliefs BS_j from the group and adds them to its own belief base (invoking its own belief revision mechanism in case of conflicting beliefs). The agent in receipt of the new beliefs may or may not disseminate them to the agents in its content, depending on the nature and purpose of the group. Once held, beliefs are retained until contradicted.

Joint beliefs. Joint beliefs are stronger than shared beliefs. To maintain the levels of cohesion found in teams each member must not only believe a joint belief but must also believe that its team members also believe it. Let us assume the agent is capable of internal actions such as *addBelief(Belief, RelevantTo)* adding *Belief* to its belief base, and recording the context that *Belief* is relevant to, and *removeBeliefs(Context)*. Upon joining a group, an agent is supplied the beliefs relevant to that context, which it stores in its belief base along with the context in which they hold. This behaviour is captured in the rule below.

> **IF** *received(from, membershipConfirm(beliefSet))*
> **THEN for each** b **in** {*beliefSet*}   *addBelief(b, from)*.

The presence of such `Context` meta-information can be used to specify boundaries on agent deliberation, thus mitigating the complexity caused by introducing another variable. When leaving a `Context` an agent might either choose to drop the beliefs relevant to that `Context` or to retain them.

---

[1] Let us refer to such an agent as a *group* to distinguish it from the agent within its `Content`.

4.2 Sharing Capabilities

Let agent Ag_i have a goal G, for which a plan P exists. However, Ag_i does not have plan P and therefore must find an agent that does. Two options available to Ag_i are to find an agent Ag_j, who has P, and either: request that Ag_j carries out the plan; or request that Ag_j sends P to Ag_i so that Ag_i can carry out the plan itself. The first possibility suggests a closer degree of co-operation between agents i and j, perhaps even the sub-ordination of agent j by agent i. Whereas, in the second possibility, agent i benefits from information supplied by j.

In the first scenario we might envisage a group in which a member (or the group agent itself) asks another member to execute the plan. In the second case, we can envisage agents i and j *sharing* a plan. This second scenario is typical if groups are to capture certain capabilities — agents who join the Content of such a group agent are sent (or at least can request) plans shared amongst the group. Either scenario can be modelled using our approach.

4.3 Joint Intentions

An agent acting in an independent self-interested way need not inform any other entity of its beliefs, or changes to them. On the other hand, an agent who is working, as part of a team, towards a goal shared by itself and all other members of the team has both an obligation and a rational interest in sharing relevant beliefs with the other team members [8]. This gives an agent a *persistent* goal with respect to a team. Such that the agent must intend the goal whilst it is the team's mutual belief that the goal is valid (not yet achieved, achievable and relevant) — it must not give up on a goal nor assume the goal has been achieved, independently. The implications of this impact on agent's individual behaviour when it learns, from sources external to the group, that the goal is no longer valid. In such a situation the team/group agent maintains its commitment to the invalid goal but informs its team members of the antecedent(s) that lead it to believe the goal is invalid. Only when the agent receives confirmation that the entire team share its belief does it drop its commitment.

The intuitive implementation of this joint intention is not via a team construct but as an extension of an agent's attributes, however, increases in expressiveness of this sort are often accompanied by increased complexity. The organisational or team construct may overcome this problem but we believe that our simple group approach is sufficient to implement joint intentions, mutual beliefs and common goals. Consider the scenario given in Fig. 5.

Agent A. On joining group T, agent A accepts goal JI and confirms its adoption of the goal. Whilst T remains a member of A's Context, A informs T of all beliefs that are relevant to JI. Finally, all communications from agent T must be acknowledged, with an indication of the agent's acceptance (or non-acceptance) of the information.

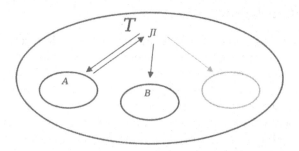

Fig. 5. Communicating Joint Intentions

A simple specification of this might be:

> **IF** $received(from, jointIntention(JI))$ **AND** $inContext(from)$
> **THEN** $achieve(JI)$ **AND** $send(from, ack(JI))$

> **IF** $belief(\varphi)$ **AND there is** x **in** {Context} $relevantTo(\varphi, x)$
> **THEN** $send(x, \mathsf{inform}(\varphi))$

> **IF** $goal(\gamma)$ **AND there is** x **in** {Context} $relevantTo(\gamma, x)$
> **THEN** $\mathsf{achieve}(\gamma)$.

Thus, an agent is obliged to inform its group of beliefs relevant to jointly held intentions and will maintain a goal whilst it remains relevant to its Context.

Agent T. Evaluates group beliefs and communicates both the adoption, and dropping, of intentions when mutual agreement is established. Since T has details of the agents in its Content and can send messages to interrogate them, it can maintain knowledge of *common* information and behaviours, and reason with this knowledge.

4.4   Roles

The concept of a role is a common abstraction used by many authors for a variety of purposes [14,19,28], including:

- to define the collective abilities necessary to achieve a global goal.
- to provide an agent with abilities suitable for team activity.
- to constrain or modify agent behaviour for conformance with team norms.
- to describe a hierarchy of authority in an organisation of agents and hence create a permissions structure.

Roles are most obviously integrated into our framework as further agents whose Content is those agents fulfilling the role and whose Context is the organisation to which the role belongs. However in some cases, in particular strict hierarchies, it may be possible to associate roles directly with the organisational agent. Below we examine a variety of such role types and consider in more detail how each could fit into our model.

Ability roles. Let plan P be a complex plan that requires abilities x,y and z if it is to be fulfilled. An agent A is created (without any domain abilities of its own) to gather together agents that have the necessary abilities. Agent A might generate a new agent in its `Content` for each of the abilities required to fulfil plan P.

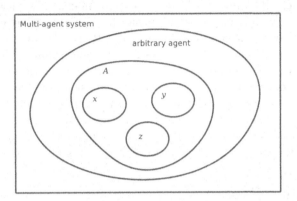

Fig. 6. Roles according to abilities

When agents with abilities x, y or z join the `Content` of agent A, A adds them to the `Content` of the appropriate group (agent), analogous to assigning roles.

A talented agent might become a member of several ability sets. The ability set, itself an agent, may be a simple container or could exhibit complex behaviour of its own. One basic behaviour might be to periodically request (of the agents in its `Content`) the execution of its designated ability. Note that, in the case of an ability that is hard to carry out, it may be provident to include many agents with that ability. Similarly, the desired ability might be a complex ability that must be subjected to further planning, resulting in a number of nested abilities.

Roles in society. Joining an institution, organisation or team of agents commonly involves the adoption of the norms of that institution, organisation or team. Whether these norms are expressed as beliefs, goals, preferences or communication protocols, our approach allows them to be transmitted between group members, particularly at the time of joining. For example, if team membership requires that members acknowledge receipt of messages then each new member of a group might be given the new rule (behaviour)

$$\textbf{IF } received(ag,\theta) \textbf{ THEN } send(ag,ack(\theta)) \ .$$

A stronger constraint might require an agent to believe all messages received from its `Context`:

$$\textbf{IF } received(ag,\theta) \textbf{ AND } ag \in \texttt{Context}$$
$$\textbf{THEN } addBelief(\theta,ag) \textbf{ AND } send(ag,ack(\theta)) \ .$$

Of course, agents can not be certain that another agent will keep with given constraints or comply with norms of the society, the most it can do is demand formal acknowledgement of its request and a commitment to do so. Group membership can be denied if an agent fails to satisfy the *entry criteria.*

Authority roles. None of the structures discussed usefully reflect hierarchies of authority. Each allow almost arbitrary group membership, with transitive and cyclic structures possible making them unsuitable for expressing a hierarchy of authority, which by its nature must be acyclic with exactly one root.

A common use for such a hierarchy is for creating channels of communication. Our approach to grouping enables communication restrictions for free, as agents may only communicate with their immediate superiors (context), or their direct subordinates (content). Communication to peers (by multicast) can only be achieved by sending a single *broadcast* message to the agent common to the contexts of the intended recipients. The receiving [superior] agent will, if it deems it appropriate, forward the message to the other agents in its content.

5   Concluding Remarks

In this paper, we have proposed a simple but clear model for multi-agent structuring in agent languages based on varieties of the logical BDI approach. Although derived from work on METATEM, we propose this as a general approach for many languages. To support this, we first show how simple and intuitive the approach is and how the underlying structures of any appropriate language can be modified. (Note that more detailed operational semantics for our grouping approach in logic-based BDI languages is given in [10].) We then showed, in a necessarily brief way, how many of the common teamwork and organisation aspects can be modelled using our approach.

In order to evaluate the approach, we have also implemented it in AgentSpeak (actually, Jason [3]) and have developed several simple examples of dynamic organisations. This simple additional layer has so far proved to be convenient and powerful. Obviously, the Content/Context approach has also been extensively used in previous work on METATEM [16,17,18]. In addition, it has been incorporated in the semantics of AIL [9], a common semantics basis for a number of languages, including AgentSpeak and 3APL; see [10] for formal details.

5.1   Future Work

Our immediate aim with this work is to apply the model to larger applications, particularly in the areas of ubiquitous computing and social organisations. This will give a more severe test for the approach and will highlight any areas of difficulty.

As mentioned above, the approach is being integrated into the AIL semantics [9], which provides a common semantics basis for a number of BDI languages. Since translations from AgentSpeak, 3APL, etc are being produced, we also aim to translate the organisational aspects used into the above model.

Finally, since the aim of the work on AIL is to provide generic verification techniques for BDI languages (that can be translated to AIL) [4]. In extending the AIL semantics, we also aim to provide verification techniques for teams, roles and organisations developed within BDI languages.

References

1. Barringer, H., Fisher, M., Gabbay, D., Owens, R., Reynolds, M. (eds.): The Imperative Future: Principles of Executable Temporal Logic. Research Studies Press (1996)
2. Bordini, R.H., Dastani, M., Dix, J., El Fallah Seghrouchni, A. (eds.): Multi-Agent Programming: Languages, Platforms and Applications. Springer, Heidelberg (2005)
3. Bordini, R.H., Hübner, J.F., Wooldridge, M.: Programming Multi-Agent Systems in AgentSpeak using Jason. Wiley, Chichester (2007)
4. Bordini, R.H., Fisher, M., Visser, W., Wooldridge, M.: Verifying Multi-Agent Programs by Model Checking. Journal of Autonomous Agents and Multi-Agent Systems 12(2), 239–256 (2006)
5. Cavedon, L., Rao, A.S., Tidhar, G.: Social and Individual Commitment. In: Cavedon, L., Wobcke, W., Rao, A. (eds.) PRICAI-WS 1996. LNCS, vol. 1209, pp. 152–163. Springer, Heidelberg (1997)
6. Cohen, P.R., Levesque, H.J.: Intention is Choice with Commitment. Artificial Intelligence 42(2-3), 213–261 (1990)
7. Cohen, P.R., Levesque, H.J.: Confirmations and Joint Action. In: Proc. International Joint Conference on Artificial Intelligence (IJCAI), pp. 951–959. Elsevier, Amsterdam (1991)
8. Cohen, P.R., Levesque, H.J.: Teamwork. Technical Report 504, SRI International, California, USA (1991)
9. Dennis, L.A., Farwer, B., Bordini, R.H., Fisher, M., Wooldridge, M.: A Common Semantic Basis for BDI Languages. In: Dastani, M., et al. (eds.) ProMAS 2007. LNCS (LNAI), vol. 4908, pp. 124–139. Springer, Heidelberg (2008)
10. Dennis, L.A., Fisher, M., Hepple, A.: Language Constructs for Multi-Agent Programming. In: Sadri, F., Saton, K. (eds.) CLIMA 2007. LNCS (LNAI), vol. 5056. Springer, Heidelberg (2008)
11. Esteva, M., de la Cruz, D., Sierra, C.: ISLANDER: an electronic institutions editor. In: Proc. 1st International Conference on Autonomous Agents and Multiagent Systems (AAMAS), pp. 1045–1052. ACM, New York (2002)
12. Esteva, M., Rodríguez-Aguilar, J.A., Sierra, C., Garcia, P., Arcos, J.L.: On the Formal Specification of Electronic Institutions. In: Sierra, C., Dignum, F.P.M. (eds.) AgentLink 2000. LNCS (LNAI), vol. 1991, pp. 126–147. Springer, Heidelberg (2001)
13. Ferber, J., Gutknecht, O.: A Meta-model for the Analysis and Design of Organizations in Multi-agent Systems. In: Proc. 3rd International Conference on Multi-Agent Systems (ICMAS), pp. 128–135. IEEE, Los Alamitos (1998)
14. Ferber, J., Gutknecht, O., Michel, F.: From Agents to Organizations: An Organizational View of Multi-agent Systems. In: Giorgini, P., Müller, J.P., Odell, J.J. (eds.) AOSE 2003. LNCS, vol. 2935, pp. 214–230. Springer, Heidelberg (2004)
15. Fisher, M.: MetateM: The Story so Far. In: Bordini, R.H., Dastani, M., Dix, J., Seghrouchni, A.E.F. (eds.) PROMAS 2005. LNCS (LNAI), vol. 3862, pp. 3–22. Springer, Heidelberg (2006)

16. Fisher, M., Ghidini, C., Hirsch, B.: Programming Groups of Rational Agents. In: Dix, J., Leite, J.A. (eds.) CLIMA 2004. LNCS (LNAI), vol. 3259, pp. 16–33. Springer, Heidelberg (2004)
17. Fisher, M., Kakoudakis, T.: Flexible Agent Grouping in Executable Temporal Logic. In: Intensional Programming II. World Scientific, Singapore (2000)
18. Hirsch, B.: Programming Rational Agents. PhD thesis, Department of Computer Science, University of Liverpool (June 2005)
19. Hübner, J.F., Sichman, J.S., Boissier, O.: A Model for the Structural, Functional, and Deontic Specification of Organizations in Multiagent Systems. In: Bittencourt, G., Ramalho, G.L. (eds.) SBIA 2002. LNCS (LNAI), vol. 2507, pp. 118–128. Springer, Heidelberg (2002)
20. Jennings, N.R., Wooldridge, M.: Applications of Agent Technology. In: Agent Technology: Foundations, Applications, and Markets, pp. 3–28. Springer, Heidelberg (1998)
21. Levesque, H.J., Cohen, P.R., Nunes, J.H.T.: On Acting Together. In: Proc. 8th American National Conference on Artificial Intelligence (AAAI), pp. 94–99. AAAI Press, Menlo Park (1990)
22. Muscettola, N., Nayak, P.P., Pell, B., Williams, B.: Remote Agent: To Boldly Go Where No AI System Has Gone Before. Artificial Intelligence 103(1-2), 5–48 (1998)
23. Noriega, P., Vázquez-Salceda, J., Boella, G., Boissier, O., Dignum, V., Fornara, N., Matson, E. (eds.): COIN 2006. LNCS (LNAI), vol. 4386. Springer, Heidelberg (2007)
24. Pynadath, D.V., Tambe, M., Chauvat, N., Cavedon, L.: Towards Team-Oriented Programming. In: Jennings, N.R. (ed.) ATAL 1999. LNCS, vol. 1757, pp. 233–247. Springer, Heidelberg (2000)
25. Rao, A.S., Georgeff, M.: BDI Agents: from Theory to Practice. In: Proc 1st International Conference on Multi-Agent Systems (ICMAS), pp. 312–319. AAAI Press, Menlo Park (1995)
26. Smith, I.A., Cohen, P.R.: Toward a Semantics for an Agent Communications Language Based on Speech-Acts. In: Proc. American National Conference on Artificial Intelligence (AAAI), pp. 24–31. AAAI Press, Menlo Park (1996)
27. Tidhar, G.: Team-Oriented Programming: Preliminary Report. Technical Report 1993-41, Australian Artificial Intelligence Institute, Melbourne, Australia (1993)
28. Vázquez-Salceda, J., Dignum, V., Dignum, F.: Organizing Multiagent Systems. Journal of Autonomous Agents and Multi-Agent Systems 11(3), 307–360 (2005)
29. Wooldridge, M., Jennings, N.R.: Intelligent Agents: Theory and Practice. The Knowledge Engineering Review 10(2), 115–152 (1995)

Adjusting a Knowledge-Based Algorithm for Multi-agent Communication for CPS

E. van Baars and R. Verbrugge

Ordina Vertis B.V., Kadijk 1, 9747 AT Groningen, The Netherlands
egon@vanbaars.com
Department of Artificial Intelligence, University of Groningen,
P.O. Box 407, 9700 AK Groningen, The Netherlands
L.C.Verbrugge@rug.nl

Abstract. Using a knowledge-based approach we adjust a knowledge-based algorithm for multi-agent communication for the process of co-operative problem solving (CPS). The knowledge-based algorithm for multi-agent communication [1] solves the sequence transmission problem from one agent to a group of agents, but does not fully comply with the dialogue communication. The number of messages being communicated during one-on-one communication between the initiator and each other agent from the group can differ. Furthermore the CPS process can require the communication algorithm to handle changes of initiator. We show the adjustments that have to be made to the knowledge-based algorithm for multi-agent communication for it to handle these properties of CPS. For the adjustments of this new multi-agent communication algorithm it is shown that the gaining of knowledge required for a successful CPS process is still guaranteed.

1 Introduction

For cooperative problem solving (CPS) within multi-agent systems, Wooldridge and Jennings give a model of four consecutive stages [2]. Dignum, Dunin-Kęplicz and Verbrugge present a more in-depth analysis of the communication and dialogues that play a role during these four stages [3,4]. At every stage one agent of the group acts as an initiator, communicating with the other agents of the group. For a successful process of CPS, the agents have to achieve an approximation of common knowledge through communication. This makes reliable knowledge-based communication essential for teamwork. Agents communicate to each other by a communication system consisting of a *connection* in a communication medium between agents, together with a *protocol* by which the agents send and receive data over this connection. To be reliable, the connection has to satisfy the *fairness* condition, leaving the protocol responsible for the *liveness* and *safety* properties [5,6]. Besides the *liveness* and *safety* properties a protocol used in teamwork has to satisfy the requirements of CPS.

Van Baars and Verbrugge [1] derive a knowledge-based algorithm for multi-agent communication. The algorithm ensures the *liveness* and *safety* property,

M. Dastani et al. (Eds.): LADS 2007, LNAI 5118, pp. 89–105, 2008.

but does not satisfy the other requirements of CPS [1]. This algorithm solves the *sequence transmission* problem [5] from one agent to a group of agents. However, the communication during CPS is not a one-way transport of data as in the *sequence transmission* problem, but a dialogue. The next message is not predefined, but depends on the answers from the receivers [4]. A CPS process starts with an initiator communicating individually to the other agents, referred to as one-on-one communication. After a successful one-on-one communication, the initiator communicates the outcome to all the agents of the group, referred to as one-on-group communication. After a successful one-on-group communication, the initiator starts to communicate one-on-one again. Although 'one-to-group' is a more common term used in for example computer science to refer to broadcasting protocols, we rather use 'one-on-group' to underline that dialogue type protocols are used.

One of the properties of CPS dialogues is that the number of messages communicated between the initiator and the other agents can differ per agent during one-on-one communication. If for example the initiator asks whether the abilities of the agents are sufficient for a goal, then some of the agents can answer directly. Other agents need more information to determine whether their abilities are sufficient and they answer with a request. This property is referred to as the *asynchronous communication* property.

Another property of a CPS process is that the initiator can change. At the different stages of CPS the initiator has to have different abilities [2,4]. If an agent has all the required abilities, then it can fulfill the role of initiator throughout the whole process of CPS. If not, then different agents can fulfill the role of initiator at different stages. During the transition from one-on-one to one-on-group communication, the initiator always stays the same, because the initiator agent during one-on-one communication is the only agent who has sufficient group knowledge to start communicating one-on-group [3]. At the transition from one-on-group to one-on-one communication, however, any agent from the group can bid to become the initiator. This property is referred to as the *changing initiator* property.

The knowledge-based algorithm from [1] cannot handle asynchronous communication, because it uses only one index. Introducing a separate index for each sender-receiver pair solves this problem, but only for the situation where the initiator does not change. The initiator is the sender and it increments the indices, the other agents are the receivers. When the initiator changes, the sender becomes one of the receivers and one of the receivers becomes the sender. This means that another agent now increments the indices, which can lead to several messages with the same index but containing different data, or to parallel communication processes. Introducing a two-index mechanism, where the sender and a receiver both increment their own index, partially solves these problems. The remaining problem is that an initiator change does not become general knowledge. The solution for this problem is a procedure that is not embedded in the algorithm. In this paper we show that the algorithm from [1] can be modified

---

[1] A simulation of the protocol can be found at www.ai.rug.nl/alice/mas/macom

to handle the asynchronous communication property and the changing initiator property. The modified multi-agent communication algorithm guarantees a stream of accumulating messages during a CPS process, meeting the requirements of CPS concerning the gaining of group knowledge.

As to the methodology of this research, we use *knowledge-based protocols* based on epistemic logic and analyse them using the formalism of *interpreted multi-agent systems*. In this formalism, one views the sender and receivers as agents, and the communication channel as the environment. For each of these, their local states, actions and protocols can be modeled. The semantics is based on runs, which can be seen as sequences of global states (tuples of local states of agents plus environment) through discrete time. This knowledge-based approach to communication protocols has been pioneered in the work of Halpern and colleagues [5,7]. Because of the use of epistemic logic, it fits very well to multi-agent systems based on BDI architectures. Nowadays in theoretical computer science, another formalism, that of strand spaces, has become very popular, especially in the context of security protocols. Halpern and Pucella have shown that strand spaces can be translated into interpreted multi-agent systems, but not vice versa, because strand spaces are less expressive: some interesting interpreted multi-agent systems cannot be expressed as a strand space [8].

The rest of the paper is structured as follows. Section 2 and section 3 present the problems that arise in the flexible context of teamwork and their possible solutions, while section 4 gives the new knowledge-based algorithm incorporating the feasible solutions. Section 5 presents a proof that approximations of common knowledge are indeed attained. Finally, section 6 closes the paper with some conclusions and ideas about further research.

2   Adjusting the Algorithm for Asynchronous Communication

To handle the asynchronous communication property, a separate index is needed for every sender-receiver communication. This solution works for the situation where the initiator stays the same. For example we take one group G consisting of three agents R_1, R_2, and R_3, $G = \{R_1, R_2, R_3\}$. Agent R_3 is the initiating (sending) agent, temporarily denoted as S_3, and the two other agents R_1 and R_2 are the receivers. The index that S_3 uses to communicate with R_1 starts at 100 and the index that S_3 uses to communicate with R_2 starts at 200. Let us work out an example. S_3 sends three messages to R_1, which are received and answered by R_1. These answers can be an answer to a question or request sent by S_3 or just an acknowledgement if S_3 sent a statement.

In the notation below, the agents are identified by the numbers 1,2 and 3. If an agent acts as a sender or receiver, then this is denoted by S1 or R1 respectively. The agents exchange messages and the arrow -> indicates the direction of each message. The messages are of the form (100,_,data). The first field contains a sequence number. The second field contains the group information. In the case of one-on-one communication the value of this field is '_' and in the case of one-on-group communication the value of this field is 'G'. The last field contains the data that is sent.

```
1. S3 (100,_,data)-> R1
2. S3 <-(100,_,answ) R1
3. S3 (101,_,data)-> R1
4. S3 <-(101,_,answ) R1
5. S3 (102,_,data)-> R1
6. S3 <-(102,_,answ) R1
```

This moves the index for the next message to be sent to R_1 to 103. S_3 communicates two messages with R_2, which are answered by R_2, as follows:

```
1. S3 (200,_,data)-> R2
2. S3 <-(200,_,answ) R2
3. S3 (201,_,data)-> R2
4. S3 <-(201,_,answ) R2
```

This moves the index for the next message to be sent to R_2 by S_3 to 202. During both these one-on-one communications, S_3 has reached the goal for this phase and is now ready to communicate the outcome one-on-group to R_1 and R_2. To announce the outcome, S_3 has to communicate two messages one-on group, which are answered by R_1 and R_2:

```
1. R1 <-(103,G,data) S3 (202,G,data)-> R2
2. R1 (103,_,answ)-> S3 <-(202,_,answ) R2
3. R1 <-(104,G,data) S3 (203,G,data)-> R2
4. R1 (104,_,answ)-> S3 <-(203,_,answ) R2
```

After this successful one-on-group communication, S_3 enters the next stage in order to communicate one-on-one again with the others in G. The indices for the next message to R_1 and R_2 are 105 and 204, respectively. Introducing a separate index for each sender-receiver pair in the communication solves the problem of the different numbers of messages sent during the one-on-one communication phase. Does this solution also work for the situation where the initiator changes after one-on-group communication?

3   Adjusting the Algorithm for Changing Initiators

The last example from the previous section ends with a successful one-on-group communication. Let us go from there while R_2 now takes over the role of initiator, temporarily denoted as S_2. The previous initiator S_3 is denoted again as R_3. The communication between S_2 and R_1 is straightforward. Because S_2 did not communicate tot R_1 before, S_2 sets a new index. The last communication between S_2 and R_3 was the message (203,_,answ), sent from R_2 to S_3. Now, S_2 wants to send some data to R_3. Which index does it have to use? One possibility could be that S_2 sets a new index for this communication, starting for example at 400. Another possibility is that S_2 continues with the index used by S_3 while communicating one-on-group to R_2. In this case, S_2 can use the same index number, 203, as used during its last answer message to S_3. Alternatively S_2 can use the next index number, 204. Let us develop these three options. The last two communication lines of the previous one-on-group communication are taken as a starting point and are repeated in the examples.

Option 1, S_2 sets new index:

```
1. R1 <-(104,G,data) S3 (203,G,data)-> R2
2. R1 (104,_,answ)-> S3 <-(203,_,answ) R2
3.                   R3 <-(400,_,data) S2
4.                   R3 (400,_,answ)-> S2
5.                   R3 <-(401,_,data) S2
```

Option 2, S_2 reuses the last index number:

```
1. R1 <-(104,G,data) S3 (203,G,data)-> R2
2. R1 (104,_,answ)-> S3 <-(203,_,answ) R2
3.                   R3 <-(203,_,data) S2
4.                   R3 (204,_,answ)-> S2
5.                   R3 <-(204,_,data) S2
```

Option 3, S_2 uses the next index number:

```
1. R1 <-(104,G,data) S3 (203,G,data)-> R2
2. R1 (104,_,answ)-> S3 <-(203,_,answ) R2
3.                   R3 <-(204,_,data) S2
4.                   R3 (204,_,answ)-> S2
5.                   R3 <-(205,_,data) S2
```

All the above options show some anomalies in the index numbering with respect to being an accumulating stream of messages. For option 1, two different consecutive communication streams run between agent 2 and agent 3. This can lead to parallel communication streams if agent 3 continues communicating as initiating agent S_3 to agent 2, while agent 3 as receiver R_3 also receives messages from S_2. Two parallel communication processes between two agents about the same process are prone to communication errors and should be avoided.

For option 2, two anomalies can occur. The first one is that in one-on-one communication the receiver increases the index with every answer instead of the sender. So, when R_3 sends an answer, it acknowledges an index it did not receive yet. The second anomaly can arise at the second time agent 2 sends a message with the same index. If the previous message was just an acknowledgement, then there is no problem. Acknowledgements do not occupy an index number, otherwise we would end up with acknowledging acknowledgements [9]. If R_2 sent data instead of just an acknowledgement to agent 3 in the first message, then agent 2 cannot send another message with the same index number. When agent 3 answers with just an acknowledgement, agent 2 does not know whether agent 3 acknowledged the first or the second message. For option 3, agent 3 might send a next message (204,_,data) to agent 2 and receive from agent 2 a message (204,_,data) instead of (204,_,answ). Thus, both agents sent a data message with index 204 and also received a data message while both agents expected an answer message. This situation should be avoided.

3.1   Two-Index Mechanism to the Rescue

How can these problems be solved? The transmission control problem (TCP) makes use of two indices per connection [9,10]. One index is configured by the sender and the other index is configured by the receiver. Thus every message contains a sequence number as well as an acknowledgement of the last consecutive sequence number that is received. Could this two-index system solve the index numbering problems? Let us look at a one-on-one communication process ending with a one-on-group communication. Agent S_3 sends two messages to agent R_1 which are answered by agent R_1, and sends one message to agent R_2 which is answered by agent R_2. Next, agent S_3 sends one message one-on-group to agent R_1 and R_2 which is answered by both agents after which agent S_3 starts communicating one-on-one to agent S_1 and S_2 again. In his first message to an agent, the sender conveys only its own sequence number. When the receiver receives this, it initiates its own sequence number and answers with a message containing this number together with the acknowledged sequence number from the sender. Thus after two messages, the sender and receiver know one another's sequence numbers. The messages are now of the form   (100,200,_,data). The first field contains the sequence number of the agent that sends the message. The second field contains the acknowledged sequence number of the message the agent is reacting to. The third field contains the group information and the last field contains the data that is sent.

```
1. R1  <-(100,_,_,data)   S3
2. R1 (200,100,_,answ)-> S3
3. R1 <-(101,200,_,data) S3 (300,_,_,data) --> R2
4. R1 (201,101,_,answ)-> S3 <-(400,300,_,answ) R2
5. R1 <-(102,201,G,data) S3 (301,400,G,data)-> R2
6. R1 (202,102,_,answ)-> S3 <-(401,301,_,answ) R2
```

This works straightforwardly, so let us look how this two-index mechanism works when the initiator changes. Lines 5 and 6 from the previous communication schema are used as starting point, and agent 2 becomes the sender. The first option with the one index mechanism is that S_2 sets a new index to communicate with R_3. There are already two indices between S_2 and R_3, so it is not necessary to set a new index. S_2 and R_3 start communicating one-on-one, continuing the use of the indices they already used during the previous one-on-group communication. This eliminates the problem of two parallel communication processes between both agents. Now two options are left for S_2 when using the two-index number mechanism. The first option is to reuse the last index number and the second option is to use the next index number. Worked out, these options look as follows.

Option 1, S_2 reuses the last index number:
```
1. R1 <-(102,201,G,data) S3 (301,400,G,data)-> R2
2. R1 (202,102,_,answ)-> S3 <-(401,301,_,answ) R2
3.                        R3 <-(401,301,_,data) S2
4.                        R3 (302,401,_,answ)-> S2
5.                        R3 <-(402,302,_,data) S2
```

Option 2, S_2 uses the next index number:

```
1. R1 <-(102,201,G,data) S3 (301,400,G,data)-> R2
2. R1 (202,102,_,answ)-> S3 <-(401,301,_,answ) R2
3.                       R3 <-(402,301,_,data) S2
4.                       R3 (302,402,_,answ)-> S2
5.                       R3 <-(403,302,_,data) S2
```

For option 1, the anomaly of the receiver increasing the index (as happened with one index) does not occur. However, the second anomaly still exists. Agent 2 still sends two messages with the same index number containing different data. For option 2, agent 2 sends two messages with the same acknowledgement number, but it increases its own sequence number. Again a similar problem can arise as with the single index mechanism. It is possible that agent 3 sends a next message, (302,401,_,data), to agent 2 while it receives from agent 2 a message (402,301,_,data) instead of (402,302,_,answ). As can be seen, the index numbering is now completely messed up. Both agents will not know how to proceed so this situation should be avoided.

3.2 Who's the 'Boss'

Using a two-index mechanism solves some but not all of the problems that arise while the initiator changes. The problems that are left have a single cause. When a new agent becomes the initiator, this is not general knowledge. Another agent from the group can start acting as an initiator while the current initiator continues acting as an initiator as well. This leads to problems between these two agents as discussed in section 3.1, but also leads to problems for the other agents in the group, continuing to act as receivers. These agents start getting one-on-one communication messages about the next stage from different agents acting as initiator. Obviously this is not a workable situation. To solve this problem, the algorithm has to provide a mechanism that prevents multiple concurrent initiators.

An initiator change takes place at the transition from a successful one-on-group communication to the next one-on-one communication process. The solution for preventing multiple concurrent initiators is that if any new agent wants to act as initiator, then this agent notifies the current initiator of this fact. Every potential new initiator sends a request with its acknowledgement of the last one-on-group message. The current initiator now knows whether there are other candidate initiators and can decide whether it continues as an initiator itself, or allows one of the other agents to act as initiator. If the current initiator decides to stay on, then it continues communicating one-on-one concerning the next stage. As soon as an agent that announced itself as a new initiator receives the first one-on-one communication message from the sender, it knows that it should not act as initiator. If the current initiator decides that one of the other agents can take over, then it sends a message one-on-one to this agent confirming that it is the new initiator. After the initiator for the next stage receives this message, it knows its new role and starts communicating messages one-on-one concerning the next stage. As soon as the other agents that announced themselves as new initiator receive the first one-on-one communication message from the new initiator, they know that they should not act as initiator. We assume that agents involved in CPS are cooperative, so if one of the other agents has better resources for being the new initiator, then the current initiator transfers the role of initiator to that agent.

Let us develop two examples. In both, the current initiator and two other agents want to act as initiator. In the first example, the initiator changes, while in the second example, the initiator stays the same. An agent announcing itself as a potential initiator for the next stage is represented by the value *init* in the data field. If the current initiator decides that another agent can have the role of initiator, then it sends a message containing *answ* into the data field.

Example 1, S_2 as initiator after init request from R_1 and R_2.

```
1. R1 <-(102,201,G,data) S3 (301,400,G,data)-> R2
2. R1 (202,102,_,init)-> S3 <-(401,301,_,init) R2
3.                       S3 (302,401,_,answ)-> R2
4.                       R3 <-(402,302,_,data) S2 (500,_,_,data)-> R1
5.                       R3 (303,402,_,answ)-> S2 <-(600,500,_,answ) R1
6.                       R3 <-(403,303,_,data) S2 (501,600,_,data)-> R1
```

Example 2, S_3 stays the initiator after init request from R_1 and R_2.

```
1. R1 <-(102,201,G,data) S3 (301,400,G,data)-> R2
2. R1 (202,102,_,init)-> S3 <-(401,301,_,init) R2
3. R1 <-(103,202,_,data) S3 (302,401,_,data)-> R2
4. R1 (203,103,_,answ)-> S3 <-(402,302,_,answ) R2
5. R1 <-(104,203,_,data) S3 (303,402,_,data)-> R2
6. R1 (204,104,_,answ)-> S3 <-(403,303,_,answ) R2
```

In the above two examples, no anomalies in the index numbering are present. The combination of the two-index mechanism with the mechanism regulating the change of initiator handles the problems that could occur when the initiator changes during the CPS process.

4 CPS Specific Algorithm

In sections 2 and 3 it was shown which adjustments had to be made to ensure the group's appropriate gain of knowledge for the asynchronous communication and changing initiators. Let us have a look at the adjusted algorithm. The messages from the algorithm from [1] have the following form:

$$K_{source}(destination, -, group, position, -, data).$$

The fields filled with "−" are the *checksum* and *window_size* fields, dealing with package mutation errors and congestion control [10,11]. As discussed in section 3, an algorithm for CPS needs an index mechanism consisting of two indices. The *window_size* is used for the sliding window [9] mechanism which is not used during dialogue. This allows us to use the *window_size* field as the second index field. Because the checksum field does not contribute to the gaining of knowledge, it is filled with "−". The first index contains the sequence number of the agent who sends the message, and the second index field contains an acknowledgement of the sequence number of the message this agent reacts to. These fields are called the *sequence* field and the *acknowledgement* field, respectively. The message used by the CPS algorithm has the following form:

$$K_{source}(destination, -, group, sequence, acknowledgement, data)$$

Here follows a description of the fields in the messages used in the CPS algorithm.

source = source port where this message is sent from $[S, R_i]$;
Ksource = the source who sends this message knows this message;
destination = destination port of message $[S, R_i]$;
group = group receivers to which the message is sent $[R_G, -]$ ("−" means that the sender communicates only to the **destination** (one-on-one communication));
sequence = sequence number of message from agent who sends this message;
acknowledgement = sequence number of message that agent is reacting to;
data = data that has to be transmitted.

The next table explains variables and functions used in the CPS algorithm:

Acknowledgement	
ack_Ri	: Used by S. Acknowledged sequence number received from Ri
seqSRi	: Used by S. Sequence number of messages S is sending to Ri
seqS	: Used by Ri. Sequence number of messages Ri is receiving from S
seqRi	: Used by Ri. Sequence number of messages Ri is sending to S
seqRi	: Used by S. Sequence number of messages S is receiving from Ri
Data	
compose()	: Used by S and Ri. Agent makes up the data it wants to send

4.1 CPS Algorithm

The algorithm consists of four parts. Both sender and receiver have an algorithm that handles incoming messages and an algorithm that handles outgoing messages. The lines in bold face are the lines from the algorithm and the lines between curly brackets contain some comments on them. The numbers at the beginning and at the end of the comments represent the line numbers at which the commented block of code begins or ends, respectively.

Sender (incoming packages)

1   **for (i = 1 to n) do**
     {*For all agents who sender is sending to, ... *}
2   **ack_Ri = seqSRi**
        {*... initialize the acknowledgement number.*}
3   **end**
     {*ack_Ri's initialized*}

4 **while true do**
   {*Get ready for receiving acknowledgements from the receivers, ... [11]*}
5   **when received** $K_{R_i}(S, -, -, seqR_i, seqSR_i, data)$ **do**
       {*You have received a package. Prepare for processing, ... [10]*}
6   **if** ($seqSR_i = ack\_R_i + 1$) **do**
           {*If this acknowledgement from R_i is equal to the next ack_R_i, ... [9]*}
7              $ack\_R_i = seqSR_i$
               {*... this is the new current acknowledgement from R_i, ...*}
8   **store** $K_S K_{R_i}(S, -, -, seqR_i, seqSR_i, data)$
               {*... store that you know that R_i knows it.*}
9   **end**
           {*[6] ... acknowledgement from R_i, and highest group acknowledgement updated.*}
10   **end**
       {*[5] ... finished processing of incoming package.*}
11 **end**
   {*[4].*}

Sender (outgoing packages)

1 **for (i = 1 to n) do**
   {*For all receiving agents.*}
2   **if not** $seqSR_i$ **do**
       {*If S did not communicate to R_i before*}
3          $seqSR_i = x$
           {*Initiate own sequence number for R_i at x*}
4   **end**
       {*$seqSR_i$ initiated.*}
5 **end**
   {*$seqSR_i$ for all receiving agents initiated.*}
6 **while true do**
   {*Start sending sequence of messages, ... [20]*}
7   **compose(data)**
       {*... ,make up the data for this package, ...*}
8   **store** $K_S(-, -, G, -, -, data)$
       {*... and store this information in your knowledge base.*}
9   **while** ($\exists\ ack\_R_i \neq seqSR_i$) **do**
       {*While not all receivers acknowledged the package with sequence $seqSR_i$, ... [15]*}
10   **for (i = 1 to n) do**
           {*... and for all receiving agents, ... [14]*}
11   **if not** $K_S K_{R_i}(-, -, G, seqR_i + 1, SeqSR_i, data)$ **do**
               {*... check if package '$seqSR_i$' has not been acknowledged yet by R_i, ... [13]*}
12   **send** $K_S(R_i, -, G, seqSR_i, seqR_i, data)$
                   {*... (re)send the package to R_i.*}
13   **end**
               {*[11] ... A package that was unacknowledged by R_i, has been resent.*}
14   **end**
           {*[10] ... A package has been resent to all agents that didn't acknowledge it.*}
15   **end**
       {*[9] ... all agents R_i have acknowledged package with sequence number $seqSR_i$.*}

```
16    for (i = 1 to n) do
      {For all receiving agents, ... [19]}
17       seqRi = seqRi + 1
         {Sequence number of next message from Ri is known. Increment seqRi.}
18       seqSRi = seqSRi + 1
         {Increment own sequence number for Ri.}
19    end
      {[16] ... Sequence numbers for and from Ri updated.}
20 end
   {[6].}
```

Receiver (incoming packages)

```
1  while true do
   {Get ready for receiving sequence of messages, ... [5]}
2     when received $K_S(R_i, G, -, seqS, seqR_i, data)$ do
      {You have received a package (from S). Prepare for processing, ... [4]}
3        store $K_{R_i} K_S(-, -, G, seqS, seqR_i, data)$
         {Store the received package.}
4     end
      {[2] ... finished processing incoming package.}
5  end
   {[1].}
```

Receiver (outgoing packages)

```
1  when $K_{R_i} K_S(R_i, -, G, x, \varnothing, data)$
   {The first message is received.}
2  seqS = x
   {The first sequence number from S is x.}
3  seqRi = y
   {Initiate own sequence number at y.}
4  while true do
   {Get ready to acknowledge incoming packages, ... [11]}
5     compose(data)
      {Make up the data for this message. (Possibly a request to act as initiator.)}
6     while not $K_{R_i} K_S(R_i, -, G, seqS + 1, seqR_i, data)$ do
      {Still not received package with 'seqS+1' (and 'seqRi'), ... [8]}
7        send $K_{R_i}(S, -, -, seqR_i, seqS, data)$
         {... (re)send data package.}
8     end
      {[6] ... You've received message seqS+1 wiht acknowledgement seqRi}
9     seqS = seqS+1
      {You know the sequence number of the next message. Increment seqS.}
10    seqRi = seqRi+1
      {Increment own sequence number, seqRi.}
11 end
   {[4].}
```

5   Analysis of Epistemic Properties of the Algorithm

For the adjustments discussed in section 2 and 3, we showed informally that they ensure the required knowledge gaining for CPS. In this section we prove that if the adjusted algorithm is used during CPS communication, then the agents achieve an approximation of general knowledge.

5.1   Logical Background: Knowledge and Time

When proving properties of knowledge-based protocols, it is usual to use semantics of interpreted systems $\mathcal{I}$ representing the behaviour of processors over time (see [7]). We give a short review. At each point in time, each of the processors is in some *local state*. All of these local states, together with the environment's state, form the system's *global state* at that point in time. These global states form the possible worlds in a Kripke model. The accessibility relations are defined according to the following informal description. The processor R "knows" φ if in every other global state having the same local state as processor R, φ holds. In particular, each processor knows its own local state; for the environment, there is no accessibility relation. The knowledge relations are equivalence relations, obeying the well-known epistemic logic $S5_n^C$ (see [7]), including the knowledge axiom $K_i\varphi \Rightarrow \varphi, i = 1, ..., n$, as well as axioms governing general and common knowledge such as $E_G\varphi \Leftrightarrow \bigwedge_{i \in G} K_i\varphi$ and $C_G\varphi \Rightarrow E_G(\varphi \wedge C_G\varphi)$. We use abbreviations for general knowledge at any finite depth. Inductively, $E_G^1\varphi$ stands for $E_G\varphi$ and $E_G^{k+1}\varphi$ is $E_G(E_G^k\varphi)$.

A *run* is a (finite or infinite) sequence of global states, which may be viewed as running through time. Time here is taken as isomorphic to the natural numbers. There need not be any accessibility relation between two global states for them to appear in succession in a run. Time clearly obeys the axioms of the basic temporal logic K_t (see [12]), in which the following principle (A) is derivable:

(A) $P(\Box\varphi) \rightarrow \Box\varphi$

To further model time, we extend $S5_n^C$ with the following mixed axiom:

KT1. $K_i\Box\varphi \rightarrow \Box K_i\varphi, i = 1, ..., n$

This axiom holds for systems with perfect recall [13]. Halpern et al. [13] present a complete axiomatization for knowledge and time, however in this article we only need the axiom KT1.

As for notation, global states are represented as (r, m) (m-th time-point in run r) in the interpreted system $\mathcal{I}$. In particular for the temporal operators, we have the following truth definitions:

$(\mathcal{I}, r, m) \models \Box\varphi$ *iff* $(\mathcal{I}, r, m') \models \varphi$ *for all* $m' \geq m$
$(\mathcal{I}, r, m) \models P\varphi$ *iff* $(\mathcal{I}, r, m') \models \varphi$ *for some* $m' < m$

5.2   Proof of the Increase of Group Knowledge

For the readability of the proof, the form of the package is shortened to $Ksource(sequence, data)$. We assume that the group stays unchanged and we assume that the sender S sends to a receiver R_i and vice versa, so the *destination* and *group* field are left out. Furthermore, we assume that no mutation errors occur, so the *checksum* field is also left out. We only use the *sequence* number in the proof; the *acknowledgement* number is left out. In the next table we present some relevant formulas with their informal meanings.

Formulas	Descriptions
$K_{R_i}(p, \alpha)$	Receiver i knows that the p-th data segment is α; similar for $K_S(p, \alpha)$
$K_{R_i}(p, -)$	Receiver i knows the value of the p-th data segment; similar for $K_S(p, -)$
$E_G(p, \alpha)$	Every agent in group G knows that the p-th data segment is α
$E_G(p, -)$	Every agent in group G knows the value of the p-th data segment
$E_G^k \varphi$	Group G has depth k general knowledge of φ
R_G	G is the current group of receivers
$P\varphi$	At some moment in the past on this run, φ was true
$\Box\varphi$	φ is now true and will always be true on this run

Theorem 1. *Let $\mathcal{R}$ be any set of runs consistent with the knowledge-based algorithm from section 4 where:*

- *the environment allows for deletion and reordering errors, but no other kinds of error;*
- *The safety property holds (so that at any moment the sequence Y of data elements received by each R_i is a prefix of the infinite sequence X of data elements on S's input tape).*

Then for all runs in $\mathcal{R}$ and all $k \geq 0, j \geq 0$ the following hold:

[Forth]: R_i stores $K_{R_i} K_S (j + k, \alpha) \rightarrow \Box K_{R_i} K_S (E_G K_S)^k (j, \alpha)$.
[Back_i]: S stores $K_S K_{R_i} (j + k, -) \rightarrow \Box K_S K_{R_i} K_S (E_G K_S)^k (j, -)$.
[Back_G]: S stores $K_S E_G (j + k, -) \rightarrow \Box K_S (E_G K_S)^{k+1} (j, -)$.

In the proof below we use a general principle from temporal logic (A), and some consequences we can derive from the assumptions of the theorem (B & C).

A $P(\Box\varphi) \rightarrow \Box\varphi$
B Because $\mathcal{R}$ is consistent with the knowledge-based algorithm, S and R_i store all relevant information from the packages that they receive. Moreover, packages that are sent have the following form: $K_{R_i}\varphi$ or $K_S\varphi$, from which the following can be concluded. If R_i receives $K_S\varphi$, then R_i stores $K_{R_i} K_S\varphi$, thus also $\Box K_{R_i} K_S\varphi$. Similarly for S.
C Under the same assumption of $\mathcal{R}$ being consistent with the knowledge-based algorithm, system $\mathcal{R}$ can be viewed as a system of perfect recall. Now we have in general that $K_S\Box\varphi \rightarrow \Box K_S\varphi$, see axiom KT1.

Proof

We prove *theorem 1* by induction on k. First we look at the situation for **k = 0**. From B follows the **Forth**-part for $(k = 0)$ namely

$$R_i \text{ stores } K_{R_i}K_S\left(j,\alpha\right) \to \Box K_{R_i}K_S\left(j,\alpha\right). \tag{1}$$

R_i sends an acknowledgement only if it received a package. Together with A and B we have:

$$\text{if } R_i \text{ sends } K_{R_i}\left(j,-\right) \text{ then } P\left(R_i \text{ stores } K_S\left(j,\alpha\right)\right), \tag{2}$$

$$\text{so } P\Box K_{R_i}K_S\left(j,\alpha\right), \text{ and } \Box K_{R_i}K_S\left(j,\alpha\right).$$

S only stores an acknowledgement if it also received it from R_i, thus it knows that R_i has sent it in the past.

$$\text{If } S \text{ stores } K_S K_{R_i}\left(j,-\right) \text{ then } K_S P\left(R_i \text{ sends } K_{R_i}\left(j,-\right)\right)\ldots \tag{3}$$

With A, C and the fact proven at (2) it can now be derived that:

$$K_S P\left(\Box K_{R_i}K_S\left(j,-\right)\right), \text{ and } K_S\Box K_{R_i}K_S\left(j,-\right), \text{ so } \Box K_S K_{R_i}K_S\left(j,-\right). \tag{4}$$

If (3) and (4) are combined, then we have the **Back_i**-part of the theorem for the j-th data segment ($k=0$).

S receives acknowledgements from all the receivers and is able to retrieve information out of this. We go back two steps and look at another knowledge level of S instead of the knowledge level between S and just one receiver.

S only stores acknowledgements it received. If S has received acknowledgements of a certain package from R_G where $G = \{1,...,n\}$ then S knows that $R_{i<i=1..n>}$ have sent these acknowledgements in the past.

$$\text{If } S \text{ stores } K_S E_G\left(j,-\right) \text{ then } K_S P\left(R_{i<i=1..n>} \text{ sends } K_{R_i}\left(j,-\right)\right)\ldots \tag{5}$$

With A, C and the fact proven at (2) it can now be deduced that:

$$K_S P\left(\Box E_G K_S\left(j,-\right)\right), \text{ and } K_S\Box E_G K_S\left(j,-\right), \text{ so } \Box K_S E_G K_S\left(j,-\right). \tag{6}$$

If (5) and (6) are combined, then we have the **Back_G**-part of the theorem for the j-th data segment ($k=0$). What knowledge about the j-th data segment emerges for $k \neq 0$? This is shown in the induction step.

Induction step. Suppose as induction hypothesis that **Back_i**, **Back_G** and **Forth** are valid for $k-1$, with $k \geq 1$. Now a proof follows that **Forth**, **Back_i**, and **Back_G** are also valid for k.

[Forth]: S only starts sending packages with position mark $(j+k)$ if it has received from all the receivers R_i an acknowledgement for package with position mark $(j+(k-1))$:

$$S \text{ sends } K_S\left(j+k,\alpha\right) \to P\left(S \text{ stores } K_S E_G\left(j+(k-1),-\right)\right). \tag{7}$$

With the **Back_G**-part of the theorem for $k-1$ and A, the following can be deduced:

$$S \text{ sends } K_S\left(j+k,\alpha\right) \to \Box K_S\left(E_G K_S\right)^k\left(j,-\right). \tag{8}$$

R_i knows this fact. So if R_i receives a package from S with position mark $j + k$, then R_i knows that S has sent this package somewhere in the past. From the fact given at (8) together with A and B, the following can be derived:

$$R_i \text{ stores } K_{R_i} K_S \left(j + k, \alpha\right) \rightarrow \Box K_{R_i} K_S \left(E_G K_S\right)^k \left(j, -\right). \qquad (9)$$

This is exactly what the **Forth**-part of the theorem says.

[**Back_i**]: R_i only sends an acknowledgement for the $(j + k)$-th data element if he stored $K_{R_i} K_S \left(j + k, -\right)$ in the past. With A, now the following can be derived:

$$R_i \text{ sends } K_{R_i} \left(j + k, -\right) \rightarrow \Box K_{R_i} K_S \left(E_G K_S\right)^k \left(j, -\right). \qquad (10)$$

S knows this fact. So if S receives an acknowledgement from R_i for the $(j + k)$-th data segment, then S knows that R_i has sent this acknowledgement in the past. Using A and B it can now be concluded that:

$$S \text{ stores } K_S K_{R_i} \left(j + k, -\right) \rightarrow \Box K_S K_{R_i} K_S \left(E_G K_S\right)^k \left(j, -\right), \qquad (11)$$

and this is exactly the **Back_i**-part of the theorem.

[**Back_G**]: S receives acknowledgements from all R_i. At a certain time S has received an acknowledgement for the $(j + k)$-th data segment from all R_i. Thus,

$$S \text{ stores } K_S E_G \left(j + k, -\right).$$

With A and B it can now be concluded that:

$$S \text{ stores } K_S E_G \left(j + k, -\right) \rightarrow \Box K_S \left(E_G K_S\right)^{k+1} \left(j, -\right), \qquad (12)$$

and this is exactly the **Back_G**-part of the theorem.

6   Conclusion and Future Work

This research falls in the tradition of using interpreted multi-agent systems to analyze communication protocols, and extends knowledge-based analysis of file transmission protocols such as [5,10,14]. Our aim has been to make communication protocols much more flexible than file transmission protocols, in order to adapt them to dialogue-based cooperative problem solving (CPS). There, more interactive inter-group communication is needed than can be achieved by simple broadcasts from an initiator to the rest of his team. In this paper a knowledge-based algorithm for multi-agent communication [1] is adjusted for dialogue communication in teamwork. It is shown how the protocol handles the different numbers of messages between the initiator and different members and the changing initiator property, guaranteeing the knowledge gain required for CPS. An algorithm supporting the dynamic properties of CPS communication provides a flexible approach for CPS.

This research complements other literature that aims to make Wooldridge's and Jennings' CPS model [2] more flexible, for example, [15] where the needed group attitudes for teamwork are adjusted to properties of the environment and the organization. Durfee et al. present another model of CPS [16]. Their idea of partial global planning interleaves plan execution with stages of gradually specifying the global plan in more detail. This seems to be an appropriate model for long term software development projects, where teams change over time. It would be interesting to see whether communication during CPS based on such more flexible models can be handled similarly to the knowledge-based algorithm presented here, by a modular approach that can be instantiated for specific models of CPS.

In the present work, we have concentrated on the types of dialogues needed during team formation. Future work will include an investigation how protocols establishing binary social commitments during plan formation can be developed and analyzed in an interpreted multi-agent systems framework. Chopra and Singh have presented relevant work on commitment protocols, based on the formalism of transition systems [17]. Lomuscio and Sergot [14] investigate the possibility of applying deontic logic in order to study agents' *violations* of file transmission protocols. We have not yet investigated this issue for our protocols, but it is interesting future research. It is also interesting to design a logic exactly suited to communication protocols such as the one-to-many protocol from [1] and the CPS adjusted algorithm given here, in a similar fashion as the sound and complete system TDL developed by Lomuscio and Woźna for authentication protocols [18]. For such a system with a computationally grounded semantics of interpreted systems, it may even be possible to develop model checking techniques in order to check relevant properties automatically.

Acknowledgements

We would like to thank three anonymous referees for their helpful comments.

References

1. van Baars, E., Verbrugge, R.: Knowledge-based algorithm for multi-agent communication. In: Bonanno, G., et al. (eds.) Proceedings of the 7th Conference on Logic and the Foundations of Game and Decision Theory, University of Liverpool, pp. 227–236 (2006)
2. Wooldridge, M., Jennings, N.R.: The cooperative problem-solving process. Journal of Logic and Computation 9(4), 563–592 (1999)
3. Dignum, F., Dunin-Kęplicz, B., Verbrugge, R.: Creating collective intention through dialogue. Logic Journal of the IGPL 9(2), 289–303 (2001)
4. Dunin-Kęplicz, B., Verbrugge, R.: Dialogue in teamwork. In: Fonseca, J.M., et al. (eds.) Proceedings of The 10th ISPE International Conference on Concurrent Engineering: Research and Applications, Rotterdam, A.A. Balkema, pp. 121–128 (2003)
5. Halpern, J.Y., Zuck, L.D.: A little knowledge goes a long way: Simple knowledge-based derivations and correctness proofs for a family of protocols. In: Proceedings of the 6th ACM Symposium on Principles of Distributed Computing, pp. 269–280 (1987); Full version including proofs appeared in Journal of the ACM 39(3), 449–478 (1992)

6. van Baars, E.: Knowledge-based algorithm for multi-agent communication. Master's thesis, Department of Artificial Intelligence, University of Groningen (2006), www.ai.rug.nl/alice/mas/macom

7. Fagin, R., Halpern, J.Y., Moses, Y., Vardi, M.: Reasoning About Knowledge. MIT Press, Cambridge (1995)

8. Halpern, J.Y., Pucella, R.: On the relationship between strand spaces and multi-agent systems. ACM Trans. Inf. Syst. Secur. 6(1), 43–70 (2003)

9. Postel, J.: Transmission control protocol (TCP). Technical Report RFC 793, Internet Society (September 1981), ftp://ftp.rfc-editor.org/in-notes/rfc793.txt

10. Stulp, F., Verbrugge, R.: A knowledge-based algorithm for the internet protocol TCP. Bulletin of Economic Research 54(1), 69–94 (2002)

11. Douglas, D.E.: Internetworking with TCP/IP. Principles, Protocols and Architectures, vol. 1. Pearson Prentice Hall, Upper Saddle River (2006)

12. Goldblatt, R.: Logics of Time and Computation. CSLI Lecture Notes, vol. 7. Center for Studies in Language and Information, Palo Alto (1992)

13. Halpern, J., van der Meyden, R., Vardi, M.: Complete axiomatizations for reasoning about knowledge and time. SIAM Journal on Computing 33(3), 674–703 (2004)

14. Lomuscio, A., Sergot, M.: A formulation of violation, error recovery, and enforcement in the bit transmission problem. Journal of Applied Logic 2, 93–116 (2004)

15. Dunin-Kęplicz, B., Verbrugge, R.: A tuning machine for cooperative problem solving. Fundamenta Informaticae 63, 283–307 (2004)

16. Cox, J.S., Durfee, E.H., Bartold, T.: A distributed framework for solving the multi-agent plan coordination problem. In: Dignum, F., Dignum, V., Koenig, S., Kraus, S., Singh, M.P., Wooldridge, M. (eds.) AAMAS, pp. 821–827. ACM, New York (2005)

17. Chopra, A.K., Singh, M.P.: Contextualizing commitment protocols. In: Nakashima, H., Wellman, M.P., Weiss, G., Stone, P. (eds.) AAMAS, pp. 1345–1352. ACM, New York (2006)

18. Lomuscio, A., Woźna, B.: A complete and decidable security-specialised logic and its application to the TESLA protocol. In: Stone, P., Weiss, G. (eds.) Proceedings of the Fifth International Joint Conference on Autonomous Agents and Multiagent Systems, pp. 145–152. ACM Press, New York (2006)

Extending the MaSE Methodology for the Development of Embedded Real-Time Systems

Iman Badr, Hisham Mubarak, and Peter Göhner

Universität Stuttgart, Institute of Industrial Automation and Software Engineering (IAS),
Pfaffenwaldring 47
70550 Stuttgart, Germany
{Iman.Badr,Hisham.Mubarak,Peter.Goehner}@ias.uni-stuttgart.de

Abstract. Embedded real-time systems play an important role in various application areas like plant automation, product automation or car electronics. In recent years, a considerable growth in the functionality has been observed. At the same time, expectations on systems' flexibility at runtime are growing steadily. The agent-oriented software engineering approach is well suited for the development of decentralised, complex software systems with high flexibility. A number of software engineering methodologies have been introduced for developing agent-oriented systems. However, none of the existing methodologies is intended for the development of embedded real-time systems. This work presents concepts that extend the Multi-agent Systems Engineering (MaSE) methodology for the development of agent-oriented embedded real-time systems. The proposed concepts have been integrated in the traditional engineering process of MasE and evaluated by applying the extended process to the development of a flexible agent-oriented embedded system for the control of an elevator model.

Keywords: Agent-Oriented Software Development, Real-Time Systems, Embedded Systems.

1 Introduction

Embedded systems are systems that are integrated logically and physically in a device or a larger system. Their application spectrum ranges from simple devices like mobile phones and house held devices up to the complex ones like aircrafts and industrial process controllers, to name a few. Regardless of the diversity of their application domain, all embedded systems are required to synchronise their execution with the technical process of the encapsulating device. Traditionally, the development of real-time systems was targeted for closed predefined hardware structures. More and more the structure of systems hardware is becoming dynamic with the addition, removal and upgrade of components. Current systems are thus required to adapt to dynamic changes in the structure of the hardware as well as to flexibly deal with unforeseeable events that may occur in the working environment. Therefore, the development of

M. Dastani et al. (Eds.): LADS 2007, LNAI 5118, pp. 106–122, 2008.

such systems represents a challenge of achieving flexibility without violating invariant requirements, especially real-time requirements which are considered crucial for these systems.

With their special nature in tackling the complexity of distributed applications and adapting their behaviour to stochastic, dynamically changing environments, software agents represent a suitable approach for developing flexible embedded systems. Such development is supposed to be based on and guided by systematic methodologies that result in exhibiting the required controlled flexibility. However, the appealing concepts of agents are not complemented with powerful comprehensive methodologies that provide the needed support along the different application domains. Concerning the embedded real-time systems domain, the available agent-oriented methodologies provide no support for indispensable features namely, timeliness and concurrency. Therefore, the employment of agents in real-time systems may lead to possible violations of the timeliness requirements. Consequently, the potential of the agent-based paradigm in dealing with complexity and adapting to dynamic conditions has not been utilised in the embedded systems field.

In order to pave the way for the employment of agents in the embedded real-time systems domain and capitalise on their flexibility, this work aims at bridging the gap between the embedded systems domain and the available agent-oriented software engineering. Towards achieving this objective, the Multi-agent Software Engineering (MaSE) methodology [1] was extended with timeliness concepts that customise it for the embedded systems domain.

This paper is organised as follows. Section 2 overviews the special requirements and conventional development trends of embedded systems. Section 3 focuses on the MaSE methodology by first reviewing the comparative study that led to its selection and then discussing its limitations in capturing the special characteristics of embedded systems. Section 4 proposes a set of extensions that overcome these limitations. Section 5 illustrates the proposed extensions with a case study. Section 6 presents concluding remarks and an outlook on future work.

2 Embedded Systems

Unlike information systems whose development is targeted basically to the satisfaction of the customer needs, embedded systems have to satisfy the goals and desires of the customer while at the same time complying with the requirements and constraints enforced by its controlled process. To illustrate, consider an embedded system of a typical automatically controlled washing machine. Such system is expected to provide a user interface that allows for acquiring the user input concerning the required washing program. In addition, it is obliged to react on the right time to the events continually emerging from the technical washing process like an event signaling the fall of the water level under a certain threshold. Failing to react to such events on the right time may cause undesired effects or for safety critical systems may bring about dangerous or even fatal effects.

2.1 Distinguishing Characteristics

In light of the previously mentioned example, two basic distinguishing characteristics of embedded systems could be identified.

2.1.1 Timeliness

To synchronise their operation with the controlled physical process, embedded systems are required to work under timing constraints that stem basically from the technical system. In other words, embedded systems are real-time systems whose input, processing and output have to be performed under predefined timing requirements, which usually result from the physical laws governing the controlled technical process. [2]. For example, an automobile engine system controls the amount of proper fuel to be injected into the combustion chamber of each cylinder. For such an example, a delay in terms of a few microseconds may lead to opening the valve at an incorrect point of time which results in the mechanical damage of the engine [3]. In general, real-time systems are classified according to the nature of their real-time requirements into soft and hard real-time systems. While soft real-time systems work under relatively flexible timing constraints which when violated can lead to lowering the performance but can still be tolerated, hard real-time systems have much more strict constraints whose violation can lead to a failure or can be dangerous.

2.1.2 Concurrency

Embedded real-time systems are concurrent by nature in that they have to react to several sensors and control multiple actuators simultaneously to achieve the required performance on the right time. Concurrency raises several challenges like scheduling, synchronisation, and communication of tasks. Tasks are either executed periodically or are triggered by events whose occurrence time is not determined a priori. Each task works under timing constraints and has to meet a certain deadline [2]. The objective of a real-time system is to satisfy the requests of all tasks in a way that all deadlines can be met. However, due to limited resources, this is not always possible. Therefore, priorities of tasks have to be considered in scheduling to make sure that time critical tasks with hard deadlines are not delayed.

2.2 Conventional Development Trends

The engineering trends of embedded systems have featured major changes all over the years. During its early stages, embedded systems were developed in an ad-hoc manner, where the system was realised by engineers having little knowledge of computer science. They tended to satisfy the requirements at hand by sketching a block diagram of the system to be implemented with special considerations to saving hardware resources at the expense of the software capacity. Software was just limited to stand-alone implementation running on a microcontroller with no operating system. With increasing market needs, more attention was given to adding software functionalities to enhance the utilisation of the system which resulted in an increasing complexity of the software [3]. Currently, the industrial trend is characterised by designing embedded systems with in-house methods that are specifically tailored to their application domain. In general, a co-design approach is adopted as a natural model for conceiving the strong interrelation between hardware and software [4].

2.3 Modelling Techniques

Due to their inherent complexity, embedded real-time systems depend heavily on computational models for their analysis and design. They serve in formally specifying the temporal and concurrent aspects of the behaviour of the system in an unambiguous manner that simplifies implementation and testing. In general, real-time systems are usually modelled by state-oriented models that stress the control and reactive aspects of the system by capturing the effect of the external events coming from the environment on the states of the system. These models attach special importance to temporal and concurrency issues. Out of the existing models, finite state machines and Petri-nets are most commonly used for modelling the behaviour of embedded systems [5].

2.4 Flexibility Requirement

The embedded systems industry is featuring exponential growth motivated by the increasing availability of cheaper and more powerful hardware components. Due to the relatively long lifetime of devices incorporating embedded systems, it is highly demanding to design an embedded system in such a way that allows for modifications to the hardware structure – by adding or removing components – with no or minimal effects on the existing software. Consequently, the conventional approach of designing closed software which is tightly coupled with the underlying hardware components does not offer sufficient flexibility in face of the new challenges. This motivates investigating new approaches of software engineering like the agent-oriented paradigm, which represents a good approach for distributed, ill-structured and dynamic systems [6].

3   The MaSE Methodology

Mulit-agent Systems Engineering (MaSE) is a generic agent-oriented software development methodology [1]. The engineering process of MaSE is based on a top-down software engineering approach that supports the analysis and design phases through seven steps, which can be performed in an iterative fashion. The whole process with the steps and the corresponding artefacts is depicted by Fig.1. As illustrated in the figure, MaSE adopts a goal-oriented analysis by deriving the system goals from a set of system requirements – whose generation is assumed to be outside the scope of MaSE. The system is next modelled as a set of roles which are assigned the identified goals. During the design phase, the identified roles are grouped together to form agents that are designed to play the incorporated roles. The design phase extends up to the deployment stage, where a decision on the distribution of agents to the available physical platforms is taken.

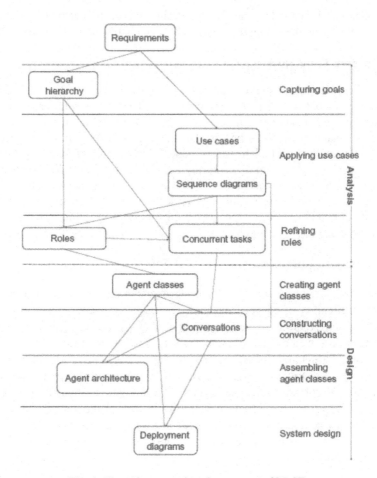

Fig. 1. The software engineering process of MaSE

3.1 The Selection of MaSE

This work builds on a previous study that resulted in the selection of MaSE as the agent-oriented methodology with the best relative potential for the embedded systems domain [7]. During the course of this work, a two-phase evaluation process was conducted.

The first phase served in deciding on an initial set of methodologies that represent good candidates for further deeper investigation out of the excessive number of the currently available methodologies that amount to twenty different methodologies [8]. The evaluation criteria for this phase considered broad aspects like the soundness of concepts, the suitability to the embedded systems domain, the coverage of the development process, and the tool support. This initial evaluation resulted in the selection of Gaia [9], MaSE [10], Prometheus [11], and PASSI [12].

During the second phase, the four methodologies were assessed against a framework of attributes according to the well-known feature-based evaluation method. The evaluation criteria covered twenty seven different features grouped into five categories that examine the support of the methodologies to aspects related to the application domain, the development process, the agent-oriented features, the system to be developed, , and the flexibility this system is supposed to exhibit. Assessing the four methodologies according to this evaluation framework resulted in the choice of MaSE as the methodology with the best relative potential for the application for the flexible embedded systems.

3.2 Limitations of MaSE for the Embedded Systems Domain

In spite of its good support for agent-oriented concepts like goals and roles, MaSE fails to capture some of the essential characteristics of the embedded real-time systems domain. By examining the applicability of MaSE to the flexible embedded systems, a number of limitations have been identified.

3.2.1 Requirements Engineering
The lack of support to the requirements engineering phase may not have a noticeable impact on the modelling of traditional information systems, whose development is based on user requirements that can be acquired based on conventional methods of software requirements engineering. However, the integrated nature of the embedded systems results in a set of constraints that stem from the technical system and from the existing system hardware. Such constraints may conflict with or limit the user requirements and need thus to be considered at the early development stages. The temporal requirements of the technical system, the response time of the computational nodes, as well as the topology of the hardware components are all examples of possible factors that can greatly constrain the required system behaviour. The formal specification of these constraints is not straightforward and should be based on a careful analysis of the physical aspects of the system. Therefore, a methodology that attempts to cater for the embedded real-time application domain has to give clear support to how requirements are to be specified in light of the enforced constraints.

3.2.2 Environmental Support
In spite of the important role played by the environment in the agent-oriented paradigm, where an agent is by definition situated in an environment with which it interacts, MaSE fails to support this feature and provides no mechanism for explicitly modelling the environment, nor for modelling the interaction between the system and its environment. Considering the embedded systems domain, the role of the environment becomes even stronger because of its integrated nature within an encapsulating device or system. Consequently, identifying the boundaries of the modelled system and designating it from its environment aids in a better understanding of the system concerned. In addition, modelling the interaction between the system and its environment is of a big significance to embedded systems due to their reactive nature, where the internal behaviour of the system is highly shaped by external events emerging from the environment.

3.2.3 Temporal Dimension of the Modelled Behaviour

While real-time requirements and constraints greatly shape the behaviour of an embedded real-time system whose performance is always judged by how far it satisfies its temporal requirements, this aspect is totally absent from the development process of MaSE and from the other methodologies that have been surveyed [7]. This is viewed as the greatest obstacle hindering the application of agent-oriented methodologies to the embedded systems domain. Hence all aspects of the system behaviour including internal behaviour of agents as well as inter-agent communications have to explicitly consider the temporal factor as a central shaping factor in the analysis and design phases.

The concurrent behaviour of the system is another aspect which is closely related to timeliness since it deals with the way the system works on satisfying several temporal requirements simultaneously. MaSE provides limited support by the concurrent tasks model generated during the analysis phase (see Fig. 1). It is assumed that each role fulfils its goals through the concurrent execution of a number of tasks. While the execution details of each task is modelled by a finite state automaton, the concurrency involved in managing the collective execution of these parallel tasks is not explicitly supported.

4 Proposed Extensions

In order to deal with the limitations of MaSE in conceiving flexibility to embedded systems, the whole engineering process has been refined as illustrated in Fig. 2.[1] First, a new phase for requirements engineering has been introduced. Second, modifications have been suggested to the already existing analysis and design phases.

4.1 Requirements Engineering Phase

Requirements serve in the identification of the qualitative along with the quantitative characteristics of the system [13]. They are usually viewed from two levels of abstraction. At a higher level of abstraction, requirements are described from the *user* perspective and are referred to as the *user requirements*. This view however is refined by the system developer in light of the existing constraints which results in a detailed modelling of system services and constraints which is referred to as the *system requirements* [14].

This twofold representation of requirements is adopted during this phase to serve in generating a refined set of systems requirements that takes the constraining effects of the technical system as well as the system hardware into consideration. This is made possible by the application of two steps that cover the modelling and the refinement of requirements, as illustrated in Fig 2.

User requirements are classified into process requirements and flexibility requirements. While the former relates to the basic operation of the system, the latter is associated with extra requirements that serve in exhibiting a degree of flexibility during operation. This classification serves in the refinement stage by exposing the

---

[1] New and modified artefacts are differentiated from conventional ones by denoting them with thick and dashed boarders respectively.

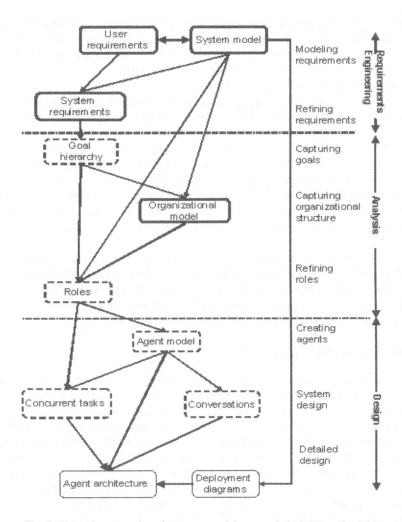

Fig. 2. The software engineering process of the extended MaSE methodology

flexibility requirements to feasibility analysis that can result in the elimination or modification these requirements, which turn out infeasible under consideration of the system constraints.

The following steps illustrate how the system requirements are modelled and refined.

1. **Elicitation and analysis of process requirements**
   This step is concerned with the classification of the user requirements into process and flexibility requirements. Process requirements are further analysed and taken as the initial set of the system requirements.

2. **Elicitation and analysis of systems constraints**
   The goal of this step is to extract the system constraints which results in the generation of the system model. This involves physical as well as behavioural

analysis of the system concerned. While the former considers the static characteristics of the technical as well as the automation system, the latter attempts to study the expected behaviour of the system based on the process requirements in order to extract the relevant constraints.

3. **Analysis of the flexibility requirements**

   At the end, the flexibility requirements which resulted from the classification of the first step undergo a feasibility test based on the generated system model with the corresponding constraints. Since different aspects of flexibility may be catered for, the system modeller is advised to focus on the required aspects of flexibility. For this purpose, this step aims at establishing a view of the required flexibility. Two modelling artefacts of the SysML [15] notation are used for this purpose: view and viewpoint diagrams. While a view captures a certain perspective of the system, a viewpoint embodies the rules for developing a certain view. The refined flexibility requirements serve in complementing the system requirements.

It is worth noting that the generation of the system requirements is a gradual process that takes place by iterating back and forth through the previously mentioned steps. The system requirements are modelled by a requirements diagram based on the SysML notation. One of the advantages of this notation is the support for associating the identified requirements with the corresponding constraints.

4.2 Environmental Support

During the requirements engineering phase, a systematic analysis of the physical structure of the automation system along with the expected behaviour of the system is carried out to extract the enforced constraints. For the sake of this analysis, the system boundaries are identified in the form of a context diagram. By defining the boundaries of the system, a distinction is made between the system and the external environment represented in the form of external terminators that may be affected by or have an effect on the analysed system. These terminators could symbolise external systems, input/output devices, or people. A decision should be made during this stage on whether to model sensors and actuators as part of the system or as external terminators.

Interactions between the system and its external environment are captured in the form of finite state machines (FSMs). The reactive nature of the system is modelled by analysing external events and how they affect the internal state of the system. This analysis of events is performed under consideration of the temporal characteristics of these events and whether they are periodic or sporadic. The resulting FSMs are complemented with a set of events descriptors.

4.3 Adding Timeliness and Concurrency Support

In this section, the extensions that serve in overcoming the drawbacks of MaSE with respect to the support of timeliness and concurrency are highlighted.

4.3.1 Extending Goals

A goal in MaSE represents a "system-level objective" which is formulated in a way that reflects what the system is trying to achieve [16]. Analysing the system from the point of view of "what" the system is trying to achieve fails to explicitly capture the essence of the embedded real-time systems whose correctness depends not only on fulfilling the required goals but also on the timeliness of that fulfillment. It follows that goals of real-time systems have to be specified in a two-fold formulation: *what* is being aimed at, and *when* it is supposed to be achieved. In other words, while identifying goals, it is important to reason about the existence of possible deadlines for these goals. A deadline can either be absolute or relative; periodic or aperiodic; at a specified point in time or during an interval. In addition, a goal may reflect a hard or a soft real-time requirement. For example, one of the goals of a fire alarm system could be the activation of alarm in no more than time t. This reflects a hard requirement which, when violated, could lead to dangerous consequences like the spread of fire. Although not all goals can be assigned temporal parameters, it is recommended to examine possible temporal requirements or constraints and to associate them with the specified goals.

4.3.2 Extending Roles

Roles in MaSE are defined by an abstract model that associates roles with the corresponding goals which they are supposed to achieve. However, this model fails to capture the internal characteristics of roles that help in achieving the assigned goals. Therefore, the role model of the Gaia methodology [17] was adopted and extended to represent these characteristics. Roles in Gaia are defined in terms of schemas compromising four attributes: permissions, activities, protocols, and responsibilities. First, permissions are access rights of this role to software or hardware resources. Second, activities and protocols represent functionalities of this role. While activities can be carried out internal to the role, protocols describe the interaction of this role and other roles. Finally, responsibilities are categorised into liveness and safety properties describing the expected behaviour that an agent playing that role should bring about and the undesired behaviour which should be avoided respectively. Under this field, the temporal constraints associated with the goals assigned to the role of concern are formulated in the form of temporal logic.

The identified role schemas are further analysed to generate a tentative time table by associating the identified activities with the corresponding temporal constraints recorded under the safety field. The dynamics of roles is then modelled by timed Petri nets [18], which support modelling concurrent events and activities and the dynamic behaviour of the role in dealing with them. Temporal requirements recorded by the time table of the role are considered and used to annotate in the associated Petri-net.

The specification of the internal behaviour of each role is described in the concurrent tasks model in section 4.4.2.

4.3.3 Organisational Model

In complement to extending goals and roles with temporal requirements, the whole system should be realised in such a way to guarantee the satisfaction of these requirements at run time. Enforcing temporal requirements at run-time is considered starting from the analysis phase by viewing the system as an organisation of agents similar to human organisations where the freedom of members in selecting their actions is controlled by the policies and rules of their organisation. This organisational view has been proposed by other agent-oriented methodologies like Gaia [19] and

Message [20]. From our point of view, a multi-agent system is conceived as a set of groups sharing a set of goals that they strive to achieve. The system as a whole as well as the individual groups is constrained by policies and rules. In order to allow for the satisfaction of these constraints, additional coordination roles may be identified. The multi-agent system is modelled during the analysis phase by an organisational model that results from the identification of groups, roles, and the governing policies (see Fig. 2). In addition, interaction patterns among organisational members are modelled by timed Petri-nets and incorporated into the organisational model.

4.4 Process-Related Extensions

In addition to the aforementioned extensions which were motivated by the need to tailor MaSE for the embedded real-time systems domain, a number of slight modifications to the process were necessary for the sake of consistency and convenience.

4.4.1 Integration of the System Model

The proposed system model which captures the constraints enforced by the underlying hardware and technical system was integrated in the engineering process. As illustrated in Fig. 2, the generation of several artefacts is based either directly or indirectly on the system model. Referring to this model during the analysis and design of the system is crucial due to the constrained nature of embedded systems.

4.4.2 The Concurrent Tasks Model

This model captures the details of the internal tasks of each role in the form of finite state machines. Traditionally, this model is generated in MaSE during the analysis phase based on the role model. Focusing on the deep details of tasks during the analysis phase can lead to immature design decisions. Consequently, in the proposed extended methodology, this generation of this model is shifted to the design phase.

To further support the specification of temporal requirements, the finite state machines are replaced with timed automata [21]. Adopting timed automata at this stage allows for keeping compatibility with the traditional notation of finite state machines, while at the same time giving the possibility to specify all relevant temporal requirements. These temporal requirements for internal tasks of each role are directly derived from the refined role model as described in section 4.3.2.

4.4.3 Detailed Design

The support of MaSE extends up to the system deployment by capturing the distribution of agents along the available platforms in the form of a UML-based deployment diagram. This step is complemented in the extended methodology by accompanying it with the generation of the agent architecture model to form the detailed design step. The role of the agent architecture diagram in MaSE is the identification of the internal architecture of agent classes. This is either done by defining components from scratch or by the reuse of existing architecture templates [1]. With respect to the embedded systems domain with its various computational platforms and limited resources, such a decision is greatly affected by the deployment platform. Therefore, in the extended MaSE methodology, the agent architecture is generated based on the deployment diagram to design the internal architecture of agents under consideration of the characteristics of the computational platform they are going to be deployed on.

5 Evaluation of the Extended MaSE Methodology

To assess its applicability to embedded systems, the extended MaSE methodology has been evaluated based on an elevator system model. This model consists of two shafts each of which consists of four floors and comprises a cabin that is controlled by a microcontroller. The two microcontrollers are interconnected to each other and to the peripherals by means of a CAN bus. On every floor, four position sensors are available at different levels to control the motion of the cabin of every shaft. These sensors serve in accelerating and decelerating the cabin while moving upwards or forwards to bring it to the correct position on the requested floor.

The traditional control of the elevator system is based on the separate control of each shaft by the corresponding microcontroller. In the case of a microcontroller failure, the corresponding cabin is left uncontrolled which can bring about bad consequences like halting the cabin between floors. Furthermore, if one of the positioning sensors breaks down, the control of the cabin fails to bring it to the required place. Therefore, a flexible control of the elevator model was required to increase the availability and robustness of the system by dynamically detecting and compensating failed components with working ones on the right time.

An agent-based embedded control has been developed for the described elevator model and has shown considerable enhancement of the system availability in case of failures. The development of the software has been guided by the extended MaSE, where the proposed concepts were shown to facilitate the analysis and design processes. A comprehensive coverage of the modelling process is beyond the scope of this work. The evaluation of the proposed concepts is rather illustrated by focusing on the new artefacts.

One of the flexibility requirements states that the system should continue to operate normally in case of the failure of one of the microcontrollers. Such requirement has to be analysed during the requirements engineering phase in light of the physical characteristics of the elevator system incorporated in the system model. By examining the system model, this requirement was shown to be doable based on the capacities and interconnectivity of the microcontrollers. However, further analysis is essential to reason about the implications of fulfilling the requirement concerned. Fig. 3 captures the model resulting from the feasibility analysis of this requirement.

As illustrated in the figure, requirements and constraints were derived to elaborate on and limit the original requirement respectively. For example, one of the derived requirements states that mutual probing between the two microcontrollers is required for the dynamic detection of a failure of one of them. Furthermore, the period of this probing has to be specified in a way that guarantees controlling the cabin whose microcontroller is not working by the other working microcontroller on the right time. As stated by the derived constraint, this period should be calculated from the distance between the consecutive sensors as well as from the velocity of the cabin to insure the

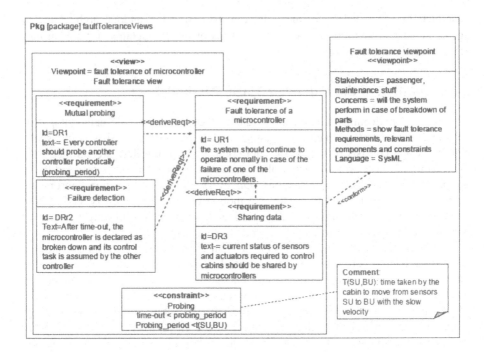

Fig. 3. Illustration of the view/viewpoint modelling of the fault tolerance aspect of flexibility

correct positioning of the cabin on the right time. Physical information like velocity and distances between each two consecutive sensors is collected and recorded in the system model.

The goal hierarchy of the system is depicted in Fig.4. Constraints that were extracted during the requirements engineering phase and incorporated in the requirements diagram are propagated to the corresponding goals in the goal hierarchy. Goal 1.1.1 is an example of a time-constrained goal which states that a passenger request has to be acknowledged within 500 ms. The distinction between hard and soft real-time requirements is visualised by colouring each of them with a different colour.

By examining the goal hierarchy, a number of roles can be identified and classified into two groups. The resulting organizational structure which is part of the organizational model is depicted in Fig.5. As illustrated in the figure, the system consists of two groups of roles. First, the shaft control group is responsible for the basic control of a single shaft through the coordination of three different roles. Second, the flexible control aims at exhibiting the required flexibility that results from the cooperation between the controllers of at least two shafts. The flexible control group is formed by at least two roles of type controller representative. This role has a dependency association with the controller role from the shaft control group. This dependency relation dictates that the controller representative role be combined with the controller role in one agent. Policies governing membership inside groups are stated in the form of group descriptors as part of the organizational model.

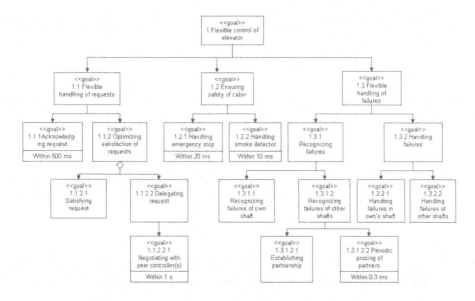

Fig. 4. The goal hierarchy of the elevator control system

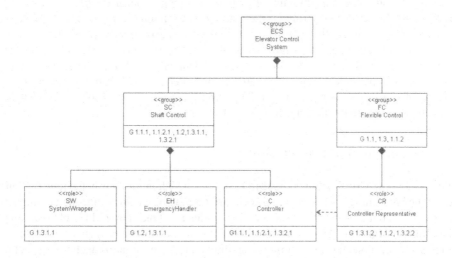

Fig. 5. The organizational structure of the elevator system

To realize the required flexible control, agents controlling their shafts by assuming the controller role form a flexible control group, in which they take on the controller representative role. This role aims at establishing a partnership with the other members of the same flexible control group. The partnership between two agents dictates the mutual probing and data exchange as illustrated by the fault tolerance (Fig.3). The dynamics of this partnership behaviour which is exhibited by the controller representative role is captured by Fig. 6. The two tokens inside the initial

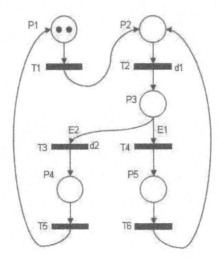

Fig. 6. A Petri-net depicting the behaviour of the controller representative role

state p1 model the number of available partnerships. This means that an agent playing this role is allowed a maximum of two other agents concurrently. Transition t2 represents the action of probing the partner by sending it a message which is controlled by time d1, that can be calculated from the probing period illustrated in Fig.3. One of two alternatives is then possible: either an acknowledgement from the partner is received or not. The former event is denoted by E1 and causes the role to continue in its periodic probing. The latter event is denoted by E2 and causes after the elapse of time-out (d2) the firing of T3. Firing t3 results in reporting the partner as defect and in assuming the control of its cabin.

6   Conclusion and Future Work

The development of flexible embedded systems – which tailor their behaviour to their dynamic environment while meeting their strict temporal requirements – is gaining an increasing attention from academia and industry. One possibility of realising flexibility is through the employment of autonomous software agents which have shown proved potential in exhibiting flexibility in the information technology field. However, the application of agents in the embedded systems domain has been hindered by the lack of concepts and methodologies that equip agents with real-time capabilities that facilitate the development of embedded real-time systems and allow for fulfilling temporal requirements at run time. This limitation of the agent-oriented software engineering has motivated this research whose objective was to extend an agent-oriented methodology for the embedded real-time systems domain.

This work is an extension to a previous study which resulted in the selection of the MaSE methodology for showing the best relative potential for the embedded systems domain based on a criteria-based evaluation specially tailored to the embedded systems domain [7]. During the course of this work, weaknesses of MaSE with respect to the development of flexible embedded real-time systems were identified and analysed. Basically, MaSE was found to suffer from a lack of support to the requirements engineering, the environmental modelling, and real-time specifications. These weaknesses have been tackled by the introduction of a requirements engineering phase which captures the timeliness constraints enforced by the underlying technical system and system hardware Environmental modelling is supported as well during the requirements engineering phase through the identify-cation of the boundaries of the system as a step in analysing its physical characteristics. In addition, timeliness support was proposed by extending goals and roles with real-time specifications. Finally, process-related modifications have been applied to MaSE to allow for the integration of the proposed concepts.

The extended methodology has been applied to the development of an agent-oriented flexible control of an elevator system model. Further application examples from the embedded systems domain are being currently worked on, such as the control for an industrial continuous wood press. Results of this practical evaluation will be used to further improve and refine the extended MaSE methodology.

Acknowledgement

This work has been carried out in the scope of the project AVE [22] on agent-oriented real-time systems. The project AVE is kindly funded by the German Research Council (DFG, Deutsche Forschungsgemeinschaft) under GO 810/15-1 and VO 937/5-1.

References

1. Wood, M.F.: Multiagent systems engineering: A methodology for analysis and design of multiagent systems. Master's thesis, School of Engineering, Air Force Institute of Technology (AU), Wright-Patterson AFB Ohio, USA (2000)
2. Lauber, R., Göhner, P.: Prozessautomatisierung 1, 1st edn. Springer, Heidelberg (1999)
3. Kopetz, H.: Real-Time Systems Design Principles for Distributed Embedded Applications. Kluwer Academic Publishers, Dordrecht (1997)
4. Voros, N.S., et al.: Hardware/Software Co-Design of Complex Embedded Systems. An Approach Using Efficient Process Models, Multiple Formalism Specification and Validation via Co-Simulation. Design Automation for Embedded Systems 8, 5–49 (2003)
5. Gajski, D., et al.: Specification and Design of Embedded Systems. P.T.R. Prentice Hall, Englewood Cliffs (1994)
6. Parunak, H.V.D.: Practical and industrial applications of agent-based systems. Environmental Research Institute of Michigan (ERIM) (1998)
7. Mubarak, H., Göhner, P., Wannagat, A., Vogel-Heuser, B.: Evaluation of agent oriented methodologies for the development of flexible embedded real-time systems in automation. atp international, issue 1/2007, Oldenbourg Industrieverlag, München (2007)
8. Henderson-Sellers, B., Giorgini, P.: Agent-Oriented Methodologies. Idea Group Publishing, Hershey (2005)

9. Zambonelli, F., Jennings, N., Wooldridge, M.: Developing Multiagent Systems: The Gaia Methodology. ACM Transactions on Software Engineering and Methodology, July 2003, vol. 12(3), pp. 317–370 (2003)
10. DeLoach, S.A.: Analysis and Design using MaSE and agentTool. In: 12th Midwest Artificial Intelligence and Cognitive Science Conference (MAICS) (2001)
11. Padgham, L., Winikoff, M.: The Agent-Oriented Software Engineering handbook. In: Bergenti, F., Gleizes, M.-P., Zambonelli, F. (eds.) Methodologies and Software Engineering for Agent Systems, July 2004, ch. 11, pp. 217–234. Kluwer Publishing, Dordrecht (2004)
12. Cossentino, M., Potts, M.: A CASE tool supported methodology for the design of multi-agent systems. In: Proceedings of the 2002 International Conference on Software Engineering Research and Practice (SERP 2002), Las Vegas, USA (June 2002)
13. Balzert, H.: Lehrbuch der Software-Technik. Band 1. 2. Auflage. Elsevier, Amsterdam (2001)
14. Sommerville, I.: Software Engineering, 6th edn. Addison-Wesley, Reading (2001)
15. OMG SysML Specification,
    http://xml.coverpages.org/OMG-SysML-Specification060504.pdf
16. DeLoach, S.A., Wood, M.: Multiagent Systems Engineering: the Analysis Phase. Technical Report, Air Force Institute of Technology, AFIT/EN-TR-00-02 (2000)
17. Wooldridge, M., Jennings, N., Kinny, D.: The Gaia Methodology for Agent-Oriented Analysis and Design. Autonomous Agents and Multi-Agent Systems 3, 285–312 (2000)
18. David, R., Alla, H.: Discrete, continuous, and hybrid Petri nets. Springer, Heidelberg (2005)
19. Zambonelli, F., Jennings, N., Wooldridge, M.: Multi-Agent Systems as Computational Organizations: The Gaia Methodology. In: Henderson-Sellers, B., Giorgini, P. (eds.) Agent-Oriented Methodologies. Idea Group (2005)
20. Garijo, F., et al.: The MESSAGE Methodology for Agent-Oriented Analysis and Design. In: Henderson-Sellers, B., Giorgini, P. (eds.) Agent-Oriented Methodologies. Idea Group (2005)
21. Carlson, J.: Languages and methods for specifying real-time systems, MRTC report, Mälardalen Real-Time Research Centre, Mälardalen University (2002)
22. AVE - Agenten für flexible und verlässliche eingebettete Echtzeitsysteme (2007),
    http://www.ias.uni-stuttgart.de/forschung/projekte/ave.html

Measuring Complexity of Multi-agent Simulations – An Attempt Using Metrics

Franziska Klügl

Department for Artificial Intelligence,
University of Würzburg
Am Hubland, 97074 Würzburg
kluegl@informatik.uni-wuerzburg.de

Abstract. The variety of existing agent-based simulations is overwhelming. However – especially when comparing agent-based simulation to other simulation paradigms, a reference frame is missing that allows characterizing shortly and discriminating between simulation models. In this contribution, I address this problem by introducing metrics for measuring properties of agent-based simulations for finally being able to characterize the complexities involved in developing such a model.

1 Introduction

Multi-agent simulation forms an innovative modeling and simulation paradigm that possesses a great potential for developing models on a level of detail and in application areas, where it was not possible neither to formulate nor to handle models before. Due to the intuitive structure of a model based on the analogy between agents and the active elements in the original system, modeling and simulation may become a research and analysis method for domain experts that ignored such approaches before.

However, there are several drawbacks that hinder people from constructing and experimenting with valid and useful multi-agent models [Klügl et al., 2004]. Most of these drawbacks are consequences of the flexible design and possibly high level of detail which is resulting in formal and conceptual arbitrariness. Meanwhile, there is a countless set of existing agent-based models which can not be compared directly. Re-implementation attempts often fail as the documentation of the models must remain incomplete. This is basically due to the fact that the particular dynamics are depending on modeling decisions on a very detailed level. A full documentation containing all necessary details mostly cannot be given within the scope of a conference or journal contribution. Thus, the actual complexity of a model is hidden.

In this paper, we will introduce one approach for characterizing the complexity of an agent-based simulation model. Sources of complexity reside in the environmental characteristics, the agent structures and dynamics, as well as in the overall organization and interaction design. Instead of discussing the sources for complexity on a coarse level, we will define metrics that can be used for measuring different aspects of agent-based models. The motivation of our attempt for

M. Dastani et al. (Eds.): LADS 2007, LNAI 5118, pp. 123–138, 2008.
© Springer-Verlag Berlin Heidelberg 2008

defining metrics is to analyze and compare aspects of complexity of agent-based simulation. At this point of research, we are not addressing issues like classical software metrics, like deriving production cost etc.

In the remainder of the paper we will shortly characterize agent-based simulation in general, followed by a coarse introduction to software metrics and especially to the state of art in agent software metrics. Before section 5 gives a list of suggestions for metrics of agent-based simulation models, we introduce examples that will be used for their illustration. After a list of example computations, a short conclusion is given.

2   Agent-Based Simulation

Agent-based simulation applies the concept of multi-agent systems to the basic structure of simulation models. Active components are identified as agents and programmed using agent-related concepts and technologies. An agent-based model consists of simulated agents that "live" in a simulated environment in virtual time. The environment may play an important role as it frames the agent behaviors and interactions. The individual environment of an agent may consist of other agents, but also may be enriched with resources or objects without agent characteristics associated with flexible, autonomous behavior [Klügl, 2001]. Agent-based simulations allow the observation of model dynamics on at least two levels: the agent level and the global level. Locality of interaction can be based on explicit representation of space or on abstract non-spatial relationships.

Agent-based simulation forms a very attractive paradigm for several simulation application domains. The most obvious is the simulation of emergent phenomena in social science, traffic, biology, etc. Emergent phenomena are "unforeseen" patterns or global behaviors [Holland, 2000] which are not derivable from properties of its constituents.

The potential of agent-based simulation is not only restricted to emergent phenomena or self-organization studies. It also forms a elegant basic paradigm for variable structure models [Uhrmacher, 1996] with changing agent numbers and agent relations.

Additionally, systems that are quite successfully treated using traditional methods can be modeled using agent-based simulation in a more precise and detailed way. A good example is the influence of human workers onto production throughput, especially integrating "intelligent" strategies to cope with non-standard situations.

Due to its attractiveness, the number of available and published agent-based simulations became uncountable. Thus, some abstract way of characterizing and classifying these models would be very useful not only for developing appropriate design methodologies, identifying best practices of use, but also for evaluation of tools, etc.

3   Metrics for Agent-Based Software

3.1   Metrics in General Software Engineering

The idea of measuring general properties of software has been attracting researcher for many years. Software metrics were proposed for this aim. They can be seen as the mapping from a piece of software to the domain of numbers. Such functions usually characterize certain properties concerning size, complexity, cost, design, etc.

The mostly known metric in software engineering, and basically the one that is generally used, is the Lines Of Code (LOC) metric that forms the basis for different heuristics about duration of implementation/modifications, cost, overall error probabilities, etc. A description of such conventional metrics can be found in [Conde et al., 1986] or [Thaller, 2000]. They also give a introduction to the Halstead metrics that are based on operator and operand numbers for predicting program volume and effort. However, their expressiveness is discussed controversially.

Also in the simulation area, early attempts for defining metrics for simulation models have been tried. For example, [Wallace, 1987] suggests a "Control and Transformation Metric" that basically consists of counting input/output variables per node combined with the number of nodes in some graphical representation.

As multi-agent systems are often implemented using/based on object-oriented programming languages, metrics for those languages may be useful also in the agent context. Structural metrics like weighted methods per class, depth of inheritance tree or coupling between object classes etc., were suggested in [Chidamber and Kemerer, 1994]. Metrics that focus on the coupling between classes can be found in [Briand et al., 1997]. However, as expected, they seem to be too low-level for being meaningful for agent-based software, as well as for agent-based simulation models.

3.2   Metrics in Agent-Based Software Engineering

From sources of complexity in agent-based system design, like discussed in [Wooldridge, 2002], only a small step seems to be necessary to suggestions of measuring complexity. Indeed, there are several suggestions. The work of Wille, Dumke and co-workers ([Wille et al., 2004], [Dumke et al., 2000]) seems to be the most extensive; however they only give a long list of informal metric suggestion without detailing a procedure for computing them. [Far and Wanyama, 2003] introduce metrics for measuring agent complexity in order to facilitate system decomposition based on a survey of sources of complexity for agent-based systems. Gómez-Sanz et al. [Gómes-Sanz et al., 2006] focus on cost estimation. They identify different descriptive variables, e.g. number of rules or number of state machines for characterizing behavior or number of mental entities or number of goals for describing the informational complexity of the agents. Gómez-Sanz et al. relate these variables to the LOC metric based on data from three EU projects, also in their early development phases. Metrics were actually applied resulting in figures that could be related to actual costs generated in these projects.

Particular metrics for measuring performance of organizational design were suggested in [Robby et al., 2006]. Another example for the use of specific metrics in agent-based system engineering is [Woodside, 2001] that evaluates scalability of systems of mobile agents.

However, agent-based simulation models can not be treated like most other agent software at least for two reasons: the first is the relevance of the simulated environment [Klügl et al., 2005], the second is determined by the relation with a reference or original system that has to be guaranteed. This becomes the more cumbersome, the more details the model has integrated. Thus, simplicity of a model is essential as a minimal set of assumptions is a prerequisite for feasible validation. The ability for comparing model complexity is thus central for evaluating model design.

4   Example Application

Before presenting our suggestions for metrics, we shortly give information about models that we will use as examples for illustration throughout the metric introduction and later to test the metrics.

Our first example is the Sugarscape model [Epstein and Axtell, 1996]. Agents move over the discrete Sugarscape map (50×50 cells), locally searching and harvesting sugar. Sugar is a renewable resource carried by every cell characterized by a maximum capacity. Only the current sugar stock is perceivable by the agents within some individual range. The cells are arranged so that two sugar hills exist. Agents possess a sugar-consuming metabolism and personal sugar storage. They always move to the next perceivable cell with maximum sugar stock that is not yet occupied. Agents may starve or die of some age limit and produce offsprings. This is the model that is described in the first chapters of the Epstein & Axtell book. In later chapters, this model is enhanced by a second resource, named spice, as a basis for modeling trade and other social phenomena. We will only deal with basic versions of the model. To show how small details affect the metrics we compare two variants of the Sugarscape model: a first one without maximum age and reproduction, the second with maximum age and sexual reproduction.

The second example we are using for illustration, is the Tribute model of R. Axelrod [Axelrod, 1995]. It consists of 10 agents arranged in a ring. Agents are randomly selected for activation. Activated agents evaluate the vulnerability of direct neighbors or neighbors of committed agents for deciding whether to demand tribute or not. The addressed agent evaluates the costs of fighting and decides for paying tribute or fighting. These actions have effect on the wealth of the involved agents and on their commitment to each other which later influencing their decision making. A global environment distributes a small value of wealth as a basic income after three activations.

These two models can be seen as basic prototypes for agent-based simulations. The Sugarscape model resembles a very simple land-use-type model where agents interact with their local environment in the first instance and only secondly with other agents depending on the resources they have acquired form their environment. Interaction is mainly mediated by the environment. The Tribute model can be seen as a representative for a second kind of models that focus on interaction-induced structures. Locality is modeled based on agent-agent relations represented in network-type structures. Interactions between agents produce some remains in the mental structures of the agents that again influences future interactions.

The third example we use for demonstration is the SBBpedes model. It was developed for a large simulation study of the pedestrian behavior in the SBB railway station Bern [Klügl and Rindsfüser, 2007]. It is particular compared to many other pedestrian simulations as the agent behavior has integrated also simple planning activities beyond pure locomotion. In contrast to the two previously sketched models, it is a model used in a successful real-world application. When entering the railway station, agents determine their destination as far as possible ahead (e.g. they cannot select the door of the train they will board when the train did not yet arrive at the platform) and then construct a coarse plan on the area-level (which stairway to take ...). This plan is executed using some standard collision-free locomotion model. Meanwhile, they continuously monitor their surrounding for determining whether it is still reasonable to pursue the coarse plan. Depending on its current situation, a simulated pedestrian adapts its plan or uses intermediate destinations on a lower level for bypassing obstacles, etc. The simulation reproduced the real situation during the most busiest morning hours with about 80 trains on 12 platforms and all together about 45000 boarding, alighting and transferring travelers. It was used for evaluating layout alternatives and a planned change in train schedule and platform assignment.

5   Suggestions for Metrics

Even this small list of three possible agent-based simulation models shows that there is a variety of dimensions for characterizing them. Examples start with environmental structures, to organizational forms, agent architectures, but also in more technical terms of agent interaction, communication language... Thus, the question arises, whether a detailed, yet informal description may help characterizing the complexities involved in the design and implementation of such an agent-based simulation. Metrics on the other hand, have the advantage of being objective and exact – if they are appropriate for capturing the intended properties. Model metrics – in analogy to software metrics – can be seen as functions that map the model to a numeric value that characterizes some property of the model.

In the following, we distinguish between overall system-level metrics, metrics for measuring the complexity of the environment. These metrics that are relevant for the complete model, will be followed by agent-level metrics and interaction metrics. Whereas the first refer to some more standard-like metrics, the other three directly address the three basic aspects of an agent-based simulation model: Environment, Agents and Interactions.

5.1   System-Level and Environmental Metrics

On the overall system level one may tackle metrics that are not surprising, starting from the population sizes and their dynamics. However, even those metrics are not trivial as their values are scenario-dependent. That means, the metrics can only be used to characterize one particular, completely specified simulation run, for characterizing a complete model, especially with stochastic elements - means over more than one run have to be used.

NAT: Number of Agent Types is a measure for heterogeneity of the model. It basically resembles the number of classes like an object-oriented metric and can be easily computed in simulation models, respectively in their implementations. However, there are different sources of heterogeneity for agent-based simulation models. With NAT we refer to the most basic one: structural differences. When every agents is using a different architecture for reasoning, then NAT equals the number of agents. When heterogeneity is based on different parameter values, the NAT metric is not very significant. For example, if parameters like thresholds or weights are set individually by some random process, they may effectively produce completely different behavior; yet all agents structurally belong to the same class and $NAT = 1$. This is the case for the Sugarscape model, where actually $k = 6$ different perception radius' may be combined with 6 different metabolism value, resulting in 36 different agents. In the SBBpedes model *all* agents are different as individual desired speed is a continuous value and drawn from a random distribution. The Tribute model is particular, in the beginning all agents are actually the same, however due to random activation and flexible decision making, the situation may become fully heterogenous. Thus, some additional metric might be interesting - especially in the case of adaptive and learning agents that counts agents that are in any form different.

NRT: Number of Resource Types like the NAT-Metric, but for passive entities of the environment.

MNA: Maximum Number of Agents is probably the most obvious measure for the size of the simulated situation – the maximum number of agents that are concurrently present during a simulation run. There is a conceptual problem when the maximum number is only adopted at the beginning of the simulation. This happens e.g. when the question is tackled how many agent can be supported by a particular environment like in Sugarscape. In such cases, one may doubt the meaningfulness of such a measure as the number of agents is intentionally set too high in the beginning. The number of agents to which the simulation is converging to, would make more sense.

Another idea may be to use the sum of agents that are existing in the simulated environment over the complete simulation time. In the SBBpedes example, the maximum number of agents concurrently simulated is about 9000, the overall number sums up to about 45000. Also this difference accents the dynamics of a system.

MNR: Minimum Number of Resources is the analogue to the maximum number of agents. We list the minimum here as often the question is addressed what minimum number of resources is needed to support a maximum number of agents.

One may argue that only resources should be counted that may be actually used by an agent – see e.g. in the Sugarscape world there are 2500 cells, but a not negligible share of them does not carry any sugar (cell capacity equals zero). In some simulations, inanimate objects are used for decorating the environment in order to produce nice animations. Whereas in the first example the relation between cells with and without sugar may be interesting, decoration elements should be ignored.

MDA: Maximum Delta of Agent Population is a measurement for the variability of population numbers over a given interval of time, typically one simulation step. It forms the rate of population change, thus it is a measure of model dynamics that is mostly only measurable during a simulation run. In models that contain probabilistic aspects related to agent lives, the actual dynamics may vary from time interval to interval as well as between runs. Also here, the initial phase with potentially higher death rates should be distinguished from the converged state.

MDR: Maximum Delta of Resource Population is the analogue to the MDA metric.

ARR: Agent-Resource Relation is the number of agents divided by the number of resources. Here mean and variation are interesting.

MRS: Maximum Resource Status Size. Resources may be differently complex. Obstacles may only possess some purely spatial attributes like extent, form and position. Other resource objects may carry sophisticated information. This metric counts the maximum number of status variables of resources. The question what are status variables, may arise. In the simple Sugarscape model, a cell possesses only one status variables, namely the sugar storage. Every cell needs two additional parameter, namely the growth rate and maximum sugar capacity. Although the latter two influence the status, they are parameter, no state variables. The state of a resource may also be used as data container for agents; for example in the SBBpedes simulation (see below) a train is a resource that carries data about length or number of doors which would be counted as parameters. On the other hand, a train object is also used to manage information about its travelers. How many have already arrived at their goal? Information like this forms the status of a train resource.

MRP: Maximum Resource Parameter. This metric computes the maximum number of parameter that influence the values of the status variables. Following the examples of MRS, the growth rate or maximum stock form parameters. Other examples are initial values. Resources may also carry (static) information used not to update the status of the resource, but used by agents to guide their behavior according to this information. This constant information items are also subsumed under this metric.

NASh: Number of Agent Shapes. This is a measure for spatial complexity. How many different geometries may agents possess? This makes only sense in simulation with map-based spatial representation.

NRSh: Number of Resource Shapes is the analogue to the NASh metric: How many different geometries do occur in the set of resources?

5.2 Agent Metrics

Whereas the metrics above aim at measuring population size and environmental complexity, the agents and their interactions naturally form another source of complexity for an agent-based model that is worthwhile being measured.

All following metrics are measures for individual agents. Thus, for characterizing a complete model, they have either to be aggregated or computed for a "typical" agent. Aggregation can consist of averaging over all agents, using the maximum or minimum, or simply summing up.

ACR: Architectural Complexity Rank. Complexity of the agent architecture might be a reasonable measure. Unfortunately, indicators for it are not obvious despite of several existing classifications for agent architectures. We suggest to simply classify the architectures into one of three sets along their complexity and use this rank as a metric:
   1. **Behavior-describing architectures** are all rule-based structures that aim at reproducing individual behavior based on directly describing it. They do not claim to resemble actual cognitive processes of decision making but are more like a black box description of observed behavior. Examples are rule- and activity-based descriptions of behavior with hardwired behavior representations.
   2. **Behavior-configuring architectures** are quite common in agent-based system as they combine pre-defined behavior structure with a flexible goal- or utility-based architecture. Behavior is described using task- or activity representations like skeletal plans. For action selection and thus actual production of agent behavior, the appropriate plan-like data structures are selected and refined based on some goals and interpreted for fitting them to the current situation of the agent. This is actually the category of BDI architectures.
   3. **Behavior-generating architectures** are using traditional AI planning from first principles. Basic representation is a set of operators with pre- and post-conditions which are selected and ordered for achieving a particular goal state. Thus, the agent generates a sequence of actions without predefined skeletons.
APM: Action Plasticity Metric. For being really sensitive, the ACR metric has to be combined with additional measures for describing the behavioral plasticity and variability. Plasticity denotes the potential adaptivity of behavior in reaction to environmental influences. This predominantly means the extent of the behavioral repertoire and the flexibility in its application. For discrete actions, this metric is computed by simply counting possible actions. When actions are parameterized, the range of the parameters has to be multiplied. As an illustration take the following example of a simple pedestrian simulation: the agents may move with a standard speed, that means *move* is one atomic action without further need for refinement. In

addition, the agents may have the possibility to turn in reaction to obstacles. The angle is a parameter for the turn action. If e.g. only turning actions with a angle of $45°$ and $90°$ in both directions are allowed, the action space metric would overall return $1 + 1 * 4 = 5$. If the angle has a continuous range, the metric would return ∞. Unfortunately, an additional continuous parameter would not affect the outcome of the metric. In this case, it could be more descriptive to introduce an additional metric describing the basic types of actions. Yet, the idea of APM consists in denoting the most basic degree of freedom in action selection.

SPK: Size of Procedural Knowledge. Another metric influencing behavior plasticity is the size of the procedural knowledge that is available for an agent. Its computation must be dependent on the particular form of architecture. One may think of several options for defining this metric aiming at finding a more or less unified definition for the different architecture classes. However, we did not find a solution that would fulfil this requirement.

Thus, we reduce the computation of SPK to the following computations: In behavior-describing architectures, SPK equals the number of rules that define the agent behavior. In behavior-configuring architectures, the number of plan skeletons is counted, including explicitly represented partial plan skeletons when they are arranged in some hierarchical structure. In these two cases, a set of additional metrics would be useful for characterizing the complexity of the rules or plan skeletons themselves, as the rules, as well as the plan skeletons may be differently complex. These metrics may count the number of conditions, generality of conditions, number of branching elements in the skeleton, etc. Metrics for rule-based systems were already developed in the early 90ies, see for example [Chen and Suen, 1994].

The computation of the SPK of behavior-generating architectures also needs some discussion: The number of possible action sequences would be the first idea for a definition. However, it would be hardly comparable to the number of plan skeletons as the latter may contain more than one paths per skeleton according to conditioned expansion in hierarchical representations. Also, the number of operators would not be a good measure, as it does not represent the potential complexity of the procedural knowledge of the agent. Despite of the potential combinatoric explosion, there seems to be no other reasonable way than to define the SPK for behavior-generating architectures as the number of reasonable possible action sequences.

NCR: Number of Cognitive Rules. Denotes the share of actions that affect the internal beliefs or status of an agent. One may also call these cognitive rules responsible for updating the mental models. They can be an interesting indicator for the reasoning complexity of the agent, although NCR is ignoring the variety of used data structures and algorithms. At least, one may derive a measure for the independence of actions from that information – as far as the environment is not used as an external memory. However, in general the usefulness of this metric can be doubted in the current form of vague definition.

5.3   Interaction-Related Metrics

Interactions between agents express dynamics and structure on the agent-system level beyond mere system size.

SPII: Sum of Public Information Items. A good measure for the size of the external interface seems to be the number of concurrently publicly accessible variables or information items.

In the Tribute model, the wealth and commitments of every agent is common knowledge. That means, every agent knows about the wealth and the commitment status of every other agent. Consequently, we have a value of $1 \times n + n \times (n-1)$ as the available information items for a single agent; For $n = 10$, the resulting metric returns 100.

Sugarscape is another example that illustrates the dilemma of this approach. Here, interaction is strictly local. Every agent interacts only with its local neighbors or the cells within its perception radius. It can only perceive the current sugar stock of such a cell. Thus, there is no global knowledge, but information is accessible in general as far as the cell is near enough to the agents position. In Sugarscape, an agent may just perceive the sugar storage of cells within their range (only in the four directions) – which consists of an area of $4 \times k$ cells. With $k = 6$ and 300 agents- this would mean that for every agent $SPII = 24$, and in the sum 7200 data items are concurrently available for all.

This kind of metric becomes more meaningful, if we divide this value by the number of actually available data containers. In the Tribute model this would result in the same value as all data units are accessible for all agents at every point in time. In the Sugarscape model we have to divide it by the number of all available status units. This results in $7200/2500 = 2.88$ - basically this means that with the initial agent numbers the intersection between two sets of perceived sugar cells contains almost 3 cells. However, after only a few steps, the population is decreasing and concentrating on the cells with higher sugar values. In a population of only 50 agents, this measure would result in a value of $50 \times (4 \times 6)/2500 = 0.48$. When the relation between environmental information and agent needs is lower than 1, it indicates that situations may occur where the perception radius of the agents do not intersect. However, as the agents concentrate on a small region, this measure might be misleading.

One might suspect that this metric might not work for purely message-based multi-agent systems. However, it is a question of abstraction. The SPII metric deals with information units independently from their mode of transfer.

NEA: Number of External Accesses. In addition to the number of available information units, an interesting property is how often external data is accessed by the agent in its behavior definition. Basically this is an abstraction from some message counting metric. Especially together with the SPII metric, this metric promises to form an interesting measure for the amount of external information that the agent may actually processes per time step. It nicely discriminates between highly interactive simulations and models where the agents only once access information and then process this potentially outdated information.

NAR: Number of Agent References. A metric addressing the coherence of the agent system is the mean number of agent references stored in the internal models. This is basically a measure for the degree of connection within the agent system. As this value may be varying over time, we may distinguish between NAR-mean and NAR-stdev. Also, minimum and maximum number of references as well as the time-related delta of these values may be interesting as they indicate the dynamics of the system in terms of relations between agents.

NRR: Number Resource References. The number of references that an agent memorizes for addressing resources. Using this metric, we can e.g. distinguish between models contain more or less detailed elements of ownership.

NMA: Number of Mobility Actions. This metric only makes sense when there is an actual map where the agents may change their local position and thus their immediate surroundings. It is measured in number of move actions per agent per time step. In combination of the SPII and NEA metrics, it shows the dynamics of relations.

This compilation of suggestions for metrics in agent-based simulations covers a variety of relevant aspects, yet is far for being complete. Metrics quantifying aspects of protocols and conversations are missing. Examples may be the number of conversations, the mean number of message per conversation, etc. Such metrics would support some form of higher level description of interactions. Another area that is under-represented are more organization-structure oriented metrics, like the number of roles, size of groups, etc. Another ides might be the distinction along different relations (acquaintance, dominance,...) between the agents.

One aspect that complicates the computation of relevant quantities are variations of a model for experimentation. As mentioned before, the numbers of agents and resources, etc. are modified during experimentations, the maximum number of agents depends on the concrete environmental conditions of the scenario, etc.

5.4   Feedback Loops and Other Missing Aspects

Although the metrics given above are attractive due to their simplicity and option for automatic, non-human-done computation, one may wonder whether they really capture the actually necessary aspects.

Even for humans, the existence of feedback loops – especially multi-level loops – is hard to determine just based on a static model specification or implementation. Every change of a status value, every interaction can be part of an feedback loop. Hidden feedback loops form the backbone for every complex problem.

If the number of positive and negative feedback loops, sub-divided into one-level and multi-level feedback loops could be determined based on human intelligence, these numbers would be really useful as a metric for complexity. Would be, because it is quite unclear how this should happen for agent-based simulations. Feedback-based analysis can be found in the *System Dynamics* methodology [Forrester, 1961]. However, such macro models are much less complex than agent-based approaches.

There are two additional aspects that we only treated very coarsely: Metrics for adaptive agents and a more detailed elaboration of metrics related to interaction dynamics. However, we suppose that these are even more complex than the metrics that we proposed there.

5.5 Language-Specific Metrics

Using traditional programming languages for implementing an agent-based simulation, clearly only general metrics can be applied. If the simulation is implemented based on a particular framework and architecture, more specific and meaningful metrics can be defined. This specially applies to the metrics related to the agents action selection module: APM (Action Plasticity Metric), the SPK (Size of Procedural Knowledge) and the NCR (Number of Cognitive Rules). However, without reference to specific architectures, the identification of such variables is quite hard. Sometimes, it even violates the requirement of objectivity and automatic computation.

Thus, in an agent-based system implemented using the JADE framework (*jade.tilab.com*), the number of *behaviors* of agent may be interesting. Such behaviors form the basic structure for behavior definition. Also for agents using the PRS architecture [Ingrand et al., 1992] or one of its legacies like JACK (*www.agent-software.com*), the number and size of Knowledge Areas per agent determines the complexity and sophisticated-ness of agent behavior. Similar metrics may be meaningful for agents designed based on the RAP architecture [Firby, 1989]. Analogous metrics may be found in any agent system and simulation when it is based on some form of high-level structure.

This is also the case with SeSAm (*www.simsesam.de*) which is used as implementation basis for all example computations in the next section. We did this to avoid tampering based on different implementation styles. In SeSAm, the behavior of agents is structured along a graph, named "reasoning engine" that contains activities – which are some form of script – and rules that are used for controlling the transition between activities. The state of an agent consists of a set of state variables with potentially complex data structures. Thus, in SeSAm, among others, the number of parallel reasoning engines, number and size of activities and rules per graph, number of variables, may provide interesting measures of the size and complexity of a model. A set of specific metrics for SeSAm has been suggested in [Bülow, 2005].

5.6 Test and Assessment

For demonstrating potential of metrics for agent-based simulation, we want to give some example computations for the models shortly described in section 4. For reducing effects of potentially hidden implementation details, all models were implemented using the same simulation environment: We used the above mentioned SeSAm, as it provides a convenient high-level languages combined with visual programming. An additional reason was, that we were quite familiar with the modeling facilities provided by it. Thus, re-implementation implied minor effort for the Sugarscape and Tribute model. The SBBpedes project was originally implemented using SeSAm.

The results of our computations are shown in table 1. One has to keep in mind that we did not aim at studying the outcome of the respective models, but we were searching for general measures of complexity for characterizing these models.

One may notice large differences in the size of the simulation in terms of agent numbers. In contrast to Sugarscape, one may notice that the SBBpedes model does not converge, the high number of agents is really an extreme value. However, for determining the number of agents where the situation converges, simulation runs had to be done – due to the random processes, the runs had to be repeated several times and simulation run times are depending on the number of agents.

One may see that the Sugarscape models show an interesting population dynamic. The number of agents is dynamic - with a higher dynamic in variant II

Table 1. Application of metrics onto three example model implementations. All models contain stochastic elements, therefore at some places only rough numbers are given, when the exact number slightly varies between two runs.

Metric	Sugarscape I	Sugarscape II	Tribute	SBBpedes
NAT	1	1	1	1+4
NRT	1	1	0	5
Initial NA	300	300	10	110
MNA	ca. 15 (conv.)	ca 1350	10	ca. 9000
MNR	2500	2500	0	140
MDA	-13, +0	-40, +74	-0, +0	-14,+21
MDR	0	0	0	0
ARR	0.12	0.56	indef.	36
MRS	1	1	0	11
MRP	2	2	0	16
NASh	1	1	1	1 + 250
NRSh	1	1	0	250
ACR	1	1	1	1+3
APM	26	27	12	∞
SPK	2	4	4	26
NCR	0	0	2	3 (plan) + 2 (move)
SPII	2.88	2.88	100	0
NEA	24 (for $k = 6$)	24	9+9=18	min. 1
NAR	0	2+23	9	0
NRR	1	1	0	1 to 8 (planned path)
NMA	1	1	0	1
SeSAm-NA	2	5	8	23
SeSAm-NR	3	7	11	59

than variant I, even higher than in the SBBpedes model. The Tribute model does not possess any form of explicit population dynamics. However, some agents become incapable of acting due to their low wealth, even when they are activated they cannot decide for fighting as they simply cannot afford to do. This is not expressed by the current set of metrics - a metric denoting the effective number of active agents would be necessary. An interesting detail is the missing resource dynamics in the SBBpedes model ($MDR = 0$). This shows an implementation detail: Trains are always existing throughout the complete simulation run. First to wait for activation, then secondly for waiting until all travelers have arrived at their particular destination.

Concerning the agent-level metrics, one may see that the agent model of SBBpedes is slightly larger than the other two and indeed the design and implementation was quite effortful especially for selecting the appropriately parameterized action.

Large differences can be found in the between the values of the different metrics in the third part concerning agent-interaction metrics. One may notice that here the entries of the SBBpedes model are mostly zero whereas the Tribute model, as well as the Sugarscape contain much higher values. However, the numbers support the characterization that we initially used to introduce these two models: Sugarscape as the example for a land-use model, Tribute as a merely interaction-based model concerning the emergence of political actors.

The SBBpedes model is larger than the others in terms of mere agent numbers as well as in extend of agent behavior. However, the interaction between agents is comparatively simple. No agent possess explicit information about other agents within its belief model. Direct interactions are seldom.

The main question that remains is - of what use are these numbers? Up to now, the metrics can be used for demonstrating "areas" (in terms of subsets of metrics) of higher complexity relative to other models. We have seen that the metrics are actually able to discriminate between models. For an absolute complexity measure, the set of isolated metrics has to be re-considered, potentially extended and solicited. Then, these basic metrics have to be weighted and combined resulting in a characteristic that can be used for supporting the management of a simulation study, for estimating simulation effort or for evaluating simulation tools.

6   Conclusion

What does complexity of an agent-based model in relation to a user (modeler, stake-holder, domain expert, etc.) mean? Basically it consists of understandability for the human and is connected with the predictability of the model dynamics and output. Understandability means clarity of structures and relations. It is also influenced by size and heterogeneity of the individual agents as well as of the overall system. Predictability refers to the effort and skills of the modeler needed for traceability of behavior and interactions. These are properties that we tried to address using the abstraction mechanism of metrics.

Despite of a lot of scientific effort, software metrics are still controversially discussed in practice. We suggested a set of metrics and illustrated them by applying them to a set of existing, and partially well-known models. Although we concentrated on mere size-related metrics, their application allowed to expose details of complexity characterizing the individual models. The metrics also allow to discriminate between two slightly different variants of the Sugarscape model. Consequently, one may state that this set of metrics seems to be a good starting point towards evaluating and comparing agent based simulation models.

Clearly, several aspects were left to future efforts. The next steps involve the development of more dynamics-related metrics and the application to more simulation models for finally reaching the goal of a short and precise characterization of agent-based simulation model complexity.

References

[Axelrod, 1995] Axelrod, R.: A model of the emergence of new political actors. In: Gilbert, N., Conte, R. (eds.) Artificial Societies: The Computer Simulation of Social Life, p. 19. UCL Press (1995)

[Briand et al., 1997] Briand, L., Devanbu, P., Melo, W.: An investigation into coupling measures for C++. In: Proceedings of the 1997 (19th) International Conference on Software Engineering, pp. 412–421 (1997)

[Bülow, 2005] Bülow, M.: Metriken für Multiagentensimulationen in SeSAm. Master's thesis, Institute of Computer Science, University of Würzburg (2005)

[Chen and Suen, 1994] Chen, Z., Suen, C.Y.: Complexity metrics for rule-based expert systems. In: International Conference on Software Maintenance, 1994, pp. 382–391 (1994)

[Chidamber and Kemerer, 1994] Chidamber, S.R., Kemerer, C.F.: A metrics suite for object oriented design. IEEE Trans. Software Engineering 20, 476–493 (1994)

[Conde et al., 1986] Conde, S.D., Dunsmore, H.E., Shen, V.Y.: Software Engineering Metrics and Models. Benjamin/Cummings (1986)

[Dumke et al., 2000] Dumke, R.R., Koeppe, R., Wille, C.: Software agent measurement and self-measuring agent-based systems. Technical Report 11, Fakultät für Informatik, Uni. Madgeburg (2000)

[Epstein and Axtell, 1996] Epstein, J.M., Axtell, R.: Growing Artificial Societies. Social Science from the Bottom Up. Random House Uk Ltd. (1996)

[Far and Wanyama, 2003] Far, B.H., Wanyama, T.: Metrics for agent-based software development. In: IEEE CCECE 2003. Canadian Conference on Electrical and Computer Engineering, May 2003, vol. 2, pp. 1297–1300 (2003)

[Firby, 1989] Firby, J.: Adaptive Execution in Complex Dynamic Worlds. PhD thesis, Yale University (1989)

[Forrester, 1961] Forrester, J.: Industrial Dynamics. Pegasus Communications (1961)

[Gómes-Sanz et al., 2006] Gómes-Sanz, J.J., Pavón, J., Garijo, F.: Estimating cost for agent-oriented software. In: Müller, J., Zambonelli, F. (eds.) AOSE 2005. LNCS, vol. 3950, pp. 218–230. Springer, Heidelberg (2006)

[Holland, 2000] Holland, J.H.: Emergence. From Chaos to Order. Oxford University Press, Oxford (2000)

[Ingrand et al., 1992] Ingrand, F.F., Georgeff, M.P., Rao, A.S.: An architecture for real-time reasoning and system control. IEEE Expert 7(6), 34–44 (1992)

[Klügl, 2001] Klügl, F.: Multiagentensimulation – Konzepte, Anwendungen, Tools. Addision Wesley (2001)

[Klügl et al., 2005] Klügl, F., Fehler, M., Herrler, R.: About the role of the environment in multi-agent simulations. In: Weyns, D., Parunak, H.V.D., Michel, F. (eds.) E4MAS 2004. LNCS (LNAI), vol. 3374, pp. 127–149. Springer, Heidelberg (2005)

[Klügl et al., 2004] Klügl, F., Oechslein, C., Puppe, F., Dornhaus, A.: Multi-agent modelling in comparison to standard modelling. Simulation News Europe 40, 3–9 (2004)

[Klügl and Rindsfüser, 2007] Klügl, F., Rindsfüser, G.: Large-scale agent-based pedestrian simulation. In: Müller, J.P., Petta, P., Klusch, M., Georgeff, M. (eds.) MATES 2007. LNCS (LNAI), vol. 4687, pp. 145–156. Springer, Heidelberg (2007)

[Robby et al., 2006] Robby, DeLoach, S.A., Kolesnikov, V.A.: Using design metrics for predicting system flexibility. In: Baresi, L., Heckel, R. (eds.) FASE 2006. LNCS, vol. 3922, pp. 184–198. Springer, Heidelberg (2006)

[Thaller, 2000] Thaller, G.E.: Software-Metriken – einsetzen, bewerten, messen, 2nd edn. Verlag Technik (2000)

[Uhrmacher, 1996] Uhrmacher, A.M.: Object-oriented and agent-oriented simulation-implications for social science applications. In: Doran, J., Gilbert, N., Müller, U., Troitzsch, K.G. (eds.) Social Science Micro Simulation- A Challenge for Computer Science. Lecture Notes in Economics and Mathematics, pp. 432–447. Springer, Berlin (1996)

[Wallace, 1987] Wallace, J.C.: The control and transformation metric: Toward the measurement of simulation model complexity. In: Thesen, A., Grant, H., Kelton, W.D. (eds.) Proceedings of the 1987 Winter Simulation Conference, pp. 597–603 (1987)

[Wille et al., 2004] Wille, C., Brehmer, N., Dumke, R.R.: Software measurement of agent-based systems - an evaluation study of the agent academy. Technical Report Preprint No. 3, Faculty of Informatics, University of Magdeburg (2004)

[Woodside, 2001] Woodside, M.: Scalability metrics and analysis of mobile agent systems. In: Wagner, T.A., Rana, O.F. (eds.) AA-WS 2000. LNCS (LNAI), vol. 1887, p. 234. Springer, Heidelberg (2001)

[Wooldridge, 2002] Wooldridge, M.: An Introduction to Multi-Agent Systems. John Wiley, Chichester (2002)

DCaseLP: A Prototyping Environment for Multi-language Agent Systems

Viviana Mascardi, Maurizio Martelli, and Ivana Gungui

Dipartimento di Informatica e Scienze dell'Informazione – DISI,
Università di Genova, Via Dodecaneso 35, 16146, Genova, Italy
{mascardi,martelli}@disi.unige.it, iva_sim@yahoo.it

Abstract. This paper describes DCaseLP, a multi-language prototyping environment for Multi-Agent Systems. DCaseLP provides tools, languages, and methodological suggestions for engineering a MAS prototype from the late requirement analysis to the prototype implementation and testing. Full support for validating the MAS model by running the prototype in the JADE platform is offered. DCaseLP and its ancestor, CaseLP, have been employed to develop many applications in collaboration with Italian companies, thus demonstrating the feasibility of the proposed approach.

Keywords: Multi-Agent System, Multi-Language, Agent-Oriented Software Engineering, Rapid Prototyping.

1 Introduction

The correct and efficient engineering of heterogeneous, distributed, open, and dynamic applications is one of the technological challenges faced by Agent-Oriented Software Engineering (AOSE). Researchers and practitioners agree that engineering a software system involves a non negligible amount of risk. The client requirements may be unstable, unclear, or incomplete, and this increases the risk to develop systems that will not match the client's desiderata. The feasibility of algorithms, be they developed from scratch for the project, or adapted to it, may not be completely known in advance, raising the risk to use algorithms that, in some scenarios, do not behave as expected. The adequacy of the output of the design stage for the implementation stage, may need to be validated in some systematic way, in order to ensure that the systems' functionalities devised during the design stage are met by the implemented system. Ignoring these and many other risks (see [4]) may cause enormous losses of time and money. According to The Standish Group report published in 1995 [26],

> *the average is only 16.2% for software projects that are completed on-time and on-budget. In the larger companies, the news is even worse: only 9% of their projects come in on-time and on-budget. And, even when these projects are completed, many are no more than a mere shadow of their original specification requirements.*

The risk for a project to fall among those that fail meeting their requirements on time, budget, and functionalities, is very high. This is particularly true when the system

M. Dastani et al. (Eds.): LADS 2007, LNAI 5118, pp. 139–155, 2008.

to develop is as complex as a MAS. However, the risk intrinsic to the development of a MAS could be mitigated by following a prototyping approach.

A prototype is not something to be delivered to a client, usually. One of the reasons is precisely the purpose of the prototype: proof of concept. It intends to show the client what the final software product will look like, in order to gain a full understanding of the client's requirements before starting the implementation of the product. Developing a working prototype does not require a great deal of time. This means early availability of parts of a product that the customer can evaluate, and the opportunity to detect any possible inaccuracies. Early detection of inadequacies allows to reduce development costs, and indeed the construction of prototypes is a well known technique for early detection. The iterative prototyping process ensures the flexibility to revise the requirements or critical design choices several times before committing to any final decision. Finally, efficiency is not a key feature: a prototype does not need to be extremely efficient, and therefore it can be produced using (not efficient) methods and tools that are suitable for validation of the initial requirements, but not necessarily for the implementation of the final product. Of course, one has to trade off between the cost of prototype development and the risks being considered.

In this paper we describe the **DCaseLP** framework for MAS prototyping. **DCaseLP** stands for *Distributed Complex Applications Specification Environment based on Logic Programming*. Although initially born as a logic-based framework, as the acronym itself suggests, **DCaseLP** has evolved into a multi-language prototyping environment that integrates both imperative (object-oriented) and declarative (rule-based and logic-based) languages, as well as graphical ones. The rationale behind **DCaseLP** is that MAS development requires engineering support for a diverse range of non-functional properties, such as understandability of the MAS at various conceptual levels, integrability of heterogeneous agent architectures, usability, re-usability, and testability.

We may rephrase B. Henderson-Sellers[1] and observe that, in order to support these properties, there are three options:

1. have a suite of inflexible methodologies, each specifically designed for supporting one or more properties, in an ad-hoc way, or
2. have a comprehensive methodology and permit a level of freedom for adapting it to the properties it must support, or
3. have a comprehensive framework that permits flexible instantiation and methodology assembly.

Creating either one pre-determined set of inflexible AOSE methodologies (option 1), or one monolithic and all-comprehensive methodology (option 2) to support all the properties relevant for MAS engineering is not feasible. Rather, we expect that different methods and approaches, harmonised in a coherent way within a unique framework, will be suitable for modelling, verifying, or implementing various properties. By providing the MAS developer with an open set of languages, where new languages can

---

[1] *Agent-oriented methodologies – the value of method engineering*, presentation held at Agentsvic, Melbourne, 2004, available at
http://www.agents.org.au/20040827AOSE-Brian.pdf

be plugged if needed, and allowing for the choice of the most suitable one to model, implement, and test each property, **DCaseLP** moves one step towards the modular approach to AOSE proposed by [17,18]. These ideas, that we applied since the beginning of our project in 1996,[2] are currently gaining a wide consensus also for the final product development and maintenance stages [16].

The languages and tools that **DCaseLP** integrates are **UML** and an **XML**-based language for the analysis and design stages, **Java**, **JESS** and **tuProlog** for the implementation stage, and **JADE** for the testing stage. Software libraries for translating **UML** class diagrams into code and for integrating **JESS** and **tuProlog** agents into the **JADE** platform are also provided.

There are many motivations behind supporting these languages as part of an integrated environment:

1. The ability to describe the MAS's architecture and interaction strategies in **UML**[3] may be exploited by any average skilled software developer who wants to generate code starting from those diagrams. He/she needs to know how to draw **UML** class and sequence diagrams, without needing a deep knowledge of the language in which code is generated. In fact, the generated code contains comments that explain what should be added inside it in order to make it executable, and make code completion easy to be faced.

2. **JESS**, the **Java Expert System Shell** [13], allows the developer to supply knowledge in the form of declarative rules that are processed by means of the Rete algorithm [11]. It is a very expressive and concise language, suitable for implementing lightweight and fast expert agents that may easily access and reason about **Java** objects.

3. Computational logic and logic programming in particular are very suitable to implement sophisticated, self-aware agents able to reason about themselves and the other agents in the MAS [20]. **tuProlog** [10] provides a light Prolog engine written in **Java**. It may be used to build rational agents that behave according to the "strong" agent notion, namely entities conceptualised in terms of mental attitudes and able to perform some reasoning about their mental state.

4. Finally, as far as the importance and usefulness of **JADE** is concerned, we may quote [2] that describes **JADE** as *"probably the most widespread agent-oriented middleware in use today."*

The paper is organised in the following way: Section 2 puts **DCaseLP** into its research context by analysing six tools that share a similar aim; Section 3 discusses the AOSE stages that **DCaseLP** addresses; Section 4 describes the libraries that **DCaseLP** provides to the user; Section 5 discusses the most recent applications of **DCaseLP**; and finally Section 6 evaluates **DCaseLP** with respect to the related work, and concludes.

---

[2] At that time, the project name was **CaseLP** – without *D*, since no support to distribution was given yet.

[3] At the time of writing, only the translation from **UML** class diagrams to code is fully supported by **DCaseLP**. We have already developed a separate translator from sequence diagrams to **Prolog** agent skeletons, `http://www.disi.unige.it/person/MascardiV/Software/WEST2EAST.html`, and we are currently integrating it in **DCaseLP**.

2   Related Work

The features that better characterise **DCaseLP** are:

- support to MAS development, from requirements to implementation and testing, thanks to the availability of libraries that semi-automatise the generation of code starting from high-level specifications;
- support to multi-language development, thanks to the availability of libraries that allow the integration of different languages within the same middleware, **JADE**;
- support to AOSE, thanks to the identification of a set of engineering steps to face during MAS development, and the availability of tools and languages for facing them.

In this section we relate **DCaseLP** to its research context by analysing six toolkits that offer a good support to these features. An evaluation of these tools and a comparison with **DCaseLP** are given in Section 6, after **DCaseLP** has been fully described.

AgentTool and AgentTool III. **AgentTool** [8] is a **Java**-based graphical development environment created by the Multiagent & Cooperative Robotics Laboratory. Currently, there is an ongoing project for releasing **AgentTool III** (**aT3**, http://macr.cis. ksu.edu/projects/agentTool/agentool3.htm) to support the design of MASs. **aT3** will be released as an Eclipse plug-in, and will provide predictive performance metrics to allow the designer to make intelligent trade-offs. It will also generate code for FIPA compliant frameworks. The *support to MAS development* provided by **AgentTool** consists of a set of editors that allow the developer to define the high-level system behavior in a graphical way: the types of agents as well as the possible communications that may take place between agents may be defined via the editors. This system-level specification is then refined for each type of agent in the system. Once the system has been completely specified, skeletal **Java** code with empty methods is produced. Once completed by hand by the developer, the **Java** agents may be run as any **Java** application. No ad-hoc monitoring and debugging facilities are provided. A good *support to multi-language specification* is provided by **AgentTool**: in fact, it allows the MAS developer to describe its MAS in a graphical way, providing an interface for specifying the goal hierarchy, use cases, sequence, role and agent diagrams. **AgentTool** allows to use different graphical languages for different specification stages. However, the language in which the high-level specifications are translated into executable code is only one: **Java**. As far as *support to AOSE* is concerned, **AgentTool** supports the Multiagent Systems Engineering (MaSE) methodology [9] that consists of capturing goals; refining roles; creating agent classes; constructing conversations; assembling agent classes; designing the system.

The INGENIAS Development Kit (IDK). The **INGENIAS Development Kit** (**IDK**), http://ingenias.sourceforge.net/, is a tool *supporting MAS development* thanks to the availability of the INGENIAS Editor, the main development tool for IN-GENIAS methodology. The editor is the replacement of Rational Rose or other **UML** based tools for those researchers that work with software agents, and supports alpha version of **AUML** protocol diagrams. As far as *support to multi-language development* in INGENIAS Development Kit is concerned, the INGENIAS Editor includes several code generation modules, among which the JADE protocol generator, that generates JADE agents that implement protocols defined with INGENIAS diagrams, and the Prolog generator, a basic, non complete, translation of INGENIAS elements to Prolog predicates. The *support to AOSE* in INGENIAS Development Kit is ensured by its adherence to the INGENIAS MAS design methodology defined by [14]. INGENIAS describes the elements that constitute a MAS, according to five viewpoints: organization, agent, goals/tasks, interactions, and environment.

The Jack Platform. JACK [24] is an agent-oriented development environment created by the Agent Oriented Software Pty Ltd, and conceived to be an environment for creating, running and integrating commercial Java-based multi-agent software using a component-based approach. JACK *supports MAS development* by supplying a lightweight implementation of the BDI architecture. Moreover, JACK provides the core architecture and infrastructure for developing and running software agents in distributed applications, and a JDE (JACK Development Environment) that offers a high-level design tool, a graphical plan editor and graphical tracing of plan execution, that provide a powerful and flexible program development environment. JACK *does not support multi-language development*: Java is the only language provided to implement both the agents' knowledge and their behaviour. MAS development in JACK *does not follow a principled AOSE methodology*, although the BDI approach offers a way to validate the model of the application.

MadKit. MadKit [15] is a highly customisable, scalable, generic multi-agent distributed platform for developing and executing distributed applications. MadKit *supports MAS development* by providing a set of tools which are useful to the developer of multi-agent applications, like the system agents, that are the main tools that a MadKit developer uses to explore, launch, visualise and trace agents; the communicator, an agent which allows to build distributed applications without being concerned about distribution; and an editor and animator of diagrams that can be used to view and manipulate information represented as graphs. A "graphic shell" launches the kernel and loads the interfaces for the various agents managing them in a global GUI. MadKit provides a *good support to multi-language development*. It is possible to program MadKit agents in several languages: Java, Python, Scheme (Kawa), BeanShell and JESS. Even if MadKit *does not follow any specific AOSE approach*, one of the software tools it provides is SEdit (Structure Editor). This tool allows the design and animation of structured diagrams containing nodes and arrows between them, and helps the MAS developer in engineering the MAS in a correct way.

The Mozart Programming System. The Mozart Programming System [25] is an advanced development platform for intelligent, distributed applications. It implements Oz 3, the latest in the Oz family of multi-paradigm languages based on the concurrent constraint model. By combining concurrent and distributed programming with logical constraint-based inference, Oz is *suitable for MAS development*. The developer that implements a distributed application must not be concerned with details regarding the underlying network, that is open and fault-tolerant. Besides this, Oz is a multi-paradigm high-level programming language which supports declarative programming, object oriented programming, constraint programming, and concurrency. Thus Mozart, being based upon Oz, *provides a true support to multi-language development*. However, graphical tools for modelling the MAS or for animating diagrams describing the architecture of the MAS are not supported by the Mozart platform: *no support to any SE methodology is given*.

The ZEUS Platform. Zeus [21] is an open source agent development tool kit written in Java and created as part of the Midas and Agentcities research projects at BT in the late 1990's and early 2000's. A version of Zeus is available under an open source license from http://sourceforge.net/projects/zeusagent. As far as *support to MAS development* is concerned, Zeus provides editors for entering the specifications of all the artifacts needed for building a MAS. In particular, it provides an Ontology Editor for specifying the ontology used by the agents in the MAS, and an Agent Editor for specifying agents and their tasks, social context, and social abilities. The Code Generation Editor allows the developer to automatically generate code from the specifications entered by means of the Agent Editor. Visualiser and deployment tools use user-friendly graphic interfaces that facilitate the MAS deployment. *Multi-language issues* are not faced by Zeus: Zeus agents are programmed by entering their characterizing features through the Agent Editor panel by means of forms that impose the usage of a Zeus-dependent input language. The Java agent code can be automatically generated when all these features have been defined. No output language other than Java is supported. Finally, as far as *AOSE support* is concerned, the approach that Zeus suggests for building a MAS consists of five stages: ontology creation, agent creation, utility agent configuration, task agent configuration, and agent implementation.

3   DCaseLP: An Integrated AOSE Approach and Environment

DCaseLP provides the languages and tools that support a MAS developer in the engineering stages from late requirements analysis to prototype testing. In the following sections we outline these engineering stages. The suggested AOSE approach is based upon existing proposals.

3.1   Modelling Stage (Analysis and Design)

The analysis stage is mainly role-driven. We share the belief that roles are the key abstraction in MAS modelling with several researchers in the AOSE field. Role modelling allows the MAS developer to specify *what* the system can do, without going into the details about *how* the system will do it. Roles are played by agent classes. To make an example, *Seller* and *Buyer* are two roles that may be played by the *fruitSeller* and *fruitBuyer* agent classes respectively, as well as by a *fruitExchanger* class that plays both of them. In order to define roles and interactions taking place among them, the MAS developer may follow the guidelines given in [5], where modularity, high cohesion, parsimony, completeness, and low coupling are used as characterising criteria for qualifying roles.

Once the role model is well understood, the developer needs to define how communication among entities playing different roles takes place; which roles should be assigned to which agent class; and how many instances of each agent class are required for the given application.

The language that DCaseLP provides to the user in order to cope with these aspects is UML, along the lines of [3,5]. The tool that allows the integration of role models defined using UML into DCaseLP consists of a set of XSL configuration files that define the rules for translating XMI representations of UML diagrams into executable code.

The first issue to address refers to the activity of defining interactions among the roles needed in the MAS under development. A "Protocol Diagram" may be defined to this aim. A suitable notation is provided by UML sequence diagrams where - according to the AUML philosophy [22] - roles are used instead of classes or objects as the entities involved in the interaction.

In order to identify the agent classes needed by the application, and assign roles to them, the developer may consider that both access points for information, expertise, and services, and entities that are responsible for controlling some kind of activity, are good agent class candidates [5]. This assignment of roles to classes may be modelled as an "Architecture Diagram", namely, a UML class diagram where UML classes may be either agent roles or agent classes (according to their stereotype), and "plays" relationships between agent classes and agent roles are defined. For each agent class defined in the modelling stage, the corresponding code implementing the class behaviour should be defined in the implementation stage.

The number of instances of each agent class depends on the MAS under development. Clearly decoupling agent classes from agent instances enforces the modularity and re-usability of the agent class model. Agent instances are assigned to their corresponding agent classes in the "Agent Diagram", a UML class diagram that includes agent classes and agent instances. When the MAS is going to be implemented, the initial state of each agent instance must be defined by encoding it in the chosen language.

3.2 Implementation Stage

The implementation of the MAS prototype must be coherent with the specification given in the previous step. Ensuring this coherence is a demanding task for the developer of the prototype, but DCaseLP may reduce this burden by providing a semi-automatic translator from UML into JESS, that is one of the implementation languages offered by DCaseLP.

During the implementation stage, the *integration of external software* comes into play. To this aim, DCaseLP follows the *Wrapper Agent* model, [12], defined by the Foundation for Intelligent Physical Agents, FIPA, with agents that act as "wrappers " for the external pieces of code. The external packages which can be accessed by the prototype are all the ones that Java, tuProlog and JESS provide interfaces for.

DCaseLP provides a set of libraries for integrating in JADE agents whose behaviour is entirely programmed in tuProlog or JESS, and not simply a way of executing tuProlog or JESS pieces of code from inside JADE agents. From a developers point of view, the difference is substantial. By "integrating tuProlog and JESS agents into JADE", we mean the ability to specify the complete behaviour of the agent, including its ability to communicate with other agents running into a JADE platform, in tuProlog and JESS and, then, execute these specifications. A developer that is able to write tuProlog or JESS code, but that is not able to program in Java (and thus, is not able to define JADE agents), can define active and communicating agents, and run them in JADE, without even knowing the structure and definition of JADE agents. This is possible because we have extended both tuProlog and JESS with primitives that allow them to communicate with agents running in a JADE platform (no matter if they are tuProlog, JESS, or pure JADE agents) in a completely transparent way. This is obviously different from, and more sophisticated than, providing the means to integrate code into JADE agents, but still constraining the developer to use and know the JADE package.

3.3   Testing and Evaluation Stage

The execution of the MAS prototype allows the MAS developer to test and evaluate the analysis, design, and implementation choices that were made during development.

DCaseLP libraries provide no direct support to MAS testing, which exploits monitoring and debugging tools offered by JADE. However, the output of this stage impacts on the previous ones where DCaseLP has an active role; for this reason we briefly discuss it. We identified a set of general evaluation criteria, which are relevant for most MAS applications, that help the MAS developer to identify the possible sources of errors made in the previous stages, according to the evaluation outcomes.

– *Load Balancing and Load Peaks*. The amount of work done by each agent in the prototype can be monitored by measuring the number of exchanged messages (for example, by using the Sniffer agent provided by JADE). By means of these measurements, the developer can identify the overloaded agents and may then decide to modify the architecture of the MAS, for example by defining a different assignment of roles to agent classes.
– *Implementation of Communication Protocols*. Implementation of the communication protocols can be tested by monitoring which messages are received by which agent, and whether there are agents that receive messages that they do not understand. If this is the case, there may be a mis-implementation of the protocols related to the roles the agents must play in the MAS.
– *MAS Topology*. During the simulation, the "neighbours" of each agent, i.e., the set of agents it can exchange messages with, can be set up. This allows the developer to experiment various interconnection topologies.

4   DCaseLP Architecture

DCaseLP has been implemented in order to provide

1. a *support to the steps* described in Section 3, and
2. a *transparent integration* between Java, JESS, and tuProlog agents running in a JADE platform (Figure 1).

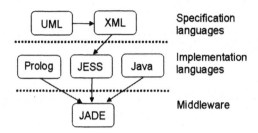

Fig. 1. DCaseLP packages

The result of our work consists of the following packages:

1. the Java UMLInJADE package that contains the Java classes and the XSL style sheets for translating UML diagrams created with any UML modelling tool[4] and exported into XMl, into (ad-hoc) intermediate XML models and, from these, to create the files containing the code for running the JESS agents into JADE.
2. the Java jessInJADE package, that contains the classes that implement JESS *agents*, to be run in the JADE environment, and whose behaviour is fully specified by means of the JESS language.
3. the Java tuPInJADE package, that contains the classes that implement tuProlog *agents*, to be run in the JADE environment, and whose behaviour is fully specified by means of the tuProlog language.

The three packages, together with their manuals and tutorials, are available from http://www.disi.unige.it/person/MascardiV/Software/DCaseLP. html. Examples of use of DCaseLP are also provided from the above URL, together with the code for the electronic commerce application discussed in Section 5.

4.1 The UMLInJADE Package

The UMLInJADE package provides the means to translate, in a semi-automatic way, the high level specification of the MAS, consisting of the Protocol, Architecture and Agent diagrams introduced in Section 3, given either in UML (usable only for Architecture and Agent diagrams) or in an XML intermediate format (available for all of them), into JESS agents.

The protocol diagram sets the interaction rules among roles that will be played by classes of agents. There is only one way to specify protocol diagrams in a format that can be automatically translated into code, namely, using our XML intermediate format. Currently, we cannot define protocol diagrams directly in ArgoUML (http:// argouml.tigris.org), which is the UML editor that we currently use for drawing UML diagrams and for exporting them into XMl. In fact, ArgoUML does not support the definition of UML sequence diagrams (and protocol diagrams are expressed using the same notation of sequence diagrams). Other UML editors such as Poseidon (http://www.gentleware.com/index.php), that support the definition

---

[4] In our experiments, we used ArgoUML.

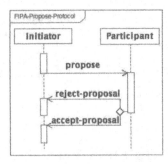

Fig. 2. FIPA propose protocol

of sequence diagrams, export them into an **XMI** format that is not compliant with our translation program. We are currently working to a definition of a new translation program from **XMI** to our **XML** intermediate format, that is compliant with **Poseidon**, in order to overcome this limitation of the current release of **DCaseLP**.

To show how our intermediate **XML** looks like, we use it to describe the propose protocol suggested by FIPA (Figure 2), where a Seller role substitutes the role of Initiator, and a Buyer role substitutes the role of Participant; a fragment of the resulting intermediate **XML** specification is shown below. The structure of our **XML** notation is trivial, with roles characterised by a role name and by the ordered list of messages that they send or receive, eventually embedded into "or", "xor", and "and" tags.

```
1    <protocoldiagram>
2    <role><name>Seller</name>
3    <msgs><msg><sender>Seller</sender>
4     <receiver>Buyer</receiver>
5     <act>PROPOSE</act></msg>
6    <xor-thread>
7    <thread><msg>
8     <sender>Buyer</sender><receiver>Seller</receiver>
9     <act>REJECT_PROPOSAL</act></msg></thread>
10    <thread><msg>
11     <sender>Buyer</sender><receiver>Seller</receiver>
12     <act>ACCEPT_PROPOSAL</act></msg></thread>
13    </xor-thread></msgs></role>
 . . . . .
n  </protocoldiagram>
```

The architecture diagram expresses the relationships that exist between roles and classes of agents. It can be specified either by means of a **UML** class diagram like the one shown in Figure 3, or in the **XML** intermediate format.

The agent diagram states which agent classes have which instances. Like the architecture diagram, it can be specified either by means of a **UML** class diagram (like the one shown in Figure 4), or in intermediate **XML** format. The UMLInJADE package defines the Specif2Code class, that is used to perform the translation from the high level description of the MAS (either given by means of **UML** and exported into **XMI**,

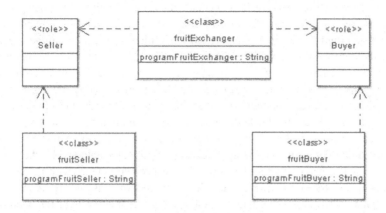

Fig. 3. An architecture diagram

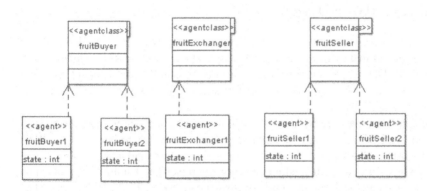

Fig. 4. An agent diagram

or by means of the intermediate XML format) into partial JESS agents that behave according to the interaction protocols, and are organised according to the architecture and agent diagrams. The Java code necessary to load and run a JESS agent into a JADE platform is also automatically generated.

The usage of UMLInJADE.Specif2Code is simple: from a command line, the developer just needs to type in javaUMLInJADE.Specif2Code and enter the information on the location of the XMI or XML files to translate, that are input by means of a set of interactive windows.

In order to execute the MAS resulting from the translation of the high level specification, the generated JESS code, that we will name JESS "skeleton" and that is put by the translator into a directory named jecode, must first be completed (see Section 4.2). The completed JESS code must be kept in the directory where it was generated and its name must not be changed, for ensuring its integration into JADE.

Once all the JESS skeletons have been completed, the JADE MAS can be built and its simulation can start. First of all, the Java "stubs" necessary for integrating the JESS skeletons into JADE, and automatically generated by the translation program taking the architecture diagram into account, must be compiled. Supposing that the Java stubs are compiled into the jacode directory, and that the MAS agent diagram is the one specified in Figure 4, then the MAS simulation in JADE can be started by entering the command `java jade.Boot fB1:fruitBuyer fB2:fruitBuyer fS1:fruitSeller fS2:fruitSeller fE1:fruitExchanger` from the jacode directory.[5] This command launches a JADE platform (first argument, `jade.Boot`) containing an agent named `fB1`, and whose behaviour is given by the JESS program integrated in JADE by the Java `fruitBuyer` stub. In the same way, there are an agent instance `fB2` with class `fruitBuyer`, an instance `fS1` with class `fruitSeller`, and so on. The names of the agent classes are directly obtained by the architecture diagram. The agent diagram has a one-to-one correspondence with the command line typed to start the simulation. In fact, the command line has one argument for each agent instance specified in the diagram, and the argument consists of the agent name separated by a colon from the agent class.

4.2 The jessInJADE Package

The `jessInJADE` package defines two classes, `jessAg` and `jessBhv`. Every JESS agent must be defined by means of a Java class that extends `jessAg`, which, in turn, extends the JADE `Agent` class by adding to it the capability, for an agent written in JESS, to exchange messages with any JADE agent. The class `jessBhv` defines the behaviour of a JESS agent.

In order to integrate a JESS piece of code into a JADE agent, we provide both the skeleton of a JESS agent, and the Java stub that is necessary to integrate the JESS agent into JADE. The `JavaStubSkeleton` code can be found in the `jessInJADE` directory. Once opened in a text editor and completed (self-explaining comments in the code indicate where the developer must add his/her own code), the `JavaStubSkeleton` behaves like a JADE agent whose only activity is to execute the JESS code obtained by editing and completing the `jessAgentSkeleton` file. This file (also found in the `jessInJADE` directory) must be edited by the developer, and completed with the JESS rules and initial facts that characterise the agent's behaviour and initial beliefs.

If the developer takes advantage of the translation process from the UML and XML specifications of protocol and architecture diagrams into JESS code, one Java stub and one JESS skeleton are automatically created for each agent class involved in the MAS. In other words, the JESS rules that characterise the agent's behaviour do not need to be encoded by the developer, since they are automatically generated in order to comply with the protocol given in the XML intermediate format. Since the protocol specifies neither the agent's initial state, nor the conditions under which a message is sent, the developer still needs to manually complete the code, but his/her work is less, and easier, than writing a JESS agent from scratch. On the other hand, the Java stub that is generated by the `Specif2Code` method, is ready to use and does not need to be edited.

The built-in predicates defined by the `jessInJADE` package include a `send` function, that sends an `ACLMessage` to an agent running in a JADE platform, and a

---

[5] We have substituted `fruitBuyer1`, etc, with `fB1`, etc, for readability.

receive function. The input of the send function is the fact ACLMessage whose template is predefined in any JessAg. The slots defined for the ACLMessage fact are the same as the one present in a JADE ACLMessage, namely communicative act (or "performative"), content of the message, sender, receiver, and eventually other arguments. The receive function returns a reference to the first ACLMessage available in the mail box of the agent, and nil if no message is available.

4.3   The tuPInJADE Package

The tuPInJADE package contains the following files:

- JadeShell42P.java and JadeShell42PGui.java represent a tuProlog agent and, as the name suggests, behave as a general "agent shell" for a tuProlog agent in JADE that incorporates a Prolog inference engine. When launched in a JADE platform, the tuProlog agent needs an input file containing the Prolog theory defining the agent behaviour. The input file may be either supplied from the command line (JadeShell42P.java), or by browsing the file system by means of a GUI (JadeShell42PGui.java).
- TuJadeLibrary.java is a Java library necessary for a tuProlog agent to communicate in a JADE platform. It defines the communicative predicates based on the facilities that JADE offers to its agents for communication in a platform and with other platforms.

Once a JadeShell42P or JadeShell42PGui agent has been loaded into a JADE platform, it looks for the tuProlog file that contains the agents's theory. This theory must define a "main" predicate that implements the agent's behaviour. If such a predicate exists, the tuProlog engine is created and, by default, it contains the standard tuProlog libraries and the theory input when loaded.

Every time that this agent is scheduled by JADE it automatically tries to prove the "main." goal. If the resolution does not succeed then an error message is displayed to the user.

The built-in predicates of tuProlog agents defined in the TuJadeLibrary include a send(Performative,Content,Receiver,Protocol,Cid) predicate, together with a blocking receive (blocking_receive(Performative, Content,Sender)) and a not blocking receive (receive(Performative, Content,Sender)).

Once a th file containing the tuProlog theory th for an ag agent has been defined, ag can be loaded into a JADE platform by typing java jade.Boot ag: tuPInJADE.JadeShell42P(th) from a command line (or java jade.Boot ag:tuPInJADE.JadeShell42PGui, for taking advantage of a GUI for browsing the file system).

5   Applications

The most recent application that we have developed with DCaseLP, described by [23], deals with an electronic implementation of different auction mechanisms.

There are many different auction mechanisms that can be classified according to their features (see for example [19]). The first distinction can be made between *open* and *sealed-bid* auctions. In the *open* auction mechanisms, the seller announces prices or the bidders call out the prices themselves, thus it is possible for each agent to observe the opponents' moves. The most common type of auctions in this class is the *ascending* (or *English*) auction, where the price is successively raised until no one bids anymore and the last bidder wins the object at the last price offered. The *descending* (or *Dutch*) auction, works in the opposite way w.r.t. the English one, and essentially belongs to the *sealed-bid* class. The *sealed-bid* auction mechanism is characterised by the fact that offers are only known to the respective bidders (as the name suggest, offers are submitted in sealed envelopes). In the *first-price* sealed-bid auction each bidder independently submits a single bid without knowing the others' bid, and the object is sold to the bidder who made the best offer. The *second-price* sealed-bid auction works exactly as the first-price one except that the winner pays the second highest bid.

Considering that the Dutch auction mechanisms is completely equivalent to the first-price sealed-bid auction, we only implemented the English, first-price sealed-bid, and second-price sealed-bid mechanisms.

Following the steps sketched in Section 3, for each auction mechanism, we have analysed the interaction between the Auctioneer role and the Bidder role, and a Protocol Diagram has been produced. In the design phase, the internal behaviour and the customisable features of each class of agent have been studied. Finally, each agent has been implemented as a tuProlog agent, and integrated into DCaseLP by exploiting the functionalities offered by the tuPInJADE package, thus achieving the goal of providing a tuProlog library of customisable agents for simulating auction mechanisms.

We have ran experiments with all the implemented mechanisms under the hypotheses, that, according to the "Revenue Equivalence Theorem" (RET, described by [27]), lead to the existence of an optimal bidder's strategy. We programmed our test bidders with these strategies and we verified that all the simulated auctions gave the same revenue to the auctioneer and the same payoff to the bidders. The fact that RET is satisfied (up to some error clearly due to discretisation) can be seen as a check for the correctness of the implementation.

The code developed as part of this application can be downloaded from http://www.disi.unige.it/person/MascardiV/Software/DCaseLP.html.

Many applications had also been developed using the ancestor of DCaseLP, CaseLP. For example, the Kicker project, based on a previous "freight train traffic" application [6], was developed within the framework of the EuROPE-TRIS Project as a result of an industrial collaboration with the Information Systems Division of Italian Railways (Ferrovie dello Stato s.p.a.), and dealt with the train dispatching problem.

Another application of CaseLP was the design and development of a working prototype of a vehicle monitoring system, which was carried out in collaboration with Elsag s.p.a. and discussed by [1].

Finally, a prototype of a multimedia, multichannel, personalised news provider, [7], was developed in collaboration with Ksolutions s.p.a. as part of the ClickWorld project, a research project partially funded by the Italian Ministero dell'Istruzione, dell'Università e della Ricerca (MIUR).

The above mentioned applications demonstrated that the CaseLP environment could be used effectively to engineer a real application modelled as a MAS in very heterogeneous domains.

We are currently working on making all these applications compliant with DCaseLP. Since CaseLP is implemented in Sicstus Prolog, and DCaseLP integrates tuProlog, the syntactic differences between these two Prolog implementations prevent us from running the applications developed with CaseLP in DCaseLP "as they are". However, the conversion from the two Prolog formats should be almost easy, and we plan to test soon DCaseLP on the applications already developed with its ancestor.

6   Conclusions and Future Work

By comparing DCaseLP with AgentTool, INGENIAS Development Kit, JACK, MadKit, Mozart, and Zeus, we may observe that all the seven systems provide a good support to MAS development (AgentTool provides a strong support to the analysis and design stages, but poor support to the deployment and testing of the MAS, while the other tools cover all the development phases). The support that DCaseLP offers to this stage is not an original contribution, since it entirely relies on the support offered by the JADE platform, which is similar to that offered by the six systems we have analysed (apart from AgentTool). The advantage of using JADE is that it is FIPA-compliant.

The multi-language development feature is very well supported by MadKit, and fairly well supported by INGENIAS Development Kit. Instead, JACK, AgentTool, and Zeus do not offer facilities for integrating agents written in languages different from the their respective agent implementation language. Mozart allows the developer to program agents using Oz 3, that offers multi-paradigm features. Obviously, developer must know Oz 3 for programming his/her MAS.

Finally, the toolkits that better face the engineering of the MAS are AgentTool and INGENIAS Development Kit, both built for supporting an existing AOSE methodology (Mase and INGENIAS, respectively). MadKit allows the developer to define diagrams that can be animated by integrating user-defined Java code, while JACK, Mozart and Zeus offer some guidelines and tools, but no AOSE support at all.

In the end, we may conclude that DCaseLP is comparable with these toolkits under most respects. An advantage of DCaseLP is that it integrates a Prolog engine, which is not supported by any of the other toolkits apart from INGENIAS Development Kit. However, while INGENIAS Development Kit provides the means for generating basic, non complete Prolog predicates from INGENIAS elements, DCaseLP provides a seamless integration of Prolog agents within the JADE platform. On the other hand, a feature that is currently missing in DCaseLP is a unifying formal semantics of the agents and the MAS, despite the language they are modelled or implemented in. In the end, DCaseLP complements the related work by taking into account Logic Programming languages, that is considered in a limited way only by one of the mentioned toolkits. The advantages of exploiting Logic Programming for implementing intelligent software agents have been depicted in the Introduction of this paper.

It is part of our future work to formally describe the meaning of protocol, architecture and agent diagrams, and their relationships with the generated JESS code. We are also working on the automatic translation of all of these diagrams into tuProlog (advances on the translation of protocol diagrams has been done as part of the "West2East" project, http://www.disi.unige.it/person/MascardiV/Software/ WEST2EAST.html, but no translation of architecture and agent diagrams has been performed yet), and on the definition of a translation program that takes as its input the XMI representations of diagrams produced by Poseidon, instead of those produced by ArgoUML.

Another direction of our research involves the integration of ontologies within DCaseLP, and the experimentation of its suitability as a tool for prototyping Service-Oriented systems. This last activity is carried out within the "Iniziativa Software Finmeccanica" project, http://www.iniziativasoftware.it/. Finmeccanica is the main Italian industrial group operating globally in the aerospace, defence and security sectors. The "Iniziativa Software", set up in April 2006, is a network of public-private laboratories where researchers from both the academia and Finmeccanica work together for applying the results obtained from the academic partners, to the industrial needs. We will also exploit the results obtained in collaboration with Finmeccanica for the industrial projects carried out within the Sistemi Intelligenti Integrati Tecnologie (S.I.I.T.) society, a non-profit consortium aimed at promoting the development of a technological district in the Italian region of Liguria, in the field of integrated intelligent systems.

Acknowledgements. This work was partially supported by the research project "Iniziativa Software CINI - Finmeccanica" and by the Italian project MIUR PRIN 2005 "Specification and verification of agent interaction protocols". The authors are grateful to the anonymous reviewers for their thoughtful and constructive comments.

References

1. Appiani, E., Martelli, M., Mascardi, V.: A multi-agent approach to vehicle monitoring in motorway. Technical report, Computer Science Department of Genova University (2000); DISI TR-00-13, Poster session of the Second European Workshop on Advanced Video-Based Surveillance Systems, AVBS (2001)
2. Bellifemine, F.L., Caire, G., Greenwood, D.: Developing Multi-Agent Systems with JADE. Wiley, Chichester (2007)
3. Bergenti, F., Poggi, A.: Exploiting UML in the design of multi-agent systems. In: Omicini, A., Tolksdorf, R., Zambonelli, F. (eds.) ESAW 2000. LNCS (LNAI), vol. 1972, pp. 106–113. Springer, Heidelberg (2000)
4. Carr, M.J., Konda, S.L., Monarch, I., Ulrich, F.C., Walker, C.F.: Taxonomy-based risk identification. Technical report. Carnegie Mellon University, Pittsburgh, Pennsylvania (1993) CMU/SEI-93-TR-6 ESC-TR-93-183
5. Collins, J., Ndumu, D.: ZEUS methodology documentation, Part I: The role modelling guide (1999), http://more.btexact.com/projects/agents/zeus/
6. Cuppari, A., Guida, P.L., Martelli, M., Mascardi, V., Zini, F.: An Agent-Based Prototype for Freight Trains Traffic Management. In: Larsen, P.G. (ed.) FM 1999. Springer, Heidelberg (1999)
7. Delato, M., Martelli, A., Martelli, M., Mascardi, V., Verri, A.: A multimedia, multichannel and personalized news provider. In: Ventre, G., Canonico, R. (eds.) MIPS 2003. LNCS, vol. 2899, pp. 388–399. Springer, Heidelberg (2003)

8. DeLoach, S.A., Wood, M.F.: Developing multiagent systems with AgentTool. In: Castel-franchi, C., Lespérance, Y. (eds.) ATAL 2000. LNCS (LNAI), vol. 1986, pp. 46–60. Springer, Heidelberg (2001)
9. DeLoach, S.A., Wood, M.F., Sparkman, C.H.: Multiagent systems engineering. Int. J. of Software Engineering and Knowledge Engineering 11(3), 231–258 (2001)
10. Denti, E., Omicini, A., Ricci, A.: Multi-paradigm Java-Prolog integration in tuProlog. Sci. Comput. Program 57(2), 217–250 (2005)
11. Forgy, C.: Rete: A fast algorithm for the many patterns/many objects match problem. Artif. Intell. 19(1), 17–37 (1982)
12. Foundation for Intelligent Physical Agents. FIPA agent software integration specification. Experimental, 15-08-2001 (2001), http://www.fipa.org/specs/fipa00079/
13. Friedman-Hill, E.: Jess in Action: Java Rule-Based Systems (In Action series). Manning Publications (2002)
14. Gomez-Sanz, J., Pavon, J.: Agent oriented software engineering with INGENIAS. In: Marík, V., Müller, J.P., Pechoucek, M. (eds.) CEEMAS 2003. LNCS (LNAI), vol. 2691. Springer, Heidelberg (2003)
15. Gutknecht, O., Ferber, J.: MadKit: a generic multi-agent platform. In: AGENTS 2000: Proceedings of the fourth international conference on Autonomous agents, Barcelona, Spain, pp. 78–79. ACM Press, New York (2000), http://www.madkit.org/
16. Henderson-Sellers, B.: Evaluating the feasibility of method engineering for the creation of agent-oriented methodologies. In: Pechoucek, M., Petta, P., Zsolt Varga, L. (eds.) CEEMAS 2005. LNCS (LNAI), vol. 3690, pp. 142–152. Springer, Heidelberg (2005)
17. Juan, T., Martelli, M., Mascardi, V., Sterling, L.: Creating and reusing AOSE features (2003), http://www.cs.mu.oz.au/~tlj/CreatingAOSEFeatures.pdf
18. Juan, T., Martelli, M., Mascardi, V., Sterling, L.: Customizing AOSE methodologies by reusing AOSE features. In: Rosenschein, J.S., Sandholm, T., Wooldridge, M., Yokoo, M. (eds.) Proceedings of the Second International Conference on Autonomous Agents and Multiagent Systems (AAMAS 2003), pp. 113–120. ACM Press, New York (2003)
19. Klemperer, P.: Auctions: Theory and practice. Princeton University Press, Princeton (2004)
20. Mascardi, V., Martelli, M., Sterling, L.: Logic-based specification languages for intelligent software agents. TPLP 4(4), 429–494 (2004)
21. Nwana, H.S., Ndumu, D.T., Lee, L.C., Collis, J.C.: ZEUS: A toolkit for building distributed multiagent systems. Applied Artificial Intelligence 13(1-2), 129–185 (1999)
22. Odell, J., Parunak, H.V.D., Bauer, B.: Representing Agent Interaction Protocols in UML. In: Ciancarini, P., Wooldridge, M. (eds.) AOSE 2000. LNCS, vol. 1957, pp. 121–140. Springer, Heidelberg (2001)
23. Roggero, D., Patrone, F., Mascardi, V.: Designing and implementing electronic auctions in a multiagent system environment. In: Proceedings of the WOA 2005, Dagli Oggetti Agli Agenti (2005)
24. The JACK Home Page. The Agent Oriented Software Group (2006), http://www.agent-software.com/shared/home/index.html
25. The Mozart Home Page. The Mozart Programming System. Last release: (June 15, 2006), http://www.mozart-oz.org/
26. The Standish Group. CHAOS (1995) (accessed on January 30, 2008), http://www.projectsmart.co.uk/docs/chaos-report.pdf
27. Vickrey, W.: Auction and bidding games. In: Recent advances in Game Theory, pp. 15–27. Princeton University Conference, Princeton (1962)

A Step Towards Fault Tolerance for Multi-Agent Systems

Katia Potiron[1,2], Patrick Taillibert[1], and Amal El Fallah Seghrouchni[2]

[1] Thales Systèmes Aéroportés
2 avenue Gay Lussac
78852 Elancourt – France
{katia.potiron,patrick.taillibert}@fr.thalesgroup.com
[2] Laboratoire Informatique de Paris 6
104 avenue du Président Kennedy
75016 Paris – France
{amal.elfallah}@lip6.fr

Abstract. Robustness, through fault tolerance, is a property often put forward in order to advocate MAS. The question is: What is the first step to be fault tolerant? Obviously the answer is: to know faults. The claim of this paper is that existing fault classification suitable for distributed systems does not fit completely MAS needs among other things because of autonomy, the main characteristic of their components. Actually autonomy is the very distinctive concept of agents and has unquestionable worthwhile properties. But do these properties have no compensation?

After these observations on the need for fault classification the question would be about its usages for fault tolerance.

To answer these questions the paper will, after a short presentation of the fault classification which prevails in fault tolerance community, show that autonomy induces a need for significant extension to this classification. It will then make a special review of this extension and present some expectations with regard to the programing of fault tolerant MAS and the behavior of two general fault handlers.

Keywords: Fault tolerance, MAS design, autonomy, Fault classification.

1 Introduction

Autonomy is one of the major characteristics of agents, and one issue of the MAS domain has been to precisely define this concept. In this paper, we consider a point that most definitions have in common: autonomy allows agents to take their decisions on their own, see for example [1,2,3].

Agents, taking their decisions on their own, gain some independence with regard to other agents. They can go on and thus survive even if no other agent is available. This aspect of autonomy makes agents more robust.

But, as a consequence of this decision making, the behavior of an agent is not completely foreseeable for the agents interacting with it. The question here can be: How to interact with autonomous agents? Agents eventually have to make

M. Dastani et al. (Eds.): LADS 2007, LNAI 5118, pp. 156–172, 2008.
© Springer-Verlag Berlin Heidelberg 2008

some assumptions about the behavior of the other agents. But what is to be done if an agent does not fulfill these expectations? In brief, agents taking their decisions by themselves can, voluntarily or not, be responsible for faults which other agents will experience.

From a software engineering point of view, autonomy can be perceived as the fact that the agent designer does not know exactly the specifications neither the internal laws nor the internal state of other agents during their execution. Even if MAS are distributed systems, Autonomy is the break point opposing their design.

Faults are a concern for MAS designers, especially because agents are interacting with unpredictable agents. To deal with faults, the designer must have some precise information on the faults MAS are subject to. *Faults* are generally defined as judged or hypothesized causes of an error. They are not dangerous when handled properly because only errors have direct effect on the system. Nonetheless, since not all faults can be detected during the system design and tests, their handling must be considered as a natural feature of computing systems. *Errors* are deviations of one or more of the external state of the system from correct service state. And *Failures* are events that occur when the delivered service deviates from the correct service. We will here be concerned by *fault tolerance* that represent all means to avoid service failures in the presence of faults. Some work on MAS was done with regard to this domain.

For example, some research on exception handling for MAS [4,5] deals with *exceptional situations*. In this researches, exceptions are detected as situations not suitable with the expectations of the agent. More practically, they are defined as the messages that materialize fault detection as it creates an error [6].

Another line of research in MAS is the replication of agents, a well-known fault tolerance method which deals particularly with physical faults [7,8]. "Prevention of harmful behaviors" [9] which deals with the emergence of harmful behaviors of agents and "fault tolerant agents communication language" which deals with crash failure detection [10] are other approaches. Some lines of research in MAS never refer to fault tolerance but gives good piece of work for it, as computational trust and reputation [11] to deal with malicious agents or planning [12] to deal with unexpected situations. In all these researches, it is not clear what kinds of fault are taken into consideration and hence their efficiency with regard to fault tolerance.

Our final goal is to find a way to build MAS where fault tolerance is naturally a property of the agents and the system (achievable without a specific effort of the designer). To obtain such a good property, fault tolerance must be "made for MAS" and hence take into account specificities of MAS, particularly autonomy of agents. The fault classification presented in this paper is our first step as it gives a tool for designers to specify and evaluate systems and agents. The paper will be organized as follow. Section 2 presents fault classification issue and method. Section 3 explains our contribution on classification of MAS faults. A study of the usefulness of such a classification is presented in section 4 and the last section concludes our paper and presents our perspectives.

2   Conventional Fault Classification

The seminal work in fault classification is the work done by [6,13,14] that began in the early 80's. To make their classification, the authors studied a wide group of faults including faults like short-circuits in integrated circuit, programmer's mistakes, electromagnetic perturbations or inappropriate man-machine interactions.

In [14], faults are classified according to seven attributes[1] (Phase of creation or occurrence, system boundaries, dimension, phenomenological cause, objective, capability, persistence). Each attribute has a set of exclusive values (for example values related to the attribute "phase of creation" are: "development" or "operational"), as shown on Tab.1.

A fault is described as a complete assignment of a single value to each attribute. Doing so the seven attributes and their values give 192 possible combinations. Not all these combinations were kept by the authors, because not all are relevant. Thus a fault cannot be malicious and accidental at the same time. The 25 faults remaining, that are named DSFaults (Distributed Systems Faults) in this paper, are illustrated in the fault classification tree presented on Fig.1.

Table 1. Attributes to describe faults and their values

Attributes	Values	Definitions
Phase of creation or occurrence	Operational	Occur during service delivery of the use phase
	Development	Occur during (a) system development including generation of procedures to operate or to maintain the system, (b) maintenance during the use phase
System boundaries	Internal	Originate inside the system boundary
	External	Originate outside the system boundary and propagate errors into the system by interaction or interference
Dimension	Hardware	Originate in, or affect, hardware
	Software	Affects software, ie., programs or data
Phenomenological cause	Natural	Caused without human participation
	Human-made	Result from human actions
Objective	Malicious	Introduced with the malicious objective of causing harm to the system
	Non-malicious	Introduced without a malicious objective
Capability	Accidental	Introduced inadvertently
	Deliberate	Result of a decision
	Incompetence	Result from a lack of professional competence by the authorized human(s), or from inadequacy of the development organization
Persistence	Permanent	Presence is assumed to be continuous in time
	Transient	Presence is bounded in time

---

[1] In [13], there were eight attributes as capability was separated into: 1) intent with deliberate and non-deliberate faults as values and 2) capability with accidental and incompetence faults as values. But the intent viewpoint appeared redundant.

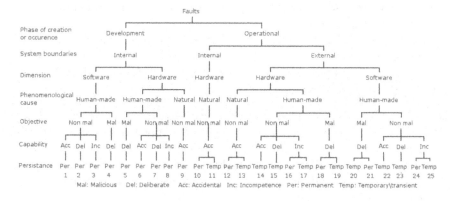

Fig. 1. Fault classes combinations

Development faults					Physical faults						Interaction faults					
1	2	3	4	5	6	7	8	9	10	11	12 13 14 15 16 17 18 19	20	21	22	23	24	25
Software flaw	Logic bomb	Errata hardware / Production defects					Physical deteriorat.				Physical interference	Intrus.	Virus	Input mistakes		

Fig. 2. Groups of fault examples

It is then possible to characterize the large number of everyday or specialized terms denoting faults as the set of fault classes they belong to. Some illustrative examples are given on the boxes at the bottom of Fig.2. The faults are also shown to belong to three *major non-exclusive groups* representing some practical points of view (two first lines of Fig.2) and described as follow:

- **Development faults:** faults occurring during development.
- **Physical faults:** faults affecting hardware.
- **Interaction faults:** external faults.

The knowledge of all possible fault classes allows the system designer to decide, during the system specifications, which fault classes should most be taken into consideration.

The next section will investigate this fault classification using a MAS point of view. As matter of fact, the fault classification presented here is, in particular, suitable for distributed systems (which MAS are) but, as explained in the introduction, MAS have some specificities (particularly the autonomy), which motivate further investigations on the fault classification. Our goal is to emphasize the pertinent faults for MAS (belonging to Fig.1) and to demonstrate that new specific faults are needed. This is the purpose of the next section.

3   MAS Faults Classification

MAS are separated components interacting each other to achieve some goal as in the case of distributed systems. What introduce the following findings:

- Since they are made of programs, MAS are vulnerable to all faults grouped as development faults;
- Since they are distributed programs, MAS are vulnerable to all faults grouped as physical faults;
- Since they are composed of interacting programs, MAS are vulnerable to all faults grouped as interaction faults.

The classification tree presented (Fig.1) is entirely relevant for MAS.

But, since MAS are composed of autonomous components we argue that an extension to the DSFaults classification is necessary. To do that, a new value is given to the first attribute of the DSFaults classification. Specific faults of MAS are investigated and classified from the agents point of view and from an "external to the MAS" point of view.

3.1 A New Value for the First Attribute "Phase of Creation or Occurrence"

The autonomy of the agents is the most salient difference between MAS and classical distributed systems. It is perceived by agents as the impossibility to predict the behavior of other agents. This unpredictability is the point studied here as possible fault source.

When considering these faults for the first time, we tried to classify them with one of the two existing values of the first classification attribute: "phase of creation or occurrence"[2]. These attributes presented into (Tab.1) are "Development faults" what means faults occurring during system development (they occur before the execution of the considered program) and "Operational faults" what means faults occurring during service delivery of the use phase (they occur when executing the considered system interacting with programs or human beings). But the result was not what we expected:

1. These faults cannot be considered as development faults because autonomy is a natural feature of agents.
2. These faults cannot be considered as operational faults because they are not linked to *service delivery* but linked to the *autonomous behavior* of the agents. Classical systems are created only with the aim of service delivery whereas for agents, created as autonomous and maybe proactive, the intent is different. This is why the faults resulting from the autonomous behavior of agents can not be considered as operational fault.

This makes us consider autonomy as a new value of the attribute "phase of creation or occurrence". *Autonomy* value will represent faults occurring during the "autonomous behavior" of an agent. When employing: "autonomous behavior" we mean all actions that autonomy allows to the agents, as for example:

- Not to respond to a request ("the power to say no") or respond negatively whether or not it is included into the interaction protocol.

---

[2] Phase of creation or occurrence is related to the moment when the fault is made.

– To make a fault in order to incapacitate another agent.
– Not doing what was promised.

Concerning the three non-exclusive fault groups (development faults, physical faults or interaction faults) presented on Fig.2, faults which first attribute is valued as "autonomy" cannot be considered as belonging exclusively to anyone. The next section will show that possible behavioral faults includes faults like intentional spam (which belong to the physical fault group), default of response (which belong to the interaction fault group) or wrong response (which belong to the development fault group). So we named these faults: *Behavioral faults* and consider it as a fourth non-exclusive group of faults presented in Fig.6.

The introduction of a new value for an attribute creates 96 new possible combinations among which the following analysis shows that 12 correspond to relevant new fault classes. As the faults perception is a matter of perspective we will present these new fault classes using two different points of view: agent centered (section 3.2) and "external to the MAS" centered (section 3.3).

3.2   Agent Centered Analysis

A behavioral fault, on an agent-centered point of view, is equivalent to the "freedom" that autonomy gives to other agents and their unpredictability. If an agent displays autonomy this is not a fault from the perspective of the agent, the considered act is a fault only for the agent in interaction with it. We give six examples to illustrate some corresponding situations.

1. An agent A, from time to time, voluntarily commits a fault to interfere with an agent B. For example sending a wrong message because it have chosen not to follow a correct interaction protocol (if the protocol was not correct it would be a development fault).
2. Voluntarily committed fault as example 1, but permanent.
3. An agent A evaluates that it has no time to respond and so agent B does not receive any answer (duration of faults is time bounded and link to the context of the agent A).
4. Not voluntarily committed fault as example 3, but not bounded in time.
5. Physical attacks between agents like temporary spam.
6. Physical attacks as example 5 but permanent.

For these faults, the values of the attributes are:

– **Phase of creation or occurrence:** *Autonomy*.
– **System boundaries:** *External*; because its source is in the other agent (an "internal to the agent" fault would be a development fault).
– **Dimension:** *Software*; autonomy comes from the agent implementation (examples 1 to 4) or *Hardware*, autonomy cannot come from hardware but can influence it (examples 5 and 6).
– **Phenomenological cause:** *Natural*; autonomy does not allow a human being to dictate its behavior to the agent.

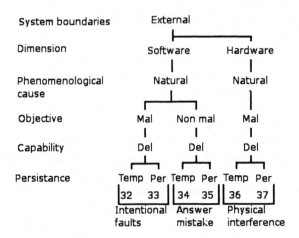

Fig. 3. External behavioral faults

- **Objective:** *Non-malicious* (examples 3 and 4) or *Malicious* (examples 1, 2, 5 and 6).
- **Capability:** *Deliberate*; results from the decision of an agent.
- **Persistence:** *Transient*; if the decision context is bounded in time (examples 1, 3 and 5) or *Permanent* (examples 2, 4 and 6).

This classification is represented by the tree of fault classes number 32 to 37 on Fig.3, for a more global view see Fig.5.

3.3 System Centered Analysis

A behavioral fault in the "external MAS"-centered point of view is comparable to the incompetence to handle the autonomy of the agents. This refers to how an agent can handle the autonomous behavior of the agents it is in interaction with. Faults are observable for an "external MAS" point of view only if an agent is incompetent to handle some autonomous behavior. This explains the introduction, with the new faults, of some new combination of values concerning the attributes objective and capability. From an external point of view the faults can be made by one agent with a malicious intent and is perceived at the user level only because of the incompetence of the system to handle the fault. We give six examples to illustrate some corresponding situations:

1. An agent overloads the network creating temporary problems considering messages transmission time.
2. Physical fault as example 1 but not bounded in time.
3. An agent is incompetent to realize its goal because of another agent reaction (request refusal) and temporarily has no other way to realize its goal.
4. Incompetence fault as example 3 but permanent.
5. An agent creates voluntarily a temporary fault to prevent another agent from accomplishing its goal.
6. Malicious fault as example 5 but permanent.

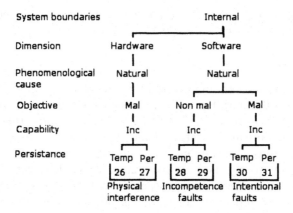

Fig. 4. Internal behavioral faults

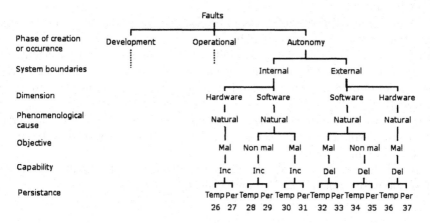

Fig. 5. New fault classes combinations

For these faults the values of the attributes are:

- **Phase of creation or occurrence:** *Autonomy*.
- **System boundaries:** *Internal*; because its source is into the MAS.
- **Dimension:** *Software*; autonomy comes from the agent implementation (examples 3 to 6),or *Hardware*, autonomy cannot come from hardware but can influence it (examples 1 and 2).
- **Phenomenological cause:** *Natural*; autonomy does not allow a human being to dictate his behavior to the agent.
- **Objective:** *Non-malicious* (examples 3 and 4) or *Malicious* (examples 1, 2, 5 and 6).
- **Capability:** *Incompetence*; results of an agent incompetence to adapt itself to the non-expectable behavior of the other agents or to changes in the environment.
- **Persistence:** *Transient*; if the decision context is bounded in time (examples 1, 3 and 5), or *Permanent* (examples 2, 4 and 6).

This classification is represented by the tree of fault classes number 26 to 31 on Fig.4, for a more global view see Fig.5.

3.4 Faults Review

To begin a review of new faults introduced, named AAFaults (Autonomous Agent Faults) in this paper, Fig.5 shows the new fault classification tree.

As shown at the bottom of Fig.3 and Fig.4 (and summarized on last line of Fig.6), some faults can be gathered into fault classes examples. Malicious software fault group is named intentional fault group, since they are faults committed intentionally by agents. External non-malicious deliberate fault group is named answer mistake, since they are committed without bad intention. Internal non-malicious incompetence fault group is named incompetence fault group, since they result from the agent incompetence with regard to other agents autonomy. Hardware fault group is named physical interference as they are close to this example class.

Moreover some behavioral faults can be classified as development, physical or interaction faults like shown on Fig.6.

Faults 26 to 31 are development faults as these faults come from agents or system incompetence to handle autonomous behavior of agents. They can create some service outage and can force system in a degraded mode or, at worst, stop the execution.

Faults 32 to 37 are interaction faults because all are external to the considered system. They can create some local service failure (not always observable from an external point of view).

Some of these faults can also be viewed as physical faults (faults 26, 27, 36 and 37) because of their influence on hardware.

Behavioral faults										
Development faults					Interaction faults					
Physical faults									Physical faults	
26	27	28	29	30	31	32	33	34	35	36	37
Physical interference		Incapability faults				Intentional faults		Answer mistake		Physical interference	

Fig. 6. Behavioral faults example classes

4 Validity of Our Approach

4.1 Faults Comparison

In order to analyze the relevance of the behavioral faults (named AAFaults) we proposed, we made a comparison to evaluate their similarity with regard to the pre-existing DSFaults. To do this, we compute a similarity measurement representing the number of common values of the attributes describing two faults, and defined as:

$$Similarity_{ab} = \sum_{ij} \delta_{ij} .$$

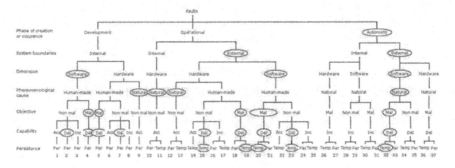

Fig. 7. Comparison of fault 32 to DSFaults

Table 2. Faults comparison

MoS \ AAF	3	4	5
26	5, 8, 9, 13, 17, 19	11	
27	**3**, 4, 6, 7, 12, 16, 18	5, 8, 9, 10	
28	8, 9, 13, 17, 22, 23	**3**, 11, 25	
29	4, 6, 7, 12, 16	10, 9, 8, 1, 2, 24	**3**
30	**3**, 4, 11, 20, 25		
31	1, 2, 5, 8, 9, 10, 21, 24	**3**, 4	
32	4, 13, 15, 18, 22, 25	19, 21, 23	20
33	2, 5, 12, 19, 23, 24	4, 18, 20	21
34	2, 11, 12, 14, 17, 19, 21, 24	13, 15, 22, 25	23
35	1, **3**, 4, 7, 9, 10, 13, 18, 22, 25	2, 12, 16, 21, 23, 24	
36	5, 11, 12, 14, 17, 21, 23	13, 15, 20	19
37	4, 7, 9, 10, 13, 15, 16, 20	5, 12, 21	18

With i (resp. j) in the set of values describing fault a (resp. b) and δ_{ij} the Kronecker symbol [3].

For example, the similarity measurement of faults 20 and 32 is shown on Fig.7.

Fault 20 is described as: "Operational, **External**, **Software**, Human-made, **Malicious, Deliberate, Temporary**".

Fault 32 is described as: "Autonomy, **External**, **Software**, Natural, **Malicious, Deliberate, Temporary**".

Their similarity score is equal to 5.

The biggest possible *similarity score* is six since the first attribute ("phase of creation or occurence") always have a different value between DSFaults and AAFaults. Results are presented on Tab.2, lines are AAFaults, columns are similarity scores and the values are the DSFaults having with AAFault the corresponding similarity score.

General review: Tab.2 shows that some DSFaults are very similar to AAFaults. But the first observation is that there are no similarity score better than 5.

---

[3] $\delta_{ij} = 0$ if i $\neq$ j; $\delta_{ij} = 1$ if i = j.

This tends to confirm the necessity of introducing AAFaults since they are not redundant what would have been the conclusion if the similarity score were 6.

Another observation that can be done is that fault number 3 (a development fault) is most present as similar fault. It is not possible to make some conclusions right now but some questions can be raised. Did this means that autonomy is, in term of software development, near to the capability to violate specifications (it is the characteristic of fault 3)? Did the fact this fault is viewed five times implies that MAS are more subject to some kind of faults than classical distributed systems?

Since different fault classes can lead to very similar errors, comparison of faults is a good mean to improve MAS fault tolerance. If behavioral faults can be considered similar to other faults in the given classification, we can think that being tolerant to these faults gives some tolerance to the other faults.

4.2   Analysis of the Difference between DSFaults and AAFaults

The similarity score study we made underlines some similarities between DS-Faults and AAFaults but also some differences that are now explained.

On natural faults: All faults introduced by our study are natural faults since autonomy is a natural component of the agents. Difference is that, for DSFaults, phenomenological cause being natural only verifies non-malicious and physical faults. Some explanation comes when taking into account the fact that agents are programs allowed to be malicious; they can act not only at physical level but also at interaction level. The consideration we made on autonomy would tend to unify humans-made faults and faults made by agents.

On malicious faults: Malicious faults are not anymore only human-made. Autonomy introduces into the MAS entities that have some specificities usually belonging to humans (autonomy and independence). Particularly in open MAS, agents are not always cooperative, they are able to decide to make malicious actions towards other agents.

One interesting point to emphasize here is behavioral faults prevention. A simple way to prevent all non-malicious behavioral faults is to send a preventing message. For example if an agent has too many messages to consider, it can send (without reading the messages to save some time) a cancel message or if it cannot deliver a result in time, ask for a delay. Prevention messages does not increase the number of messages exchanged since they are only used for exceptional situations and since a fault handling mechanism is required anyway. However this is not well suitable to malicious faults, because the prevention can be useless if a fault is made with a malicious objective.

On interaction faults: Half of AAFaults are interaction faults. They are really close to interaction DSFaults; one outstanding point is that they differ according to their classification as natural (Fig.5). The closeness of DSFaults and AAFaults drives us towards the conclusion that, at least for interaction faults, some DSFault tolerance methods can be used, or adapted to MAS in order to handle groups of interaction faults belonging to DSFaults and AAFaults. These adapted methods could be able to handle interaction faults due to autonomy as well as those due to operational context.

All these observations lead to the consideration that faults related to agent autonomy can be treated partly as human interaction faults and partly as development or physical faults because their effects will be very similar.

Preliminary conclusion. We have seen first that the autonomy of the agents is source of faults. But theoretically, with fault comparison and connection it seems possible to consider that if agents are tolerant to behavioral faults they can be tolerant to some other faults (particularly development and interaction faults) making it possible to factorize the processing necessary to tolerate these faults. It seems that, contrary to what would be expected, fault tolerance methods used for distributed systems cannot guaranty the handling of behavioral faults because of the fundamental difference of assumptions made by interacting with autonomous agents. But some practical tests must be done to confirm these expectations.

Since the aim of this paper is to study fault tolerance suitable for MAS the next section will present some perspectives based on the classification and factorization of faults.

5   Prospects about Building Fault Tolerant MAS

As said in introduction the goal we had by making this fault classification was to find a way to build fault tolerant MAS. The presented fault classification was done to identify the faults MAS may be subject to, and also to permit MAS designers and developers to specify fault tolerance with regard to the needed properties (presented in subsection 5.1.) and to analyze the adapted handlers (presented in section 5.2.).

5.1   Specifying Fault Tolerance for Agents and Platforms

Specifications: A necessary step for a MAS designer would be to choose which faults the system (all the MAS including the agents and the platform) must be tolerant to. Especially a significant piece of work must be done on defining which faults must be handled by the platform or by the agents. The classification will then facilitate MAS specifications. Following are some examples of specification of faults depending on MAS specificities:

- The platform would have to deal with all physical faults 5 to 19 plus 26, 27, 36 and 37 (because the platform is low level and aware of hardware problems). But agents will have to handle the interaction faults not contained into physical faults as 20 to 25 plus 28 to 35. And development faults must be handled at their corresponding level (development faults occurring respectively into the platform/agent handled at the platform/agent level).

- In a close MAS, if there are no malicious agents there are no reason that faults 26, 27, 30 to 33, 36 and 37 occur.
- For some other MAS, it will not be considered that agents can commit physical faults. So faults 26, 27, 36 and 37 have no reason to be taken into consideration by agent designer.

Diagnosis: The next issue of fault tolerance is diagnosing faults. As other programs, MAS would have to make some assumptions on faults they face because of the difficulty to diagnose exactly the faults. Doing so they will be able to choose the corresponding fault handler. For practical purpose, general diagnosis methods exist. Some are particularly based on temporal duration of faults [15] and evaluate faults as permanent, intermittent or transient to evaluate appropriate handler. This is to be worth studied.

Choice and monitoring of the handlers: After fault diagnosis an agent (or a sentinel [16,4]) would have to choose some handlers to manage faults (note that in this article the term handler refers to any method permitting to handle faults). This could be a way of using this classification. It is possible to classify handlers with the same attributes and same values that the faults they can handle. Making so, the choice of the handler can be done by matching diagnosed properties of a fault and classification of the handlers.

After a presentation of our generic protocol, the next section will present an example of study of the faults handled by two handlers.

5.2   Specifying Generic Handlers

Since creating agents interacting with autonomous agents is a really important point for MAS to be fault tolerant, one of our work has been to find a generic protocol to handle some possible issues in agents communications. Looking for a generic protocol permit to facilitate the development of the agents and make a step to generate automatically fault tolerant agents whereas specific handlers are an extra work for the designer as well as a source of fault.

ReSend protocol is a protocol presented by the authors in [17]. It was designed for agents to handle some interaction faults based on the argument that a retry method can be used in a cooperative way. By retry we mean the method consisting in trying to send another time a message for which the agent has not received an expected answer.

The agent can obtain some useful information at its knowledge level using a method quite similar to a retry: When an agent thinks that it should have received a response to a message sent before, it can send another message encapsulating the previous one to explain the issue to the other agent. The used performative, to "explain the issue to the other agent", correspond to an "expressive" speech act as defined in [18].

The message encapsulation makes our method different from a retry and not confusable with a stutter (repetition of the same message potentially due to a development fault). It is thus possible to the agent to identify the moment the

Table 3. ReSend description

Name	ReSend
Description	*ReSend* allow an agent i to tell an agent j that i desires that j process the expression ϕ sent before for which one i had not perceived any realization.
Message	The ReSend performative contains the expression ϕ corresponding to the performative sent before the agent i considers an exception.
Formal model [19]	$\langle i, resend(j,\phi)\rangle \equiv \langle i, inform(j, U_i\phi \wedge I_i\phi)\rangle$ $FP: I_i\phi \wedge U_i(B_j I_i\phi \vee B_j\phi)$ $RE: B_j I_i\phi$

	Phase of creation or occurrence			System boundaries		Dimension		Phenomenological cause		Objective		Capability			Persistence	
	Development	Operational	Autonomy	External	Internal	Software	Hardware	Natural	Human-made	Non malicious	Malicious	Accidental	Deliberate	Incompetence	Permanent	Transient
Retry		♦		♦		♦	♦	♦	♦			♦				♦
ReSend	♦	♦	♦	♦		♦	♦	♦	♦			♦	♦			♦

Fig. 8. Summary table for handled faults for Retry and ReSend

fault appeared and then diagnose it with their common knowledge. For example, if an agent does not receive any response to a request and use our method to handle this fault, the other agent can respond that it has already answered to the request and that the first message may have been lost.

A formal description is given by Tab.3.

We classified this protocol with regard to the values of the attributes of the faults it can handle and compared it with the retry method, the results are summarized in Fig.8. Note that the following study and table present the values for which the handlers are potentially adapted. We do not guaranty that the following handlers can handle every single fault having the corresponding values.

The *retry method* is possibly suitable for faults with the following values:

- **Phase of creation or occurrence:** suitable for *operational* faults as a loss of a message; not suitable for development fault (since the same message will be treated as a message received at a bad time or by the same faulty instruction) and not suitable for autonomous behavior (since sending the same message have no other value than sending a new request and will not make the agent change its internal state since it gives no new information).
- **System boundaries:** suitable for *external* faults since the method is made to handle faults at the communication level.

- **Dimension:** not suitable for *software* faults for the same reason that it is not suitable for development faults.
- **Phenomenological cause:** not a discriminating attribute since the method is suitable for all its values.
- **Objective:** suitable for *non-malicious* faults since the other agent will only try to help with the fault if it wants to.
- **Capability:** not suitable for *deliberate* faults since it does not imply any possible change in the internal state of the other agent, and not suitable for *incompetence* faults since it will be treated always by the same instruction.
- **Persistence:** not suitable for *permanent* faults since sending the same message if nothing in the environment change will change nothing.

Hence, the retry method is adapted for faults 13 and 14.

The *ReSend method* is possibly suitable for faults with the following values:

- **Phase of creation or occurrence:** suitable for *operational* faults as a loss of a message, suitable for *development* fault since the message will be treated as a new message and so by another instruction and suitable for *autonomous* behavior since sending a message corresponding to an expressive speech act have a different meaning than sending the same request and will influence the internal state of the agent as it gives new information.
- **System boundaries:** suitable for *external* faults since the method is made to handle faults at the communication level.
- **Dimension** and **Phenomenological cause:** not discriminate attributes since the method is suitable for all the values of the attributes.
- **Objective:** suitable for *non-malicious* faults since the other agent will only try to help with the fault if it wants to.
- **Capability:** suitable for *accidental* faults since some of this faults are temporary, suitable for *deliberate* faults since it implies a change in the internal state of the other agent, and not suitable for *incompetence* faults since it will be treated always with the same abilities.
- **Persistence:** not suitable for *permanent* faults since sending a message, if nothing in the environment or in the internal state of the agent change, will change nothing.

Hence, the ReSend method is adapted for faults 11, 13, 14, 15, 19, 20, 22, 23, 28, 32, 34 and 36.

6   Conclusion

After a summary of the existing fault classification which prevails in fault tolerance community, this paper has shown that autonomy induces a need of significant extension to this classification. To do so, it studied one of the consequence of autonomy that the behavior of an agent is not completely foreseeable for the other interacting agents. It implies that agents taking their decisions by themselves can, voluntarily or not, be responsible for faults which other agents will experience.

Then the paper has pointed out the pertinent faults and demonstrated which specific faults were possible for MAS. Autonomy was added as a value of "phase of creation" attribute, representing faults occurring during an autonomous behavior. We defined a new group of faults named *Behavioral faults*. The paper has also presented a special review of these 12 faults.

Finally this paper pointed out some prospects concerning the use of our classification to determine what faults must be handled by agents to be able to interact with autonomous agents in a dependable way and presented a complete study and comparison of two generic handlers.

Future work may be done to give a complete analysis of the faults that may be handled by the agent or the platform, to study an exhaustive list of generic handlers and to obtain fault tolerance as a natural property of MAS with as less as possible efforts from the designer.

We would conclude citing [13]: "More combinations may be identified in the future".

Acknowledgments

We acknowledge the comments received from Caroline Chopinaud, Sylvain Dekoker, Paul-Edouard Marson and Michaël Soulignac.

References

1. d'Inverno, M., Luck, M.: Understanding autonomous interaction. In: Wahlster, W. (ed.) 12th European Conference on Artificial Intelligence, pp. 529–533. John Wiley and Sons, Chichester (1996)
2. Hexmoor, H.: Stages of autonomy determination. In: IEEE Computer Society (ed.) IEEE Transactions on Systems, Man, and Cybernetics, pp. 509–517 (2001)
3. Castelfranchi, C., Falcone, R.: From automaticity to autonomy: the frontier of artificial agents. In: Hexmoore, H., Castelfranchi, C., Falcone, R. (eds.) Agent Autonomy, pp. 103–136. Kluwer Academic Publishers, Dordrecht (2003)
4. Klein, M., Dellarocas, C.: Exception handling in agent systems. In: Etzioni, O., Müller, J.P., Bradshaw, J.M. (eds.) Proceedings of the Third International Conference on Autonomous Agents (Agents 1999), Seattle, WA, USA, pp. 62–68. ACM Press, New York (1999)
5. Platon, E., Sabouret, N., Honiden, S.: A definition of exceptions in agent-oriented computing. In: O'Hare, G., O'Grady, M., Dikenelli, O., Ricci, A. (eds.) Engineering Societies in the Agent World 2006 (2006)
6. Laprie, J.-C.: Dependable computing and fault tolerance: Concepts and terminology. In: 15th IEEE Symposium on Fault-Tolerant Computing (FTCS-15), Vuibert, pp. 2–11 (1985)
7. Fedoruk, A., Deters, R.: Improving fault-tolerance by replicating agents. In: Proceedings of the first international joint conference on Autonomous agents and multiagent systems: part 2, Bologna, Italy, pp. 737–744. ACM Press, New York (2002)
8. Guessoum, Z., Faci, N., Briot, J.P.: Adaptive replication of large-scale multi-agent systems: towards a fault-tolerant multi-agent platform. In: Proceedings of the fourth international workshop on Software engineering for large-scale multi-agent systems, St. Louis, Missouri, pp. 1–6. ACM Press, New York (2005)

9. Chopinaud, C., Fallah-Seghrouchni, A.E., Taillibert, P.: Prevention of harmful behaviors within cognitive and autonomous agents. In: European Conference on Artificial Intelligence, pp. 205–209 (2006)
10. Dragoni, N., Gaspari, M.: Crash failure detection in asynchronous agent communication languages. Autonomous Agents and Multi-Agent Systems 13(3), 355–390 (2006)
11. Sabater, J., Sierra, C.: Review on computational trust and reputation models. Artificial Intelligence Review 24(1), 33–60 (2005)
12. de Weerdt, M., ter Mors, A., Witteveen, C.: Multi-agent planning: An introduction to planning and coordination. In: Handouts of the European Agent Summer School, pp. 1–32 (2005)
13. Avizienis, A., Laprie, J.C., Randell, B., Landwehr, C.: Basic concepts and taxonomy of dependable and secure computing. In: IEEE Computer Society (ed.) IEEE Transactions on dependable and secure computing, pp. 11–33 (2004)
14. Arlat, J., Crouzet, Y., Deswarte, Y., Fabre, J.C., Laprie, J.C., Powell, D.: Tolérance aux fautes. In: Akoka, I.W.J. (ed.) Encyclopédie de l'Informatique et des Systèmes d'Information, Vuibert, pp. 241–270 (2006)
15. Lin, T.H., Shin, K.G.: A bayesian approach to fault classification. In: ACM SIGMETRICS Performance Evaluation Review archive, vol. 18(1), pp. 58–66. ACM Press, New York (1990)
16. Hägg, S.: A sentinel approach to fault handling in multi-agent systems. In: Second Australian Workshop on Distributed AI in conjunction with the Fourth Pacific Rim International Conference on Artificial Intelligence, pp. 181–195 (1996)
17. Potiron, K., Taillibert, P., Fallah-Seghrouchni, A.E.: Gestion des exceptions dans les conversations entre agents autonomes. In: Actes des Journées Francophones sur les Systèmes MultiAgent (JFSMA 2007), pp. 211–220 (2007)
18. Searle, J.R.: Speech Acts: An Essay in the Philosophy of Language (1969)
19. FIPA: FIPA communicative act library specification. In for Intelligent Physical Agents, F. (ed.) Rapport technique (2000)

The Webbridge Framework for Building Web-Based Agent Applications

Alexander Pokahr and Lars Braubach

Distributed Systems and Information Systems
Computer Science Department, University of Hamburg
{pokahr,braubach}@informatik.uni-hamburg.de

Abstract. Web applications represent an important category of applications that owe much of their popularity to the ubiquitous accessibility using standard web browsers. The complexity of web applications is steadily increasing since the inception of the Internet and the way it is perceived changes from a pure information source to a platform for applications. Many different web frameworks exist that support recurring and tedious development tasks in order to simplify the process of building web applications. Most of the currently available web frameworks adhere to the widely accepted Model 2 design pattern that targets a clean separation of model, view and controller parts of an application in the sense of MVC. Nevertheless, existing frameworks are conceived to work with standard object-oriented business applications only and do not respect the particularities and possibilities of agent applications. Hence, in this paper a new architecture, in accordance with the Model 2 design pattern, is proposed that is able to combine the strengths of agent-based computing with web interactions. This architecture is the basis for the Jadex Webbridge framework, which enables a seamless integration of the Jadex BDI framework with state-of-the art JSP technology. The usage of web technology in combination with agents is further exemplified by an electronic bookstore case study.

1 Introduction

One key reason for the popularity of web applications is that they can be accessed via browsers in a standardized way. In this respect, they facilitate the execution of arbitrary applications without the need for installing or updating software components. These properties make web applications desirable even for more advanced and complex business tasks. Intelligent agents have been used for enterprise scale applications [2,4,11] for quite a long time. Nevertheless, few works exist that aim at a systematic integration of agent and web technology allowing to easily build web-based agent applications. Despite the many agent frameworks available, only limited support exists on how to build agent applications employing the web as user interface. Such a setting requires answering some fundamental questions about how interactions should be managed between the web and the application layer and what responsibilities agents should overtake in such a scenario.

M. Dastani et al. (Eds.): LADS 2007, LNAI 5118, pp. 173–190, 2008.
© Springer-Verlag Berlin Heidelberg 2008

A systematic integration between both layers will reduce the gap between the request/response style of browser-based interaction and the autonomous and concurrent nature of agent-based task execution. It will allow exploiting the full power of the agent paradigm to build the application logic and tie the web interface seamlessly to it. For example, in the backend of a logistics transportation system, agents could concurrently negotiate with different subcontractors for establishing a complex multimodal transportation route while processing a single user request. In this paper we propose an architecture and a corresponding framework, which provide such a systematic integration and therefore foster the efficient development of web-based agent applications.

The rest of the paper is structured as follows. In the next section an architecture for building web-based agent applications will be presented. In section 3 the realization of the architecture within the Jadex Webbridge framework is described. Thereafter, an example application will be discussed in section 4, which illustrates the usage of the web framework in a typical e-commerce scenario. In section 5 our approach will be discussed in the context of existing approaches including non-agent based frameworks as well as related agent-based solutions. Finally, we will conclude the paper with a summary and an outlook on planned future work in section 6.

2   Architecture

The aim of this paper is to integrate an agent-based approach with web application technology. Main focus is to increase efficiency and usability for developers confronted with the task to build a web-based agent application. While interoperability with web browsers could be hand-crafted into agent applications, a generic web/agent framework allows developers to concentrate on the application problem, abstracting away from technical details.

The primary objective of the approach is to separate the agent-specific parts of an application from the web-specific parts such as HTML pages. This enables modularization and maintainability of the code-base during development and additionally supports the specialization of developers (e.g. web engineers vs. agent programmers). During building the web representation, the developer should not be concerned with agent-specific aspects, whereas during the development of the business logic using agents, details of the web layer should not be of great importance.

To achieve the desired independence between the web front-end and the agent application an extra layer has to be introduced, which performs the necessary mediation operations. This "glue tier" therefore allows to transparently map between details of the agent and the web layer (cf. Fig. 1). In its general form, the problem and its solutions are not specific to agent applications. As can be seen from the large number of web frameworks today (cf. section 5), a multitude of design choices exists for an implementation of mediation layers between a web front-end and some application logic. The design and implementation of the specific agent-oriented solution proposed in this paper is influenced by existing

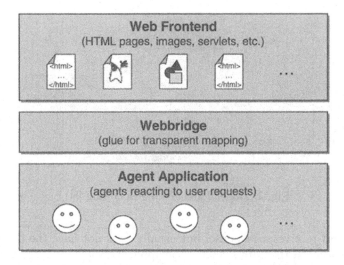

Fig. 1. The Webbridge as glue between agent and web layer

approaches and frameworks, but is motivated by the fact that the application programmer should only be concerned with the abstract and intuitive concepts of the agent paradigm. To this end, a well-established design pattern for conventional web applications is used as a starting point and is extended in a way suitable for developing agent-based applications.

2.1 Traditional Model 2 Architecture

Foundation of the proposed architecture is the widely used and accepted Model 2 design pattern [8], which adopts the Model-View-Controller (MVC, cf. [12]) approach for web development. The main idea behind this pattern is the separation of concerns, where each of the three proposed aspects plays a fundamentally different role. The model represents the domain-specific representation of the data on which the application operates. It is used by the view, which has the purpose to render the data in a user-friendly manner. In between, the controller serves as a connector that translates interactions with the view into actions to be performed on the model. By separating an application into the three distinct parts the application components become more manageable and can be reused or exchanged independently of each other, e.g. alternative views could be used for rendering a data model.

In contrast to the MVC pattern which was conceived for desktop applications with a toolkit-based user interface, Model 2 transfers the original ideas to the web and adapts them to the request/reply-based interaction pattern of web browsers. Model 2 has been conceived by web developers who realized that it is quite difficult to use the original MVC architecture for web applications, because the view part cannot play an active role in the system. All actions in Model 2 are caused by a user that interacts with its browser. The browser then sends

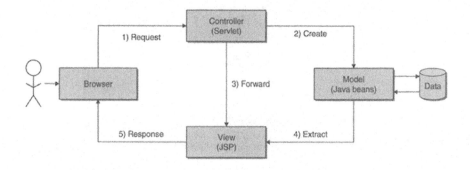

Fig. 2. Model 2 architecture (following [8])

a request and receives a response, but usually does not have the possibility to react to changes in the data model of the application.

In Model 2 the data model is kept in data bases and the data is cast into Java beans [9] for transmission and presentation. The view is typically expressed within JavaServer Pages (JSPs) [7] and the controller is represented by servlets [6]. A typical Model 2 scenario for Java web applications is depicted in Fig. 2. A browser request is issued by a user and invokes a controller servlet (1). This servlet performs the request processing, produces results in form of Java beans (2) and additionally decides which JSP to forward the request to (3). The only responsibility of the JSP is rendering the result page by utilizing the data generated from the servlet (4). The generated view is then sent back to the browser and presented to the user (5). This architecture takes advantage of the predominant strengths of both techniques, using JSP to generate the presentation layer and servlets to perform computation-intensive tasks.

As stated above the Model 2 architecture provides several benefits and allows for building complex web applications in a clean way. Additionally, its practical importance is emphasized e.g. by many non agent-based web frameworks that build on it and refine and extend its basic functionality. Hence, the direct usage of the Model 2 architecture would be beneficial but is hindered by the tight technology coupling via servlets and JSPs. Modifications to the Model 2 architecture are necessary for employing the advantages of agent technology for web-based applications. These modifications should be carefully designed to preserve the benefits of the architecture and to enable the developer to continue using established technologies such as JSPs and JavaBeans, which have proven their value for web-based applications.

2.2   Extending Model 2 for Agents

In a web-based agent application, the agents are responsible for the execution of the application logic. In the traditional Model 2 architecture, the application logic is executed by the controller, which is realized as a Java servlet. To achieve the seamless integration of agents with the web, a conservative extension of the

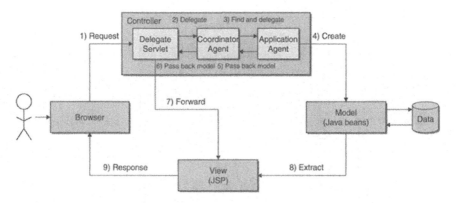

Fig. 3. Agent-based Model-2 architecture

Model 2 architecture is proposed, which allows the execution of agent behavior inside the controller. This extension allows the application functionality to be designed and implemented with different interacting agents. As only the controller is changed with respect to the original Model 2 architecture, the web front-end can still be realized using the well established JSP and JavaBeans technologies.

Figure 3 shows the extended Model 2 architecture proposed in this paper. To avoid application logic being scattered between the agents and the controller servlet, web requests from the browser (1) that require the execution of application logic are completely forwarded to the agent layer. Forwarding is performed in a two-step process. First the request is transferred from the *delegate servlet* to a generic *coordinator agent* (2), which acts as a mediator between the agent system and the web layer. The coordinator is responsible for finding an *application agent* that is able to process the request (3). If no suitable agent is available, the coordinator can also decide to create a new agent instance for the request. Once a suitable application agent has been identified, the coordinator sends a message to the agent, which contains the details about the request. As the request is transformed to an agent message by the coordinator, the application agent does not need to know, if the request comes from the web layer or another source. After the application agent has processed the request and generated the model data (4), it sends the result back to the coordinator (5), which forwards it to the servlet (6). Finally, a JSP page is selected (7), which reads the results created by the application agent (8) and displays it to the user (9).

3   Framework Realization

To simplify the development of applications following the architecture presented above, a generic software framework has been developed based on the Jadex BDI (belief-desire-intention) agent system [3,16]. The framework, called Jadex Webbridge, enables application developers to focus on the three core aspects of an application, i.e. the application logic using agents, visualization via JSP

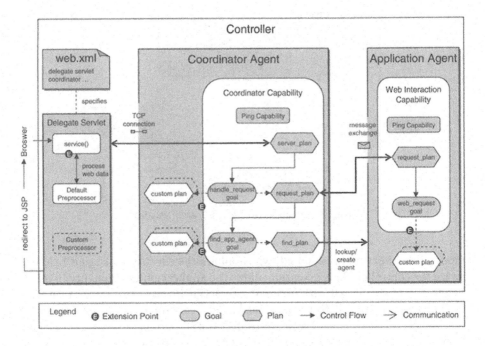

Fig. 4. Framework components

pages, and the domain data utilizing Java objects. The sources, binaries and documentation of the framework can be obtained as an add-on to the Jadex BDI agent system as described at the corresponding web page.[1] In addition, a simple example application can be directly accessed online.[2]

Following the presented architecture, the delegate servlet and the coordinator agent are responsible for mediating between these elements. Both have been realized as generic reusable components as part of the Webbridge framework. They are accompanied by a generic agent module, called web interaction capability, which can be included by the developer into application agents and handles all communication aspects with the coordinator. In the following subsections, the purpose and operation of each of these three main components of the Webbridge framework is described. The basic structure of these components and their interplay is shown in Fig. 4, which zooms further into the Controller part of Fig. 3.

3.1   Delegate Servlet

The delegate servlet has the purpose of transferring the processing of web requests to the agent layer and to finally trigger the creation of a result page. It

---

does so by forwarding web requests to a coordinator agent using a determinate TCP connection. To tell the servlet how to establish the connection, the address of the coordinator agent can be specified in the configuration file of the web application (web.xml). After the request has been processed, the delegate servlet obtains the result from the coordinator agent and forwards the data to suitable JSP page. The application objects that are contained in the result from the application agent are copied into the forwarded request, such that they are accessible from within the selected JSP page. A default JSP page can be defined in the application configuration, but can be overridden in the result, in case different pages should be displayed depending on the outcome of the request processing.

An important responsibility of the delegate servlet is to ensure that application data (represented as Java objects) can seamlessly be exchanged between the web and the agent layer. A generic XML encoding for JavaBeans is provided, such that application objects can easily be included in the result obtained from the agent layer. On the other hand, the values of parameters in the web request are restricted to simple strings, as sent by the browser. To be able to include application objects into web pages, the framework provides an extensible pre-processing mechanism (cf. Fig. 4, left), which automatically converts string values from the web request into corresponding application objects.

3.2   Coordinator Agent

The handling of web requests in the agent layer could be based on many different strategies. Those strategies can be implemented by the developer by providing application specific implementations of the coordinator agent. A default implementation of the coordinator agent is provided as part of the framework, which is based on reusable components providing useful extension points and therefore supporting the easy implementation of alternative application specific strategies. In the default strategy that is used, when the developer does not provide own extensions, the coordinator agent forwards web requests from the delegate servlet as messages to a specific application agent instance belonging to the corresponding web session. In this strategy, the kind of application agent suitable for handling a specific request can be defined in the web application configuration file, such that the application developer does not have to alter the code of the coordination agent, unless another strategy is desired. The application agent type is included in the request sent from the delegate servlet to the default coordinator agent. When no application agent of the requested kind exists for the corresponding session, the default coordinator agent will automatically create a new instance. Moreover, unused application agents are automatically removed from the agent platform after a configurable session timeout.

As different applications may have different requirements regarding the request handling, the default strategy is realized in a way that allows it to be easily extended or adapted. The coordinator agent functionality is implemented in a reusable module called coordinator capability (cf. Fig. 4, middle). It exposes an interface in the form of goals that are created during the handling of a request.

Moreover, the capability already contains default plans to handle these goals. To specify different courses of action, the developer may include the capability in a custom agent and define alternative plans for handling these goals. When the coordinator receives a request, a handle_request goal is automatically created, containing the details of the request. The default plan for handling this goal starts by creating another goal find_app_agent with the purpose of finding (and maybe creating) a suitable application agent. In order to check if the desired application agent already (or still) exists the default find plan uses a simple ping mechanism, which is readily available via the included Ping capability. After an agent has been found or newly created, the plan sends a message with the request data to this agent. The default plan for handling the find_app_agent goal realizes the session handling described above.

The two goals provide different entry points for extending or changing the request handling. By defining new plans for the find_app_agent goal, developers can realize different strategies for how a web request gets dispatched to application agents. Alternatively, by directly reacting to the handle_request goal, plans can be created to process web requests without the need for additional application agents (e.g. doing all processing in the coordinator agent or delegating to other software components). Alternative plans can be developed to handle various types of requests in different situations. For the selection of suitable plans, BDI-style reasoning is applied, such that e.g. plans get selected according to pre- or context-conditions and alternative plans are tried, when some selected plan fails.

3.3 Web Interaction Capability

Using the default strategy described in the last section, web requests are forwarded by the generic coordinator agent as messages to an application agent, which is implemented by the application developer. To simplify the development of application agents, the Webbridge framework provides a reusable module, called web interaction capability (cf. Fig. 4, right), which manages the communication with the coordinator agent. The web interaction capability is included in an application agent and automatically handles request messages sent by the coordinator. For each message a goal of type web_request is created, which has to be handled by plans, created by the application developer. The result of the goal processing is automatically communicated back to the coordinator.

From the viewpoint of application developers, the web interaction capability converts web requests into goals that belong to the application agent. Therefore, the details of the web request handling are abstracted away from agent programmers allowing them to focus on the behavior of the application agent by setting up custom plans to handle the different kinds of web_request goals.

3.4 Application Development

To further illustrate the purpose of the framework components, this section presents important activities that can be employed for building a web-based agent application using the framework. The main purpose of the Webbridge framework is to support the interactions of a user with the application agents. Therefore, the web interface development for the application should be based on a use-case analysis of the user with the system. In this respect, first those interactions have to be identified that are handled via the web. Depending on the application scenario other interaction forms such as email might be necessary as well. Then, the semantics of the individual interactions have to be defined in terms of the requested actions, the used application concepts, the response possibilities and the allowed protocol flow in general. These specifications are subsequently used to develop the web and agent tier quite independently and additionally provide the link between both.

For the connection between the web and agent tier, the application objects have to be designed and implemented. The application objects play an important role in the development, because these objects serve as glue between the view and agent parts of the application. These objects are used in both and are exchanged between them. The application objects store beliefs of the agents and are used in the presentation tier to provide dynamic content which is extracted out for textual presentation. This approach allows for a homogeneous and transparent view on the data in the whole framework.

The main tasks for realizing the web tier consist in designing the request and result web sites. Request web sites provide interaction points via forms and have to deliver form data to the processing agents. To facilitate the transformation of the plain text of the forms into meaningful application objects usually custom web data preprocessors have to be constructed that will be automatically invoked by the Webbridge framework. Result pages are produced as responses to user requests and therefore have the purpose to render the processing outcomes in a user-friendly way. Therefore, for each result page the required application objects have to be specified, from which necessary information can be extracted and incorporated into the generated page.

For the agent tier one preparatory task consists in defining a strategy for web request processing. This strategy has to specify which agent types are generally responsible for processing web requests and what agent instances handle which requests. As default strategy the Webbridge framework provides a session-oriented model in which agent instances are created for each user visiting a site. If this is not sufficient and a more elaborate scheme is needed existing extension points in the Webbridge architecture can be exploited. The second task for realizing the agent tier concerns the provision of the application logic for processing web requests. This task is supported by the underlying idea that web requests are transformed to agent goals, which can be handled in the same way other goals are processed. The realization of the application logic further has to consider, which application objects are required in the web tier. Thirdly, the dialog control of the application has to be realized by ensuring that actions can only invoked when the context allows this. This task is simplified by the general BDI mechanisms that allow pre- and context conditions being specified for plans. Hence, the validity of a request can be declaratively specified and is automatically verified by the system.

For the development of the web and agent tiers existing IDEs such as the eclipse wtp (web tools platform) can be used. This is possible for the web tier because the Webbridge framework does not change the syntax / semantics of any of the web documents. Similarly, the development of Webbridge agents does not alter the syntax / semantics of Jadex agents and therefore the IDE's standard XML editor for the agent definition files and the IDE's Java editor for the plans is satisfactory. Moreover, the configuration and deployment of the web tier and the agent-based application logic can be performed following the standard procedures for Java web applications and Jadex agents, respectively.

To conclude, the Webbridge framework provides a set of concepts and components allowing to partition an application into a web and an agent tier. Tasks on the web tier do not differ from traditional web development and also on the agent tier most of the web interaction complexities are hidden via the Webbridge framework.

4   Example Application

In this section, important aspects of an example application developed with the Jadex Webbridge framework are explained. The application represents an electronic bookstore and is inspired by the book "Developing Intelligent Agent Systems: A Practical Guide" [15]. In this scenario customers are allowed to search for and order books through a web-based user interface. Other use cases of customers of the system include managing their account/profile and checking the state of an order. Additionally, the system performs several backend tasks. It has to manage a stock of books and to reorder books from wholesalers in certain intervals.

The application development of the bookstore was guided by the Prometheus methodology [18] and consisted mainly of an analysis, design and implementation of the problem domain. The analysis and design of the application generally followed the descriptions of the book and refined the modeling artifacts until they could be directly implemented. The complete application logic of the system was realized in a multi-agent system as a set of collaborating agents that interact with each other to provide the overall bookstore functionality.

A typical functionality in the bookstore scenario, treated here in more detail, is the management of the shopping cart allowing a customer to add, remove items and finally to check out. In this respect the sales assistant agent is of vital importance as it represents a personal shopping assistant for a customer. For each customer arriving at the web site an individual sales agent is created, which means that the default Webbridge strategy that creates session agent on demand is sufficient and therefore employed.

To show how the web/agent interaction is supported by the Webbridge framework, in the following important code snippets from the bookstore application will be presented and explained next.

```
1   <web−app xmlns="http://java.sun.com/xml/ns/j2ee" version="2.4" ...>
2     <servlet>
3       <servlet−name>DelegateServlet</servlet−name>
4       <servlet−class>jadex.bridge. delegate . DelegateServlet </servlet−class>
5       <init −param>
6         <param−name>agent_container</param−name>
7         <param−value>localhost:9090</param−value>
8       </init−param>
9       <init −param>
10        <param−name>session_agent_type</param−name>
11        <param−value>jadex.bookstore.SalesAssistant</param−value>
12      </init−param>
13      <init −param>
14        <param−name>webdata_preprocessor</param−name>
15        <param−value>jadex.bookstore.BookstorePreprocessor</param−value>
16      </init−param>
17      ...
18    </servlet>
19    ...
20    <servlet−mapping>
21      <servlet−name>DelegateServlet</servlet−name>
22      <url−pattern>/</url−pattern>
23    </servlet−mapping>
24    ...
25  </web−app>
```

Fig. 5. Web.xml application configuration cutout

4.1 Application Configuration

The basic configuration of the web related parts of the bookstore application defines which web requests are managed by what parts of the agent tier and therefore provides the necessary link between both parts. This configuration is defined the within the standardized web.xml file [7], which mainly determines which servlets are responsible for what URLs.

Figure 5 shows a relevant cutout of the bookstore web.xml and mainly consists of servlet descriptions and their URL-mappings respectively. In the example, only the specification of the DelegateServlet and its mapping are shown. It uses the default DelegateServlet of the Webbridge framework (lines 2-18) and additionally defines several parameter values (lines 5-16). Among these are the contact address of the coordinator agent (lines 5-8), the class name of the application agent type (lines 9-12) and the class name of the bookstore specific webdata preprocessor (lines 13-16). In the mapping part it is defined that the DelegateServlet is the default handler for all page requests (lines 20-23). If some parts of the application should be generated by other means e.g. via normal

```
1   public class BookstorePreprocessor extends DefaultWebdataPreprocessor {
2       public Request preprocessWebdata(HttpServletRequest request) {
3           Request  agentrequest     = super.preprocessWebdata(request);
4
5           if (request.getRequestURI().indexOf("addOrderItem")!=−1) {
6               int isbn     = Integer.parseInt(request.getParameter("isbn"));
7               int amount = Integer.parseInt(request.getParameter("amount"));
8               OrderItem  item    = new OrderItem(isbn, amount);
9               agentrequest.addParameterValue("item", item);
10          }
11          ...
12          return agentrequest;
13      }
14  }
```

Fig. 6. Mapping HTTP request parameters to application objects

JSPs more specific mappings can be defined which have precedence over the DelegateServlet. In the bookstore example, e.g. further JSPs containing general information about the store and contact details have been defined in the full web.xml definition.

In general, the Webbridge framework uses an established and standardized way for the web application configuration. Therefore, the application can be deployed using an arbitrary web container such as Apache Tomcat[3] or IBM WebSphere[4]. Webbridge specific settings are defined in form of parameters of existing elements.

4.2   Preprocessing of Web Requests

Starting point of the scenario is that a human user is surfing at the web site of the electronic bookstore and decides to order some books after her fancy. When adding a book to the shopping cart an "addOrderItem HTTP request" is automatically generated by the browser. The request contains the item's ISBN and the amount of items to be added and is processed by the delegate servlet.

For seamless integration between the web and the agent layer, the application agent (i.e. the sales assistant agent of the bookstore) should not be required to handle details of HTTP-based interaction, such as parsing URL-patterns and MIME-encoding of request parameters. Therefore, the handling of these details is performed in the delegate servlet, which forwards only domain-level information based on the defined application concepts. The mapping between data received from a web form and domain-level objects are achieved using the extensible preprocessing mechanism provided by the Webbridge framework.

---

[3] http://tomcat.apache.org/
[4] http://www.ibm.com/software/websphere

```
 1   <agent name="SalesAssistant">
 2       <capabilities >
 3           <capability  name="webcap" file="WebInteraction"/>
 4       </capabilities >
 5
 6       <goals>
 7           <achievegoal name="web_request">
 8               <assignto ref="webcap.web_request"/>
 9               <parameter name="type" class="String"/>
10               <parameter name="request" class="jadex.bridge.onto.Request"/>
11               <parameter name="response" class="jadex.bridge.onto.Response"
12                   direction ="out"/>
13           </achievegoal>
14       </goals>
15
16       <plans>
17           <plan name="additem_plan">
18               <parameter name="item" class="OrderItem">
19                   <value>$goal.request.getParameterValue("item")</value>
20               </parameter>
21               <body>new AddOrderItemPlan()</body>
22               <trigger>
23                   <goal ref="web_request">
24                       <parameter ref="type">
25                           <value> "addOrderItem"</value>
26                       </parameter>
27                   </goal>
28               </trigger>
29           </plan>
30       </plans>
31   </agent>
```

Fig. 7. XML definition file excerpt from the SalesAssistant agent

In the bookstore scenario the data from the "addOrderItem" web form are represented as simple strings, while the sales assistant agent only handles bookstore application concepts containing objects such as an OrderItem. Therefore, the domain-dependent BookstorePreprocessor is used by the delegate servlet to extract the values from the request (see fig. 6, lines 6, 7) and create a new domain object of type OrderItem (line 8). The ordered item is subsequently added to the agent-based request (line 9) which will be sent to the coordinator agent.

The preprocessing facility of the Webbridge framework therefore solves the problem of different representations within the web and the agent tier in a generic manner by converting textual data to directly processable application objects.

4.3   Request Execution in the Agent Layer

The coordinator agent processes the request by determining if it belongs to an ongoing conversation. In this case the request will be directly transformed into an agent message and forwarded to the corresponding application agent. Otherwise the coordinator first needs to instantiate a new application agent whose type is specified directly within the request. In this example, sales assistant agents are responsible for handling the user interaction, i.e. for each web session a corresponding sales assistant agent is created, which stays alive until the user leaves the site (as determined by a lack of activity for some time).

The agent definition file of the sales assistant is shown in Fig. 7. It includes the Webbridge functionalities via the web interaction capability (line 3). This capability mainly exports the web_request goal so that it is sufficient for the sales assistant agent to react on all domain-dependent kinds of web_request goals. In order to do this it is necessary that the web_request goal is declared and connected to the exported original one within the capability (lines 7-13). The goal exposes two in-parameters containing the domain-dependent goal type (line 9) and the agent-based web request (line 10) and one out-parameter for the agent-based response (line 11, 12).

The application code is contained in plans, which are used to process the web_request goals that are automatically created by the generic web interaction capability. The reasoning engine uses the goal parameters to find matching plans, which are executed in turn until one plan produces a suitable result. In the example, the additem_plan (lines 17-29) matches web_request goals of type addOrderItem (line 24-26). Because of the preprocessing described earlier, the agent only has to cope with application specific objects like the OrderItem (lines 18-20). The plan body (omitted here) whose creation is specified within the plan head (line 21) contains the agent-based application logic to handle the customer request. One purpose of this plan is simply to update the shopping cart of the customer and store the result in the response object of the goal. In making use of the advantages of the agent-based design, the sales assistant agent further interacts with other agents in the backend of the bookstore application. It checks the availability of the item by querying a so-called stock manager agent and at the same time determines possible delivery options by negotiating with a delivery manager agent. The results of these possibly lengthy additional interactions are not passed back to the user in the context of the initial web request. Instead, they are stored locally in the beliefbase of the sales assistant, which is then able to instantly present this information to the user, if requested.

The example highlights the general capability of the Webbridge framework reducing the effort of processing a web request. This is achieved by a transformation of the request to an agent goal retaining the full flexibility of agent reasoning capabilities. Furthermore, extension points within the webbridge architecture allow the realization of different strategies with respect to the assignment of request to agents.

```
1   <%@page contentType="text/html; charset=ISO-8859-1"%>
2   <%@page import="de.vsis.bookstore.UserContext" %>
3   <%@page import="de.vsis.bookstore.CustomerOrder" %>
4   <%@page import="de.vsis.bookstore.OrderItem" %>
5   <% UserContext ctx = (UserContext) request.getAttribute("context"); %>
6   <jsp:include page="header.jsp" flush="true"/>
7       <h1>Keep track of your order:</h1>
8       <div>
9         Current orders of customer <%= ctx.getCustomerID() %>
10        <ol>
11        <%
12          CustomerOrder[] orders = ctx.getCustomerOrders();
13          for (int i =0; i< orders.length; i++) {
14            OrderItem[] items = orders[i].getOrderItems();
15            for (int j =0;j< items.length; j++) {
16              %><li><%= items[j].getIsbn() %>
17              ( <%= items[j].getArrivalDate() %>)</li><%
18            }
19          }
20        %>
21        </ol>
22      </div>
23  <jsp:include page="footer.jsp" flush ="true"/>
```

Fig. 8. JSP page for the shopping cart of a customer

4.4   Result Page Generation

The visual part of the bookstore front-end is developed using JSP technology. This means, that the application logic in the agent layer produces dynamic application objects, which are used in the web layer to fill in the gaps of HTML templates, specified in the JSP language. Fig. 8 shows one such JSP page, specifically the order status page. It has the purpose to display the current orders of a customer together with the expected delivery dates. When the user requests the order status, the sales assistant agent will retrieve the corresponding information from the database. The information is stored in the user context, represented as a list of customer orders, each containing a list of order items.

The JSP page therefore imports the required context, order, and item classes from the bookstore domain model (lines 2-4). The context object that is produced by the sales assistant agent is obtained from the request (line 5). The information in the context about open orders and order items is used to generate HTML code for the list of open orders and associated delivery dates (lines 12-19).

The Webbridge framework simplifies the development for web designers / programmers, because the JSP pages do not have to deal with agent-related aspects of the application. This is achieved by supporting an application dependent domain model, which allows representing all required domain data in form of Java objects. These Java objects are managed by the agents in the backend (e.g. stored in beliefs or an external database) and are made available to the web layer by the Webbridge framework.

5 Related Work

Regarding agents and the web, there are basically two different strands of related work that need to be considered. On the one hand, a huge amount of work has been carried out in the context of traditional Model 2 Java web frameworks. In this area many different frameworks have emerged that are able to satisfy nearly any kind of developer needs. One of the first and best-known frameworks is Jakarta Struts [5], which is still widely used and also features a large developer community. Struts directly adopts the Model 2 pattern and introduces user-defined actions that perform the work of the application and finally create Java beans that can be processed in the view. Due to some limitations of Struts many fundamentally different Model 2 approaches such as Spring MVC [13] and JavaServer Faces (JSF) [10] have been proposed. A detailed comparison of many traditional web frameworks can be found e.g. in [8]. To be able to use the existing web frameworks in combination with agent technology it is necessary to embed the agents in a web framework friendly manner. This approach is e.g. followed by the Agentis AdaptivEnterprise Suite [17], which converts agents into J2EE application server components and makes them accessible for web frameworks in this way. Nevertheless, this approach limits the exploitation of agent technology as important functionalities such as the application flow and dialog management are typically handled by web frameworks cannot be delegated to the agent layer.

On the other hand, approaches need to be investigated that build up a web framework especially for agent technology and are therefore directly comparable with our architecture. Stunningly, this strand of research is nearly non-existent today. Instead, in the agent community a large body of research has been carried out in the field of interface agents aiming at the improvement of human computer interaction e.g. [14] but this does not directly contribute to the problem addressed in this paper. The only generic approach is provided by the JACK WebBot solution[5] which can be used to equip JACK agent applications with a web front-end. The approach is similar to ours as also the controller part represents the mediator component between the web and the agent layer. Although the WebBot architecture is very flexible, it does not provide a clean framework approach. Instead, the agent programmer has to design and implement generic functionalities such as agent session management by herself and cannot make use of predefined modules for that purpose. Additionally, it does not allow consistently using the same application objects on all tiers and hence requires tedious conversions being done by the application instead of the framework.

Besides the WebBot architecture, also some ad-hoc solutions exist, which use external interfaces provided by an agent platform (e.g. the JadeGateway class in

---

[5] http://www.agent-software.com

JADE [1] or the HabitatGateway class in Tryllian's ADK[6]). As such interfaces only provide generic access to the agent platform, most of the technical details concerning the connection of agents with the web layer have to be handcrafted by the developers in these approaches.

6   Conclusion and Outlook

This paper has presented an architecture and a framework for simplifying the development of web-based agent applications as these kinds of systems gain steadily more importance in the context of business solutions. To achieve an integration between the web and the agent world a novel agent-based architecture conformant to the well-known Model-2 design pattern has been proposed. The agentified Model 2 architecture intentionally refines only a small part of the original architecture by refining the *controller component*. This allows a developer to use agents for the application functionality while preserving the usability of the existing and well suited Model 2 techniques for rendering (JSPs) and model representation (JavaBeans). One crucial aspect of this extended architecture is the partitioning of the controller into three distinct functionalities: *delegate servlet, coordinator agent* and *application agents*. The delegate has the main purpose to forward business tasks that originate from browser requests to the coordinator agent. The coordinator processes requests by distributing them to domain-dependent application agents. A main advantage of the proposed generic architecture consists in the separation of concerns established by Model 2. The architecture therefore cleanly detaches the web layer from the agent layer and facilitates their largely independent development.

Moreover, the Jadex Webbridge framework has been presented, which implements the aforementioned architecture. The main characteristic of this framework is the support for agent technology in the context of web applications. The framework provides ready-to-use and extensible functionalities realizing the delegate servlet and the coordinator agent. Additionally a web interaction module (capability) is provided that encapsulates the generic functionalities needed by application agents. This capability transfers web requests to web_request goals which can be handled in the same way as any other ordinary agent goal. The capability automatically handles all interactions with the coordinator and reduces the task of the agent developer to writing plans for the domain logic of pursuing web_request goals.

Future work will be targeted at improving the processing of web interactions. Currently, web interactions are short-lived meaning that request goals are created whenever a user issues a new browser request so that the interaction state has to be preserved within the agent's beliefs. A more advanced approach would allow to treat a conversation as a whole e.g. within a plan allowing the agent to manage the interaction in a similar sense as normal message-based protocols. This would extend the semantics of an interaction goal from a short-term interaction to a whole workflow (e.g. the book buying use case in the example presented).

---

[6] http://www.tryllian.com

References

1. Bellifemine, F., Caire, G., Greenwood, D.: Developing Multi-Agent systems with JADE. John Wiley & Sons, Chichester (2007)
2. Benfield, S., Hendrickson, J., Galanti, D.: Making a strong business case for multi-agent technology. In: Proc. of Autonomous Agents and Multiagent Systems (AAMAS 2006), pp. 10–15. ACM Press, New York (2006)
3. Braubach, L., Pokahr, A., Lamersdorf, W.: Jadex: A BDI Agent System Combining Middleware and Reasoning. In: Software Agent-Based Applications, Platforms and Development Kits, pp. 143–168. Birkhäuser Verlag, Basel (2005)
4. Castro, J., Kolp, M., Mylopoulos, J.: Developing agent-oriented information systems for the enterprise. In: Proc. of the 2nd Int. Conf. on Enterprise Information Systems (ICEIS 2000), pp. 9–24. ICEIS Secretariat (2000)
5. Cavaness, C.: Programming Jakarta Struts. O'Reilly Media, Sebastopol (2004)
6. Coward, D.: Java Servlet, Specification Version 2.3. Sun Mircosystems (2001)
7. Delisle, P., Luehe, J., Roth, M.: JavaServer Pages, Specification Version 2.1. Sun Mircosystems (2006)
8. Ford, N.: Art of Java Web development: Struts, Tapestry, Commons, Velocity, JUnit, Axis, Cocoon, InternetBeans, WebWorks. Manning Publications (2003)
9. Hamilton, G.: JavaBeans, Specification Version 1.01. Sun Mircosystems (1997)
10. Holmes, J., Schalk, C.: JavaServer Faces: The Complete Reference. McGraw-Hill Osborne Media, New York (2006)
11. Jennings, N.R., Wooldridge, M.J.: Agent Technology - Foundations, Applications and Markets. Springer, Heidelberg (1998)
12. Krasner, G., Pope, S.: A description of the model-view-controller user interface paradigm in the smalltalk-80 system. Journal of Object Oriented Programming 1(3), 26–49 (1988)
13. Ladd, S., Davison, D., Devijver, S., Yates, C.: Expert Spring MVC and Web Flow. APress (2006)
14. Maes, P.: Agents that reduce work and information overload. Communications of the ACM 37(7), 30–40 (1994)
15. Padgham, L., Winikoff, M.: Developing Intelligent Agent Systems: A Practical Guide. John Wiley & Sons, Chichester (2004)
16. Pokahr, A., Braubach, L., Lamersdorf, W.: Jadex: A BDI Reasoning Engine. In: Bordini, R., Dastani, M., Dix, J., El Fallah Seghrouchni, A. (eds.) Multi-Agent Programming: Languages, Platforms and Applications, pp. 149–174. Springer, Heidelberg (2005)
17. Taylor, P., Evans-Greenwood, P., Odell, J.: Agents in the enterprise. In: Australian Software Engineering Conference (ASWEC 2005), pp. 9–24. IEEE, Los Alamitos (2005)
18. Winikoff, M., Padgham, L.: The Prometheus Methodology. In: Methodologies and Software Engineering For Agent Systems, pp. 217–234. Kluwer, Dordrecht (2004)

Specifying Interaction Space Components in a FIPA-ACL Interaction Framework

Ernesto German and Leonid Sheremetov

Mexican Petroleum Institute
Eje Central Lazaro Cardenas 152, San Bartolo Atepehuacan,
Distrito Federal, Mexico
{egerman,sher}@imp.mx

Abstract. Despite the acceptance of FIPA-ACL as a standard for agent communications, there exist a gap between its specification and infrastructures supporting interactions among agents. The hypothesis we study in this paper is that interaction space components must be specified and described in depth by taking into account an explicit six-layered FIPA-ACL communication model. Based on this model, generic components are developed for a FIPA-ACL interaction framework. An implementation of interaction components is described within the CAPNET agent platform in an integrated way with the agent interaction architecture. The use of interaction space components for engineering agent interactions is illustrated by example.

Keywords: FIPA-ACL, Interaction Framework, Interaction Space.

1 Introduction

Communication is central to Multi-Agent System (MAS), for without it, any benefits of interaction vanish and the agency degenerates into a collection of individuals with a chaotic behaviour. Going far beyond dealing with communication issues at the level of data and physical message transport, Agent Communication Languages (ACL) are complex structures composed of different components that specify the message content syntax and meaning, message parameters such as the sender and receiver, and the pragmatics of the intention of the message. Furthermore, interaction also includes interpretation and validation that the message has been correctly interpreted.

In spite of many efforts on designing flexible and robust agent interactions, very little attention has been paid so far on providing support for runtime processing of such interactions using higher level concepts than messages. Indeed, current MAS infrastructures (such as languages, toolkits, frameworks and platforms) are limited mostly to simple message sending and receiving for processing agent interactions [1]. Although interaction protocol is a higher level concept than messages, they are supported at runtime only for controlling the sequence of messages but not for processing the whole set of activities involved in ACL interaction. Nevertheless, the increasing

M. Dastani et al. (Eds.): LADS 2007, LNAI 5118, pp. 191–208, 2008.
© Springer-Verlag Berlin Heidelberg 2008

complexity of MAS integration requires more effective interactive behaviors based on message semantics and pragmatics [2], [3].

Though FIPA-ACL has become a standard to engineer agent-to-agent interactions, two main objectives of this language, autonomy and interoperability, are not addressed in MAS engineering. Our experience in developing MAS with current FIPA-ACL infrastructures shows that interactions typically have been engineered using ad-hoc communication assumptions made for reasons of communication efficiency or developer convenience [4], [5]. Furthermore, awareness of these assumptions is critical to properly interpret and understand messages at runtime, becoming autonomy and interoperability almost impossible to achieve [6]. So, while application specific agents are useful to test and validate different approaches to develop agents, their interaction components are extremely difficult to generalize, re-use and extend for agents integration in open networking applications without participation of their developers.

Till now, the FIPA communication model has focused more on how agents could communicate by separately specifying different components. However, little work has been done on explicitly specifying organization and integration of these components to enable message processing by agents. In our previous work a FIPA-ACL interaction framework was described through three high level concepts: interaction space, interaction models and interaction architecture [7].

The focus of this paper is the specification of the interaction space components and their implementation within the CAPNET agent platform. We deal with the problems of implementing and interpreting interactions by explicitly arranging and engineering different layers found in the FIPA-ACL specification[1]. The paper considers a six-layered communication model which is inspired in a recently revised FIPA communication model [8]. These layers go from physical transport and encoding to internal agent processing of syntax, semantics and pragmatics of messages.

In particular, we think that explicit support for interaction components helps to fill the gap between FIPA-ACL specification and implementation of runtime interaction processing. To facilitate the engineering of MAS interactions we developed interaction space components as an important step to address the previously mentioned problems of interaction engineering. Our approach considers that these interaction components are worth when integrated in an agent interaction framework.

The structure of the paper is the following. In section 2 the specification of an explicit FIPA communication model is provided. Section 3 describes the generic interaction space components composing each layer of the model. Section 4 gives details of the interaction space components implementation within the CAPNET agent platform. In section 5 the process of instantiation of interaction space components in an agent application is illustrated by example from MAS managing transportation logistics of offshore oil platforms. It is also explained how these components are useful to validate interactions at runtime by the agent interaction architecture. Finally, some related works are discussed and conclusions are given.

---

[1] Foundation for Intelligent Physical Agents. FIPA Communicative Act Library Specification http://www.fipa.org/specs/fipa00037/ and FIPA ACL Message Structure Specification http://www.fipa.org/specs/fipa00061/

2 FIPA Communication Model

The standard FIPA Communication model starts on top of the OSI reference model [9] extending the application layer. In Fig. 1, the components of this model are shown. An envelope encapsulates FIPA-ACL messages before they are transmitted over a Transport Protocol. Messages are units of communication expressed in FIPA-ACL. Each message stores the content of the communication, which is expressed in a Content Language. The content contains symbols which belong to an ontology named in the message. Interaction protocols are components engaged in controlling sequences of related messages in order to maintain conversations between agents. Envelope, message and content are encoded using data structures (EnvelopeEncodingScheme, ACLEncodingScheme, CLEncodingScheme) such as XML, string formats and bit efficient schemas, rather than binary codifications.

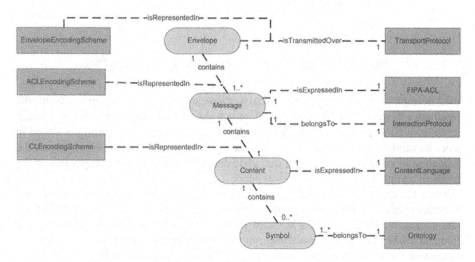

Fig. 1. Components of the FIPA communication model

The engineering perspective developed in this paper (Fig. 2), is inspired in a recently revised FIPA communication model [8], and supports six FIPA-ACL computation layers: Message Transport, Message Encoding, Content Expression Syntax, Content Expression Semantics, Communicative Acts and Interaction Protocols. At the message transport layer, agents look for and use asynchronous message transport services to interchange messages through physical network protocols. At the layer of message encoding, the message structure and encoding are validated because agents serialize messages through the network. Furthermore, message information such as agent identifiers, type of message and payload require parsers. The layer of content expression syntax is a layer where agents recognize the entities built-in into the content of messages by determining whether the content structure is correct in accordance with a common content language representation.

The layer of content expression meaning (semantics) refers to the use of ontologies to validate the meaning of content by explicitly representing domain symbols. At the

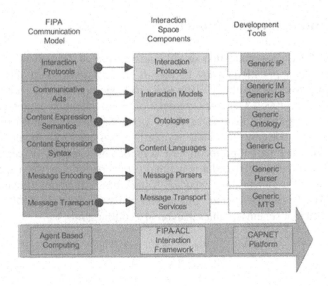

Fig. 2. FIPA communication model: an engineering perspective

layer of communicative acts agents have to manage messages taking into account the pragmatics of each type of communicative act. Almost all communicative acts entail access to a Knowledge Base (KB) where application domain information is stored in order to validate their pragmatics. Interaction protocols is the layer where occurs the validation of communications that use a pre-defined sequence of messages among the involved agents.

From the engineering perspective, we focus on interaction space components and activities required for validating and interpreting messages at each layer of the model. The approach based on layers is taken to better organize and build the interaction components because it lets specifying not only components themselves but also computation in the context of runtime message validation process described in [7]. In the following sections, we describe the components needed at each layer and their implementation within the CAPNET agent interaction framework.

3   Interaction Space Components

The Interaction Space (IS) is an environment that stores interaction components of the agent that can be accessed in order to validate interactions at runtime. It is integrated by the following components: message transport services, message parsers, content languages, ontologies, interaction models, interaction protocols and a knowledge base. Interaction space extends FIPA-ACL interaction infrastructure and forms a part of agent architecture (Fig. 2). An Interaction Model (IM) represents a modular unit permitting the validation of a simple interaction. IM includes five modules for programming validation of content syntax and semantics, feasibility preconditions, rational effect of messages and interaction termination. Interaction models let programmers design and implement validation code for different communicative acts taking into account the requirements of both communication and application. In each module of the interaction models, components of the interaction space are resolved and used at runtime. For example, a content language component is invoked in the module to validate syntax of content and an ontology component is invoked in the module to validate semantics of content.

The Agent Interaction Architecture (AIA) is defined as a component to control creation and processing of interactions through validation of interaction models within the interaction space of an agent. Transport services and message parsers components are also invoked within the AIA.

3.1 Message Transport Service

Let us consider the layers of the interaction space. The first layer is composed of message Transport Services (TS). TSs are components that agents use to exploit several available network infrastructures. Concrete networking technologies are available along distributed computing infrastructures so that different TSs could be implemented for exploiting the advantages of each type of technology such as SOAP-XML for web services-based agents, HTTP for web-based agents and TCP for remote object-oriented agents. Since some of these communication services are commonly used in known MAS infrastructures, in this framework they are considered to be part of the interaction space like specific components that will be invoked dynamically when agents need their services.

Although each TS has its own implementation features they can be implemented using common interfaces in order to be added to the interaction space of the agent. Basically, this type of services must provide functionality to process the sending and receiving of transport messages. Transport-message is the communication unit at this layer of the model and includes FIPA-ACL message as the payload and the envelope.

3.2 Message Parser

At the layer of message encoding, each message is either encoded or decoded[2] by a component called a message parser. The main activity of parsers is to find out whether the structure of the message complies with FIPA-ACL. This is a first level of syntactic validation of the message. Typically, several message parsers can be available as software components. These parsers must be implemented following a well defined interface to generate and parse messages represented through different codification schemas specified by FIPA[3]. The information about parser components is explicitly available in the interaction space. With this information, agent interaction architecture can dynamically analyze the message requirements applying the specific parser.

3.3 Content Language

Agent communication is designed to represent the content of messages following certain common criteria in such way that content can be understood by both sides of

---

[2] Encode means what is usually called "generate" or "format" and decode is similar to parse.
[3] See FIPA-ACL Message Representation Library at http://fipa.org/specs/fipa00068/index.html

Table 1. Content entities for FIPA-ACL communicative acts

Communicative act	Content entities
accept-proposal, agree, cfp, failure, propose, refuse, reject-proposal, request-when, request-whenever	action, proposition
request, cancel	action, message
confirm, disconfirm, inform, inform-if, query-if	proposition
inform-ref	object reference
not-understood	action, message, proposition
propagate, proxy	object reference, message, proposition
query-ref, subscribe	object reference

the communication. Since agents could manage different content languages, similar basic elements should be used. Based on the specification of each communicative act of FIPA-ACL, five content entities that can be part of message content are implicitly defined: actions, propositions, domain objects, references to objects and FIPA-ACL messages (Table 1).

We define a Generic Content Language (GCL) component based on the basic content entities. The GCL also contains a set of content objects which are useful to build message content combining one or more basic entities. Every concrete CL should give only one content object per communicative act. For example the *"request-when"* communicative act combines an action and a proposition in the content. So that the *request-when* content object must be composed of such two entities. Since every entity and content object is designed to be used in a serialized way in messages, they must give two functions. The first one is used to serialize the entity in an encoded format in such way that it can be part of the message. The second one does the opposite task: from a serialized representation gets the entity information and re-builds the entity. The validation criteria for each concrete CL are left to the CL programmer's choice because they depend on the particular requirements of each type of entity.

3.4 Ontology

The communication model of FIPA-ACL is based on the assumption that two agents try to interact sharing a common ontology of the domain in order to give meaning to the entities represented in a message's content. For a given domain, agents can decide to access ontologies explicitly represented and stored. In this paper, we consider that ontologies engineering must share common design lines. That is why, we propose to define a Generic Ontology (GO) as software component. Based on GO, concrete ontologies can be built and added as part of the interaction space of agents and can be accessed to validate the semantics of message's content at runtime.

The GO is basically formed by all content entities given by generic content language but messages. GO has two parts. In the first one, collections for actions, propositions, domain objects and object references store the information about the domain. In the second part, there are a set of validation functions for each type of content entity forming the ontology and one validation function for each type of communicative act. The criteria for internal organizing, storing and validating the entities in the ontology are left open for developers of concrete implementations.

3.5 Interaction Model

An interaction model is a key concept of the framework for implementing the communicative acts layer of the FIPA Communication model. An IM is seen as an interaction component for validating single-message interactions. For each communicative act, the IM is composed of the modules covering five validation phases: validation of the content structure with a specific content language, validation of content semantics with a specific ontology, validation of feasibility preconditions, validation of rational effect, and validation of the termination conditions.

Depending on the interaction requirements of each agent, different interaction models implemented according with supported interaction capabilities such as communicative acts, content languages and ontologies are required. Each IM is stored in the interaction space to be automatically used when messages fit its requirements. The idea is that IMs can be as reusable for different application agents as possible or at least ready to be refined by specializing functionality.

When agents interact and try to achieve pragmatics of communicative acts (feasibility preconditions and rational effects), almost always they have to store, query or modify concrete information about the application. The knowledge base (KB) is an interaction space component used to complete several types of interactions.

Being consistent with the knowledge model (composed of a basic set of content entities) given by the FIPA-ACL and followed in both the generic CL and generic ontology, the KB must give the possibility of managing actions, propositions and domain objects in order to allow agents to reason about the requirements of communicative acts. For example, when a request message is going to be sent or is being received, the agent has to check whether or not the action is stored in its KB. Regardless any concrete implementation of the KB, this software component must provide functions to add, query and remove actions, propositions and domain objects.

3.6 Interaction Protocol

The framework requires interaction protocols to attend interactions composed of more than one message. To build concrete IPs, we propose to define a generic interaction protocol as a component with IP common attributes. The specification for a Generic Interaction Protocol (GIP) is given by a unique name of IP, a name of the content language, a name of the ontology and the implementation engaged in controlling the execution sequence and states of the IP. Each agent is able to know the set of protocols it can use at runtime when interactions occur because they are stored in the interaction space. How IPs are invoked and executed is a matter of agent interaction architecture and it is out of the scope of this paper.

4 CAPNET Interaction Space

The current version 2.0 of the CAPNET agent platform [10] is empowered with the interaction framework described in this paper (Fig. 2). In the CAPNET, each type of interaction component is implemented following an object oriented design. The *InteractionSpace* class is a container of concrete objects representing capabilities that can be used dynamically by the validation process of the AIA.

Each concrete component has its own unique descriptive information so that message attributes can be used to resolve at runtime invocation of the correct component, depending on the communication requirements. Each interaction component is engineered by following interfaces and base classes that represent generic component functionality. Components can be implemented by reusing and extending them, thus exploiting the runtime polymorphic advantages for checking and resolving types.

4.1 Message Transport Services

To help the messaging system to work dynamically (and eventually to make agents more autonomous) CAPNET transport services are implemented by following the *IGenericTransportService* interface (Fig. 3-a). This interface defines methods for sending (*sendMessage*) and receiving (*receiveMessage*) messages. The base class *BaseTransportService* declares attributes for transport service type (*MTSType*) and address (*address*).

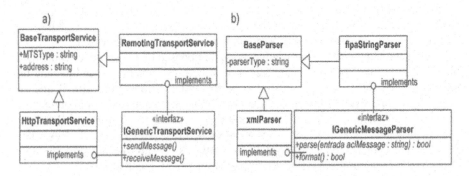

Fig. 3. CAPNET Message Transport Services (a) and Parsers (b)

At the moment, we have implemented two concrete message transport services. In the first one (*RemotingTransportService*), we configure a TCP connection by using distributed .NET framework remote objects for intranet agent applications. The second service (*HttpTransportService*) is an HTTP server infrastructure based on request-response connections to send and receive messages beyond local area networks and for web based agent applications. One single instance of each TS should be added to the interaction space to make them available at runtime.

4.2 Message Parsers

In the CAPNET implementation, the *IGenericMessageParser* interface describes the generic functionality of parser components. Two methods are described to cover the parsing of messages: from the side of the sender agent, *format* should be used for converting a message to its textual representation ready to be communicated by a transport service. *Parse* is the method for checking message syntax and for recovering the message information from a textual representation when a message is received by the receiver agent. As shown in Fig. 3-b, the basic class *BaseParser* can be extended by concrete classes like *xmlParser* and *fipaStringParser*. While the former parser serializes messages by using XML formats and conventions, the latter represents messages in string format.

4.3 Content Languages

CAPNET CLs design is based on the Generic Content Language specification and is implemented by the *GenericCL* class (see Fig. 4-a). *GenericCL* class has a *CLName* attribute to assign a unique identifier of the CL. Also this class is composed of a set of basic entity classes (explained in section 3.3) that implements the *ISerialization* interface supporting methods for serialization syntax validation (*validateDescription*) and for converting the entity to a serializable format (*setDescription*).

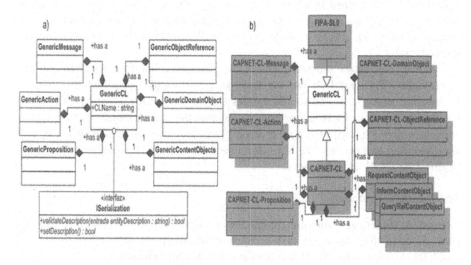

Fig. 4. CAPNET Content Language implementation

Following these design rules, we have developed two concrete CL classes in the CAPNET (Fig. 4-b). *CAPNET-CL* [11] is a proprietary language based on FIPA-RDF0 to represent the syntax of entities. *FIPA-SL0* is the implementation of the FIPA-SL0 specification. Both CLs inherit from *GenericCL* class and implement each entity by the *ISerialization* interface.

4.4 Ontologies

For engineering ontologies, CAPNET offers the *GenericOntology* class which is composed of several common ontology attributes (Fig. 5). Ontologies must have a unique name for identifying them in the interaction space (*OntoName*). The attribute *CLName* is the name of the content language, the entities managed by the ontology

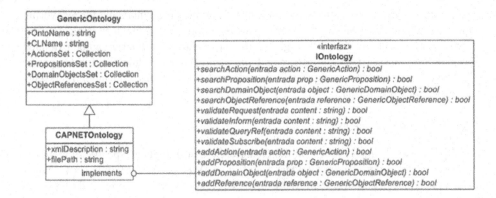

Fig. 5. Design of ontologies in CAPNET

belong to. As established in the Generic Ontology, this software component contains collections for storing actions, propositions, domain objects and references to domain objects (*ActionsSet*, *PropositionsSet*, *DomainObjectsSet* and *ObjectReferencesSet* respectively).

Concrete ontologies must implement the *IOntology* interface to offer common functionality. This interface has functions to search entities (*searchAction*, *search-Proposition*, and so on) and to add entities (*addAction*, *addProposition*, and so on). Finally, the interface includes methods to validate the content object of each type of communicative act supported by the ontology (*validateInform*, *validateRequest*, *validateQueryRef*, and so on). We have developed the *CAPNETOntology* concrete class by using the *CAPNET-CL* entities.

4.5 Interaction Models

Interaction Models are software components based on the *GenericInteractionModel* class. Some of them are illustrated in Fig. 6-a. When a message is going to be processed, the AIA looks for an IM that fits the message requirements.

To control the execution of concurrent IMs at runtime, a set of common attributes identified for interaction models were implemented. *InteractionId* is a unique number to internally identify each individual interaction. *IMName* is used to identify the communicative act of the interaction. The field *message* indicates what message the IM object is related to at runtime. *CLName* and *OntologyName* attributes store the names of the content language and ontology used to represent and validate syntax and semantics of the entities included in the message content. The same type of communicative act can be implemented by different interaction models combining different content languages and ontologies because an agent can participate in different application domains. Each IM developed for a specific agent must implement the *IInteractionModel* interface where the five phases of IM validation cycle are defined (*validateCL*, *validateOntology*, *validateFP*, *validateRE* and *validateTermination*).

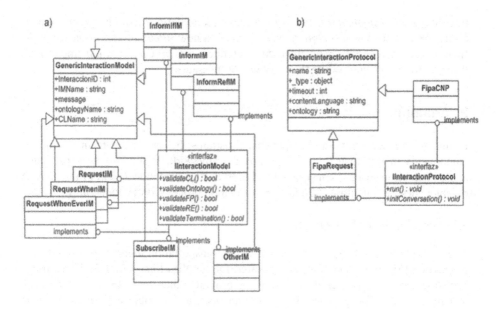

Fig. 6. CAPNET Interaction models (a) and protocols (b)

4.6 Knowledge Base

The CAPNET KB was implemented by the *KnowledgeBase* class. This component is formed by collections to store actions, propositions and domain objects derived from generic classes. Moreover, in our implementation we have found two special types of collections to temporally store monitors. Monitors are propositions and domain objects to be monitored at runtime and are useful to implement some interaction models like *request-when*, *request-when-ever*, *subscribe*, *inform-if* and *query-if* making the agent be aware of entities that have changed their attributes.

Although, having a knowledge base in the agent interaction space can help the agent to perform internal reasoning activities, in this paper we focus on the necessary functionality to carry out interactions. In this sense, the knowledge base class has methods to *add*, *search* and *remove* specific entities and methods to *add*, *update* and *remove* entity monitors when interactions take place at runtime.

4.7 Interaction Protocols

Each interaction protocol is implemented as a software component that includes necessary attributes to dynamically determine its execution. We propose the *GenericInteractionProtocol* base class to encapsulate such attributes that agent interaction architecture can read when messages require the use of a specific IP.

In the case of the CAPNET IP development, the base class considers that each IP has a unique name (such as FIPA-REQUEST, FIPA-CNP, and so on), a timeout (a configurable amount of time the agent is going to wait for the next message in the sequence), content language and the ontology as shown in Fig. 6-b. Concrete IP classes inherit from the base class and also should implement the *IInteractionProtocol* interface where *run* and *initConversation* methods are defined to allow agents concurrently execute several IPs. *Run* is used to create a new thread of execution when the IP is instantiated in the agent interaction architecture. *InitConversation* implements the real strategy of controlling the sequence of messages.

5 Example

In this section we show an example that illustrates the use of the main interaction components in the context of the proposed framework. It shows how a particular agent interaction space is constructed and used during execution as part of the AIA. A complete description of the AIA and the validation process can be found in [8].

5.1 Description of the Example

The example is an excerpt from the MAS for transportation logistics of offshore oil production [5]. Boats and ships are required for supplies transportation. These transportation services are offered by third party providers that the MAS have to find out and request for. This scenario represents an open and flexible environment where heterogeneous agents should interact by using different interaction components. An example MAS is composed of several oil platform agents that request specific supplies to a supplier agent. Supplier agent receives requests, looks for the requested supplies, and negotiates the marine transport services offered by transport agents. To engineer the interactions we have built agents by using the interaction space components of the CAPNET platform. The example is coded in Visual Basic .NET compatible with the .NET framework 1.1. Table 2 shows the interaction components incorporated in each type of agents.

Table 2. Interaction Space components

Agents	TSs	Parser	CLs	Ontology	IMs	IPs
Supplier	http TCP-Remoting	XML FIPA-string	CAPNET-CL FIPA SL0	transport supply	request requestWhen inform	FIPA-request, FIPA-Contract-Net
Platform	TCP-remoting	XML FIPA-string	CAPNET CL FIPA SL0	supply	request inform	FIPA-request
Transport	http	XML FIPA-string	CAPNET CL FIPA SL0	transport supply	requestWhen inform	FIPA-request, FIPA-Contract-Net

5.2 Instantiation of Interaction Space Components

The *supplier* agent has two transport services (*http* and *TCP-Remoting*) because it needs to interact with *Platform* (internal) and *Transport* (external) agents. In the prototype, agents use *XML* and *fipa-string* parsers to validate syntax of FIPA-ACL messages. Resolving which parser will be used is a task done dynamically by the agent interaction architecture by checking the message field encoding for every message and by invoking the required parser component. TSs and parsers are stored in collections of the interaction space (*ts* and *p* in code 4).

When created, application agents get object instances of the *CAPNETCL* and *FI-PASLO* classes and store them in the interaction space (Code 1). Interacting with CAPNET management agents (Agent Management System and Directory Facilitator), they use *FIPASLO* as content language and while communicating among themselves they exchange messages codified in *CAPNET-CL*.

Code 1. The content languages instances are created

```
capnetcl = New CAPNETCL(CONTENT_LANGUAGE_CAPNET-CL)
sl0 = New FIPASL0(CONTENT_LANGUAGE_SL0)
cl = New Hashtable
cl.Add(capnetcl.CLName, capnetcl)
cl.Add(sl0.CLName, sl0)
```

The MAS works with *transport* and *supply* domain ontologies. The *Supplier* and *Transport* agents load both ontologies. *Platform* agents only need *supply* ontology (Code 2). Internally, these ontologies are based on the *CAPNETOntology* class and uses *CAPNET-CL* to represent concrete entities. The *supply* ontology defines the *planningSupply* action to allow *Platform* agents request supplies from *Supplier* agent. This ontology also declares domain object references that can be considered as valid supplies in this domain. In the *transport* ontology the *transportSupplies* action also is defined to negotiate transport services among *Supplier* and *Transport* agents. Every action is also stored in the KB in order to be executed at runtime (Code 4).

Code 2. Segment of the supply ontology creation

```
ontSupp = New CAPNETOntology("supply", capnetcl.CLName)
PlanSupplyAct = New
CAPNETCL.RDFOAction("planningSupply")
PlanSupplyAct.setact("planningSupply")
PlanSupplyAct.setactor("SupplyAgent")
ontSupp.AddAction(PlanSupplyAct)
Dim d1, d2, d11 As CAPNETCL.RDFObjectRef
d1 = New CAPNETCL.RDFObjectRef ("PERF-WATER", "No")
ontSupp.AddObjectReference(d1)
d2 = New CAPNETCL.RDFObjectRef ("DRINK-WATER", "No")
ontSupp.AddObjectReference(d2)
d11 = New CAPNETCL.RDFObjectRef("BUMP-A", "No")
ontSupp.AddObjectReference(d11)
Dim o As New Hashtable
o.Add(ontSupp.OName + ontSupp.CLName, ontSupp)
```

The agents require several interaction models in order to execute specific communication acts supported by the MAS (Code 3). For example, *Platform* agents use *requestIM* for requesting the action *planningSupply* to *Supplier* agent (and whatever supported action). Typically when they request the action, they receive the answer as an inform message that is managed by an *InformIM*. This interaction can also be carried out by applying the *fipa-request* interaction protocol when synchronous communication is preferred. In other interactions, *Supplier* agent uses *requestWhenIM* to ask *Transport* agents to execute the action *transportSupplies* for the supplies assigned to it only when the required supplies are ready to be transported. When each interaction component and collection is created, the agent programmer must create the *InteractionSpace* instance as it is shown in Code 4.

Code 3. Creation of Interaction Models

```
requestWhenIM = New RequestWhenIM(ACL_REQUEST_WHEN)
requestIM = New RequestIM(ACL_REQUEST)
InformIM = New InformIM(ACL_INFORM)
Dim IM As New Hashtable
IM.Add(requestIM.IMName + capnetcl.CLName +
ontoSupp.OName, requestIM)
IM.Add(requestWhenIM.IMName + capnetcl.CLName +
ontoSupp.OName, requestWhenIM)
IM.Add(IIM.IMName + capnetcl.CLName + ontoSupp.OName,
InformIM)
```

Code 4. Creation of the Interaction Space of agents

```
Dim actions As New Hashtable
actions.Add(PlanSupplyAct.Name, PlanSupplyAct)
Dim kb As New KBManager(Props, Objects, actions)
iSpace As New InteractionSpace(ts,p,kb,cl,o,IPs,IM)
```

5.3 Example of Message Validation Processing

Let us illustrate the message validation process by example of *Supplier* agent receiving a *request* message from the *Platform* agent. Fig. 7 shows a fragment from its AIA within the CAPNET Basic Agent illustrating how components are instantiated and invoked by the validation process at runtime.

The interaction starts on the side of the *Platform* agent requesting the *planningSupply* action. While sending the message, the messaging mechanism invokes the *TCP-Remoting* TS as indicated in the message by the programmer. On the side of the *Supplier* agent also connected to a *TCP-Remoting*, the message is received by the messaging mechanism. After that, messaging gets the *XML parser* to validate the structure of this message because the message is encoded with XML syntax. Then, if it is correct, the mechanism looks for an interaction model in order to satisfy the message requirements (related to the type of communicative act, name of CL and name of ontology). If an IM is registered in the Interaction Space, it clones the registered object and returns the IM copy to messaging (*requestIM* in this case).

Every phase of the IM is executed by the corresponding engines of the validation process. It depends upon the agent's role what validation cycle the architecture will

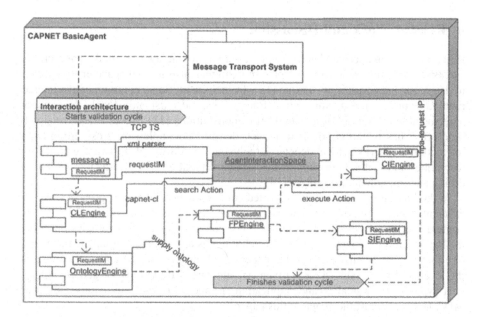

Fig. 7. Agent interaction architecture of the *Supplier* agent receiving *request* message

follow. In the example, the receive validation cycle is activated in order to process the received message. The validation is made by an instance of the *requestIM* class. The interaction model is passed to the CLEngine component which enqueues the interaction model and asynchronously invokes its *validateCL* module. The *CAPNET CL* component is cloned from the IS and is used to validate the *requestContentObject* by invoking its *validateDescription* method.

The results of the validation are stored in the CLEngine and are made available for the validation cycle. If the IM validation fails then the message does not comply with the syntax of that content language. If validation is successful then the interaction model is passed to the ontology engine component where the IM *validateOntology* module is invoked. The meaning of the content is validated in this module by getting a copy of the *supply* ontology component from the IS and by invoking its *validateRequest* method where the requested action description (*planningSupply*) is validated as part of the ontology.

For the next phase, the validation process passes the IM to the Simple Interaction Engine (SIEngine). This engine invokes the interaction model *validateRE* module. In this module, the requested action (*planningSupply*) is obtained from the message content, searched in the KB (where the capability is implemented by an executable action) and executed. The receive validation cycle finishes when the *validateTermination* is invoked and results are communicated back to the *Platform* agent. For composed interactions, the processing mechanism is similar to the simple interaction but when the rational effect is validated, the interaction model is delivered to the engine for composed interactions (CIEngine) in order to be managed by an interaction protocol.

6 Related Work and Discussion

Research work in agent technology is focused on moving away from the hand-crafted agents to the agents able to participate in particular institutional space enabling them to determine capabilities at runtime [12]. In such institutions, communicative interactions take place in open interaction frameworks and exist only thanks to common agreements on the basis of a shared set of conventions [13]. Nevertheless, relatively little effort has been put so far to model, design, and implement crosscutting agent interaction concerns which depend largely on the ability of software engineering techniques and methods to support the explicit separation of concerns throughout the design and implementation stages [14].

In the literature, there are also reported communication layered approaches like the efficient agent communication in wireless environments presented in [15] and the communication model based on interactions, conversations and ontologies described in [16] which only covers specific issues but not as an integrated complete infrastructure that we have considered in this paper. We follow a layered approach similar to the levels defined in the Model Driven Architecture (MDA) [17] for generic component types, type instances and application instances. A rigorous comparison with MDA levels is out of the scope of this paper.

Concerning presented approach, we briefly emphasize three issues i) how autonomy is improved, ii) what type of interoperability is enabled and iii) interaction engineering concerns. Our approach to agent's autonomy is oriented to process interactions. Agents are able to determine by themselves whether or not they can process unforeseen messages at runtime depending on their own interaction capabilities. This is achieved by having both explicitly represented interaction components and an interbuilt agent interaction architecture. It is fairly different from that of representative works like Jadex and Jason presented in [18], which employ a reasoning architecture for deducing agent's actions from internal domain model but not for processing ACL interactions.

Interoperability refers to the programmer's ability to take into account at design time the interaction capabilities of the agents in order to reduce interaction among software developers. It permits development of agent interactions using common interaction space components. Upper level of interoperability could be reached when agents developed within different agent infrastructures try to interoperate using the same interaction components. To reach this level of interoperability we need other platforms implement interaction components following the proposed generic components. Then experiments could be provided to test this issue in practice. Our work is different than other similar approaches found in the literature [19] [20] because it provides interoperability for each layer of the communication model.

Finally, the use of interaction space components releases developers from writing bulk of code to validate each stage of communication. Agent interaction architecture is provided once by the basic agent and it takes the control of agent interaction processing. Without it, development of interactions would require writing code to control each scenario of message processing and for each agent in the MAS. That technique of programming is inflexible, repetitive and prone error because validation of messages at each layer is completely a duty of the developer. As an outcome, we promote the separation of concerns by reusing, extending and sharing different interaction components.

7 Conclusions

In this paper we pointed out the interaction space components that are required to carry out message processing at runtime within the FIPA-ACL interaction framework. We organized the FIPA-ACL communication model through six layers to accomplish agent interactions: transport services, message parsers, content languages, ontologies, communicative acts and interaction protocols. Based on this model, interaction components were identified as part of each layer and arranged as core components of our FIPA-ACL interaction framework.

We proposed that every interaction component should be stored into the agent interaction space as software components that could be accessed at runtime by the agent architecture. Interaction components were defined as generic software components in order to specify their basic functionality in accordance with the expected activities they have to manage at each layer of the communication model. These interaction components are implemented within the CAPNET agent platform. We show by example of the MAS for offshore oil platform logistics how the interaction components can be created in CAPNET agents.

The experiments to measure productivity and the level of maturity of the software that can be produced with this approach are in progress. The first results show that though the interaction architecture is time consuming for each layer of the validation process, this effect on the efficiency is diminished by the concurrency model which is managed by the multi-threaded interaction architecture for each validation engine, so that multiple messages can be processed at the same time and in the correct order. On the other hand, the results also show that developers can reuse IS components at each layer of the interaction model reducing considerably the time to build agent interactions. We are convinced that proposed agent interaction architecture improves autonomy, interoperability and interaction engineering of complex MAS.

Acknowledgments. The first author would like to thank CONACYT and the IMP for supporting the Ph. D. studies that originated this research.

References

1. Winikoff, M.: Implementing Commitment-Based Interaction. In: International Conference on Autonomous Agent and Multi-Agent Systems (AAMAS 2007), Hawaii (May 2007)
2. Omicini, A., Ossowski, S., Ricci, A.: Coordination Infrastructures in the Engineering of Multiagent Systems. Methodologies and Software Engineering for Agent Systems – An AgentLink Perspective. In: Bergenti, F., Gleizes, M., Zambonelli, F. (eds.) Coordination Infrastructures in the Engineering of Multiagent Systems, Kluwer, Dordrecht (2004)
3. Serrano, J.M., Ossowski, S.: On the Impact of Agent Communication Languages on the Implementation of Agent Systems. In: Klusch, M., Ossowski, S., Kashyap, V., Unland, R. (eds.) CIA 2004. LNCS (LNAI), vol. 3191, pp. 92–106. Springer, Heidelberg (2004)
4. Sheremetov, L., Martínez, J., Guerra, J.: Agent Architecture for Dynamic Job Routing in Holonic Environment Based on the Theory of Constraints. In: Mařík, V., McFarlane, D.C., Valckenaers, P. (eds.) HoloMAS 2003. LNCS (LNAI), vol. 2744, pp. 124–133. Springer, Heidelberg (2003)

5. Sheremetov, L., Contreras, M., Valencia, C.: Intelligent Multi-Agent Support for the Contingency Management System. J. of Expert Systems with Applications 26(1), 57–71 (2004)
6. Chaib-Draa, B., Dignum, F.: Trends in Agent Communication Language. Computational Intelligence 18(2), 89–1015 (2002)
7. German, E., Sheremetov, L.: An Agent Framework for Processing FIPA-ACL Messages Based on Interaction Models. In: Luck, M., Padgham, L. (eds.) AOSE 2007. LNCS, vol. 4951, pp. 88–102. Springer, Heidelberg (2008)
8. Poslad, S.: Review of FIPA Specifications, IEEE FIPA Revision of FIPA Specifications Group, Foundation for intelligent Physical Agents (September 2006), http://www.fipa.org
9. Zimmermann, H.: OSI Reference Model–The ISO Model of Architecture for Open Systems Interconnections. IEEE Transactions on Communications 28(4), 425–432 (1980)
10. Contreras, M., Germán, E., Chi, M., Sheremetov, L.: Design and Implementation of a FIPA Compliant Agent Platform in. NET. J. of Object Technology 3(9), 5–28 (2004)
11. Sheremetov, L., Batyrshin, I., Filatov, D., Martínez-Muñoz, J.: An Uncertainty Model for Diagnostic Expert System Based on Fuzzy Algebras of Strict Monotonic Operations. In: Gelbukh, A., Reyes-Garcia, C.A. (eds.) MICAI 2006. LNCS (LNAI), vol. 4293, pp. 165–175. Springer, Heidelberg (2006)
12. Dignum, F., Dignum, V., Thangarajah, J., Padgham, L., Winikoff, M.: Open Agent Systems? In: Luck, M., Padgham, L. (eds.) AOSE 2007, vol. 4951, pp. 73–87. Springer, Heidelberg (2008)
13. Fornara, N., Vigano, F., Colombetti, M.: Agent Communication and Institutions Reality. Agent Communication, State of the Art Survey. In: van Eijk, R., Huget, M., Dignum, F. (eds.) AC 2004. LNCS (LNAI), vol. 3396, pp. 1–17. Springer, Heidelberg (2005)
14. Garcia, A., Chavez, C., Choren, R.: Enhancing Agent-Oriented Models with Aspects. In: International Conference on Autonomous Agents and Multi Agent Systems (AAMAS 2006), Japan (May 2006)
15. Helin, H., Laukkanen, M.: Efficient Agent Communication in Wireless Environments. In: Unland, R., Klusch, M., Calisti, M. (eds.) Software Agent-based Applications, Platforms and Development Kits, pp. 307–330. Birkhäuser, Basel (2005)
16. van Aart, C.: Organizational Principles for Multi-Agent Architectures, pp. 139–176. Birkhäuser, Basel (2005)
17. Kleppe, A., Warmer, J., Bast, W.: MDA Explained, The Model Driven Architecture: Practice and Promise. Addison-Wesley, Reading (2003)
18. Bordini, R., Dastani, M., Dix, J., El Fallah Seghrouchni, A. (eds.): Programming Multi-Agent Systems. Kluwer Academic Publishers, Dordrecht (2005)
19. Pasha, M., Faroog-Ahmad, H., Ali, A., Suguri, H.: Semantic Grid Interoperability Between OWL and FIPA SL. In: Shi, Z.-Z., Sadananda, R. (eds.) PRIMA 2006. LNCS (LNAI), vol. 4088, pp. 714–720. Springer, Heidelberg (2006)
20. Suguri, H., Kodama, E., Miyazaki, M.: Assuring Interoperability in Heterogeneous, Autonomous and Decentralized Multi-Agent Systems. In: Proceedings of 6th International Symposium on Autonomous Decentralized Systems (ISADS 2003), pp. 17–24. IEEE Computer Society, Los Alamitos (2003)

Enabling the Reuse of Platform-Dependent Agents in Heterogeneous Agent-Based Applications

Giancarlo Fortino, Alfredo Garro, and Wilma Russo

Department of Electronics, Computer and Systems Science (DEIS),
University of Calabria, Rende (CS), 87036 Italy
{g.fortino,garro,w.russo}@unical.it

Abstract. There is an increasing interest in the development of applications which involve agents operating on (mobile) agent-based platforms of different types (heterogeneous agent-based applications). In this context, a relevant and emerging issue concerns the possibility of integrating platform dependent agents (i.e. agents which were specifically developed for a particular agent platform) in these applications. This issue becomes particularly important in the development of *inter-organization* agent-based applications where different organizations, which usually adopt different agent platforms and related applications for offering their services, may attempt to join to constitute a new (virtual) organization or, simply, to jointly offer new services to users. This paper presents a solution for enabling the reuse of platform-dependent agents in heterogeneous agent-based applications. The proposed solution is a natural enhancement of JIMAF and makes it the only full-fledged interoperability approach which, without requiring any modification to the platforms made interoperable, fully addresses the main interoperability issues of migration, execution, and communication among heterogeneous mobile agent platforms and also provides platform-dependent agent-based code reuse.

1 Introduction

Open and heterogeneous computing environments, like those based on the Internet, require suitable software engineering paradigms and technologies for designing and implementing applications which usually involve distributed and heterogeneous components collaborating on common goals or competing to maximize their results.

Agents [20] are one of the most diffuse paradigms for tackling the development of distributed applications, as witnessed by both the large number of available agent platforms [1, 2, 7, 8, 13, 16, 17, 24] and the variety of platform-dependent agent-based applications [5]. However, agents developed for a specific agent platform are usually not able to execute on, migrate to, and communicate with agents operating on other different platforms.

To allow for the development of heterogeneous agent-based applications (i.e. applications which involve agents operating on agent-based platforms of different types), several solutions which attempt to address the interoperability issues of execution, migration, and communication have been proposed [4, 11, 22, 28, 30, 6, 14, 21, 23])

M. Dastani et al. (Eds.): LADS 2007, LNAI 5118, pp. 209–224, 2008.

but only few [6, 14, 21, 23] do not require to access and modify the platforms as they provide interoperability by adding an application-level adaptation layer which is able to support the development of heterogeneous agent-based applications.

Another relevant and emerging issue concerns the possibility of using code (agents) which was specifically developed for a particular agent platform (i.e. platform-dependent and *non-interoperable* agents) in a heterogeneous agent-based application. In fact, the development of *inter-organization* agent-based applications is becoming increasingly important as different organizations, which usually adopt different agent platforms for implementing specific applications and offering specific services, may attempt to join to constitute a new (virtual) organization or, simply, to jointly offer new services to users. This goal can be achieved by either completely developing *ex novo* applications or by developing new heterogeneous agent-based applications which also reuse the existing platform-dependent agent code.

This paper presents a solution for integrating platform-dependent code in heterogeneous agent-based applications. The proposed solution is a *natural* enhancement of the Java-based Interoperable Mobile Agent Framework (JIMAF) [9, 10, 18], a framework which can be layered atop available Java-based agent platforms [19]. JIMAF allows for the development of Interoperable Mobile Agents (IMAs) which are able to execute on heterogeneous Java-based agent platforms, to migrate among them and to communicate regardless of the platforms on which the agents operate. The enhancement proposed in this paper makes JIMAF the only full-fledged interoperability approach which, without requiring any modification to the platforms which are made interoperable, fully addresses the main interoperability issues as well as provides platform-dependent code reuse.

In particular, the proposed solution exploits wrapping techniques [11, 14, 25] by means of special agents called Interoperable Wrapper Agents (IWAs). IWAs act as mediators capable of interacting both with JIMAF-based agents (i.e. interoperable agents programmed by using JIMAF), exploiting JIMAF-based communication mechanisms, and with platform-dependent agents by using platform-dependent communication mechanisms.

The remainder of this paper is organized as follows. Section 2 explains the main JIMAF-based components of a heterogeneous agent-based application which also involves platform-dependent agents. Section 3 describes a case study of a virtual organization in the insurance domain which highlights the easiness of using JIMAF for the development of new heterogeneous agent-based applications which are capable of reusing exiting platform-dependent agents. Section 4 discusses the more relevant solutions presented in the literature which address the important issue of integrating platform-dependent agents in heterogeneous agent-based applications; finally, conclusions are drawn and future works delineated.

2 Definition and Implementation of a Heterogeneous Agent-Based Application

The main JIMAF-based components of a heterogeneous agent-based application which also involves platform-dependent agents are shown in Figure 1. In particular,

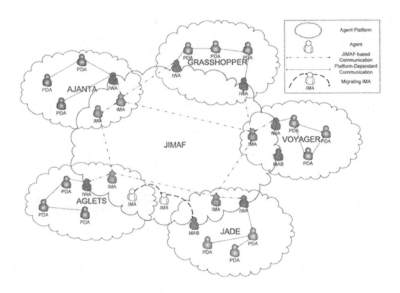

Fig. 1. Architecture of a JIMAF-based Application

the components which support the interoperability issues of execution, migration and communication are the following:

- Interoperable Mobile Agents (IMAs), which are JIMAF-based agents able to migrate, execute, and communicate atop each platform made interoperable by JIMAF (currently Aglets [1], Ajanta [2], Grasshopper [13], Voyager [24], and JADE [17]). These agents constitute the *interoperable part* of the heterogeneous agent-based application written according to JIMAF.
- Mobile Agent Bridges (MABs), which are special-purpose stationary IMAs, provided by JIMAF and capable of supporting the migration of IMAs between heterogeneous agent platforms; in particular a MAB is capable of receiving a migrating IMA from a source agent platform and injecting it into the heterogeneous target agent platform.

The components which enable the use of Platform-Dependent Agents (PDAs), which are agents already available and/or developed ad hoc for a specific platform to fulfil specific services and/or tasks, are the Interoperable Wrapper Agents (IWAs). IWAs are special JIMAF-based agents which wrap PDAs and are then capable of communicating both with PDAs of the specific platforms and with IMAs, thus enabling the reuse of platform-dependent agents in a heterogeneous agent-based application.

Communication between IMAs and PDAs is mediated by IWAs, whereas communication among IMAs is based on asynchronous messages enabled by a proxy-based infrastructure.

In the next Subsections the main aspects related to the definition and implementation of the above-mentioned components are presented.

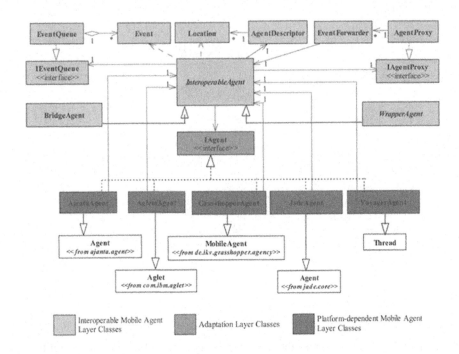

Fig. 2. The UML class diagram of the JIMAF framework

2.1 Programming Interoperable Mobile Agents

The solution to the interoperability problem offered by JIMAF consists in programming Java-based agents (IMAs) which are able to execute on heterogeneous Java-based agent platforms, to migrate among them and to communicate regardless of the platforms on which the agents operate.

IMAs are programmed by using the Java classes provided by the JIMAF framework (see Figure 2) according to an event-driven agent model. In particular, an IMA is composed of: (i) a platform-neutral High-Level Part (HLP), which does not change during the agent lifecycle and defines the specific behaviour of the agent; (ii) a Low-Level Part (LLP), which depends on the specific agent platform where the agent is operating and changes when the agent migrates to an agent platform of a different type (heterogeneous migration).

As the LLP is provided by JIMAF, to define the behaviour of an IMA it is necessary to only define its HLP by extending the *InteroperableAgent* class to specify the lifecycle of the IMA. In particular, the lifecycle of the IMA is driven by its LLP in the context of which it is always executed (i.e. the LLP lends its thread to the HLP). The lifecycle is enclosed in the *onArrival, run* and *onDeparture* methods of the HLP invoked by the LLP, in this precise sequence. These methods must be overridden and the events, to be handled and/or generated by the IMA for proactively driving its tasks and lifecycle or communicating with other IMAs, must be specified. Figure 3 reports a skeleton of the HLP of an IMA which describes each of the above-mentioned methods and highlights how to extend them.

```
import jimaf.interoperable.*;

public class AnInteroperableMobileAgent extends InteroperableAgent {
  /* TODO: declare additional application -dependent data structures here */
  /* TODO: declare additional application -dependent methods here */

  public AnInteroperableMobileAgent(AgentDescriptor ad /*, additionalParams*/) {
    super(ad);
    /* TODO: set additionalParams here */
  }

  public void onArrival(){
    /* The onArrival method, which is invoked when an IMA is created and when a migrating
     * IMA arrives at a new location, provides the creation of the proxy component
     * communication among IMAs and the binding/rebinding of an IMA to its proxy */
    super.onArrival();
    /* TODO: add additional operations here */
  }

  public void run(){
    /* The run method implements the execution of the Event Processing Cycle (EPC) that
     * cyclically picks up an event from the event queue of the IMA, processes it according
     * to the IMA behaviour (as defined in the handleEvent method),and ends when an
     * event of the Move or Termination type is processed */
    /* TODO: add additional operations here */
    super.run();
  }
  public void onDeparture(){
    /* The onDeparture method handles the migration of the IMA, if any, or its termination */
    /* TODO: add additional operations here */
    super.onDeparture();
  }

  public void  handleEvent(Event ev){
    /* The handleEvent method specifies what are the events that an IMA is able to
     * handle and how an IMA handles each of these events */
    /* TODO: add the handling of additional events here */
    super.handleEvent(ev); // to handle the "migrate", "terminate", and "info" events
  }
}
```

Fig. 3. The Java Skeleton of the HLP of an IMA

```
String[] argsAd=new String[]{hostName,userName,serverName,agentName,serverPort,type};
AgentDescriptor ad = new AgentDescriptor(argsAd);
AnInteroperableAgent myIMA_HLP = new AnInteroperableAgent(ad /*, additionalParams*/);
APlatformDependentAgent myIMA_LLP = new APlatformDependentAgent(myIMA_HLP, /*,
additionalParams*/);
myIMA_LLP.start();
```

Fig. 4. The creation of an IMA

During its lifecycle an IMA can create other IMAs, communicate with IMAs and migrate through heterogeneous agent platforms. The following describes how these main tasks are programmed: while the creation task is exemplified in Figure 4, the other tasks are exemplified in Figure 8 of Section 3 in reference to the case study.

The creation of an IMA (see Figure 4) requires the creation of: (i) an *AgentDescriptor* which contains the information related to the agent's identity; (ii) the HLP of the IMA by passing the *AgentDescriptor* as a parameter; (iii) the LLP of the IMA, which depends on the specific agent platform on which the IMA is being created, by passing the HLP as a parameter.

An IMA can communicate with other IMAs through asynchronous messages implemented as asynchronous events (JIMAF events) which are created by specifying the sender, the receiver, the event type, and an object representing its content, and sent by invoking the *send* method provided by the *InteroperableAgent* class. In particular, the proxy URL of the receiver, which must be known by the sender, can be obtained by invoking the *lookup* method of the *InteroperableAgent* class.

An IMA can send an event to itself for proactively driving its tasks and lifecycle. To migrate, an IMA sends itself an event of the *migrate* type which specifies the target location in its content. This event (transparently) allows for both homogeneous (i.e. the source and the target platforms are of the same type) and heterogeneous migration. Homogeneous migration of an IMA is fully supported by its LLP, exploiting the specific mechanisms of the source agent platform, whereas heterogeneous migration is fully supported by an infrastructure based on Mobile Agent Bridges (MABs). MABs are provided by JIMAF and are capable of receiving a migrating IMA from a source agent platform and injecting it into the heterogeneous target agent platform [9].

2.2 Programming Interoperable Wrapper Agents

JIMAF exploits wrapping techniques for enabling the reuse of platform-dependent agents in the context of a heterogeneous agent-based application. The provided solution is based on Interoperable Wrapper Agents (IWAs). An IWA is a special JIMAF-based agents which wraps platform-dependent agents and acts as a mediator capable of interacting both with the IMAs by using JIMAF-based events as well as with the platform-dependent agents by using the platform-dependent communication mechanisms.

In particular, an IWA is a stationary IMA whose HLP is constituted of a class which extends the *WrapperAgent* abstract class furnished by JIMAF (see Figure 2) and whose LLP depends on the hosting platform.

```
import jimaf.interoperable.*;

public class AnInteroperableWrapperAgent extends WrapperAgent {
  /* TODO: declare additional application -dependent data structures here */
  /* TODO: declare additional application -dependent methods here */

  public AnInteroperableWrapperAgent(AgentDescriptor ad /*, additionalParams*/) {
    super(ad);
    /* TODO: set additionalParams here */
  }

  public void onArrival(){
    super.onArrival();
    /* TODO: add additional operations here */
  }

  public void run(){
    /* TODO: add additional operations here */
    super.run();
  }

  public void onDeparture(){
    /* TODO: add additional operations here */
    super.onDeparture();
  }

  protected Object translate(Event evtReq){
    /* TODO: extend the translate method to support the adaptation of the communication
     * content from JIMAF-based events to platform-dependent formats */
  }

  protected Event constructReply(Object rs){
    /* TODO: extend the constructReply method to support the adaptation of the
     * communication content from platform-dependent formats to JIMAF-based events */
  }

  public void handleEvent(Event ev){
    /* TODO: extend the handleEvent method to handle the JIMAF-based events sent
     * by an IMA to the IWA for requesting the services offered by the platform-dependent
     * agents wrapped by the IWA */
    super.handleEvent(ev);
  }
}
```

Fig. 5. The Java Template class of an IWA

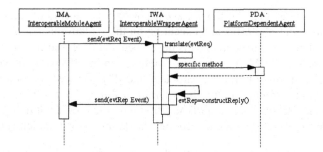

Fig. 6. Sequence diagram of the interaction between an IMA and a PDA, mediated by an IWA

As an IWA is a stationary IMA, its lifecycle, creation and communication with IMAs are as described in Section 2.1. In addition, in order to allow an IWA to access all the platform-dependent communication mechanisms which are required for interacting with platform-dependent agents, the *WrapperAgent* class must be properly extended by overriding the *translate, constructReply* and *handleEvent* methods. Figure 5 reports a skeleton of the HLP of an IWA which describes each of the above-mentioned methods and highlights how to extend them.

A general interaction between an IMA and a PDA, mediated by an IWA, in which the interaction initiator is the IMA, is shown in Figure 6. In particular, the IMA sends its request (evtReq) to the IWA that, in turn, translates its content into a platform-dependent format through the *translate* method and incorporates this content into a platform-dependent request which is sent to the PDA. As soon as the IWA obtains the reply from the PDA, it constructs the reply event (evtRep) through the *constructReply* method and sends this event to the IMA.

3   A Case Study

The following describes a JIMAF-based solution for implementing a complex insurance service offered by a virtual organization. In particular, the proposed JIMAF-based application concerns the problem of determining the price that a user must pay for a complex insurance product which comprehends policies of various types and is offered by a *virtual insurance company* which is composed of different insurance companies, each of which is specialized in a particular insurance service (e.g. automotive, life, home and medical insurance). The price of the complex product required by the user is determined from the price of each component, as established on the basis of the user's data (age, sex, income, etc.) by the insurance company which handles that kind of product within the *virtual insurance network*. Each insurance company has a proprietary agent-based pricing service running on a specific agent platform.

This problem could be effectively approached through the mobile agent paradigm by employing a mobile agent which, on the basis of both the insurance products which compose the complex insurance product and the user's data, migrates to the locations of each member insurance company of the *virtual insurance network*, and determines the price of the complex product by exploiting the local available pricing services. As demonstrated in the literature [27], such a solution is particularly effective for reducing the time necessary to complete an otherwise complex task. However, this solution requires that the mobile agent not only is capable of migrating among heterogeneous agent platforms and executing on these platforms but also of interacting with the platform-dependent agents developed and deployed for offering the specific pricing services; JIMAF, due to its features, can be effectively exploited for the implementation of this solution. In particular, the JIMAF-based solution for pricing a complex insurance product offered by a *virtual insurance company* is not expensive as it exploits the already available PDAs (*PricingAgents*) for handling the pricing services, and easy to develop as it only requires the definition and implementation of:

- an IMA (*RoamingInsuranceAgent*) which, according to the composition of the complex insurance product to price, roams through the heterogeneous agent platforms where the single pricing services are managed by the *PricingAgents*, contracts the price of each single insurance product and departs for the next location;
- a set of local IWAs (*PricingWrapperAgents*), one for each type of platform which may be included in the itinerary. Each *PricingWrapperAgent* mediates the communication between the *RoamingInsuranceAgent* and a local platform-dependent *PricingAgent* by using the wrapping techniques as illustrated in Section 2.2. In particular, at each location of the itinerary, the *RoamingInsuranceAgent* interacts through JIMAF-based events with the local *PricingWrapperAgent*, which, in turn, interacts with the local *PricingAgent* through the interaction mechanisms provided by the specific platform.

Figure 7 reports the class diagram of a JIMAF-based solution for an itinerary which includes Aglets, Ajanta, Grasshopper, JADE, and Voyager platforms highlighting the *PricingWrapperAgent* and the *PricingAgent* for the JADE platform.

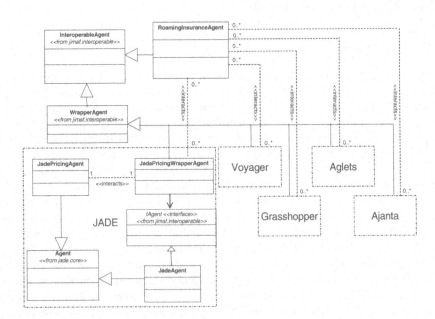

Fig. 7. The JIMAF-based solution for pricing a complex insurance product offered by a *virtual insurance company*

In the following subsections the programming of the *RoamingInsuranceAgent* and the *PricingWrapperAgent*s is described to show both the definition of the behaviors of the identified agents and the use of the relevant features of JIMAF described in Section 2:

- event-based programming of an IMA and IWA for the proactive driving of their behaviour and for their intercommunication;
- programming of heterogeneous transparent migration of an IMA through the generation of events of the *migrate* type;
- communication between IMAs (*RoamingInsuranceAgent*) and PDAs (*PricingAgent*s) mediated by IWAs (*PricingWrapperAgent*s).

The complete code of this JIMAF-based application can be requested from the JIMAF website [18].

3.1 Programming the RoamingInsuranceAgent

The specification of the behavior of the *RoamingInsuranceAgent* requires only the definition of its HLP (see Section 2.1) as the LLP of an IMA, which depends on the agent platforms hosting it during its lifecycle, is already provided by JIMAF (currently for the Aglets, Ajanta, Grasshopper, JADE, and Voyager platforms). In particular, the definition of the HLP, given the skeleton reported in Figure 3, was carried out by specifying, along with the definition of application-dependent data structures and auxiliary methods, the *onArrival* and the *handleEvent* methods whose implementation is reported in Figure 8.

In the *onArrival* method the *RoamingInsuranceAgent* performs the following activities: (i) after its creation, it computes its itinerary on the basis of the description of the complex insurance product to be priced and finally migrates onto the first platform of the itinerary; (ii) after each subsequent migration, it constructs an event (*PriceRequest*) to be sent to the *PricingWrapperAgent* which is running on the current hosting platform; this event contains the URL of the proxy of the *RoamingInsuranceAgent* (*URLSender*), the URL of the proxy of the *PricingWrapperAgent* (*URLReceiver*), the event type (*PriceRequest*), and the event content (*evtArgs*) related to the user's data for pricing the specific insurance product; (iii) after the completion of its itinerary, it computes the price of the complex insurance product through the *computeTotalPrice* method at the starting location (*startingLocation*).

In the *handleEvent* method the *RoamingInsuranceAgent* reacts to the following events:

- the *PriceReply* event by extracting the single product price from the content of the event, which was sent by a *PricingWrapperAgent*, and by adding it to the gathered prices. In addition, if the itinerary has not been completed, the *RoamingInsuranceAgent* generates a migrate event with itself as target (*URLSender=URLReceiver*) and the next location of the itinerary as content; otherwise, the agent generates and sends a *Finish* event to itself;
- the *Finish* event by generating a migrate event for migrating to the *startingLocation* on which the gathered prices will be analyzed to compute the total price of the complex insurance product.

```
public void onArrival(){
    super.onArrival();
    if (roamingStarted==false) { // the agent is starting the roaming task
        startingLocation = getInfo().getCurrentLocation();
        if (locationsToVisit>=1) {
            roamingStarted=true;
            URLSender = myInfo.getName(); URLReceiver = myInfo.getName();
            evtTag = "migrate";
            evtArgs = (Location)(itinerary.elementAt(locationIDNumber));
            send(new Event(URLSender, URLReceiver, evtTag, evtArgs));
        }
    } else if (roamingComplete==false) { // the agent is carrying out the roaming task
        URLSender = myInfo.getProxyURL();
        AgentDescriptor AgDReceiver = (AgentDescriptor)
            (pricingWrapperAgents.elementAt(locationIDNumber));
        URLReceiver = AgDReceiver.getProxyURL();
        evtTag = "PriceRequest";
        evtArgs = priceQueries.elementAt(locationIDNumber);
        send(new Event(URLSender, URLReceiver, evtTag, evtArgs));
    }
    else // the roaming task has been completed and
         // the agent returned on the starting location
        computeTotalPrice();
}
public void handleEvent(Event ev){
    if (ev.getTag().equals("PriceReply")){
        prices.add(locationIDNumber, analysePrice(ev.getArgs()));
        locationIDNumber++;
        if(locationIDNumber==locationsToVisit) {
            roamingComplete=true;
            URLSender = myInfo.getName(); URLReceiver = myInfo.getName();
            evtTag = "finish";
            evtArgs = null;
            send(new Event(URLSender, URLReceiver, evtTag, evtArgs));
        }
        else { // the itinerary has not been completed
            URLSender = myInfo.getName(); URLReceiver = myInfo.getName();
            evtTag = "migrate";
            evtArgs = (Location)(itinerary.elementAt(locationIDNumber));
            send(new Event(URLSender, URLReceiver, evtTag, evtArgs));
        }
    }
    else if (ev.getTag().equals("finish")){
        URLSender = myInfo.getName(); URLReceiver = myInfo.getName();
        evtTag = "migrate"; evtArgs = startingLocation;
        send(new Event(URLSender, URLReceiver, evtTag, evtArgs));
    }
    super.handleEvent(ev);
}
```

Fig. 8. The *onArrival* and the *handleEvent* methods of the *RoamingInsuranceAgent* class

3.2 Programming the PricingWrapperAgents

As discussed in Section 2.2, for each platform which can be visited by the *RoamingInsuranceAgent*, a specific *PricingWrapperAgent* was developed. In particular, each *PricingWrapperAgent* was defined by extending the *WrapperAgent* class so to obtain its HLP as its LLP is furnished by JIMAF.

The *PricingWrapperAgent*s defined for Aglets, Grasshopper, Voyager, and Ajanta exploit similar communication mechanisms based on synchronous messages. In particular, the definition of their HLP, on the basis of the skeleton reported in Figure 5, was carried out by specifying, along with the application-dependent data structures and auxiliary methods, the *translate*, *constructReply* and the *handleEvent* methods whose implementation with reference to Ajanta is reported in Figure 9.

```
protected Object translate(Event evtReq){
  return evtReq.getArgs();
}
protected Event constructReply(Object rs){
  return new Event(myInfo.getProxyURL(), URLPartner,"PriceReply", rs);
}
public void  handleEvent(Event ev){
  if (evtReq.getTag().equals("PriceRequest")){
    String PRICE_REQUEST = (String) translate(evtReq);
    URLPartner = evtReq.getURLSender();
    try{
      Object rs = null;
      IAjantaPricingAgent IajantaPricingAgent = null;
      try{
        NRAccess nameReg = agHost.getNameReg();
        AgentNREntry agentNR = (AgentNREntry)
        nameReg.lookup(AjantaPricingAgentURN);
        AgentServerNREntry serverNR = (AgentServerNREntry)
        nameReg.lookup(agentNR.getServerURN());
        URL rmiRegURL = serverNR.getRMIRegURL();
        String lookupString = "//"+ rmiRegURL.getHost()+":" + rmiRegURL.getPort()+"/"+
        AjantaPricingAgentURN.toString();
        IajantaPricingAgent = (IAjantaPricingAgent) Naming.lookup(lookupString);
        rs = IajantaPricingAgent.priceRequest(PRICE_REQUEST);
      }
      catch(Exception e){System.out.println(e);}
      Event evtRep = constructReply(rs);
      send(evtRep);
    }catch(Exception e){e.printStackTrace();}
  }
  super.handleEvent(ev);
}
```

Fig. 9. The *translate, constructReply* and the *handleEvent* methods of the *AjantaPricingWrapperAgent*s class

```
protected Object translate(Event evtReq){
  String myURL = getInfo().getName();
  String evtTag = Integer.toString(PRICE_REQUEST);
  Object evtArgs = evtReq.getArgs();
  return new Event(myURL,null,evtTag,evtArgs);
}

protected Event constructReply(Object rs){
  String myURL = getInfo().getName();
  String evtTag = "PriceReply";
  Object evtArgs = ((Event)rs).getArgs();
  return new Event(myURL,URLPartner,evtTag,evtArgs);
}

public void  handleEvent(Event ev){
  if (evt.getTag().equals("PriceRequest")){
    URLPartner = evt.getURLSender();
    Event priceRequest = (Event) translate(evt);
    IAgent myLLP = getSpecificAgent();
    myLLP.send(pricingServiceLookUpString,priceRequest);
  }
  else if (evt.getTag().equals(Integer.toString(PRICE_REPLY))){
    Event priceReply = costructReply(evt);
    send(priceReply)
  }
  super.handleEvent(ev);
}
```

Fig. 10. The *translate, constructReply* and the *handleEvent* methods of the *JadePricingWrapperAgent* class

As JADE only provides communication mechanisms based on asynchronous messages, the HLP of the *PricingWrapperAgent* for JADE (*JadePricingWrapperAgent* class) does not directly exploit the platform-dependent communication mechanisms but delegates their exploitation to its LLP. Figure 10 shows the *translate, constructReply* and the *handleEvent* methods implemented by *JadePricingWrapperAgent* class. In particular:

- the *translate* method extracts the event content (i.e. the data for pricing the specific insurance product) and returns a JIMAF event which can be exploited for the generation of a suitable ACL-message to be sent to the *JadePricingAgent*;
- the *constructReply* method generates a JIMAF *PriceReply* event whose content has been obtained from the data provided by the *JadePricingAgent*;
- the *handleEvent* method handles: (i) the *PriceRequest* event by invoking the translate method and transmitting the obtained event to the *JadePricingAgent* through the *send* method of the LLP which exploits the asynchronous communication mechanism of JADE; (ii) the PRICE_REPLY event by invoking the *constructReply* method and transmitting the obtained event to the *RoamingInsuranceAgent*.

4   Related Work

The development of heterogeneous agent-based applications requires to address different interoperability issues, the most relevant ones concerning how to allow agents to migrate among, to execute on, and to communicate from/to heterogeneous agent platforms, without neglecting security concerns. In [9], proposals which address these issues were discussed and compared with JIMAF.

In this section the solutions presented in the literature, which address the other important issue of using *non-interoperable* code (i.e. code which was specifically developed for a particular agent platform) in the context of a heterogeneous agent-based application, will be discussed and compared with the solution provided by JIMAF. In particular, two main classes of approaches can be identified, the first one concerns those approaches which carry out agent *code translation* among specific heterogeneous platforms, and the second one concerns approaches based on the direct or mediated interaction of heterogeneous agents (*universal servers, middle agents, standards-based*).

Approaches based on *code translation* [30, 15] enable the use of code developed for a specific platform by migrating and executing on this platform agents coming from heterogeneous platforms and which have been previously converted for enabling their execution. In particular, in [30] the use of *converters* able to *dynamically translate* agents from a source agent platform into a different target agent platform is proposed and exemplified by defining a converter between the Aglets and the Voyager platforms. While this solution does not require changing the already available agents, it only partially addresses the interoperability issues as it does not support communication interoperability between agents running on heterogeneous platforms. In [15] a middleware approach for supporting interoperability of migration and execution among heterogeneous agent platforms is presented. The approach is centred on the concept of *incarnation agent*: when a mobile agent decides to migrate to a different type of mobile agent platform, an incarnation agent is created. Such an agent: (i) extracts the procedure and execution status of the migrating agent; (ii) translates them into a common representation; (iii) migrates to the destination agent platform;

(iv) creates, at the destination platform, a new agent by applying to the common representation obtained for the migrating agent the translation rules specific of the destination platform. For migrating on a platform of a different type, an agent must therefore be partially reprogrammed as it must explicitly invoke a migration function for triggering the described process.

Approaches based on direct or mediated interaction of heterogeneous agents encompass solutions focused on the exploitation of *universal servers* [28], *standards* [22, 11, 29, 3], and *middle agents* [12, 25, 26].

A definition of a *universal server* which is able to host agents coming from different agent platforms is presented in [28]. This approach does not require any modification to the previously developed agents which, reaching the *universal server*, can interact both locally with any other agent hosted on the *universal server* and remotely with agents whose type is that of the origin agent platform. However, the agents which reach the *universal server* cannot migrate back, thus losing the important capability of mobility.

Standards-based approaches can be based on *agent-specification* [22, 11], *protocol-definition* [29] and *web service technologies* [3].

The most significant *agent-specification* based approaches are MASIF (Mobile Agent Systems for Interoperability Facility) [22] and FIPA (Foundation of Intelligent and Physical Agents) [11]. These approaches require that the agent code is compliant with the standards or, if the agent code is not compliant, they require the development of a wrapper agent which then acts as a mediator between the non-standard entity and the standard compliant agents [11]. Although *agent-specification* based approaches are not restricted to any specific technology or programming language, the main obstacle to their wide adoption is that most of the currently available agent platforms are not compliant with these standards and, to become compliant, agent platforms must be radically modified both in their architecture and programming model.

A *protocol-definition* solution is presented in [29] where it is proposed an agent interaction technique which involves ontologies, representation in UML of ontology-specific content language, and dynamic exchange of interaction protocols. This technique regards only FIPA compliant agents which, however, need to be reprogrammed on the basis of the proposed agent architecture; moreover, as for *specification-based* approaches, wrapper agents must be developed for supporting the use/reuse of non-FIPA-compliant entities [11].

An approach based on *web service technologies*, which provides an adaptation layer among heterogeneous agent platforms, is proposed in [3]. In particular, while interactions among heterogeneous agent platforms are mediated by web services, which interact by using SOAP messages so enabling communication among heterogeneous agents, heterogeneous migration is based on a *code translation* technique.

Several approaches for supporting code reuse in the context of heterogeneous agent-based applications rely on interactions, among heterogeneous agents, mediated by *middle agents* [12, 25, 26].

In [12] a multi-agent system *interoperator* is defined, which is an entity that only enables agents of heterogeneous platforms to dialogue with each other without being aware of the interoperator itself. An interoperator which only allows agents in the RETSINA system to communicate with OAA (Open-Agent Architecture) agents and vice-versa is also described.

In [25] and [26] different types of *middle agents* (Brokers, Facilitators, and Matchmakers) are introduced. In particular, Brokers and Facilitators mediate the communication between agents by adapting, if necessary, the formats of the exchanged messages. The proposed *middle agents* exploit a shallow-parsing template approach which relaxes the constraint that interacting agents must share a common language for describing the content and format of messages. However, it is worth noting that, in order to communicate with another agent using the proposed approach, an agent must be able to interact with a middle agent by adopting a specific communication protocol, a common capability description language, and a common ontology.

The solution provided by JIMAF for supporting the use of platform-dependent code in heterogeneous agent-based applications belongs to the class of approaches centred on *middle agents*. In particular, a JIMAF-based Interoperable Wrapper Agent (IWA) can be seen as a special kind of *middle agent* which wraps platform-dependent agents and acts as a mediator capable of interacting both with the JIMAF-based Interoperable Mobile Agents (IMAs) by using JIMAF-based events as well as with the platform-dependent agents, by using the platform-dependent communication mechanisms. As an IWA is a special IMA devoted to this mediation task, this solution is naturally and fully integrated in the solution offered by JIMAF to address the main interoperability issues of migration, execution, and communication among heterogeneous mobile agent platforms.

5 Conclusions

Due to the increasing interest in applications involving agents operating on heterogeneous agent platforms (heterogeneous agent-based applications), several solutions, which attempt to address the main interoperability issues of execution, migration, and communication among heterogeneous agent platforms, have been proposed.

In this paper we have presented a solution to another relevant and emerging issue concerning the possibility of enabling the reuse of platform-dependent agents in a heterogeneous agent-based application. In particular, the proposed solution relies on special agents called Interoperable Wrapper Agents (IWAs) which act as mediators capable of interacting both with JIMAF-based agents, i.e. Interoperable Mobile Agents (IMAs) programmed by using the JIMAF framework, and with Platform-Dependent Agents (PDAs). This solution is an enhancement of JIMAF which makes JIMAF the only full-fledged approach to interoperability as it fully addresses the main interoperability issues while providing platform-dependent agents reuse. The relevance of this enhancement has been demonstrated through a significant case study which highlights the ease, effectiveness and efficacy of developing heterogeneous agent-based applications which are also able to reuse exiting platform-dependent agents.

Efforts are currently underway to: (i) support the development of wrapper agents by means of a semi-automatic process for the generation of the code skeleton of the wrapper agents; (ii) evaluate the effectiveness of the features of interoperability and code reuse offered by JIMAF so to support the development of heterogeneous agent-based applications in several business domains; (iii) investigate the effectiveness of the exploited wrapping techniques for granting the access to the resources of the agents platforms.

References

1. Aglets mobile agent system, documentation and software (2002),
   http://aglets.sourceforge.net/
2. Ajanta mobile agent system, documentation and software (2003),
   http://www.cs.umn.edu/Ajanta/
3. Artail, H., Kahale, E.: MAWS:A platform-independent framework for mobile agents using Web services. Journal of Parallel and Distributed Computing 66, 428–443 (2006)
4. Bellavista, P., Corradi, A., Stefanelli, C.: Corba solutions for interoperability in mobile agent environments. In: Proceedings of the 2nd International Symposium on Distributed Objects and Applications (DAO 2000), Antwerp, The Netherlands, September 21-23, 2000, pp. 283–292 (2000)
5. Bellifemine, F., Caire, G., Poggi, A., Rimassa, G.: JADE, a white paper. J. Exp. in search of innovation 3(3), 6–19 (2003)
6. Braun, P., Trinh, D., Kowalczyk, R.: Integrating a New Mobility Service into the Jade Agent Toolkit. In: Karmouch, A., Pierre, S. (eds.) MATA 2005. LNCS, vol. 3744, pp. 354–363. Springer, Heidelberg (2005)
7. Cybele Agent Infrastucture, documentation and software (2007),
   http://www.opencybele.org
8. FIPAOS Agent Platform, documentation and software (2003),
   http://sourceforge.net/projects/fipa-os/
9. Fortino, G., Garro, A., Russo, W.: Achieving Mobile Agent System interoperability through software layering. In: Information and Software Technology, pp. 322–341. Elsevier B.V., Amsterdam (2008)
10. Fortino, G., Garro, A., Russo, W.: Enhancing JADE Interoperability through the Java-based Interoperable Mobile Agent Framework. In: Proceedings of the 5th IEEE International Conference on Industrial Informatics (INDIN); Special session on Agent Theories and Practice for Industry (ATPI), Vienna, Austria (July 2007)
11. Foundation of Intelligent and Physical Agents, documentation and specifications (2007),
    http://www.fipa.org
12. Giampapa, J.A., Paolucci, M., Sycara, K.: Agent interoperation across multiagent system boundaries. In: Proceedings of the 4th International Conference on Autonomous Agents, pp. 179–186. ACM Press, New York (2000)
13. Grasshopper mobile agent system, IKV++ GmbH, documentation and software (2003),
    http://www.grasshopper.de/
14. Grimstrup, A., Gray, R., Kotz, D., Breedy, M., Carvalho, M., Cowin, T., Chacon, D., Barton, J., Garret, C., Hofmann, M.: Toward Interoperability of Mobile-Agent Systems. In: Suri, N. (ed.) MA 2002. LNCS, vol. 2535, pp. 106–120. Springer, Heidelberg (2002)
15. Hasegawa, T., Cho, K., Kumeno, F., Nakajima, S., Ohsuga, A., Honiden, S.: Interoperability for mobile agents by incarnation agents. In: Proceedings of the 2nd Int. Joint Conference on Autonomous Agents and Multiagent Systems, pp. 1006–1007. ACM Press, New York (2003)
16. JACK Agent Platform, documentation and software (2007),
    http://www.agent-software.com/shared/products/index.html
17. JADE, Java Agent DEvelopment framework, documentation and software (2007),
    http://jade.tilab.com
18. JIMAF (Java-based Interoperable Mobile Agent Framework), documentation and software (2006), http://lisdip.deis.unical.it/software/jimaf/
19. Lakos, J.: Large Scale C++ Software Design. Addison-Wesley, Reading (1996)

20. Luck, M., McBurney, P., Preist, C.: A Manifesto for Agent Technology: Towards Next Generation Computing. Autonomous Agents and Multi-Agent Systems 9(3), 203–252 (2004)
21. Magnin, L., Pham, V.T., Dury, A., Besson, N., Thiefaine, A.: Our Guest Agents are Welcome to Your Agent Platforms. In: Proceedings of the Symposium on Applied Computing (SAC 2002), Madrid, Spain, March 10-13, pp.107–114 (2002)
22. MASIF (Mobile Agent System Interoperability Facility) specification, OMG TC Document orbos/98-03-09 (1998),
    ftp://ftp.omg.org/pub/docs/orbos/98-03-09.pdf
23. Misikangas, P., Raatikainen, K.: Agent migration between incompatible agent platforms. In: Proceedings of the 20th Int'l Conference on Distributed Computer Systems, Taipei, Taiwan, April 10-13, 2000, pp. 4–10. IEEE Computer Society Press, Los Alamitos (2000)
24. Objectspace Voyager, documentation and software (2003),
    http://www.recursionsw.com/products/voyager
25. Payne, T., Paolucci, M., Singh, R., Sycara, K.: Facilitating Message Exchange though Middle Agents. In: Proceedings of the 1st Int. Joint Conference on Autonomous Agents and Multiagent Systems. ACM Press, New York (2002)
26. Payne, T., Singh, R., Sycara, K.: Communicating agents in open multi-agent systems. In: Proceedings of the 1st GSFC/JPL Workshop on Radical Agent Concepts (WRAC), McLean, VA, USA (2002)
27. Picco, G.: Mobile Agents: An Introduction. Journal of Microprocessors and Microsystems 25(2), 65–74 (2001)
28. Pinsdorf, U., Roth, V.: Mobile Agent Interoperability Patterns and Practice. In: Proceedings of 9th Annual IEEE Int'l Conference and Workshop on the Engineering of Computer-Based Systems (ECBS), Lund, Sweden, April 8-12, pp. 238–244 (2002)
29. Purvis, M.K., Cranefield, S., Nowostawski, M., Ward, R., Carter, D., Oliveira, M.A.: Agentcities interaction using the opal platform. In: Proceedings of the Workshop on Challenges in Open Agent Systems, 1st Int. Joint Conference on Autonomous Agents and Multiagent Systems. ACM Press, New York (2002)
30. Tjung, D., Tsukamoto, M., Nishio, S.: A Converter Approach for Mobile Agent Systems Integration: A Case of Aglets to Voyager. In: Proceedings of the 1st Int. Workshop on Mobile Agents for Telecommunication Applications (MATA 1999), Ottawa, Canada, October 6-8, pp. 179–195 (1999)

Introducing a Process Infrastructure
for Agent Systems

Christine Reese, Matthias Wester-Ebbinghaus,
Till Dörges, Lawrence Cabac, and Daniel Moldt

University of Hamburg, Department of Informatics,
Vogt-Kölln-Str. 30, D-22527 Hamburg
http://www.informatik.uni-hamburg.de/TGI

Abstract. Within open distributed systems the realization of a spanning application is an open problem. While the local functionality can be implemented based on established approaches, the overall control of the processes to form a consistent and correct application remains difficult. Workflow management systems (WFMS) are one solution for process control. In combination with distributed systems further issues have to be solved and are investigated here under different perspectives like Petri nets (to provide a true concurrency semantics of the concepts) and agents (to provide a powerful middleware and a more abstract modeling paradigm than objects or components).

In this paper we coin the phrase *process infrastructure*. The idea is to provide all means to model, build, control and maintain the processes within open agent networks as special distributed systems by combining the above mentioned concepts and techniques. To gain such a powerful process infrastructure, we started to build prototypes, which stepwise introduce some implementations of the advanced concepts. The potential of our proposed solution lies in its flexibility and rigorous formal precision. Thanks to the latter the models are directly executable. The approach introduces autonomous and adaptive handling of processes in specific units (agents), which use and produce the necessary infrastructure to handle processes in different contexts on all levels.

1 Introduction

Collaborative business scenarios raise the question of how to integrate the cooperating enterprises. One has to deal with cross-organizational processes characterized by distributed entities that have distinct (and purposefully hidden) local knowledge in addition to the common global knowledge within the network. The corresponding localization of data, behavior and decision making requires an exact conceptualization of the organization-spanning business processes that explicitly includes the participants' information and communication technologies.

Several authors (see Section 2.2, *Related Work*) propose to integrate the concepts of agents, workflows and traditional computer science techniques to build better applications. Multi-agent applications represent an important subclass of

M. Dastani et al. (Eds.): LADS 2007, LNAI 5118, pp. 225–242, 2008.

such distributed, concurrent and large applications. The overall goal of our work is to improve the development of multi-agent systems. In [1,2,3] we presented (parts of) the conceptual framework. Now we present the concept of a *process infrastructure* for open agent networks together with an implemented workflow agent as its key component. The conceptual lifecycle and implementation details have not been published before. The workflow agent encapsulates a process to allow for autonomous and flexible handling of system spanning processes, enabled through the process infrastructure. The process infrastructure facilitates the instantiation, maintenance, modification and termination of processes at the conceptual and the technical level.

We start with an approach to processes, workflow and multi-agent systems (MAS) and the basic concepts in Sections 2 and 3. The specification of our process infrastructure is presented in Section 4, followed by a short glimpse at a running prototype and application examples in Section 5.

2   Processes, Workflows and Multi-agent Systems

First of all, we introduce our terminology and outline the underlying concepts as well as their interconnections. Then we elaborate on related work in the areas of (distributed) workflow management systems and present concepts stemming from the field agent networks.

2.1   Terminology

In the domain of system-spanning cross-organizational *process management*, our focus is on open agent networks. We provide a generic *infrastructure* for the support. This infrastructure is made up of *agents* as the technical term for flexible and autonomous encapsulated entities with problem-solving capabilities. Agents make up *multi-agent systems* which are our target technology environment. The agents designed here rely on well-established mechanisms of *workflow management* and enrich those.

Processes and Petri Nets. We use Petri nets for both modeling and programming purposes. Petri nets have operational semantics that makes them specifically tailored for process-oriented models. They are a well-known means for modeling the concepts of concurrency, independence, precedence and conflict when regarding activities. The term *process* has a specific meaning in Petri net terminology. Petri net processes are a recognized alternative for describing the behavior of Petri nets by firing sequences. Processes are themselves Petri nets from the class of causal nets, where no forward branching is allowed for the places. We refer to [4] for a thorough introduction to Petri nets.

Reference nets (introduced by Kummer in [5], in German) as a higher-order Petri net formalism show some extensions compared to conventional colored Petri nets. They implement the *nets-within-nets* paradigm where a surrounding net (the system net) can have *nets as tokens* (the object nets). To facilitate communication between nets, *synchronous channels* permit a fusion of two transitions at a time for the duration of one occurrence and thus enable bi-directional information flows. In addition, reference nets may carry complex Java inscriptions and consequently offer the possibility of *Petri net-based Programming* – using the multi-formalism Petri net editor and simulator RENEW as an integrated development environment.

Agents. The Petri net-based multi-agent framework MULAN (introduced by Rölke et al. in [6]) allows for the modeling and execution of multi-agent applications with reference nets. The CAPA extension by Duvigneau et al. [7] expands the MULAN specifications to reach compliance with the FIPA[1] standards. An agent has a specific behavior which is based on its goals, its knowledge and its environment. The behavior of MULAN and CAPA agents is specified using reference nets called *protocol nets*. Agents are hosted on *platforms* that are connected through a technical communication infrastructure and together form the multi-agent system. Agents communicate asynchronously in terms of the agent communication language FIPA-ACL and domain specific ontology. One factor defining the interrelationships between the agents are services, where agents can be service providers or consumers. We deal with different types of agents according to the roles they embody and the services they offer. The agents use a (distributed) *directory service* in order to identify and contact companions. This service is named *directory facilitator* (DF), and together with the *agent management system* (AMS), is standardized by the FIPA.

Workflow Management Systems. A workflow is "the computerized facilitation or automation of a business process, in whole or part" as defined by the WfMC[2] in the workflow reference model. A Workflow is composed of *tasks*, an executable task with case data is called a *workitem* and a workitem that is assigned all necessary resources and a user to do the work is called an *activity*. Each workitem in a workflow instance is communicated to *users* according to their capabilities and rights (modeled as their *roles*). The execution of activities is *managed*: it can be monitored, controlled or stopped. Management systems for *distributed or inter-organizational workflows* are particularly interesting. A plethora of products, research efforts and projects exist that address this aspect (see Section 2.2, *Related Work*).

One especially suitable possibility to handle the arising complexity of such systems is agent-based workflow management. Another basic way to handle complexity is to use nested structures, as it is possible with the nets-within-nets concept provided by reference nets. Additionally, Petri nets are eminently apt to represent workflows. Van der Aalst introduced Workflow Petri nets and published

---

[1] FIPA: Foundation for Intelligent Physical Agents. http://www.fipa.org (2007)

[2] WfMC: Workflow Management Coalition (WfMC). http://www.wfmc.org/

on verification and analysis of those: [8,9,10]. Jacob used reference nets to design and implement a workflow management system which runs locally but provides an rmi interface for clients [11].

2.2 Related Work

The general aim to support distributed, heterogeneous or open systems is addressed from several directions in different approaches. We believe that the outcomes are converging towards general flexible infrastructures providing support for processes. Grid technology combined with Service Oriented Architectures is one of those approaches. For example Böhme and Saar [12] address integration of services based on different communication frameworks in order to develop an open software platform for adaptive services discovery, creation, composition and enactment. They do not look at FIPA agents although they are easy to integrate since agents can also provide services described in WSDL[3]. Their notion of workflow does not stress the *management* part as specified by the WfMC. Distributed workflows related to Grid technology are researched for example by Burchard et al. [13]. In this area, it is important to distinguish between *concepts* and *realization* of concepts. The concepts for agents and Web Services are different, but both concepts can be realized using the technologies of the other. So we need to distinguish between concepts and techniques. For example, Blake names dynamic service composition "agent based workflow services" [14]. He refers to agents as concepts, whereas the FIPA sees agents as a means of realization. Also, the term workflow in this work does not refer to workflow *management* notions of the WfMC.

In the sense of general distributed workflow management, a lot of related work exists, even agent-based or using Petri nets. None of these aims at providing process support to open agent networks, however, parallel development of similar ideas occurred as the field is quickly evolving: (a) van der Aalst tried to handle complexity through inheritance: [15,16] (b) Blake's work with respect to inter-organizational workflows [17] is related to ours, but focuses on automatic configuration and management of low-level services; (c) Buhler and Vidal cover adaptive and distributed workflows: [18,19]; (d) the CrossFlow European project[4] [20], its main point is to out-source parts of a process and to connect several WFMS for this purpose; (e) Purvis et al. developed Jbees [21], using Web Services [22], agents and Petri nets. This approach is similar to ours. However, it does not support the intensive use of agent concepts as middleware technology for the implementation. Purvis in [23] does the same steps we published in [2]: transfer the workflow terminology to agent terminology (f) ADEPT is a general flexible distributed workflow control (see [24,25]), not aimed at intra-agent process control and not aimed at a general service for agents in open environments. ADEPT is designed to combine dynamic workflow changes with a distributed

---

[3] WSDL: Web Service Description Language. http://www.w3.org/TR/wsdl20/ (2007)

[4] CrossFlow: Cross-organizational workflow support in virtual enterprises esprit project 28635. http://www.crossflow.org/flyer.html (Last visited: Jan 2008)

execution of workflows, taking performance issues into account [26]. Bauer, Reichert and Dadam also work on distributed WFMS under the aspect of load balancing [27]. (g) Also related to our work is the work by M.P. Singh et al. [28]. One principal point in their research is the investigation of longest running workflows.

2.3   Agent Networks

Since the early stages of standardization for agent communication through FIPA, open test environments were provided. To facilitate the vision of the possibilities of general open agent environments as a competition technique to Web Services and conceptually on a higher level than these, the European project Agentcities was created. Agentcities provided an open agent testbed for agent-based services and cooperations (which is now offline). A central node provides directory services for platforms, agents and services. The successor openNet[5] introduces a hierarchical and scalable network approach. Both agent networks introduce special agents that need to be provided by each participating agent platform and make up the network as such.

3   Conceptual Scope

This section introduces the basic ideas and concepts before in the next sections a prototype is designed. Some technical aspects are mentioned here since tools generally have an impact on the ideas (compare notion of a *Think Tool* in [29]). Furthermore, this section spans a frame of possible implementations. Sect. 4 chooses one possibility which is refined, until it reaches the concrete prototype described in Sect. 5.

To summarize, using the introduced concepts and techniques, we design a process infrastructure for open agent networks using MULAN as a conceptual view on agent systems and CAPA as an agent platform. We use Petri nets to define the behavior of agents as well as for the definition of the precedence relation of workflows.

3.1   What Is an Infrastructure for Agent Networks?

An *infrastructure* in the sense of our work consists of (a) technical aspects with a certain quality-of-service, (b) preconditions for participants *and* (c) a sufficient amount of participants because the infrastructural services are not useful as such, but become useful through usage. The *process infrastructure for open agent networks* as far as developed here focuses on point a: enactment services for system spanning processes as well as monitoring and explicit representation of processes, enabling a holistic view on spanning processes. Spanning processes

---

[5] openNet (agent network). http://x-opennet.net/ (2005) (Last visited: Jan 2008)

and fragmented processes are two views on the same thing which is inherent to distributed systems.

We now consider the infrastructure that could result from a synthesis of Agentcities and openNet: agents and agent-based services are supported by providing technical services with a certain quality (such as servers for directory services under fix addresses) under certain preconditions (such as specifications on how to connect and what agents to provide) *and* by assembling a certain amount of users. The explicit support of spanning processes as described above is missing. The standard interaction protocol specifications of FIPA could be seen as an existing support for processes, but apart from that there is no support for application specific processes.

3.2   WFMS and Agents

On the way from pure forms of organizing a complex software (workflow management system or multi-agent system) to an integrated process infrastructure for agents, we merge workflow management technology and agent technology in the following way:

Level 1. Starting point: multi-agent systems on the one hand and workflow management systems on the other.

Level 2. Use agents to provide a flexible architecture for a workflow management system.

Level 3. Change the interface of the resulting agent-based workflow management system so that agents can use it.

Level 4. Develop some generic services using the workflow management functionality to provide process *management* for a special kind of multi-agent system. The interactions and processes would be organized using the workflow management functionality so that it is possible to explicitly describe overall execution processes, observe them and manage changes and instantiation of processes. The resulting multi-agent system would be said to use a *process infrastructure*.

Level 5. Transfer the characteristics of inter-agent processes to intra-agent communication regarding complex agents, supporting the notion of agents encapsulating sub-agents, or distributedly implemented agents on logical platforms.

3.3   Design Approach

The design is done with the approach "Petri net-based agent oriented software engineering" (PAOSE, described in [30] and [31]). This approach uses mainly the following diagrams: use case diagrams and agent interaction protocol diagrams (AIP) from (A)UML, and multi-agent diagrams based on class diagrams. All diagram types are supported as drawing plugins within RENEW, the AIP plugin allows for Petri net code generation and round-trip engineering.

3.4   Central Concepts in Relation to the Technical Framework

The envisioned process infrastructure has some special conceptual requirements to the framework. Following some of those developed within the project will be mentioned.

- The relation between two agents where one agent created the other needs special attention, because the creator agent should be especially trusted by the created agent. CAPA does not support this natively but it can be simulated by a special interaction design where a reactive initialization protocol can only be invoked once in the created agent.
- An agent that represents a complex part of a system needs to have a defined agent-internal communication framework. In CAPA, this consists of the notion of a *Decision Component* – a reference net that can provide bidirectional communication channels to protocol nets, that is having access to the agent's knowledge base and that can establish connections to legacy systems or a GUI component of an agent.
- The connection to an existing agent network is not exactly necessary for the conceptual development of an agent-based workflow management system, but the process infrastructure is especially meant for the use in such a network. The main precondition for the framework here is the FIPA compliant message transport integrated in CAPA from beginning on. In order to implement the prototype, CAPA was extended to join Agentcities [32] and to openNet [33].
- In order to realize the concept agent-implemented-by-agents, ongoing work aims at nesting CAPA agents one into the other.

3.5   Distribution of Agents and Processes

We transfer the basic idea of nested structures to agents: one agent is implemented using several agents which henceforth are internal agents. The surrounding agent acts as a platform for the internal agents. The first step to this viewpoint is to consider the protocol nets as agents, communicating with other protocol nets via the previously mentioned decision components, using the knowledge base as a common resource. Another viewpoint is to regard a multi-agent system as one distributedly implemented agent, either with or even without an explicit representation of that single agent. Stockheim et al. present a holonic way to structure multi-agent systems using one agent that represents a multi-agent system: multi-multi-agent systems [34]. Our approach works differently by regarding the constituting parts as *within* the representative part which is not necessarily the only part that communicates with outside agents.

In this idea, one workflow management system (WFMS) agent is made up of several specialized agents, and one level higher, several WFMS agents can be combined to implement one distributed WFMS agent. In an open agent network, the directory services would be used for dynamic addressing of distributedly implemented WFMS agents.

A process as such may be distributed through fragmentation. Fragmentation of Petri nets for workflows has been elaborated in previous work: [2,3]. Workflow fragment nets as introduced in the cited work are place-bordered Petri nets, arranged in star shape with a control Petri net which represents the overall workflow. Conflicts can be handled using a distributed lock mechanism.

3.6   Vision: Process Control within Agents

An arbitrary agent bears part of the overall process control within itself. All such parts of process control together form a global workflow management system (in analogy, all sending and receiving facilities within each agent in a MAS form the overall message transport system). To reach this in the long run, we aim at the transfer of the process control between agents to the process control within an agent. Such a generic process control would change the communication, coordination and cooperation of agents in open networks.

This can be reached by building a hierarchical MAS where the super-MAS implements a distributed WFMS and each simple MAS implements a local WFMS. The workflow views of the subordinate ones culminate in the super-MAS.

All the features of extensive process support would apply to agent-internal processes as well as to interactions between agents. Regarding agent interactions, managed processes are as ubiquitous as a transport service and each agent, not only special agents like in the level before, can use the service with respect to initiate, monitor, control, change or stop processes while the rights and roles are a means to organize information.

4   Process Infrastructure

The following concepts are developed in three steps. First, an agent-based workflow management system corresponding to Level 3 in Sect. 3.2 is designed, then the mobile workflow agent is described and as the third step, the process infrastructure within an open agent network like openNet is described.

Using the concepts introduced in this section, a process infrastructure can be developed to control / monitor multi-agent systems.

4.1   An Agent-Based Workflow Management System

For the agent-based workflow management system, the following three types of roles were identified: (1) agent roles: e.g. workflow management system (WFMS), workflow engine (WFE), workflow enactment service (WFES), accountmanager, database agents for tasks, workflows; (2) user roles refine the agent role "user", e.g. administrator or task executor; and (3) application specific roles are refinements of user role "task executor". WFMS is an agent that conceptually *contains* the constituting agents WFE, WFES etc. (compare [1]).

The design process of interactions resulted in interactions for session handling, subscription with WFMS for up-to-date workitem and activity lists, instantiation and finishing of workflows as well as interactions to handle workitems and activities.

The ontology contains simple concepts such as "workitem" or predicates to make statements like "current workitems of". Agent actions like "instantiate workflow" are special concepts that are used to define request messages.

4.2   The Workflow Agent

Additional flexibility is added to the system by introducing an agent that represents a workflow as such. This workflow agent represents an additional indirection and a flexible connection between the creation (instantiation), the execution and changes to a workflow instance: the workflow agent knows the circumstances of creation (instantiation) including information about the requester, the home management system and the workflow definition. The workflow agent also knows the circumstances of (possibly distributed) execution. The workflow agent can be given extra constraints besides the mere execution as well as extra degrees of freedom regarding changes. When a change is to be made or a decision to be taken about the future execution, all this information can be used by the workflow agent. The goal of the workflow agent is to get its workflow specification executed satisfying the initiator of the workflow while having constraints like the abilities of the environment to execute certain tasks. The workflow agent is pro-active each time the workflow agent starts a conversation. Depending on the constraints and the environment, the workflow agent decides about the next conversation and other agents to contact.

To distribute the execution of a workflow, the workflow agent may be implemented through various workflow fragment agents (using star shape as mentioned in paragraph *Distribution of Agents and Processes*) or as a mobile agent.

A design decision for the prototype is to let the local workflow enactment service (WFES) create a workflow agent instead of, e.g. the external user creating a workflow agent to act on the user's behalf. This way, the workflow agent can be seen as a trusted part of the WFMS.

The workflow agent makes the interaction of WFES and workflow engine (WFE) agents more flexible. Possibilities to reassign the work of executing a workflow (meaning mainly the conflict-solving) include: (a) The mobile workflow agent just transports the workflow definition and gives it to the local WFE for execution (we choose this for a prototype). (b) The workflow agent transports and executes the workflow definition and subsequently interacts with the local WFES which knows about specifics of the local environment (WFMS) like users and their capabilities. Intermediate positions are possible with different granularities, such as the workflow agent giving tasks one-by-one to the local WFE.

The workflow agent is equipped with initial information which cannot be changed from the outside after creation (such as a workflow definition and creator address).[6] The different sub-goals of the workflow agent (finding an appropriate WFMS to execute the workflow, traveling, execution and finishing the workflow and finally going back to the creation place) are coordinated in a life cycle.

4.3 Workflow Management for Open Agent Networks

As described in Sect. 2.3, open agent networks provide technology for an infrastructure where directory services, identity services and message transport services are combined and provided.

An agent-based workflow management system as introduced as Level 3 in Sect. 3.2 could be deployed in an open agent network to design agent applications with some processes organized by the workflow management service. An agent that wants to use this WFMS needs to have access to such an agent network, and needs to be aware of the interaction protocols the WFMS prescribes.

A process infrastructure as introduced as Level 4 could provide a workflow view on all distributed processes in an agent network. A workflow view includes views on the current state of running processes as well as on planned and past processes (logging).

In a process infrastructure as envisioned in Level 5, each agent can use a generic process control for its internal processes, especially for but not restricted to the case that the implementation of an agent is again distributed.

5   Realization

This section introduces the realized prototype as well as four examples in order to illustrate the concepts detailed in the paper.

5.1   The Agent-Based Workflow Management System

To summarize, the agent-based workflow management system can manage users, roles, task definitions, form specifications, sub workflows and rules to combine roles and tasks to rights. Users (Executors or Administrators) can log in and change configurations or execute tasks in running workflows. This means, that the basic usage scenario of a WFMS is supported. This agent-based WFMS is qualitatively different from other WFMS because the underlying concepts and techniques are particularly flexible and powerful.

The following scenarios were realized beside some internal scenarios not listed here: Login / Logout; Connect to / Disconnect from Dispatcher; Instantiate Workflow; Offer Workitem / Activity List; Request Workitem; Confirm / Cancel Activity; Workflow End Reached.

The ontology is specified using Protégé[7] with a code generator for Java classes. It contains 8 predicates, 24 concepts and 24 agent action concepts.

---

[6] Changes to the workflow at run-time depend on the abilities of the workflow agent. If it incorporates the necessary functionality, the workflow in its narrower meaning can be changed by the workflow agent itself.

[7] Protégé: http://protege.stanford.edu/ (Last visited: Jan 2008)

5.2   The Workflow Agent

Upon workflow instantiation, the WFES creates a workflow agent, the coarse lifecycle is shown in Fig. 1. Five main states of the Workflow Agent are displayed: created, arrived (pending), idle, workflow execution and done. The state idle is the most interesting state: here the decision component of the workflow agent is active and decides on the next pro-active action, depending on the agent's knowledge about its home platform, about the workflow execution status and about the next appropriate WFMS where to execute (part of) the workflow definition. Transitions between states represent interactions that consist of several intermediate states. Within these interactions, the agent's knowledge about the workflow status, about the next appropriate WFMS, and about the home platform are used. Numbers on those interaction transitions denote an example decision sequence. The agent is able to pro-actively (3) search for appropriate workflow management systems that offer execution functionality for its workflow. If an appropriate WFMS is known to the agent, it can decide to (4) migrate to the corresponding platform. Upon arrival the agent needs to localize and is then able to enter its idle state on this platform. Here, the workflow (or parts thereof) can be executed (6) by the local workflow enactment service (WFES) and a workflow engine (WFE). The workflow agent awaits some sort of execution information (7) from the engine. Steps three to seven can be iterated until the workflow is completely processed. Then the agent can (8) migrate back to its home platform and (10) terminate the execution of the workflow. The interaction transitions map to protocol reference nets and the two migration interactions include a suspension state as in the basic FIPA lifecycle for agents.

To implement the workflow agent, the ontology was completed with the additional concept to communicate a workflow-state, two concepts for agent-internal knowledge representation as well as two additional predicates used by the workflow enactment service agent to initialize the freshly created workflow agent.

Figure 2 shows an example interaction sequence diagram of the workflow agent. Generally, messages are indicated with the performative and the named agent action. On Platform 1, the workflow enactment service agent (WFES) and the workflow definition database agent are involved as well as the FIPA standard agents AMS (agent management service) and DF (directory facilitator). The workflow agent is created by the AMS and receives its initialization information which is only possible once. Numbers map to numbers in Fig. 1. Each activation (except from (7)) on the workflow agent life-line represents a *pro-actively started* interaction and the life-line parts in between represent the idle state of the workflow agent (except from (6) to (7)). On Platform 2, the workflow management system agent (WFMS) represents the whole system to other agents that are not logged in and is therefore contacted first by the workflow agent. The answer contains the address to the subrole agent workflow enactment service (WFES) on Platform 2, so after the migration the workflow agent contacts it directly to ask for the appropriate workflow engine (WFE) agent to enact its workflow. The execution of the workflow by the WFE agent on platform 2

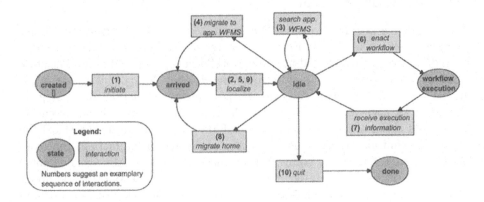

Fig. 1. Coarse Lifecycle of the Workflow Agent

requires some interactions (not displayed in the figure) involving WFMS subrole agents as well as users that are logged into the WFMS.

5.3   Application Examples

This section will give four examples in order to illustrate the concepts detailed in the paper. The order of the examples represents development and evolution over time.

The Phoneshop [11] is an application that models the ordering, data checking, payment and shipping of phones. It is implemented as a workflow application in the RENEW workflow engine by Jacob [11] in one overall workflow and two sub-workflows (one for payment data checking and one for shipping details). Employees can log in via an RMI (Remote Method Invocation) client application and are informed about tasks and activities. The Phoneshop offers possibilities of control and monitoring on the process level and allows to gather structured and unstructured data through task-forms, manual tasks, triggering of external application and automatic execution of tasks as sub-workflows. Forms, tasks and roles of participants and rules for execution are defined in a data base. Workflows are defined as reference workflow nets. These introduce the concept of a task transition into the Petri net formalism, which allows for notification of executors, cancellation and confirmation of task execution.

The Agent-Based Settler Game serves as a complex example for the design and implementation of an application with distributed processes using agent technology [32,35]. It is a board game where player agents compete for resources of different kinds like currencies (wood, wool, grain etc.), building space on an island board or status (e.g., having the longest road). For several years now this serves as an application with the right degree of complexity to illustrate

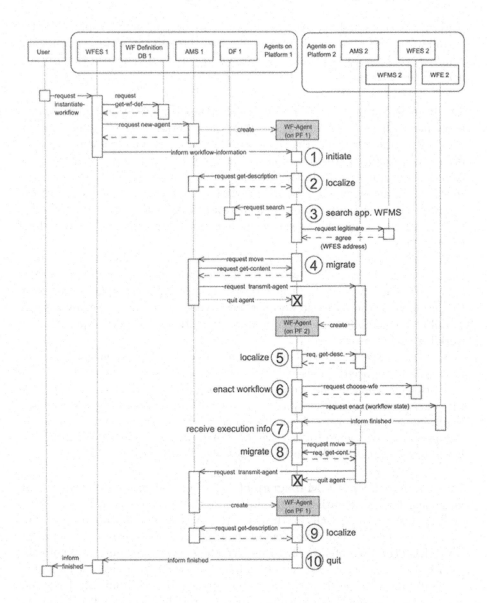

Fig. 2. Sample Interactions of the Workflow Agent

agent-based software development using the PAOSE approach (Petri net-based agent oriented software engineering), designed along the agent role abstractions and the processes of agent interactions. Each interaction protocol (IP) is implemented as multiple protocol reference nets (one for each participant of the IP) so that the overall process and decision taking is completely distributed. While very powerful concepts and approaches were used for designing this application, the overall workflows were only implicitly modeled through the entirety of all agent behaviors, e.g. interaction protocols are not executed, but instead the protocol nets within each agent.

The Travel Agency. In the Travel Agency example application, a user requests a complex service (book a trip), resulting in a workflow to be executed. This workflow consists of parts that cannot be executed within the Travel Agency itself, like booking a room is done via a hotel and booking a flight is done through an airline. So the instantiated workflow is not completely specified and the workflow agent searches the DF for workflow management services that *can* execute (parts of) the workflow and migrates there. The remote WFMSs offer the experts and the environment where it is possible to execute some parts of the workflow.

Usually, this is solved by two workflows depending on each other: a travel agency cannot *book* a room, but can request to book a room or to reserve a room at a hotel. The workflow agent now offers the possibility to explicitly represent the interface of the different workflow environments to each other by a single workflow. The details of the execution remain hidden within the respective local workflow management system.

The Travel Agency is based on the agent based workflow management system prototype introduced in this paper. It prototypically shows that the concepts of multi-agent applications, which have a strong process-oriented character, and the concepts from workflow systems can be combined. Agent applications such as the Settler Game offer flexibility, while workflow applications such as the Phoneshop have a clear process-oriented design. In the Travel Agency processes have been designed to offer both, clearness and flexibility.

The Change Request Management. In [36] we envision an integrated environment for collaborative, distributed work, which can eventually lead to an agent technology-based IDE for the development of agent applications. One fragment of the IDE is the management of change requests in software development, which has been presented in [37]. However, the presented example did not sufficiently cover flexibility, extensibility, adaptability, the possibility for individual configuration and the distribution of the application environment. The agent processes were defined by the underlying control that was handled by a conventional workflow system. The process infrastructure introduced in this work provides the missing features on the way to a full fletched and flexible distributed development environment for agent applications.

This kind of usage of our process infrastructure should allow for the support of application processes by software processes.

Implementing these processes with agents allows to introduce the desired flexibility etc. that is needed for such applications, which are distributed and should also support distributed coordination and cooperation.

6   Conclusion

Building on our previous work, which introduced a multi-multi-agent systems architecture enriched with a WFMS-like interface, in this paper we present the conceptual framework for a *process infrastructure* of open agent networks as well as the central modeling, implementation, and prototyping ideas and concepts for a specific instantiation of such an architecture.

On the conceptual level the result of this paper is the presentation of a specific vision of a *process infrastructure* for open agent networks. It summarizes and gives an overview over a research project that lasted three years. To obtain the overview, most technical details were omitted. Compared to the previous publications, this paper shapes the term *process infrastructure* regarding the specific vision, elaborates the workflow agent and makes the central modeling ideas explicit.

On the technical level the result of this project is a model and a prototype of an agent based workflow management system with an especially flexible architecture and a mobile agent representation of instantiated workflows. The underlying agent framework CAPA was connected to the open agent network openNet, thus realizing an agent-based workflow management system as described as the third level in Section 3.2 (*WFMS and Agents*) and the mobile workflow agent realizes parts of the fourth level towards the vision of the process infrastructure (Level five).

As the overall structuring concepts agents and multi-agent systems are used. The intensive use of abstraction and hierarchical, but flexible structuring of such multi-agent systems allows to implement a process infrastructure, which encompasses the necessary features to cope with the requirements to conceptually cover distributed, autonomous, concurrent, and complex applications. Therefore, we presented the notion of a *process infrastructure for open agent networks.*

The main advantage of our process infrastructure is that it is based on homogeneous and powerful techniques mentioned above. This allows for the implementation of a powerful system for the controlling and monitoring of complex applications. An important component is the workflow agent, which provides flexibility and autonomy of processes. We provide a general means to model and build systems based on true concurrency formalism, which is structured by agent concepts in such a way that processes can be adapted to the application's requirements. While the overhead for small applications is relatively large, the principle architecture should scale very well. In this direction further research has been done, but the realm has not been fully explored yet. The conceptual framework is applied within two other projects: a distributed integrated development environment mentioned in the Change Request Management example and a new approach of software development, i.e. organization oriented software development. While the first research area is targeted more towards practical application, the second area relies more on the conceptual framework to allow for expressive modeling of ULS (Ultra Large Systems). Both applications are directed to support the modeling on Levels four and five. This will allow for an IT-alignment. Thus we work for a smooth support of complex applications by an expressive framework, which incorporates the means to model and implement all central issues of such systems in a direct way.

References

1. Reese, C., Markwardt, K., Offermann, S., Moldt, D.: Distributed business processes in open agent environments. In: Manolopoulos, Y., Filipe, J., Constantopoulos, P., Cordeiro, J. (eds.) ICEIS 2006 - Proceedings of the Eighth International Conference on Enterprise Information Systems: Databases and Information Systems Integration, Paphos, Cyprus, May 2006, pp. 81–86 (2006)
2. Reese, C., Ortmann, J., Offermann, S., Moldt, D., Lehmann, K., Carl, T.: Architecture for distributed agent-based workflows. In: Henderson-Sellers, B., Winikoff, M. (eds.) AOIS 2005. LNCS (LNAI), vol. 3529, pp. 42–49. Springer, Heidelberg (2006)
3. Reese, C., Ortmann, J., Offermann, S., Moldt, D., Markwardt, K., Carl, T.: Fragmented workflows supported by an agent based architecture. In: Carbonell, J., Siekmann, J. (eds.) AOIS 2005. LNCS (LNAI), vol. 3529, pp. 200–215. Springer, Heidelberg (2006)
4. Girault, C., Valk, R.: Petri nets for systems engineering: a guide to modelling, verification and applications. Springer, Heidelberg (2003)
5. Kummer, O.: Referenznetze. Logos Verlag, Berlin (2002)
6. Rölke, H., Moldt, D., Köhler, M.: Modelling the structure and behaviour of petri net agents. In: Colom, J.-M., Koutny, M. (eds.) ICATPN 2001. LNCS, vol. 2075, pp. 224–241. Springer, Heidelberg (2001)
7. Duvigneau, M., Moldt, D., Rölke, H.: Concurrent Architecture for a Multi-agent Platform. In: Giunchiglia, F., Odell, J., Weiß, G. (eds.) AOSE 2002. LNCS, vol. 2585, pp. 59–72. Springer, Heidelberg (2003)
8. Aalst, W.v.d.: Workflow verification: Finding control-flow errors using petri-net-based techniques. In: Business Process Management, pp. 161–183 (2000)
9. Aalst, W.v.d.: WOFLAN: A Petri-net-based workflow analyser. In: Desel, J., Silva, M. (eds.) ICATPN 1998. LNCS, vol. 1420. Springer, Heidelberg (1998)
10. Aalst, W.v.d.: Verification of workflow nets. In: Application and Theory of Petri Nets. LNCS, pp. 407–426. Springer, Heidelberg (1997)
11. Jacob, T., Kummer, O., Moldt, D., Ultes-Nitsche, U.: Implementation of workflow systems using reference nets – security and operability aspects. In: Jensen, K. (ed.) Proc. of CPN (2002), August 28–30, vol. 560. DAIMI PB, Aarhus, Denmark (2002)
12. Böhme, H., Saar, A.: Integration of heterogenous services in the adaptive services grid. In: Proceedings GSEM 2005, Erfurt, Germany. LNI, pp. 220–232 (2005)
13. Burchard, L.O., Schneider, J., Linnert, B.: Distributed workflow management. In: Proceedings of the Workshop Grid-Technologie für den Entwurf technischer System (2005)
14. Blake, M.B., Gomaa, H.: Object-oriented modeling approaches to agent-based workflow services. In: de Lucena, C.J.P., Garcia, A.F., Romanovsky, A.B., Castro, J., Alencar, P.S.C. (eds.) SELMAS 2003. LNCS, vol. 2940, pp. 111–128. Springer, Heidelberg (2004)
15. Aalst, W.v.d.: Inheritance of Business Processes: A Journey Visiting Four Notorious Problems. In: Petri Net Technology for Communication-Based Systems. LNCS, vol. 2472 / 2003, pp. 383–408. Springer, Heidelberg (2003)

16. Aalst, W.v.d., Anyanwu, K.: Inheritance of interorganizational workflows to enable business-to-business E-commerce. In: Proceedings of the Second International Conference on Telecommunications and Electronic Commerce (ICTEC 1999), Nashville, Tennessee, pp. 141–157 (1999)
17. Blake, M.: An agent-based cross-organizational workflow architecture in support of web services. In: Proceedings of the 11th IEEE WETICE 2002, Pittsburgh, PA, June 2002. IEEE Computer Society Press, Los Alamitos (2002)
18. Buhler, P., Vidal, J.M.: Towards adaptive workflow enactment using multiagent systems. Information Technology and Management Journal 6(1), 61–87 (2005)
19. Buhler, P.A.: A Software Architecture for Distributed Workflow Enactment with Agents and Web Services. PhD thesis, Department of Computer Science and Engineering, College of Engineering and Information Technology, University of South Carolina (2004)
20. CrossFlow, W.: Cross-organisational workflow crossflow esprit e/28635: Architecture description (d3a). Report, CrossFlow consortium (1999)
21. Fleurke, M., Ehrler, L., Purvis, M.: Jbees – an adaptive and distributed framework for workflow systems. In: Ghorbani, A., Marsh, S. (eds.) Workshop on Collaboration Agents: Autonomous Agents for Collaborative Environments (COLA), National Research Council Canada, Institute for Information Technology, pp. 69–76 (2003)
22. Savarimuthu, B.T.R., Purvis, M., Purvis, M., Cranefield, S.: Agent-based integration of web services with workflow management systems. The Information Science Discussion Paper Series 2005/05 (2005)
23. Purvis, M., Purvis, M., Haidar, A., Savarimuthu, B.T.R.: A distributed workflow system with autonomous components. In: Barley, M., Kasabov, N. (eds.) PRIMA 2004. LNCS (LNAI), vol. 3371, pp. 193–205. Springer, Heidelberg (2005)
24. Reichert, M., Dadam, P.: A framework for dynamic changes in workflow management systems. In: DEXA Workshop, pp. 42–48 (1997)
25. Reichert, M., Rinderle, S., Dadam, P.: Adept workflow management system: Flexible support for enterprise-wide business processes. In: van der Aalst, W.M.P., ter Hofstede, A.H.M., Weske, M. (eds.) BPM 2003. LNCS, vol. 2678, pp. 370–379. Springer, Heidelberg (2003)
26. Reichert, M., Bauer, T., Dadam, P.: Enterprise-wide and cross-enterprise workflow management: Challenges and research issues for adaptive workflows. In: Enterprise-wide and Cross-enterprise Workflow Management: Concepts, Systems, Applications (1999)
27. Bauer, T., Reichert, M., Dadam, P.: Intra-subnet load balancing in distributed workflow management systems. Int. J. Cooperative Inf. Syst. 12(3), 295–324 (2003)
28. Singh, M.P., Huhns, M.N.: Multiagent systems for workflow. International Journal of Intelligent Systems in Accounting, Finance and Management 8, 105–117 (1999)
29. Moldt, D.: Petrinetze als Denkzeug. In: Farwer, B., Moldt, D. (eds.) Report FBI-HH-B-265/05: Object Petri Nets, Process, and Object Calculi, University of Hamburg, Department for Computer Science, pp. 51–70 (2005)
30. Cabac, L., Dörges, T., Duvigneau, M., Reese, C., Wester-Ebbinghaus, M.: Application development with Mulan. In: International Workshop on Petri Nets and Software Engineering (PNSE 2007), pp. 145–159 (2007)
31. Moldt, D.: Paose: A way to develop distributed software systems based on Petri nets and agents. In: Barjis, J., Ultes-Nitsche, U., Augusto, J.C. (eds.) Proceedings of The Fourth International Workshop on Modelling, Simulation, Verification and Validation of Enterprise Information Systems (MSVVEIS 2006), Paphos, Cyprus, May 23-24, 2006, pp. 1–2 (2006)

32. Reese, C., Duvigneau, M., Köhler, M., Moldt, D., Rölke, H.: Agent–based settler game. In: Agentcities Agent Technology Competition, Barcelona, Spain (2003)
33. Offermann, S., Ortmann, J., Reese, C.: Agent based settler game. In: Pechoucek, M., Steiner, D., Thompson, S. (eds.) openNet Networked Agents Demonstration for AAMAS 2005. Part of NETDEMO, demonstraion at international conference on Autonomous Agents and Multi Agent Systems, AAMAS-2005, pp. 129–130 (2005)
34. Stockheim, T., Nimis, J., Scholz, T., Stehli, M.: How to build multi-multi-agent systems: the Agent.Enterprise approach. In: 6th International Conference on Enterprise Information Systems (ICEIS 2004), Porto, Portugal (2004)
35. Cabac, L., Duvigneau, M., Köhler, M., Lehmann, K., Moldt, D., Offermann, S., Ortmann, J., Reese, C., Rölke, H., Tell, V.: PAOSE Settler demo. In: First Workshop on High-Level Petri Nets and Distributed Systems (PNDS) 2005, University of Hamburg, Department for Computer Science (2005)
36. Lehmann, K., Cabac, L., Moldt, D., Rölke, H.: Towards a distributed tool platform based on mobile agents. In: Eymann, T., Klügl, F., Lamersdorf, W., Klusch, M., Huhns, M.N. (eds.) MATES 2005. LNCS (LNAI), vol. 3550, pp. 179–190. Springer, Heidelberg (2005)
37. Markwardt, K., Moldt, D., Offermann, S., Reese, C.: Using multi-agent systems for change management processes in the context of distributed software development processes. In: Sadiq, S., Reichert, M., Schulz, K. (eds.) The 1st Int. Workshop on Technologies for Collaborative Business Process Management, pp. 56–66 (2006)

Facilitating Agent Development in Open Distributed Systems

Mauro Gaspari[1] and Davide Guidi[2]

[1] Dipartimento di Scienze dell'Informazione, University of Bologna, Italy
[2] Knowledge Media Institute, The Open University, United Kingdom

Abstract. One of the main reasons behind the success of the Web is that many "regular users" are able to create Web pages that, using hyperlinks, incrementally extend both the size and the complexity of the Web itself. The development of agents in the Web infrastructure should ideally be driven by the same paradigm: users being able to write simple or advanced agents. These agents will then provide capabilities using a set of resources, such as standard Web pages, Web services and, of course, other agents. However, agents providing advanced services will never be developed in the same way as Web pages have been created in the past. In fact programming agents is a complex task that needs adequate skills and tools in order to be carried out successfully. As a consequence, only few people are currently able to contribute to their development. The question that arises is whether this gap could be possibly reduced in the future. In this paper we address this question presenting NOWHERE, an open agent communication infrastructure which facilitates the programming task in open distributed multi-agent systems.

1 Introduction

Agent platforms usually provide a programming environment and common services to applications developed as agents. These environments can include high-level programming tools for the development of intelligent agents capable of reasoning, planning, and acting in a changing environment, together with communication mechanisms supporting agent interaction. This paper focuses just on communication facilities, which have a fundamental role to increase the power of agents in open distributed Multi-Agent Systems (MAS). Agent platforms embed specific tools to support inter-agent communication. Many of them are based on the speech act theory, which is also the approach followed by the current standard, the FIPA ACL [6]. Jade [1], for instance, is one of the most used agent platforms both in academia and in industry, and uses FIPA ACL to provide communication facilities. While FIPA ACL includes human like high-level primitives, it does not have specific features for geographically distributed MAS where agents may crash or simply become unreachable for a while. In fact, if we aim to develop robust implementations of agents in these systems, we have to consider agent failures, and a number of extra speech act primitives should be added to the agent code. Additionally, several low-level issues should be considered, such

M. Dastani et al. (Eds.): LADS 2007, LNAI 5118, pp. 243–260, 2008.

as detecting failures, establishing correct timeouts, establishing correct actions to handle failures and so on. As a result of having to deal with these issues the programming task is more difficult and the high-level programming style of the speech act based approach is partially lost.

In this paper, we try to tackle this problem presenting NOWHERE, a modular and open agent communication infrastructure, which has been designed to facilitate the programming task in open, geographically distributed, multi-agent systems. NOWHERE supports a simple programming model which facilitates the development of agents in open distributed systems and works in a reasonable class of application domains. This model supports communication among Knowledge-Level (KL) agents [8], which are agents only concerned with the use, request and supply of knowledge, exploiting an advanced ACL (FT-ACL) [3]) including high-level primitives to deal with failures of agents. Using Knowledge-Level agents, the available communication primitives are those of the ACL, and the programmer does not have to explicitly handle many low-level issues, such as network, timeout and concurrency related problems. Thus the programming task becomes simpler.

This paper is organized as follows. In Section 2 we give a sketch of the NOWHERE platform architecture and we present how the FT-ACL primitives have been embedded in a real programming language (Java). Then we compare our approach with a state-of-the-art agent architecture, presenting some details of the FIPA contract-net specification implemented using Jade and NOWHERE. We conclude the paper with a few remarks.

2   The NOWHERE Platform

In the NOWHERE platform each agent consists of two main components: a *Dispatcher*, that provides the Knowledge Level layer, and a *Facilitator*, a separate component that deals with low-level aspects, such as sending and retrieving messages providing fault tolerance. These two components communicate together by means of the TCP protocol, using a simple *Connector* interface. While the *Dispatcher* is a relatively simple component that mainly provides ACL primitives to a specific programming language, the *Facilitator* hides the whole complexity of the platform, as shown in Figure 1.

NOWHERE differs from other agent architectures in the way it manages faults. The `Facilitator` component contains a failure handler mechanism that is able to discover crashes of agents. It is based on a set of *transparent* timeouts that are automatically managed by the architecture.

In order to physically send messages, the Facilitator uses a pluggable Network Layer. Using different Network Layers as plugins, NOWHERE can be adapted to very different scenarios. Currently NOWHERE features a Jabber Network Layer and a JXTA Network Layer. Using the Jabber Network Layer it is possible to exploit the Jabber protocol (or the Google Talk protocol) to send and receive messages. Due to the fact that the Jabber network follows a client/server model, the resulting architecture will be very fast, providing support for agents with

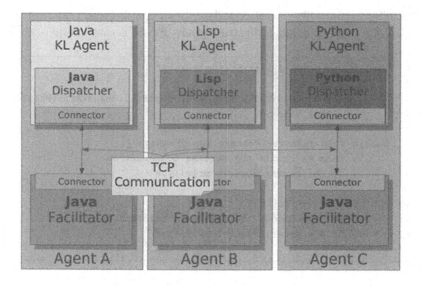

Fig. 1. The NOWHERE architecture

realtime properties. On the other hand, using the decentralised JXTA Network Layer, the resulting architecture will provide better scalability, with more latency in the communication. Of course other Network Layer plugins, such as ad-hoc ones, can be added.

2.1 NOWHERE's Agent Communication Language

NOWHERE is designed to support various kinds of communication primitives based on FT-ACL [3]. It includes a subset of FIPA communication acts based on the speech-act theory [13] extended with multicast content-based requests of knowledge. Thus, currently it is not FIPA compatible. The base language that we present is the NOWHERE *core language*[1] that supports asynchronous, non-blocking primitives.

One of the main features of FT-ACL is the ability to deal with crash failures of agents. According to a well known classification of process failures in distributed systems [10], an agent is *faulty* in an execution if its behaviour deviates from the one coded in the running algorithm; otherwise, it is *correct*. A faulty agent *crashes* if it stops prematurely and does nothing from that point on. FT-ACL manages faults considering only crash failures. This is a common fault assumption in distributed systems, since several mechanisms can be used to detect more severe failures and to force a crash in case of detection. FT-ACL deals with crash failures of agents allowing the programmer to choose which actions to invoke for each interaction they perform in the MAS, using a continuation based mechanism.

---

[1] NOWHERE also supports an *extended language* that uses blocking primitives for the development of realtime agents in sequential programming languages [9].

The following Java-like pseudo code describes a sample `genericRequest` primitive, like for example `askOne`, illustrating how FT-ACL continuations work.

```
1   public static void main(String args[]) {
2       ... some code ...
3       genericRequest(recipientAgent, content, onAnswer, onFail);
4       ... other code ...
5   }
6   public void onAnswer(Message replyMessage){
7       // Here we handle the success continuation
8       // of the genericRequest primitive
9   }
10  public void onFail(){
11      // Here we handle the failure continuation
12      // of the genericRequest primitive
13  }
```

In the code presented above there is a main function (`main`, lines 1-5) that at some point sends a message to the agent `recipientAgent` using the performative (*i.e.*, message type) `genericRequest` (line 3). A typical request primitive is usually implemented using only two arguments: the recipient (`recipientAgent`) and the content of the request that must be sent (`content`). Instead, using the FT-ACL style, a communication primitive also includes a success and a failure continuation, `onAnswer` and `onFail` respectively. These parameters are functions that allow the programmer to specify the success and the failure continuation associated to `genericRequest`. Due to the fact that the language uses non-blocking primitives, after the execution of `genericRequest`, the control flow immediately passes to the next instructions, contained in the "`... other code ...`" block, line 4. When the reply message is received, the success continuation `onAnswer` (lines 6-8) is executed, with the parameter `replyMessage` instantiated with the reply. Otherwise if a communication error arises, then the failure continuation `onFail` (lines 10-13) will be executed. Note that the behaviour of the success continuation `onAnswer` is specific for a request performative. If we consider other types of performative the role of the success continuation can be different. For example the success continuation can be activated when a message is received by the recipient agent to acknowledge that an inform performative is successfully executed. The interaction patterns supported by FT-ACL for different classes of performatives are described in details in [4].

Agents written using FT-ACL are also easy to program because these Knowledge Level properties hold ([3]):

(1) The programmer does not have to manage physical addresses of agents explicitly.
(2) The programmer does not have to handle communication faults explicitly.
(3) Communication is Starvation free.
(4) Communication is Deadlock free.

Although NOWHERE communication primitives are deadlock free, it is not guaranteed that applications implemented in NOWHERE are deadlock free in general. For example, if an agent implements a shared resource using a wrong allocation policy, then a resource deadlock may occur.

2.2 Language Primitives

Language primitives are those of FT-ACL [3]. They support inter-agent communication and provide mechanisms to exchange messages and invoke services. A `Message` object encapsulates the content of the communication in a language-independent way, so that agents written in different languages are able to exchange messages, for example with the `inform` primitive. Simple or complex capabilities can be shared among agents using a `Service` object. Services differ from messages because they have a description that holds information about several aspects, including the name of the service, its parameters and the data types used. These services are described using a subset of WSDL [2], the standard XML format for Web services. Technically, we use the Type, Message and PortType parameters to describe the service. The remaining parameters (Binding, Port and Service) are used to describe how to physically access the service. Instead, NOWHERE uses its own low level network to access these services.

Services are invoked with specific FT-ACL communication primitives, for instance `askOne`, `askEverybody` and `tell`. Intuitively, all the primitives that deal with requests of knowledge. In the NOWHERE architecture, a service description is contained in a `Description` object. To invoke a service and to send a reply NOWHERE provides a `Request` and a `Response` template, that can be retrieved from the description object. Both the `Request` and the `Response` templates are objects containing relevant information extracted from the service description, such as the name of the parameters of the service. In order to invoke a service (to provide a response), a `Request` (a `Response`) template must first be filled in with the correct information. Due to the fact that these templates contain part of the service description, they simplify the actions of invoking and replying to a service.

The communication primitives provided by NOWHERE are shown in Table 1. Due to space constraints we only present the details of those used in the subsequent case study. The interested reader will find a detailed description of all the implemented performatives in [9].

One-to-one knowledge exchange
Communication between two agents can be achieved using the `inform` primitive, the very basic communication method provided by NOWHERE. The syntax of this primitive is:

```
inform(recipientAgent, message)
```

where `recipientAgent` is the unique ID (identifier) of the recipient agent and `message` represents the message containing the information to be sent. The

Table 1. Language Primitives

One-to-one knowledge exchange

```
inform(recipientAgent, message)
informACK(recipientAgent, message, onAnswer[, onFail])
```

Using functions to manage specific messages

```
handler(message, function)
```

Managing Services

```
Description loadDescription(WSDL_Description)
Description makeDescription(targetNS, operation,
    parameters, returnParameters)
```

Using functions to manage specific services

```
handler(request, function)
```

Providing and Requesting services

```
askOne(recipientAgent, request, onAnswer[, onFail])
tell(recipientAgent, response)
```

Service publishing

```
register(description)
```

Anonymous service request

```
askEverybody(request, onAnswer[, onFail])
allAnswers()
```

---

inform primitive is used to send a message to another agent, without any feed-back about the delivery status. No actions are undertaken by the sender agent if the recipient receives the message, as well as no actions are performed if the message is not delivered for some reason.

Request/Response Performatives
To invoke a service, a Description object (that stores the data about the service) must first be generated from a standard WSDL file. The loadDescription primitive is provided for this purpose. It parses a WSDL file either from a local resource or from the Web, returning a NOWHERE Description object. The

askOne primitive must be used to invoke a service provided by another agent. The syntax is:

> askOne(recipientAgent, Request, onAnswer[, onFail])

The **recipientAgent** parameter represents the target agent, while the name of the service, together with its parameters, is contained in the **Request** object. The **onAnswer** and the **onFail** parameters are the associated continuations. They represent the names of the functions that will handle the answer and the failure, respectively. The NOWHERE architecture automatically calls one of these two functions, depending on the result of the service invocation.

Anonymous interaction mechanism
NOWHERE provides support for multicasting a service invocation to a set of agents. This mechanism is also known as content-based request of knowledge, because a service is invoked specifying its content rather than the name of the agent that provides it. This behavior is realized by the **askEverybody** primitive, whose syntax is:

> askEverybody(Request, onAnswer, onFail)

The parameters are the same as in the **askOne** primitive seen before, except that in this case the recipient agent is not specified. It is the facilitator that will send the request to all (and only) the agents that provide the specified service. Every time that a reply is received, the **onAnswer** function will be called. Instead, the **onFail** function will be called only if no agents replied at all. Inside the **onAnswer** function it is possible to check if the current reply is the last one using the **allAnswers** predicate. The **allAnswers** is a Boolean predicate that returns **true** if the current response is the last reply for the associated **askEverybody**, **false** otherwise.

3   Transparent Timeouts

Timeouts are used to provide a framework that can be adaptable to different situations. The timeouts used in NOWHERE are called "transparent timeouts" because they are managed by the architecture itself, so that the user does not have to deal with them. In NOWHERE, timeouts are countdown timers that are activated when a certain primitive is issued or, in some cases, received. Each timeout is associated to a custom message containing an action to do when the countdown timer reaches zero. Usually the action is to execute the failure continuation for the associated primitive.

Every timeout object contains:

– A message, which encodes the action to be taken when the countdown timer reaches zero.
– Two extra parameters: the **agentType** and **agentReactiveness**.

The message associated with every countdown timer is automatically sent using the Facilitator when the countdown reaches zero.

The value for the countdown is calculated using the properties `agentType` and `agentReactiveness` which are associated to each agent. The `agentType` property can be considered an upper bound of the time that the agent will wait. It defines the maximum time that an agent will wait for external replies. If no replies are given during this time, then the failure continuation is fired. The `agentReactiveness` is instead the minimum time that an agent will wait for an answer.

Every communication primitive can be associated to a custom couple of `agentType` and `agentReactiveness` properties. The `agentReactiveness` property affects how the interaction with the recipient agent will be managed by the Facilitator. A low value will force the Facilitator to check the recipient agent very frequently, in order to promptly find crashes. On the other hand, using high values the Facilitator will accept network lags or temporary failures of the recipient agent. For the implementation of the `askOne` communication primitive, these properties are managed using the following algorithm:

---

1 - The Agent executes the `askOne` primitive.
2 - The associated Facilitator sends the message containing the primitive.
3 - The Facilitator starts a countdown timer set to the lower value between `agentReactiveness` and `agentType`.
4 - When the Facilitator receives the reply before that the countdown reaches zero, it will halt the countdown and forward the received message to the dispatcher (**the success continuation fires**).
5 - When the Facilitator receives a `NeedMoreTime` message before that the countdown reaches zero, the `agentType` value will be decremented by the actual number of milliseconds already passed since the countdown started. The algorithm **continues to step 3**.
6 - When the countdown reaches zero, the message associated to the countdown timer will be forwarded to the Dispatcher (**the failure continuation fires**).

The algorithm has a loop (lines 3-5) which will end with the success or failure continuation, in lines 4 and 6. The `NeedMoreTime` message is automatically generated and managed by the Facilitator. Timeouts are contained in the `CountdownRepository`, a structure that provide two basic mechanisms: `stop`, to halt a specific timer, and `restart`, to restart it.

In order to explain this algorithm we introduce a simple scenario, in which AgentA executes an `askOne` primitive in order to invoke a service from AgentB. Four different cases can be obtained:

1. AgentB replies in due time: the time waited by AgentA for the reply is less than the maximum allowed time set by AgentA (`agentType`). This case is illustrated in Figure 2, where FA and FB indicate the Facilitator of AgentA and the Facilitator of AgentB respectively.

2. AgentB has already crashed when AgentA invokes the service. This case is illustrated in Figure 3.
3. AgentB receives the request, but it crashes (or a network error occurres) before replying, so that AgentA never receives a proper reply. This case is illustrated in Figure 4.
4. AgentB does not reply in due time, that is AgentA does not receive the reply in the maximum allowed time (specified by agentType). This case is considered in Figure 5.

Step	Time	AgentA AgentType: 4000 msec Reactiveness: 500msec		AgentB
1	T0 = 0	AgentA asks AgentB for service S. (FA starts its timer: 500 ms up to 4000 ms)	→	AgentB begin to compute the service. (FB starts its timer: <500ms, up to <4000 ms)
2	T1 < 500 ms	(FA restarts its timer)	←	(FB sends a NeedMoreTime message and restarts its timer)
3	T2 < T1 + 500 ms	(FA restarts its timer)	←	(FB sends a NeedMoreTime message and restarts its timer)
4	T3 < T2 + 500 ms	AgentA executes the success continuation (FA stops its timer)	←	AgentB sends the reply (FB stop its timer)

Fig. 2. Success Invocation of a Service

Step	Time	AgentA AgentType: 4000 msec Reactiveness: 500msec		AgentB
1	T0 = 0	AgentA asks AgentB for service S. (FA starts its timer: 500 ms up to 4000 ms)	→	AgentB begin to compute the service. (FB starts its timer: <500ms, up to <4000 ms)
2	T2 = 500 ms	AgentA executes the failure continuation (FA stops its timer)		Crash or Network error occurred (If FB not crashed then FB stops its timer)

Fig. 3. Failure Invocation of a Service (AgentB is already Crashed)

The agentType parameter associates an agent to a specific class of agents with similar interactive characteristics. In principle, any numeric value can be associated to this parameter using the setAgentType primitive. NOWHERE suggests a predefined set of default values:

- *Real Time Agent*, for agents that need a reply in 2 seconds.
- *Web Agent*, for agents that need a reply in 4 seconds.
- *Worker Agent*, for agents that need a reply in 1 minute.

Step	Time	AgentA AgentType: 4000 msec Reactiveness: 500msec		AgentB
1	$T_0 = 0$	AgentA asks AgentB for service S. (FA starts its timer: 500 ms up to 4000 ms)	→	AgentB is crashed or not reacheable
2	$T_2 = 500$ ms	AgentA executes the failure continuation (FA stops its timer)		

Fig. 4. Failure Invocation of a Service (AgentB Crashes before Replying)

- *Truster Agent,* for agents that can wait indefinitely for a reply. This is needed for example when the sender agent wants to dispatch a task and it does not know a priori how much time the task will take. Of course, if the recipient crashes before receiving a reply, the Facilitator of the sender agent will fire a failure continuation.

These values were defined according to the work made by Nielsen in [11], one of the standard reference for the Web usability.

Step	Time	AgentA AgentType: 4000 msec Reactiveness: 500msec		AgentB
1	$T_0 = 0$	AgentA asks AgentB for service S. (FA starts its timer: 500 ms up to 4000 ms)	→	AgentB begin to compute the service. (FB starts its timer: <500ms, up to <4000 ms)
2	$T_1 < 500$ ms	(FA restarts its timer)	←	(FB sends a NeedMoreTime message and restarts its timer)
3	$T_2 <$ $T_1 + 500$ ms	(FA restarts its timer)	←	(FB sends a NeedMoreTime message and restarts its timer)
4	$T_3 <$ $T_2 + 500$ ms	(FA restarts its timer)	←	(FB sends a NeedMoreTime message and restarts its timer)
...	...	...	...	...
n	$T_n = 4000$ ms	AgentA executes the failure continuation (FA stops its timer)		(FB stop its timer)

Fig. 5. AgentB does not Reply in Due Time

4   Case Study: The FIPA Contract Net Protocol

The purpose of this case study is to compare the solution obtained using the NOWHERE approach to the solution provided by Jade, a state-of-the-art agent platform. We choose a slightly modified version of the classic Contract Net protocol [14], fully described in the FIPA specification [7]. The Contract Net protocol allows an agent to distribute tasks among a set of agents by means of negotiation. The modified version considers only a single manager agent, the Initiator, and a set of worker agents, the Responders. Moreover, the FIPA Contract Net also includes rejection and confirmation communicative acts which are not modeled in this case study.

In the following we just recall the basic principles of the protocol, described in detail in the FIPA specification. A representation of this protocol is given in Figure 6 which is based on extensions to UML1.x [12]. The sequence diagram describes the inter-agent transactions needed to implement the protocol, where the diamond symbol indicates a decision that can result in zero or more communications being sent, depending on the conditions it contains.

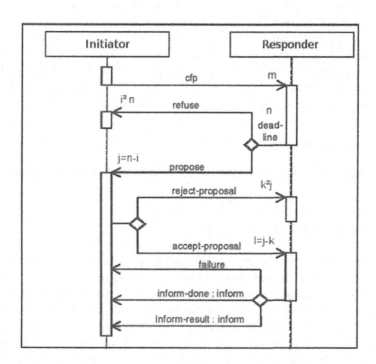

Fig. 6. FIPA Contract Net protocol (source: FIPA specification)

According to the FIPA specification, the Initiator agent sends a call for proposal (cfp) act, soliciting a proposal from every other m agents, specifying the task to be done. Responders receiving the call for proposals are viewed as potential contractors and are able to generate n responses. Of these, j are proposals to perform the task, specified as propose acts. The Responder's proposal includes the preconditions that the Responder is setting out for the task, which may be the price, time when the task will be done, etc. Alternatively, the $i=n\text{-}j$ Responders may refuse to propose. Once the deadline passes, the Initiator evaluates the received j proposals and selects agents to perform the task; one, several or no agents may be chosen.

Being a FIPA compliant platform, Jade adheres as much as possible to FIPA specifications. For this reason Jade implements ad-hoc mechanisms for the FIPA Contract Net, providing facilities that simplify the programming task. In fact, the task of the programmer is just to extend the two Java classes provided for the Initiator and for the Responder role. In order to handle proposals from Responder agents, for example, the developer must only write the proper code inside a function named `handlePropose`. The Jade architecture will then invoke this function properly, for each received proposal. In the Jade platform these ad-hoc mechanisms are called *behaviours*, and are used to easily implement well defined actions, like doing repetitive tasks (using the CyclicBehaviour), simultaneously executing different tasks (using the ParallelBehaviour) or, as in this example, starting a FIPA Contract Net interaction protocol.

For the comparison we proceed in this way: first we introduce the algorithm used in the Jade platform (adapted from an example found in the Jade software distribution) and then we provide an equivalent solution for the NOWHERE architecture. For space limitations, we only analyze the Initiator agent. However, the Responder agent is based on a straightforward reactive algorithm.

4.1   The Initiator Agent - Jade

The algorithm implemented by the Initiator agent is composed of 3 main steps:

1. Find the set of available Responder agents;
2. Send a cfp message to Responder agents;
3. Select and accept the best proposal;

1 & 2 - Find the set of available agents and send a cfp message to them.
The source code for the first two steps is presented in Figure 7. In the Jade platform the task of finding other agents is delegated to the Directory Facilitator component. In order to find other agents, the Initiator should first fill in a Service Description object (lines 1-2). The Service Description object contains information about the resource that we want to find. In this case we used a *type* tag to identify Responder agents. (line 2). The next block of code, lines 3-10, performs a query on the Directory Facilitator and retrieves a list of the available Responder agents. The second step is to send a cfp message to every Responder agent found in the previous step. In lines 11-18 a proper cfp message is created, specifying every collected agent as receiver, if there are any (line 11). Additionally, the agent sets a maximum timeout of 10 seconds for the proposals (line 17) and the name of the task to be dispatched (line 18). The newly created message is then automatically sent using the `ContractNetInitiator` behaviour in the third step.

```
   // Step 1: Find the set of available Responder agents
1  ServiceDescription sd = new ServiceDescription();
2  sd.setType("Responder");
3  DFAgentDescription df = new DFAgentDescription();
4  df.addServices(sd);
5  DFAgentDescription[] agentList = null;
6  try {
7     agentList = DFService.search(this, df);
8  } catch (Exception e) {
9     e.printStackTrace();
10 }
11 if (agentList != null && agentList.length > 0) {
   // Step 2: Send a cfp message to Responder agents
12    ACLMessage msg = new ACLMessage(ACLMessage.CFP);
13    for (int i = 0; i < agentList.length; ++i) {
14       msg.addReceiver(((DFAgentDescription)agentList[i]).getName());
15    }
16    msg.setProtocol(FIPANames.InteractionProtocol.FIPA_CONTRACT_NET);
17    msg.setReplyByDate(new Date(System.currentTimeMillis() + 10000));
18    msg.setContent("dummy-action");
```

Fig. 7. Initiator Agent - Jade solution - first fraction

3 - Select and accept the best proposal
The code used for the third step is shown in Figure 8. Again, replies from Responder agents are managed exploiting Jade's FIPA Contract Net behaviour. The messages are handled using the **handleAllResponses** function (lines 20-44). This function is automatically called by the Jade infrastructure when all the replies have been received. The code in lines 21-38 selects the best proposal, sending a REJECT message to the less competitive replies. The proposal are simply evaluated comparing them against the **bestProposal** variable that stores in every iteration the best proposal received. Replies to the Responder agents are stored in the **acceptances** Java Vector, and are then automatically sent. Finally, the code in lines 39-42 accepts the best proposal received.

4.2 The Initiator Agent - NOWHERE

The solution developed for the NOWHERE platform is shown in Figure 9. Thanks to the anonymous interaction mechanism, there is no need to search for Responder agents. The cfp message can be sent directly to all the Responder agents, that are automatically discovered. In this case the anonymous interaction mechanism relies on an agent capability, that is used to find Responder agents. This capability is provided by all the agents that want to act as Responder agents, and it is described by an external WSDL file, which can be something similar to the one presented in Figure 10. This WSDL description is then loaded in the architecture using the **loadDescription** primitive (line 2),

```
    // Step 3: Managing replies from Responder agents
19    addBehaviour(new ContractNetInitiator(this, msg) {
20       protected void handleAllResponses \
         (Vector responses, Vector acceptances) {
21          int bestProposal = -1;
22          AID bestProposer = null;
23          ACLMessage accept = null;
24          Enumeration e = responses.elements();
25          while (e.hasMoreElements()) {
26             ACLMessage msg = (ACLMessage) e.nextElement();
27             if (msg.getPerformative() == ACLMessage.PROPOSE) {
28                ACLMessage reply = msg.createReply();
29                reply.setPerformative(ACLMessage.REJECT_PROPOSAL);
30                acceptances.addElement(reply);
31                int proposal = Integer.parseInt(msg.getContent());
32                if (proposal > bestProposal) {
33                   bestProposal = proposal;
34                   bestProposer = msg.getSender();
35                   accept = reply;
36                }
37             }
38          }
    // Step 4: Evaluate the proposals and accept the best offer
39          if (accept != null) {
40             accept.setPerformative(ACLMessage.ACCEPT_PROPOSAL);
41             acceptances.addElement(accept)
42          }
43       } // This closes the addBehaviour function (line 19)
44    }); // This closes the if branch of line 11, Fig. 7
45 }
```

Fig. 8. Initiator Agent - Jade solution - second fraction

which returns a `Description` object from a WSDL file. The code in line 4 sets the timeout to 10 seconds, accordingly to the Jade's version. A `Request` object is then instantiated with proper values and sent to Responder agents using an `askEverybody` primitive (lines 5-7). The `handlePropose` function (lines 9-20) will then be called every time the Initatior agent will receive a reply. As in the Jade solution, this function will select the best proposal, sending a REJECT message to the less competitive agents (line 17). Being a synchronized method, the `handlePropose` function will avoid concurrency problems when accessing the `bestProposal` variable.

4.3 Discussion

The first thing to observe is that the solution obtained with Jade exploits a set of ad-hoc facilities to manage interactions in the Contract Net protocol. Even using

```
1   bestProposal = -1;
2   Description cfp = loadDescription("http://maya.unibo.it/cnp.wsdl");
3   public void startAgent() {
4       this.setAgentType(10000);
5       Request r = cfp.getRequest();
6       r.setParameter("taskName", "dummy-action");
7       askEverybody(r, "handlePropose", null);
8   }
9   public synchronized void handlePropose(Message m) {
10      Response r = cfp.retrieveResponseFromMessage(m);
11      int proposal = (Integer) r.getParameter("proposal");
12      if (proposal > bestProposal) {
13         bestProposal = proposal;
14         bestProposer = m.getSender();
15      }
16      else
17         inform(m.getSender(), new Message("REJECT_PROPOSAL")
18      if (allAnswer() && bestProposer != null)
19         inform(m.getSender(), new Message("ACCEPT_PROPOSAL")
20  }
```

Fig. 9. Initiator Agent - NOWHERE solution

these facilities for Jade the source code of the solution based on NOWHERE is much compact.

Analyzing in details the Jade solution, we can observe that two main features are provided by the Jade's FIPA Contract Net behaviour:

- the facility to automate some tasks, like to automatically reply to Responder agents with rejection or acceptance of proposals storing the answers in a vector (Fig. 8, lines 30 and 42);
- the facility that allows the developer to consider just the correct proposals in the handleAllResponses function, so that the developer does not have to deal with faulty agents.

While these features make the programming task easier, Jade provides them only for the Contract Net implementation. On the contrary, the NOWHERE approach provides a general purpose built-in mechanism which can be used in many contexts. The anonymous interaction mechanism, for example, can be used to send a message to every agent in the network that satisfies a set of specific criteria (such as to be a Responder agent). Regarding failures, both solutions add functions to handle low-level communication problems, implementing an appropriate handleFailure function. Again, the NOWHERE architecture provides these features as built-in. Thus they can be used for implementing any kind of interaction protocol. The general idea behind NOWHERE is to simplify the agent programming task, allowing the developer to concentrate in writing the code he/she is working on, avoiding as much as possible the need to explicitly

```
<?xml version="1.0" encoding="UTF-8"?>
<definitions name="contractNetProtocol"
  targetNamespace="http://www.maya.ei.unibo.it/wsdl/cnp.wsdl"
  xmlns:tns="http://www.maya.ei.unibo.it/wsdl/cnp.wsdl"
  xmlns:xsd="http://www.w3.org/2001/XMLSchema">
  <message name="DoTaskRequest">
    <part name="taskName" type="xsd:string"/>
  </message>
  <message name="DoTaskResponse">
    <part name="taskResult" type="xsd:string"/>
  </message>
  <portType name="DoTask">
   <operation name="doTask">
    <input message="tns:DoTaskRequest"/>
    <output message="tns:DoTaskResponse"/>
   </operation>
  </portType>
</definitions>
```

Fig. 10. The Contract Net Protocol WSDL Description

write code to handle failures. Moreover, the NOWHERE architecture provides a fault tolerant system that implements a much more sophisticated algorithm than a simple communication timeout. With regard to inter-agent communication, is important to note that NOWHERE agents can be realised in any programming language including AI languages or knowledge representation languages, provided that they react to a well defined protocol based on the standard primitives of the ACL. Further advantages of using FT-ACL primitives is that they satisfy a set of well defined properties [3]. The resulting communication will then be free from problems like communication deadlock and starvation.

The FIPA contract net protocol does not take into consideration failures of Responder agents receiving the ACCEPT_PROPOSAL message. However, using the continuations mechanism, it is easy to add this feature. A transaction mechanism can be realized using the (more lightweight) continuations, for example with following pseudocode:

```
21 public void askProposer(String proposer)
22    askOne(proposer, acceptRequest, contractNetOk, getNextProposal)
23 public void getNextProposal()
24    if (proposal.hasNext())
25       askProposer(proposals.next())
```

The askProposer function (line 21-22) is used to send a request for the acceptation of the proposal to a Responder agent, whose name is specified as a parameter. The contractNetOk function will be executed if the Responder agent replies correctly. Otherwise, the getNextProposal function (lines 23-25) is executed. The effect of the compensation is to restart the acceptation phase, sending a request to the agent author of the second best proposal, and so on.

5 Conclusions

In this paper we have presented NOWHERE, a communication infrastructure that facilitates agent development supporting Knowledge Level agents. Inter-agent communication is performed by means of an advanced Agent Communication Language (FT-ACL) based on the speech act theory, as well as other popular ACLs such as FIPA ACL [6] and KQML [5]. However, the expressive power of these languages is very different. For example, FIPA ACL sends every communication performative as content of asynchronous message passing. On the contrary the FT-ACL performatives used in NOWHERE can be classified according to a few well defined patterns [4], each one with a different concurrent semantics. Every performative implements a complex behaviour that is fundamentally different from a simple send primitive. The comparison between different solutions to the Contract Net Protocol, provided in this paper, helps to highlight the effects of the adoption of this approach.

References

1. Bellifemine, F., Poggi, A., Rimassa, G.: Jade: a fipa2000 compliant agent development environment. In: AGENTS 2001: Proceedings of the fifth international conference on Autonomous agents, pp. 216–217. ACM Press, New York (2001)
2. Christensen, E., Curbera, F., Meredith, G., Weerawarana, S.: Web services description language (wsdl) 1.1 (2001), http://www.w3.org/TR/wsdl
3. Dragoni, N., Gaspari, M.: Crash failure detection in asynchronous agent communication languages. Autonomous Agents and Multi-Agent Systems 13(3), 355–390 (2006)
4. Dragoni, N., Gaspari, M.: Performative patterns for designing verifiable acls. In: Klusch, M., Rovatsos, M., Payne, T.R. (eds.) CIA 2006. LNCS (LNAI), vol. 4149, pp. 375–387. Springer, Heidelberg (2006)
5. Finin, T., Labrou, Y., Mayfield, J.: KQML as an Agent Communication Language. In: Software Agents, pp. 291–316. MIT Press, Cambridge (1997)
6. FIPA Communicative Act Library Specification, Document number: SC00037J (2002), http://www.fipa.org/
7. FIPA Contract Net Interaction Protocol Specification (2002), http://www.fipa.org/specs/fipa00029/SC00029H.pdf
8. Gaspari, M.: Concurrency and Knowledge-Level Communication in Agent Languages. Artificial Intelligence 105(1-2), 1–45 (1998)
9. Guidi, D.: A communication infrastructure to support knowledge level agents on the web. Technical Report UBLCS-2007-06, Department of Computer Science, University of Bologna (2007)
10. Mullender, S.: Distributed Systems. Addison-Wesley, Reading (1993)

11. Nielsen, J.: Usability Engineering. MA Academic Press, London (1993)
12. Odell, J., Parunak, H.V.D., Bauer, B.: Representing agent interaction protocols in UML. In: Wooldridge, M.J., Weiß, G., Ciancarini, P. (eds.) AOSE 2001. LNCS, vol. 2222, pp. 121–140. Springer, Heidelberg (2002)
13. Searle, J.: Speech Acts. Cambridge University Press, Cambridge (1969)
14. Smith, R.G.: The Contract Net Protocol: High Level Communication and Control in a Distributed Problem Solver. IEEE Transactions on Computers 29(12), 1104–1113 (1980)

simpA: A Simple Agent-Oriented Java Extension for Developing Concurrent Applications

Alessandro Ricci, Mirko Viroli, and Giulio Piancastelli

DEIS, Alma Mater Studiorum – Università di Bologna, Italy
{a.ricci,mirko.viroli,giulio.piancastelli}@unibo.it

Abstract. More and more aspects of concurrency and concurrent programming are becoming part of mainstream programming and software engineering, as a result of several factors, such as the widespread availability of multi-core / parallel architectures and Internet-based systems. Java has been one of the first mainstream languages providing a first-class native support for multi-threading, with basic low level *fine-grained* concurrency mechanisms. Besides this fine-grained support to concurrency, the identification of higher-level—more *coarse-grained*—support is important as soon as programming and engineering complex concurrent applications is considered, helping to bridge the gap between system design, implementation and testing.

Accordingly, in this paper we present simpA, a library-based extension of Java which introduces a high-level coarse-grained support to prototyping complex, multi-threaded / concurrent applications: Java programmers are provided with an *agent-oriented* abstraction layer on top of the basic OO layer to organize and structure applications.

1 Introduction

The widespread diffusion and availability of parallel machines given by multicore architectures is going to have a significant impact in mainstream software development, shedding a new light on *concurrency* and *concurrent programming* in general. Besides multi-core architectures, Internet-based computing and Service-Oriented Architectures / Web Services are further main driving factors introducing concurrency issues in the context of a large class of applications and systems, no more related only to specific and narrow domains, such as high-performance scientific computing.

As noted in [20], if on the one hand concurrency has been studied for about 30 years in the context of computer science fields such as programming languages and software engineering, on the other hand this research has not had a strong impact on mainstream software development. As a main example, Java has been one of the first mainstream languages providing a first-class native support for multi-threading, with basic low level concurrency mechanisms. Such a support has been recently extended by means of a new library added to the JDK with classes that implement well-known and useful higher-level synchronisation mechanisms such as barriers, latches, semaphores, providing a *fine-grained* and efficient control on concurrent computations [10]. Besides this fine-grained support

M. Dastani et al. (Eds.): LADS 2007, LNAI 5118, pp. 261–278, 2008.

to concurrency, it appears more and more important to introduce higher-level abstractions that "help build concurrent programs, just as object-oriented abstractions help build large component-based programs" [20]. Agents and multi-agent systems (MASs)—in their most general characterisation—are very promising abstractions for this purpose, natively capturing and modelling decentralisation of control, concurrency of activities, and interaction / coordination of activites: therefore, they can be considered a good candidate for defining a paradigm for mainstream concurrent programming, beyond OO.

Accordingly, in this paper we present simpA, a library-based extension of Java which provides programmers with agent-oriented abstractions on top of the basic OO layer, as basic building blocks to define the architecture of complex (concurrent) applications. simpA is based on the A&A (Agents and Artifacts) meta-model, recently introduced in the context of agent-oriented programming and software engineering as a novel basic approach for modelling and engineering multi-agent systems [17,19]. *Agents* and *artifacts* are the basic high-level coarse-grained abstractions available in A&A (and simpA): the former is used in A&A to model (pro)-active and activity-oriented components of a system, encapsulating the logic and control of such activities, while the latter is used to model function-oriented components of the system, used by agents to support their activities.

The remainder of the paper is organised as follows. Section 2 describes in more detail the basic abstraction layer introduced by the A&A meta-model; Section 3 describes the simpA framework and technology; Section 4 provides some discussion about the overall approach. Finally, Section 5 and Section 6 conclude the paper with related works and a brief sum up.

2   Agents and Artifacts

As recently remarked by Liebermann [11]:

> "The history of Object-Oriented Programming can be interpreted as a continuing quest to capture the notion of *abstraction*—to create computational artifacts that represent the essential nature of a situation, and to ignore irrelevant details."

Metaphors and abstractions continue to play a fundamental role for computer science and software engineering in general, in providing suitable conceptual means to model, design and program software systems. The metaphors and abstractions at the core of A&A are rooted in human cooperative working environments, investigated by socio-psychological theories such as Activity Theory (AT) [12]. This context is taken here as a reference example of a complex system, where multiple concurrent activities are carried on in a coordinated manner, interacting within some kind of working environment: humans do work concurrently and cooperatively in the context of the same activities, interacting both directly, by means of speech-based communication, and indirectly, by means of artifacts and tools that are shared and co-used. In such systems, it is possible to easily identify two basic kinds of entity: on the one side human workers, as the entities

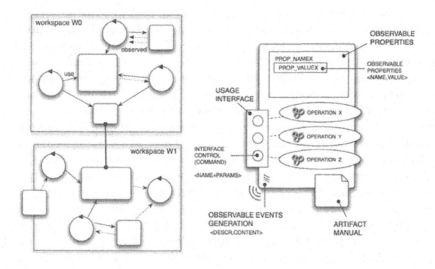

Fig. 1. *(Left)* An abstract representation of an application according to the A&A programming model, as a collection of agents (circles) sharing and using artifacts (squares), grouped in workspaces. *(Right)* An abstract representation of an artifact, with in evidence the usage interface, with commands (control) to trigger the execution of operations, the observable properties and the manual.

responsible of pro-actively performing some kinds of activity; on the other side artifacts and tools, as the entities that workers use to support their activities, being resources (e.g. an archive, a coffee machine) or instruments mediating and coordinating collective activities (e.g. a blackboard, a calendar, a task scheduler).

By drawing our inspiration from AT and human working environments, A&A defines a coarse-grained abstraction layer in which two basic building blocks are provided to organise an application (system), *agents* and *artifacts*. On the one hand, the agent abstraction—in analogy with human workers—is meant to model the (pro-)active part of the system, encapsulating the logic and the control of activities. On the other hand, the artifact abstraction—analogous to artifacts and tools in human environments—is meant to model the resources and the tools created and used by agents during their activities, individually or collectively. Besides agents and artifacts, the notion of *workspace* completes the basic set of abstractions defined in A&A: a workspace is a logic container of agents and artifacts, and can be used to structure the overall sets of entities, defining a topology of the working environment and providing a way to frame the interaction inside it (see Fig. 1, left).

2.1   Agent and Artifact Abstractions: Core Properties

In A&A the term "agent" is used in its etymological meaning of an entity "who acts", i.e. whose computational behaviour accounts for performing *actions* in some kinds of environment and getting information back in terms of *perceptions*. In A&A agents' actions and perceptions concern in particular the *use* of artifacts and direct communication with other agents. The notion of *activity* is used to group related actions, as a way to structure the overall (possibly complex) behaviour of the agent. So an agent in A&A is an *activity-oriented* component, in the sense that it is designed to encapsulate the logic, execution and control of some activities, targeted to the achievement of some objective. As a state-full entity, each agent has a *long-term memory*, used to store data and information needed for its overall work, and a *short-term memory*, as a working memory used to store temporary information useful when executing single activities.

An agent can carry on multiple activities concurrently, and each activity functions as a scope for actions, perceptions and local information useful only for the specific activity. Here it's worth remarking that the notion of agent in simpA is not meant to be comparable with models and architectures as typically found in the context of *goal-oriented* / cognitive agents platforms, such as *Jason* [3], 2APL [5], Jadex [15] or alike: here the objective is not maximising flexibility and autonomy so as to play in unpredictable and complex environments, but having a basic simple abstraction which would make it natural and straightforward to design and program complex active behaviours, providing some strong encapsulation properties for state and control of activities.

Dually to agents, artifacts are *function-oriented* components, i.e. designed to provide some kind of functionality that can be used by agents. The functionality of an artifact is structured in terms of *operations*, whose execution can be triggered by agents through artifact *usage interface* (see Fig. 2, left). Similarly to the notion of interface in case of objects or components, the usage interface of an artifact defines a set of operation controls that agents can use to trigger and control operation execution (like the control panel of a coffee machine), each one identified by a label (typically equals to the operation name to be triggered) and a list of input parameters. In this *use* interaction there is no control coupling: when an agent triggers the execution of an operation, it retains its control (flow) and the execution of the operation on the artifact is carried on independently and asynchronously. This property is a requirement when the basic notion of agent autonomy is considered.

The information flow from the artifact to agents is modelled in terms of *observable events* generated by artifacts and perceived by agents. Besides the controls for triggering the execution of operation, an artifact can define some *observable properties*, as labelled tuples whose value can be inspected by agents dynamically, without necessarily executing operations on it (like the display of a coffee machine).

So, from the programmer's perspective, agents and artifacts provide two radically different programming models to specify their computational behaviour: the former as active entities encapsulating tasks to do and a related agenda of activities, the latter as passive entities encapsulating a state and procedure-based behaviour but not the control of such a behaviour, which is exposed and governed by agents through the usage interface.

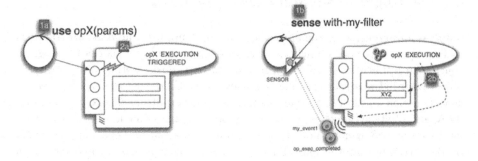

Fig. 2. An agent using an artifact, by triggering the execution of on operation (left, step 1a) and observing the related events generated (right, step 1b)

2.2   Agent-Artifact Interaction: Use and Observation

The interaction between agents and artifacts mimics the way in which humans use their artifacts. Let's consider a coffee machine, for a simple but effective analogy. The set of buttons of the coffee machine represents the usage interface, while the displays used to show the state of the machine represent artifact observable properties. The signals emitted by the coffee machine during its usage represent observable events generated by the artifact.

The interaction takes place by means of a *use* action (stage 1a in Fig. 2, left), which is provided to agents so as to trigger and control the execution of an operation over an artifact. The observable events possibly generated by the artifact executing an operation are collected by agent *sensors*, that are those parts of the agent (body) connected to the environment where the agent is situated. Sensors play here a fundamental role, that of *perceptual memory*, whose functionality accounts for keeping track of stimuli arrived from the environment, possibly applying filters and specific kinds of "buffering" policy. Besides the generation of observable events, the execution of an operation by an artifact typically results in updating the artifact inner state and possibly artifact observable properties (Fig. 2, right).

Then, a *sense* action is provided to agents to explicitly retrieve / be aware of the observable events possibly collected by their sensors (stage 1b in Fig. 2, right); in other words, there is an "active sensing" model for managing perceptions, since sensing—making the agent aware of the stimuli collected by the sensors—is an action that must be explicitly performed by the agent itself.

As mentioned previously, no control coupling takes place between an agent and an artifact with the execution of an operation. However, the triggering of an operation is a synchronisation point between the agent (user) and the artifact (used): if the use action is successfully executed, then it means that the execution of the operation on the artifact has started.

3   The simpA Framework and Technology

simpA is an extension of the Java platform that supports the A&A abstractions as first-class concepts, namely, as basic high-level building blocks to program concurrent applications[1]. This approach contrasts most existing ones modifying object-oriented abstractions (classes, objects, methods) to model concurrency aspects—such as e.g. [2]. Rather, we introduce a new abstraction layer based on A&A, and use true object-orientation to model any basic low-level data structure used to program agents and artifacts, and any information kept and exchanged by them through interactions. This approach leaves concurrency and high-level organisation aspects orthogonal to the object-oriented abstraction layer: we argue that this approach could lead to a more coherent programming framework for complex applications.

simpA extension is realised as a library, exploiting Java annotations to define the new programming constructs required: consequently, a simpA program can be compiled and executed using the standard Java compiler and virtual machine, without the need of a specific extension of the Java framework (preprocessors, compilers, class loaders, or JVM patches). This choice has the advantage to maximise the reuse of an existing widely diffused platform (Java). Indeed, on the one side using the library / annotations solution to implement a language and a platform extension has some revelant drawbacks, which derive from the fact that agents and artifacts are not true real first-class abstractions for the language and the virtual machine. Accordingly, part of the ongoing work is devoted towards the definition and the prototype implementation of a new full-fledged language and platform independent from Java. On the other side, we exploited annotations here to clearly distinguish and separating the implementation of agent and artifact concepts from the object-oriented part, and at the same time to enforce encapsulation at the language level for defining such parts: so, for example, activities are defined as annotated parts of the agent (class), without the need of creating further classes.

In the remainder of the section we give a more concrete taste of the A&A approach by describing how an application based on agents and artifacts can be designed and programmed on top of simpA. Table 1 reports the source code of a simple application, used here as a reference to exemplify the programming of agents and artifacts. The application creates a simple Cafeteria workspace, composed by a single Waiter agent using two instances of a CoffeeMachine artifact. The CoffeeMachine artifact mimics the behaviour of a coffee machine: it can be used to make either coffee or tea. Essentially, it provides a usage interface with controls for selecting the type of drink (coffee or tea) first, then for making the drink. Then, while making the drink, it provides a usage interface to adjust the sugar level and possibly to stop the operation (for short drink). The Waiter agent is programmed with the objective to make coffee and tea by exploiting two different coffee machines, and to deliver either both if they are

---

[1] simpA technology is open-source and is available at simpA web site http://www.alice.unibo.it/simpa

ready within a certain amount of time, or just the coffee if the tea production
lasts too long.

A simpA application is typically booted by setting up the workspace(s), creating an initial set of artifacts—two CoffeeMachines in the example—and spawn-
ing the initial set of agents—a single Waiter in this case. For this purpose,
the Simpa class and the ISimpaWorkspace interface provide suitable services to
initialise and configure the working environment, composed by one or multiple
workspaces. In the example there is one single workspace in a single node: actually it is possible to create multiple workspaces possibly spread among different
network nodes and agents can join and work simultaneously in multiple (possibly
remote) workspaces.

This example is part of the basic examples provided in simpA distribution,
available on simpA web site.

3.1 Defining Agents

A requirement in simpA was to make the approach as agile as possible, min-
imising the number of classes to be introduced for defining both agents and
artifacts. For that reason a one-to-one mapping has been adopted: just one class
is needed to define an agent template or an artifact template. Accordingly, to
define a new agent (template), only one class must be defined, extending the
alice.simpa.Agent base class provided by simpA API. The class name corresponds to the agent template name. The elements defining an agent, activities
in particular, are mapped into class elements, suitably annotated. By defining a
template, it is possible at runtime to spawn an instance of such type of agent.
The execution of an agent consists in executing the activities as specified in its
template, starting from the main one.

Agent long-term memory is realised as an associative store called *memo-space*,
where the agent can dynamically attach, associatively read and retrieve chunks
of information called *memo*. A memo is a tuple, characterised by a label and
an ordered set of arguments, either bound or not to some data object (if some
is not bound, the memo is hence partially specified). A memo-space is just a
dynamic set of memos: a memo is identified by its label, and only one instance
of a memo can exist at a time. Each agent has internal actions to atomically and
associatively access and manipulate the memo space: to create a new memo, to
get / remove a memo with the specified label and / or content, and so on. It
is worth remarking here that instance fields of an agent class are not used: the
memo-space is the only data structure adopted for modelling agent long-term
memory.

Agent activities can be either *atomic*—i.e. not composed by sub-activities—or
structured, composed by some kinds of sub-activity. Atomic activities are implemented as methods with the @ACTIVITY annotation, with no input parameters
and with void return type. The body of a method specifies the computational behavior of the agent corresponding to the accomplishment of the activity. Method
local variables are used to encode data-structures representing the short-term
memory related to the specific activity. By default, the main activity of an agent

is called `main`, and must be defined by every new agent template. By referring to the example reported in Table 1, a `Waiter` agent has four atomic activities: `makeOneCoffee`, `makeOneTea`, `deliverBoth`, `deliverJustCoffee`.

Structured activities can be described as activities composed (hierarchically) by sub-activities. The notion of *agenda* is introduced to specify the set of the potential sub-activities composing the activity, referenced as *todo* in the agenda. Each todo specifies the name of the subactivity to execute, and optionally a pre-condition. When a structured activity is executed, the todos in the agenda are executed as soon as their pre-conditions hold. If no pre-condition is specified, the todo is immediately executed. Then, multiple sub-activities can be executed concurrently in the context of the same (super) activity. A structured activity is implemented by methods with an `@ACTIVITY_WITH_AGENDA` annotation, containing todo descriptions as a list of `@TODO` annotations. Each `@TODO` must specify the name of the related sub-activity to execute and optionally a `pre` property specifying the precondition that must hold in order to execute the todo. A todo can be specified to be *persistent*: in that case, once it has been completely executed, it is re-inserted in the agenda so as to be possibly executed again. This is useful to model cyclic behaviour of agents when executing some activity. Todo preconditions are expressed as a boolean expression, with and / or connectors (represented by , and ; symbols, respectively) over a basic set of predefined predicates. Essentially, the predicates make it possible to specify conditions on the current state of the activity agenda, in particular on *(i)* the state of the sub-activitities (todo), if they completed or aborted or started, and on *(ii)* the memos that could have been attached to the agenda. Besides holding information useful for activities, memos are used then also to coordinate activities, by exploiting in the specification of a pre-condition the predicate (`memo`), which tests the presence of a memo in the agenda.

By referring to the example reported in Table 1, the `Waiter` has a structured `main` activity, with four todos: making a coffee (`makeOneCoffee`) and making a tea (`makeOneTea`), as activities that can be performed concurrently as soon as the main activity starts, and then either delivering the drinks (`deliverBoth`) as soon as both the drinks are ready, or deliver just the coffee (`deliverJustCoffee`) if tea is not available after a specific amount of time. At the end of the activities, the primitive `memo` is used to create memos about the drinks (labelled with `drink1` and `drink2`), annotating information related to the fact that coffee and tea are done. In the case of `makeOneTea` activity, the memo `tea_not_ready` is created instead if the agent does not perceive that tea is ready within a specific amount of time. In `deliverJustCoffee` and `deliverBoth` activities the primitive `getMemo` is used instead to retrieve the content of a memo.

To perform their activities agents typically need to interact with their working environment, in particular with artifacts by means of *use* and *sense* actions as described in previous section. For this purpose, the `use` and `sense` primitives are provided respectively to trigger the execution of an operation over an artifact, and for perceiving the observable events generated by the artifact as effect of the execution. Before describing in detail agent-artifact interaction, in next subsection we describe how to program artifacts.

3.2 Defining Artifacts

Analogously to agents, also artifacts are mapped onto a single class. An artifact template can be described by a single class extending the `alice.simpa.Artifact` base class. The elements defining an artifact—its inner and observable state and the operations defining its computational behaviour—are mapped into class elements, suitably annotated. The instance fields of the class are used to encode the inner state of the artifact and observable properties, while suitably annotated methods are used to implement artifact operations.

For each operation control listed in the usage interface, a method annotated with `@OPERATION` and with `void` return type must be defined: the name and parameters of the method coincide with the name and parameters of the operations to be triggered.

Operations can be either *atomic*, executed as a single computational *step* represented by the content of the `@OPERATION` method, or *structured*, i.e. composed by multiple atomic steps. Structured operations are useful to implement those services that would need multiple interactions with—possibly different—agents, as users of the artifact, and that cannot be provided "in one shot". The execution of an operation can be figured out then as a process composed by linear execution of atomic operation steps. Operation steps are implemented by methods annotated with `@OPSTEP`, and can be triggered (enabled) by means of the `nextStep` primitive specifying the name of the step to be enabled and possibly its parameters. For each operation and operation step a *guard* can be specified, i.e. a condition that must be true in order to actually execute the operation / step after it has been enabled (triggered). Guards are implemented as boolean methods annotated with the `@GUARD` annotation, with same parameters as the operation (step) guarded. The step is actually executed as soon as its guard is evaluated to true. Guards can be specified also for an operation, directly. Also *temporal* guards are supported, i.e. guards whose evaluation is true when a specific delta time is elapsed after triggering. To define a temporal guard, a `tguard` property must be specified inside the `@OPSTEP` annotation in the place of `guard`: the property can be assigned with a long value greater than 0, indicating the number of milliseconds that elapse between triggering and actual execution.

Multiple steps can be triggered as next steps of an operation at a time: As soon as the guard of a triggered step is evaluated to true, the step is executed—in mutual exclusion with respect to the steps of the other operations in execution—and the other triggered steps of the operation are discarded. If multiple steps are evaluated to be runnable at a time, one is chosen according to the order in which they have been triggered with the `nextStep` primitive. It is worth remarking that, in the overall, multiple structured operations can be in execution on the same artifact at the same time, but with only one operation step in execution at a time, enforcing mutual exclusion in accessing the artifact state.

Table 1. An example of simpA application, composed by a single `Waiter` agent using two instances (`cmOne` and `cmTwo`) of the `CoffeeMachine` artifact

```java
public class TestCafeteria {
  public static void main(String[] args){
    ISimpaWorkspace wsp =
               Simpa.createWorkspace("Cafeteria");
    wsp.createArtifact("cmOne","CoffeeMachine");
    wsp.createArtifact("cmTwo","CoffeeMachine");
    wsp.spawnAgent("waiter","Waiter");
} }

public class Waiter extends Agent {

  @ACTIVITY_WITH_AGENDA({
    @TODO(activity="makeOneCoffee"),
    @TODO(activity="makeOneTea"),
    @TODO(activity="deliverBoth",
          pre="completed(makeOneCoffee),
              completed(makeOneTea)"),
    @TODO(activity="deliverJustCoffee",
          pre="completed(makeOneCoffee),
              memo(tea_not_ready)"),
  }) void main(){}

  @ACTIVITY void makeOneCoffee() throws Exception {
    SensorId sid = linkDefaultSensor();
    ArtifactId id = lookupArtifact("cmOne");

    use(id, new Op("selectCoffee"));
    use(id, new Op("make"), sid);
    sense(sid, "making_coffee");

    Perception p = null;
    IPerceptionFilter filter = new GenericFilter(
                 "property_updated", "sugarLevel");

    focus(id, sid);
    do {
      use(id, new Op("addSugar"));
      p = sense(sid, filter);
    } while (p.doubleContent(1) < 0.5);

    Perception p1 = sense(sid,"coffee_ready",5000);
    memo("drink1", p1.getContent(0));
  }

  @ACTIVITY void makeOneTea() throws Exception {
    SensorId sid = linkDefaultSensor();
    ArtifactId id = lookupArtifact("cmTwo");

    use(id, new Op("selectTea"));
    use(id, new Op("make"), sid);
    try {
      Perception p = sense(sid, "tea_ready", 6000);
      memo("drink2", p.getContent(0));
    } catch (NoPerceptionException ex) {
      memo("tea_not_ready");
      throw new ActivityFailed();
    }
  }

  @ACTIVITY void deliverBoth() {
    log("delivering "+
        getMemo("drink1").getContent(0) + " " +
        getMemo("drink2").getContent(0));
  }

  @ACTIVITY void deliverJustCoffee() {
    log("delivering only "+
        getMemo("drink1").getContent(0));
  }
}
```

```java
@ARTIFACT_MANUAL(
  states={"idle","making"},
  start_state="idle" )
class CoffeeMachine extends Artifact {

  @OBSPROPERTY String selection = "";
  @OBSPROPERTY double sugarLevel = 0.0;

  int nCupDone = 0;
  boolean makingStopped;

  @OPERATION(states={"idle"})
  void selectCoffee() {
    updateProperty("selection", "coffee");
  }

  @OPERATION(states={"idle"})
  void selectTea() {
    updateProperty("selection", "tea");
  }

  @OPERATION(states={"idle"})
  void make() {
    if (selection.equals("")) {
      signal("no_drink_selected");
    } else {
      makingStopped = false;
      switchToState("making");
      signal("making_" + selection);
      nextStep("timeToReleaseDrink");
      nextStep("forcedToReleaseDrink");
    }
  }

  @OPSTEP(tguard=3000)
  void timeToReleaseDrink() {
    releaseDrink();
  }

  @OPSTEP(guard="makingStopped")
  void forcedToReleaseDrink() {
    releaseDrink();
  }

  private void releaseDrink() {
    signal(selection + "_ready", drink, sugarLevel);
    updateProperty("selection", "");
    updateProperty("sugarLevel", 0);
    switchToState("idle");
  }

  @GUARD boolean makingStopped() {
    return makingStopped;
  }

  @OPERATION(states={"making"})
  void addSugar() {
    double sl = sugarLevel + 0.1;
    if (sl > 1){ sl = 1; }
    updateProperty("sugarLevel", sl);
  }

  @OPERATION(states={"making"})
  void stop() {
    makingStopped = true;
  }
}
```

To be useful, an artifact typically should provide some level of *observability*. This is achieved either by generating observable events through the `signal` primitive or by defining observable properties. In the former case, the primitive generates observable events that can be observed by the agent using the artifact—i.e. by the agent which has executed the operation. An observable event is represented by a tuple, with a label (string) representing the kind of the event, and a set of arguments, useful to specify some information content. In the latter case, observable properties are implemented as instance fields annotated with the `OBSPROPERTY` annotation. Any change of the property by means of the `updateProperty` primitive would generate an observable event of the type `property_updated(PropertyName)` with the new value of the property as content. The observable events is observed by all the agents that are *focussing* (observing) the artifact. More on this will be provided in next subsection, when describing agent-artifact interaction.

Finally, the usage interface of an artifact can be partitioned in labelled states, in order to allow a different usage interface according to the specific functioning state of the artifact. This is realised by specifying the annotation property `states` when defining operations and observable properties, specifying the list of observable states in which the specific property / operation is visible. The primitive `switchToState` is provided to change the state of the artifact (changing then the exposed usage interface).

In the example reported in Table 1, the `CoffeeMachine` artifact has two basic functioning states, `idle` and `making`, with the former used as starting state. In the `idle` state, the usage interface is composed by `selectCoffee`, `selectTea` and `make` operations, the first two used to select the drink type and the third one to start making the selected drink; in the `making` state, the usage interface is composed by `addSugar` and `stop` operations, the first used to adjust the sugar level during drink-making and the last possibly to stop the process for having shorter drinks. Also, the artifact has two observable properties, `selection` which reports the type of the drink currently selected, and `sugarLevel` which reports current level of sugar: when, for example, `selection` is updated by `updateProperty`, an observable event `property_updated("selection")` is generated. The operations `selectCoffee` and `selectTea` are atomic, instead `make` is (can be) structured: if a valid drink selection is available, then two possible alternative operation steps are scheduled, `timeToReleaseDrink` and `forcedToReleaseDrink`. The first one is time-triggered, and it is executed 3 seconds after triggering. The second one is executed as soon as `makingStopped` guard is evaluated to true. This can happen if the agent user executed the `stop` operation while the coffee machine is making the coffee. In both cases, step execution accounts for releasing the drink, by signaling a proper event of the type `coffee_ready` or `tea_ready`, updating the observable properties value and switching to the `idle` state.

Some other artifact features are not described in detail here for lack of space. Among them we mention: *linkability*—which accounts for dynamically composing artifacts together through *link interfaces*, which are interfaces with operations that are meant to be invoked (*linked*) by other artifacts—and *artifact manual*—which concerns the possibility to equip each artifact with a document, written by the artifact programmer, containing a formal machine-readable semantic-based description of artifact functionality and usage instructions (operating instructions). The manual can be inspected dynamically by agents (by means of a specific action called readManual): this is a first step enabling scenarios—typically in the context of open systems—where agents would be able to select and use artifacts that are added dynamically to their working environment, without having a pre-programmed knowledge about their functionality and use [21]. The interested reader is forwarded to the documentation available at simpA web site.

3.3   Agent-Artifact Interaction

Artifact *use* is the basic form of interaction between agents and artifacts. Actually, also artifact instantiation and artifact discovery are realised by means of using proper artifacts—a *factory* and a *registry* artifacts—, which are available in each workspace. However two high-level auxiliary actions are provided, **makeArtifact** and **lookupArtifact**, which encapsulate the interaction with such artifacts.

Following the A&A model, artifact use by a user agent involves two basic aspects: (1) executing operations on the artifact, and (2) perceiving—through agent sensors—the observable events generated by the artifact.

Agents execute operations on an artifact by using the interface controls provided by the artifact usage interface. The use basic action is provided for this purpose, specifying the identifier of the target artifact, the operation to be triggered and optionally the identifier of the sensor used to collect observable events generated by the artifact. When the action execution succeeds, the return parameter returned by use is the operation unique identifier. If the action execution fails—because, for instance, the interface control specified is not part of artifact usage interface—an exception is generated. An agent can link (and unlink) any number of sensors (of different kinds) by means of specific internal actions (linkSensor, unlinkSensor, and linkDefaultSensor, to link a new default type of sensor), according to the strategy chosen for sensing and observing the environment.

In order to retrieve events collected by a sensor, the sense internal action is provided. The action suspends the execution of the activity until either an event is collected by the sensor, matching the pattern optionally specified as a parameter (for data-driven sensing), or a timeout is reached, optionally specified as a further parameter. As a result of a successful execution of a sense, the event is removed from the sensor and a perception related to that event—represented by an object instance of the class Perception—is returned. If no perception is sensed for the duration of time specified, the action generates an exception of the kind NoPerceptionException. A custom filter for pattern matching can be specified (with classes implementing IPerceptionFilter): by default pattern-matching is based on regular-expression patterns, matched over the event type (a string).

Finally, a support for *continuous observation* is provided. If an agent is interested in observing every event generated by an artifact—including those generated as a result of the interaction with other agents—two primitives can be used, focus and unfocus. The former is used to start observing the artifact, specifying a sensor to be used to collect the events and optionally the reg-ex filter to define the set of events to observe. The latter one is used to stop observing the artifact.

In the example reported in Table 1, in the makeCoffee activity the agent uses the coffee machine cmOne (discovered by the lookupArtifact action) by executing first a selectCoffee operation, ignoring possible events generated by such operation execution, and then a make, specifying a sensor to collect events. Then the agent, by means of a sense, waits to observe a making_coffee event, meaning that the artifact started making coffee. The agent then interacts with the machine so as to adjust the sugar level: this is done by focussing on the artifact and acting upon the addSugar operation control, until the observable property reporting the sugar level reaches 0.5. Then the activity is blocked until coffee_ready event is perceived. While performing a makeOneCoffee activity, the agent carries on also a makeOneTea activity: as a main difference there, if the agent does not observe the tea_ready event within six seconds after having triggered the make operation, then a memo tea_not_ready is inserted and the activity fails (by means of the generation of an exception).

3.4 Inter-Agent Interactions

simpA provides also a very basic support for direct communication between agents, with a tell(ReceiverId,Msg) primitive to send a message to another agent, and a listen(SensorId,Filter)—analogous to focus primitive—to specify sensors to be used to collect the messages). So, also for direct communication, sensors and sensing primitives are exploited to collect and be aware of perceptions, in this case related to the arrival of a message.

4   Discussion

The main objective of simpA is to simplify the prototyping of complex applications involving elements of concurrency, by introducing high-level abstractions on top of the basic object-oriented layer.

As a first benefit, the level of abstraction underlying the approach is meant to promote an agile design of the application and then to reduce the gap between such design and the implementation level. At the design level, by adopting a task oriented approach as typically promoted by agent-oriented methodologies [8], the task-oriented and function-oriented parts of the system are identified, driving to the definition of the agents and artifacts as depicted by the A&A model, and then to the implementation in simpA.

Then, the approach aims at providing agile but quite general means to organise and manage complex active and passive behaviours. For active behaviours, the notion of activity and the hierarchical activity model adopted in the agent abstraction make it possible to describe articulated active behaviours in a quite synthetic and readable way, abstracting from the complexity related to threads creation, management and coordination. Besides the notion of activity, the very notion of agent as the state-full entity responsible for activity execution strengthen the level of encapsulation adopted to structure active parts. For passive behaviours, the model of artifact adopted allows the programmer to specify complex functionalities (operations) possibly shared and exploited by multiple agents concurrently, without the need to explicitly use lower-level Java mechanisms such as synchronised blocks or wait / notify synchronisation primitives. On the one side, mutual exclusion in accessing and modifying artifact inner state is guaranteed by having only one operation step in execution at a time. On the other side, possible dependencies between operations can be explicitly took into account by defining the operation (step) guards.

Besides the individual component level, the approach has been conceived to simplify the development of systems composed by multiple agents that work together, coordinating their activities by exploiting suitable *coordination artifacts* [14]. More generally, the problems that are typically considered in the context of concurrent programming involving the interaction and coordination of multiple processes—examples are *producer-consumer, readers-and-writers, dining-philosophers*—can be naturally modelled in terms of agents and artifacts, providing solutions that in our opinion are more clear and "high-level" with respect to those mixing object-oriented abstractions—threads and low-level synchronisation mechanism—as in the case of Java. For instance, producers-consumers problems are naturally modelled in terms of producer and consumer agents sharing and exploiting a bounded buffer artifact; readers-and-writers problems in terms of reader and writer agents that use a suitably designed rw-lock coordination artifact to coordinate their access to a shared resource; dining-philosophers, in terms of a set of philosopher agents sharing and using a table, which encapsulates and enforces those coordination rules that make it possible to handle mutual exclusion in using chopsticks and to avoid deadlock situations. For the interested readers, these and other problems are included among the examples provided in simpA distribution, not reported here for lack of space.

Finally, the notion of artifact can be naturally used also to model and program GUI components in applications: actually simpA provides a direct support to develop graphical user interfaces as artifacts mediating the interaction between human users and application agents. Generally speaking, such kinds of artifacts expose a usage interface both for humans—in terms of GUI controls—and for agents, and generate observable events that can be observed by agents, which can, in turn, change the GUI through its usage interface. Examples about GUI realised as artifacts are provided in simpA distribution.

5   Related Works

simpA model and technology are strictly related to the research work on CARTAGO [18] and artifacts in general [17]. While simpA introduces a specific programming model for programming agents, CARTAGO is focussed solely on artifacts—programming and API for agents to use them—and conceptually it can be integrated with heterogeneous agent platforms, including cognitive agent platforms, extending them to support artifact-based environments.

The artifact abstraction at the core of simpA and CARTAGO is a generalisation of *coordination artifacts*—i.e. artifacts encapsulating coordination functionalities, introduced in [14]. In A&A artifacts are the basic building blocks that can be used to engineer the working environments where agents are situated: agent environment then play a fundamental role here in engineering the overall MAS as first-order entity that can be designed so as to encapsulate some kind of responsibility (functionality, service). This perspective is explored in several research works appeared recently in MAS literature: a survey can be found in [22]. By providing a general-purpose programming model for artifacts, simpA gives the possibility to program any kind of coordination artifacts, from simple synchronizers (such as latch, barriers, etc.) to more complex ones, such as tuple spaces [7] or tuple centres [13]. Actually, an important difference with respect to existing coordination technologies for distributed systems is that these ones are *not* typically designed for agent models / platforms, but for object-oriented environments or a-like, and so without agent autonomy in mind. For instance, JavaSpaces [6] provides API to exploit kinds of tuple spaces in Java applications, providing operations which can directly block the control flow of the thread invoking the operation: an example is given by the *take* or *in* operation. Conversely, artifacts realised in simpA, including coordination artifacts like tuple spaces, are designed and programmed following the basic programming model for artifacts defined by A&A, which explicitly preserve agent autonomy in agent-artifact interaction.

Quite obviously, simpA is not the first approach providing an agent-oriented abstraction layer on top of the flat Java. JADE[2] is probably the most known and used case, providing a general-purpose middleware that complies with the FIPA specifications for developing peer-to-peer distributed agent based applications. A main conceptual and practical difference between simpA and JADE concerns the high-level first-class abstractions adopted to organise a software system: in JADE there are agents interacting by means of FIPA ACL, in simpA there are agents and artifacts. Then, besides the support for FIPA ACL, JADE adopts a behaviour-based programming model for programming agents. From this point of view, activities in simpA are similar to behaviours in JADE, with the main difference that in simpA the definition of structured activities composed by sub-activities is done declaratively by defining the activity agenda, while in JADE is done operationally, by creating and composing objects of specific classes. Besides JADE, other well-known agent-oriented platforms have been developed as an extension of the Java platform: we cite here JACK[3], and JADEX [15], which differently from JADE and simpA provide a first-class support for programming

---

[2] http://jade.tilab.com/
[3] http://www.agent-software.com/

intelligent agents, based on the BDI architecture and the FIPA standards. These approaches—as most of the other cognitive agent programming platforms—are typically targeted to the engineering of distributed intelligent systems for complex application domains, not for concurrent programming in general.

Finally, simpA is strongly related to the research in the context of object-oriented concurrent programming (OOCP), extending the basic OO paradigm toward concurrency[4]. In this context, a large amount of approaches have been proposed since the beginning of the 80's; it is not possible to report here a full list of all the approaches: the interested reader is forwarded to surveys such as [4,23]. Among the main examples, *active objects* [9] and *actors* [1] have been the root of entire families of approaches. The approach proposed in this paper shares the aim of actor and active objects approaches, i.e introducing a general-purpose abstraction layer to simplify the development of concurrent applications. Differently from actor-based approaches, in A&A and simpA also the passive components of the systems are modelled as first-class entities (the artifacts), besides the active parts (actors in actor-based systems). Differently from active-object-based approaches—where typically active objects are objects with further capabilities—, in simpA a strong distinction between active and passive entities is promoted: agents and artifacts have completely different properties, with a clear distinction at the design level of their role, i.e. encapsulating pro-active / task-oriented behaviour (agents) and passive / function-oriented behaviour (artifacts).

6   Conclusion

More and more concurrency is going to be part of mainstream programming and software engineering, with applications able to suitably exploit the inherent concurrency support provided by modern hardware architecture—such as multi-core architectures—and by network-based environments and related technologies, such as Internet and Web Services. This calls for—quoting Sutter and Larus [20]—"higher-level abstractions that help build concurrent programs, just as object-oriented abstractions help build large componentised programs".

Along this line, in this paper we presented simpA, a library extension over the basic Java platform that aims at simplifying the development of complex (concurrent) applications by introducing a simple high-level agent-oriented abstraction layer over the OO layer. Future work will be devoted on finalising a formal model for simpA basic programmming model on the one side, and defining a full fledged simpA language and virtual machine on the other side, independent from the Java language.

---

[4] In the context of the object-oriented research community, a first paper on simpA has been presented at the conference "Principle and Practice of Java Programming" (PPPJ'07) [16]. Given the context, that paper focusses more on the features of simpA with respect to existing approaches in the context object-oriented / Java-based concurrent programming.

References

1. Agha, G.: Actors: a model of concurrent computation in distributed systems. MIT Press, Cambridge (1986)
2. Benton, N., Cardelli, L., Fournet, C.: Modern concurrency abstractions for C#. ACM Trans. Program. Lang. Syst. 26(5), 769–804 (2004)
3. Bordini, R.H., Hübner, J.F., Vieira, R.: Jason and the golden fleece of agent-oriented programming. In: Bordini, R.H., Dastani, M., Dix, J., El Fallah Seghrouchni, A. (eds.) Multi-Agent Programming: Languages, Platforms and Applications, pp. 3–37. Springer, Heidelberg (2005)
4. Briot, J.-P., Guerraoui, R., Lohr, K.-P.: Concurrency and distribution in object-oriented programming. ACM Comput. Surv. 30(3), 291–329 (1998)
5. Dastani, M., Hobo, D., Meyer, J.-J.: Practical extensions in agent programming languages. In: Proceedings of the Sixth International Joint Conference on Autonomous Agents and Multiagent Systems (AAMAS 2007). ACM Press, New York (2007)
6. Freeman, E., Hupfer, S., Arnold, K.: JavaSpaces: Principles, Patterns, and Practice. The Jini Technology Series. Addison-Wesley, Reading (1999)
7. Gelernter, D.: Generative communication in Linda. ACM Transactions on Programming Languages and Systems 7(1), 80–112 (1985)
8. Iglesias, C., Garrijo, M., Gonzalez, J.: A survey of agent-oriented methodologies. In: Müller, J., Singh, M.P., Rao, A.S. (eds.) ATAL 1998. LNCS (LNAI), vol. 1555, pp. 317–330. Springer, Heidelberg (1999)
9. Lavender, R.G., Schmidt, D.C.: Active object: an object behavioral pattern for concurrent programming. In: Pattern languages of program design 2, pp. 483–499. Addison-Wesley Longman Publishing Co., Inc., Boston (1996)
10. Lea, D.: The java.util.concurrent synchronizer framework. Sci. Comput. Program. 58(3), 293–309 (2005)
11. Lieberman, H.: The continuing quest for abstraction. In: Thomas, D. (ed.) ECOOP 2006. LNCS, vol. 4067, pp. 192–197. Springer, Heidelberg (2006)
12. Nardi, B.A.: Context and Consciousness: Activity Theory and Human-Computer Interaction. MIT Press, Cambridge (1996)
13. Omicini, A., Denti, E.: From tuple spaces to tuple centres. Science of Computer Programming 41(3), 277–294 (2001)
14. Omicini, A., Ricci, A., Viroli, M., Castelfranchi, C., Tummolini, L.: Coordination artifacts: Environment-based coordination for intelligent agents. In: Proceedings of the 3rd International Joint Conference on Autonomous Agents and Multiagent Systems (AAMAS 2004), vol. 1, pp. 286–293. IEEE computer Society, Washington (2004)
15. Pokahr, A., Braubach, L., Lamersdorf, W.: Jadex: A bdi reasoning engine. In: Bordini, R., Dastani, M., Dix, J., Seghrouchni, A. (eds.) Multi-Agent Programming, Kluwer, Dordrecht (2005)
16. Ricci, A., Viroli, M.: simpA: An agent-oriented approach for prototyping concurrent applications on top of java. In: Amaral, V., Veiga, L., Marcelino, L., Cunningham, H.C. (eds.) Proceedings of the 5th International Conference, Principles and Practice of Programming in Java (PPPJ 2007), Lisbon, Portugal, September 2000, pp. 185–194 (2000)

17. Ricci, A., Viroli, M., Omicini, A.: Give agents their artifacts: The A&A approach for engineering working environments in MAS. In: Durfee, E., Yokoo, M., Huhns, M., Shehory, O. (eds.) 6th International Joint Conference Autonomous Agents & Multi-Agent Systems (AAMAS 2007), pp. 601–603 (2007)

18. Ricci, A., Viroli, M., Omicini, A.: CArtAgO: A framework for prototyping artifact-based environments in MAS. In: Weyns, D., Parunak, H.V.D., Michel, F. (eds.) E4MAS 2006. LNCS (LNAI), vol. 4389, pp. 67–86. Springer, Heidelberg (2007)

19. Ricci, A., Viroli, M., Omicini, A.: The A&A programming model and technology for developing agent environments in MAS. In: Dastani, M., El Fallah Seghrouchni, A., Ricci, A., Winikoff, M. (eds.) Programming Multi-Agent Systems. LNCS (LNAI), vol. 4908, pp. 89–106. Springer, Heidelberg (2008)

20. Sutter, H., Larus, J.: Software and the concurrency revolution. ACM Queue: Tomorrow's Computing Today 3(7), 54–62 (2005)

21. Viroli, M., Ricci, A.: Instructions-based semantics of agent mediated interaction. In: Proceedings of the 3rd International Joint Conference on Autonomous Agents and Multiagent Systems (AAMAS 2004), vol. 1, pp. 102–109. IEEE Computer Society, Washington (2004)

22. Weyns, D., Parunak, H.V.D. (eds.): Journal of Autonomous Agents and Multi-Agent Systems. Special Issue: Environment for Multi-Agent Systems, vol. 14(1). Springer, Heidelberg (2007)

23. Yonezawa, A., Tokoro, M. (eds.): Object-oriented concurrent programming. MIT Press, Cambridge (1986)

Author Index

Lecture Notes in Artificial Intelligence (LNAI)

Vol. 4870: J.S. Sichman, J. Padget, S. Ossowski, P. Noriega (Eds.), Coordination, Organizations, Institutions, and Norms in Agent Systems III. XII, 331 pages. 2008.

Vol. 4869: F. Botana, T. Recio (Eds.), Automated Deduction in Geometry. X, 213 pages. 2007.

Vol. 4865: K. Tuyls, A. Nowe, Z. Guessoum, D. Kudenko (Eds.), Adaptive Agents and Multi-Agent Systems III. VIII, 255 pages. 2008.

Vol. 4850: M. Lungarella, F. Iida, J.C. Bongard, R. Pfeifer (Eds.), 50 Years of Artificial Intelligence. X, 399 pages. 2007.

Vol. 4845: N. Zhong, J. Liu, Y. Yao, J. Wu, S. Lu, K. Li (Eds.), Web Intelligence Meets Brain Informatics. XI, 516 pages. 2007.

Vol. 4840: L. Paletta, E. Rome (Eds.), Attention in Cognitive Systems. XI, 497 pages. 2007.

Vol. 4830: M.A. Orgun, J. Thornton (Eds.), AI 2007: Advances in Artificial Intelligence. XIX, 841 pages. 2007.

Vol. 4828: M. Randall, H.A. Abbass, J. Wiles (Eds.), Progress in Artificial Life. XII, 402 pages. 2007.

Vol. 4827: A. Gelbukh, Á.F. Kuri Morales (Eds.), MICAI 2007: Advances in Artificial Intelligence. XXIV, 1234 pages. 2007.

Vol. 4826: P. Perner, O. Salvetti (Eds.), Advances in Mass Data Analysis of Signals and Images in Medicine, Biotechnology and Chemistry. X, 183 pages. 2007.

Vol. 4819: T. Washio, Z.-H. Zhou, J.Z. Huang, X. Hu, J. Li, C. Xie, J. He, D. Zou, K.-C. Li, M.M. Freire (Eds.), Emerging Technologies in Knowledge Discovery and Data Mining. XIV, 675 pages. 2007.

Vol. 4811: O. Nasraoui, M. Spiliopoulou, J. Srivastava, B. Mobasher, B. Masand (Eds.), Advances in Web Mining and Web Usage Analysis. XII, 247 pages. 2007.

Vol. 4798: Z. Zhang, J.H. Siekmann (Eds.), Knowledge Science, Engineering and Management. XVI, 669 pages. 2007.

Vol. 4795: F. Schilder, G. Katz, J. Pustejovsky (Eds.), Annotating, Extracting and Reasoning about Time and Events. VII, 141 pages. 2007.

Vol. 4790: N. Dershowitz, A. Voronkov (Eds.), Logic for Programming, Artificial Intelligence, and Reasoning. XIII, 562 pages. 2007.

Vol. 4788: D. Borrajo, L. Castillo, J.M. Corchado (Eds.), Current Topics in Artificial Intelligence. XI, 280 pages. 2007.

Vol. 4775: A. Esposito, M. Faundez-Zanuy, E. Keller, M. Marinaro (Eds.), Verbal and Nonverbal Communication Behaviours. XII, 325 pages. 2007.

Vol. 4772: H. Prade, V.S. Subrahmanian (Eds.), Scalable Uncertainty Management. X, 277 pages. 2007.

Vol. 4766: N. Maudet, S. Parsons, I. Rahwan (Eds.), Argumentation in Multi-Agent Systems. XII, 211 pages. 2007.

Vol. 4760: E. Rome, J. Hertzberg, G. Dorffner (Eds.), Towards Affordance-Based Robot Control. IX, 211 pages. 2008.

Vol. 4755: V. Corruble, M. Takeda, E. Suzuki (Eds.), Discovery Science. XI, 298 pages. 2007.

Vol. 4754: M. Hutter, R.A. Servedio, E. Takimoto (Eds.), Algorithmic Learning Theory. XI, 403 pages. 2007.

Vol. 4737: B. Berendt, A. Hotho, D. Mladenic, G. Semeraro (Eds.), From Web to Social Web: Discovering and Deploying User and Content Profiles. XI, 161 pages. 2007.

Vol. 4733: R. Basili, M.T. Pazienza (Eds.), AI*IA 2007: Artificial Intelligence and Human-Oriented Computing. XVII, 858 pages. 2007.

Vol. 4724: K. Mellouli (Ed.), Symbolic and Quantitative Approaches to Reasoning with Uncertainty. XV, 914 pages. 2007.

Vol. 4722: C. Pelachaud, J.-C. Martin, E. André, G. Chollet, K. Karpouzis, D. Pelé (Eds.), Intelligent Virtual Agents. XV, 425 pages. 2007.

Vol. 4720: B. Konev, F. Wolter (Eds.), Frontiers of Combining Systems. X, 283 pages. 2007.

Vol. 4702: J.N. Kok, J. Koronacki, R. Lopez de Mantaras, S. Matwin, D. Mladenič, A. Skowron (Eds.), Knowledge Discovery in Databases: PKDD 2007. XXIV, 640 pages. 2007.

Vol. 4701: J.N. Kok, J. Koronacki, R. Lopez de Mantaras, S. Matwin, D. Mladenič, A. Skowron (Eds.), Machine Learning: ECML 2007. XXII, 809 pages. 2007.

Vol. 4696: H.-D. Burkhard, G. Lindemann, R. Verbrugge, L.Z. Varga (Eds.), Multi-Agent Systems and Applications V. XIII, 350 pages. 2007.

Vol. 4694: B. Apolloni, R.J. Howlett, L. Jain (Eds.), Knowledge-Based Intelligent Information and Engineering Systems, Part III. XXIX, 1126 pages. 2007.

Vol. 4693: B. Apolloni, R.J. Howlett, L. Jain (Eds.), Knowledge-Based Intelligent Information and Engineering Systems, Part II. XXXII, 1380 pages. 2007.

Vol. 4692: B. Apolloni, R.J. Howlett, L. Jain (Eds.), Knowledge-Based Intelligent Information and Engineering Systems, Part I. LV, 882 pages. 2007.

Vol. 4687: P. Petta, J.P. Müller, M. Klusch, M. Georgeff (Eds.), Multiagent System Technologies. X, 207 pages. 2007.

Vol. 4682: D.-S. Huang, L. Heutte, M. Loog (Eds.), Advanced Intelligent Computing Theories and Applications. XXVII, 1373 pages. 2007.

Vol. 4676: M. Klusch, K.V. Hindriks, M.P. Papazoglou, L. Sterling (Eds.), Cooperative Information Agents XI. XI, 361 pages. 2007.

Vol. 4667: J. Hertzberg, M. Beetz, R. Englert (Eds.), KI 2007: Advances in Artificial Intelligence. IX, 516 pages. 2007.

Vol. 4660: S. Džeroski, L. Todorovski (Eds.), Computational Discovery of Scientific Knowledge. X, 327 pages. 2007.

Vol. 4659: V. Mařík, V. Vyatkin, A.W. Colombo (Eds.), Holonic and Multi-Agent Systems for Manufacturing. VIII, 456 pages. 2007.

Vol. 4651: F. Azevedo, P. Barahona, F. Fages, F. Rossi (Eds.), Recent Advances in Constraints. VIII, 185 pages. 2007.